More praise for
Black Sheep One

"As an executive producer of *Black Sheep Squadron*, I had a chance to know Pappy. Bruce has caught the man and helped define the legend. Great reading!"
—STEPHEN J. CANNELL
Author of *King Con*

"Bruce Gamble's *Black Sheep One* is the seminal work on this legendary American hero. It puts to rest the controversies that still brew around Boyington's adventures."
—ERIC HAMMEL
Author of *Aces Against Japan*

"I last saw Greg Boyington eighteen months before his death, and he looked about two hundred years old. Now, thanks to Bruce Gamble's excellent work, it's possible to understand what was behind each wrinkle and crease in that craggy face. *Black Sheep One* is not only a superb aviation biography—it's one of the finest biographies I've ever read. Period."
—BARRETT TILLMAN
Author of *On Yankee Station*

*Please turn the page
for more reviews. . . .*

"Biographer Bruce Gamble, who presented an authoritative history of VMF-214 in *The Black Sheep,* has now applied his meticulous research to recounting the upbringing, actual achievements, and tragic postwar decline of VMF-214's famous commander. . . . Gamble's detailed, warts-and-all treatment of Boyington sets a number of records straight, but the figure he depicts is no less heroic for his human failings. . . . The author recounts remarkable deeds that still stand on their own merits, performed by a three-dimensional character who remains one of history's true originals."
—*Aviation History*

"*Black Sheep One* is a superb biography of a true American original. 'Pappy' Boyington found fame at several points in his tumultuous life. . . . Aviation historian and retired naval flight officer Bruce Gamble provides the full story of this colorful figure."
—*Veterans Voice*

"A 'warts-and-all' story of a WWII Medal of Honor winner whose life after the conflict had debilitating lows as well as exciting highs."
—*Wings of Gold*

By Bruce Gamble:

THE BLACK SHEEP: *The Definitive Account of Marine Fighting Squadron 214*

BLACK SHEEP ONE
The Life of Gregory "Pappy" Boyington

Bruce Gamble

PRESIDIO

BALLANTINE BOOKS • NEW YORK

A Presidio Press Book
Published by The Ballantine Publishing Group
Copyright © 2000 by Bruce D. Gamble

www.ballantinebooks.com

ISBN 0-89141-801-6

Manufactured in the United States of America

First Ballantine Books Edition: March 2003

10 9 8 7 6 5 4 3 2 1

For Margaret
whose love and patience are as boundless as the sky

Contents

Acknowledgments

This would never have been possible without God's grace. That said, it was made all the more possible and worry-free thanks to the unflagging support of my wife. I am indebted to many other people for their help. Gregory Boyington Jr. gave authorization for copies of his father's flight training record, university transcripts, and service/medical records; William Hallenbeck's daughters provided family information; Lars and Ramona Granath kindly copied photographs; Keith Boyington and his wife, Dolores, provided family background, photographs, and a copy of *Pappy Boyington, World War II Ace*, LP recording; E. J. McCarthy, executive editor, and Craig Schneider, copy editor, gave their expert guidance. Additional manuscript review was done by Dan Ford, June Gamble, Margaret Gamble, Hill Goodspeed and Henry Sakaida, who went above and beyond with their enthusiastic help. I am also grateful to the following people for their assistance with research: David Ails, Everett Anderson, Dennis Bergstrom, Cary Bickel, M.D., Mark Burken, Nancy Compau, Sandy Cordell, Dan Crawford, Jack Dyer, Candace Gregory, Christy Harrington, Gary Hawn, Elizabeth Jacox, Brian Kamens, Robert Kleopfer, Dennis Letourneau, Ben Levario, Richard Long, Tom Lubbesmeyer, Gregory McCormick, Mike Miller, Mikell Mowreader, Frank Olynyk, James Radford, M.D., Marilyn Roth, William Seacrest, Jennifer Shakal, Brandon Short, Sandy Smith, Barrett Tillman, Irv Thomas, Eric Voelz, Cindy Wagner, and Brandon Wood.

Prologue

A typically mild afternoon graced the San Joaquin Valley as two gentlemen in their sixties drove toward Fresno from opposite directions. Good friends for many years, they shared much in common, having been born just four months apart on central Pennsylvania farms in neighboring counties, though they didn't meet until the summer of '43. A pair of skinny marine lieutenants, they had been assigned to the same room in a bachelor officers' quarters near San Diego, and within minutes discovered their mutual background. They had traveled aboard the same ship to the South Pacific, joined the same fighter squadron as replacements, flown combat missions together, gone on leave together, lost several friends together. Their names even rhymed—Fred and Ned.

Now, entirely by coincidence, they approached Fresno from hundreds of miles apart. Neither was aware of the other's plans, yet fate would bring them together for an unforgettable reunion.

Completing a five-hour trip from his home near Los Angeles, sixty-six-year-old Fred Losch drove down Columbia Drive East and pulled into the driveway of an expensive house near the Sunnyside golf course. His former squadron commander, Greg Boyington, lived here with his fourth wife, Josephine. A day earlier, Losch had talked to Jo on the phone and learned that Greg was not well. He asked if it would be all right if he drove up and said hello to "Gramps," using Boyington's nickname from the war. Jo invited him to come.

Glancing at the beautiful house and landscaping, Losch knew subconsciously that it was mostly Jo's place. She had divorced a wealthy highway contractor before marrying Greg, who in his own right had enjoyed only short-lived moments of financial success. His life had been a series of monumental highs and lows, with alcohol almost always present, but thanks to Jo the past several years had been among his best. A decade earlier a network television series based on his best-selling autobiography, *Baa Baa Black Sheep,* had run for three seasons, ensuring him of lasting fame as one of the most colorful personalities of World War II.

Losch had not been fond of the television show, which was now off the air except in small syndicated markets. He objected to Hollywood's depiction of his fighter squadron as a bunch of misfits. That Boyington had taken an active role in perpetrating the myth made it worse. Yet, the public's response to the action-adventure show had been favorable, and at least Losch understood Boyington's motives—he needed the money. After ten years, loyalty and friendship had overcome any lingering disapproval.

While Fred was meeting Jo, Ned Corman and his wife drove from their Lake Tahoe home to her daughter's house in Fresno. Raised on a dairy farm in the little hamlet of Zion, Pennsylvania, Corman had joined Pan American Airlines after the war and eventually retired as a captain in 747s. He, too, looked forward to calling on his former squadron commander, having become reacquainted with Boyington a few years earlier. Ned was no fan of the television series, either, but he was sympathetic after hearing the Old Man's frank admissions about alcoholism.

Reaching Fresno, Ned tried to contact Boyington but was disappointed to learn from Jo that he was sick. He was at a hospice, she said, adding that Fred Losch had just arrived and they could all visit Greg together. Ned agreed to meet them early that evening.

At the prearranged time, Fred and Jo parked on a quiet, tree-lined street in a residential neighborhood on Fresno's northwest side and met Ned on the sidewalk. The friends warmly greeted each other, then crossed a manicured lawn to an attractive, sprawling ranch house. Double doors opened to a tiled foyer, where Jo paused to enter their names in a guest book before steering the men down the hall to the last bedroom on the right.

Turning into the open door, Losch and Corman might have noticed the room's comfortable furnishings, or admired the outside view through a sliding glass door of the pool and palms and banana trees, but their attention was drawn to the pallid figure lying on the hospital bed. The homey bedspread covering him did not soften their shock at how emaciated he appeared.

The two old marines could scarcely believe this was the same bullnecked wrestler they had met on a sweltering tropical island in the South Pacific. Tanned then, powerful and stocky, Boyington had already made a name as one of the best fighter pilots in the corps. The new lieutenants had laughed at his hell-raising, admired his love of fighting. He was a brilliant tactician, and it didn't matter to them that he drank—drunk or sober, he could fly rings around anybody. They teasingly called him "Gramps" because he was already thirty, but deep down they idolized him. As Corman said later, "He was just a little *god* to us."

But here he was. The man before them was what remained of the incessant smoker, unable to quit even after an operation for cancer cost him part of a lung twenty years earlier. Here was the man who had consumed more alcohol than anyone could calculate. Medically, it was amazing he had lasted this long. Inevitably the cancer had returned, metastasizing through the lymphatic system, invading his lungs to the point that he could scarcely breathe. Poor circulation and lack of oxygen left his skin ashen, his hands cold. Cancer had run amok, pulling the life out of fatty tissue, then muscle, so that his once full cheeks and broad nose and lips had all but disappeared. His skull protruded through his sunken face, and his hair, once thick and curly, hung in pitiful strands. His body was shutting down by the hour.

Astonished by the realization of what cancer had done, Corman and Losch had no idea of what to say. Not so the old fighter pilot, who was well aware of what would soon happen. He surprised them by speaking first in a rasping whisper, shredding what little composure they had managed to keep. Perhaps seeing them as young lieutenants again, he said with calm acceptance: "Ah, here's a couple of my boys, coming to say good-bye."

1

Rough and Tumble

The vista that greeted Meriwether Lewis and William Clark as they trekked through Lolo Pass was breathtaking. Leading a congressionally funded expedition across the Bitterroot Range of the Rocky Mountains in September 1805, they became the first known whites to admire the soaring granite peaks and swift, cold rivers of what would later become the panhandle of Idaho. It had taken them sixteen months to come this far, and another year would pass before they returned to their own civilization. Meanwhile, the Shoshone Indians who guided them through the mountains surely saw the white men's presence as a sign that more would follow.

More did, just a trickle, barely noticeable at first. French trappers and missionaries arrived from Canada, giving their descriptive names to some of the tribes, the Nez Percé and Coeur d'Alene among them. For years the hardy trappers and devout reformers were the only newcomers to venture into the unforgiving mountains, but other settlers were eventually drawn by the promise of abundant resources and spectacular beauty. Then came the Civil War, after which the westward expansion mushroomed, precipitated by the joining of the Union Pacific and Central Pacific railroads in 1869. The banging home of a ceremonial gold spike completed an engineering feat that changed the Indians' ways forever—and changed the land.

From the transcontinental railroad a network of tracks

spread across the West like a crazy web. Adventure seekers, industrialists, and immigrants looking for the American Dream rode the rails and wagon trails to newly accessible regions. The seekers surveyed vast regions of timber, found gold and silver, discovered bonanzas of natural bounty; the industrialists found ways to exploit these finds and extract the riches from the land. As the railroads brought more people, the towns grew in proportion, requiring ever greater quantities of lumber.

In 1902, a trained timber estimator named Joseph Boyington left his children in Eau Claire, Wisconsin, and moved to the "stovepipe" of Idaho, not far from the trail blazed by Lewis and Clark. The surrounding mountains held an enormous belt of white pine, reputedly the largest stand in the world, providing plenty of opportunity for a "timber cruiser" such as he. If a landowner wished to sell acreage to a lumber company, Boyington could determine how much usable timber it held, depending on the size of trees the company wanted to log. By traversing the property at specified distances, or "chains," and counting the trees meeting the desired diameter, he could estimate the total board feet of lumber and assess its value.

The lure of opportunity brought Boyington to Dalton Gardens, a peaceful neighborhood of small farms and apple orchards north of Coeur d'Alene. Back in Eau Claire, he had farmed and was proprietor of a wholesale feed and flour business in addition to estimating lumber. A wife named Hannah had been with him at one time, though for the past fifteen years she had not been listed as a member of his household. Of his four children, the three youngest remained in Eau Claire to work or complete their education; the eldest left for Evanston, Illinois, and enrolled in the school of dentistry at Northwestern University.

This was Charles Barker Boyington, born on August 31, 1875. He completed his schooling in 1897, then clerked in Eau Claire until a bookkeeping job took him to Montana for a few years. After a visit to Eau Claire, he left again in 1902 to pursue a doctor of dental science degree. Three years later—making him nearly thirty—he collected his diploma in a ceremony at the Garrick Theater on Randolph Street, then left Evanston for the promise of the West. His destination: Coeur d'Alene, Idaho, a picturesque lakeside town on the western slopes of the Rocky Mountains, just a few miles from his father's home.

Charles Boyington did not own a horse, buggy, or riding equipment. Thus, like most people doing business in town, he walked. Setting up his first practice, he hung his shingle outside an office in the Dollar Block, then equipped his workplace with the latest furniture, including a fancy dental cabinet of dark wood. There was an autoclave for sterilizing tools, an upright telephone with its separate earpiece, a steel cuspidor, and an elaborate belt-driven hand tool that turned drilling and grinding attachments.

Soon after opening the practice, Boyington posed for a photograph beside his barber-style dentist's chair. His short hair was neatly combed, his face fully shaven, drawing attention to a long, straight nose and prominent chin. In this and later photographs he did not smile widely enough to show his own teeth, though his broad mouth had an amicable turn at the corners.

Within a few years his practice was earning a handsome income of about $300 per month—this during a time when a new three-room house on five acres outside town could be bought for $500. Charles put his money into property, purchasing a house on West Foster Avenue, and later mortgaging two more lots with a dwelling on Eleventh Street. Considering the value of the properties and the small lien on his expensive dental equipment, he had already accumulated a respectable net worth.

Such a successful dentist would have been considered a catch for the eligible ladies of Coeur d'Alene, but there was the stigma of divorce: Boyington had been married briefly to heavyset Maude Poore in Montana, a failed union that produced no children. He maintained a low profile for several years, then, at the age of thirty-six, applied for a license to marry Grace Barnhardt Gregory, a twenty-three-year-old with long, dark tresses who had recently arrived in Coeur d'Alene. If his decision seemed impulsive to some, at least the age disparity was nothing new; at about the same time, the county clerk signed a permit for a forty-two-year-old woman to wed a codger of sixty-eight.

Grace may have simply turned his head. She was full figured, with round cheeks that dimpled when she flashed a bright smile. She wore her long hair piled high, in the current style, and was accustomed to fashionable dresses.

Her story began in Monticello, a small crossroads in eastern Iowa, where she was born on January 11, 1888. She was the youngest of six children raised by burly, mustachioed William Gregory and his wife, Ellen. Grace was eight when they moved to Mitchell, South Dakota, where William worked as a road master for the Chicago, Milwaukee & St. Paul Railroad. Misfortune visited the Gregorys in 1901 when fifteen-year-old John was killed accidentally by gunfire at a local shooting gallery; more turmoil followed when William junior divorced his wife. Another son, Forrest, died in 1908 of peritonitis.

Despite the tragedies, or perhaps because of them, Grace was animated, cavorting with a large group of friends. The young ladies wore full-length skirts and high-collared blouses, the young men dressed as dandies. She was a racy teen, sneaking with friends behind the Corn Palace to smoke and probably drink. A talented pianist, in her late teens she traveled some nine hundred miles to enter the music program at a "normal school," the equivalent of a teachers' college, in Detroit, Michigan. The curriculum at the Thomas Normal Training School prepared her for a career in music education, but instead of teaching, she worked in theaters after her 1909 graduation, providing piano accompaniment to motion pictures before the advent of the "talkies."

Evidently she had been hired to play in Coeur d'Alene, either at the Rex Theater or some saloon, when she met Charles Boyington sometime after 1910. They appeared at the courthouse for a marriage license on December 27, 1911, then wasted little time once the union was approved. A traditional church wedding would have been unsuitable because of Charles's divorce, so they stood before justice of the peace Roger Wearne, a boarder at Wolf Lodge. The ceremony was performed on New Year's Day 1912, with Florence and Fred Tiffany (Grace's sister and brother-in-law) as witnesses. There is no indication that anyone else attended.

Charles bought Grace a piano on credit for five dollars a month, and they lived comfortably on his income, but whatever matrimonial bliss they enjoyed was brief. Grace was pregnant by early March, after which a terrible change apparently came over Charles. One night, according to Grace, Charles shoved her into a corner with his fist, then grabbed both her wrists and twisted them while calling her "all sorts of vile and vulgar names." He did not strike her again during the pregnancy, but the verbal abuse continued, "so often," she claimed, "that it would be almost impossible for anyone to remember."

There was little joy for the expectant mother when she reached full term in early December 1912. Snow covered the ground during the first few days of the month, followed by rain on the fourth, a Wednesday. The temperature climbed into the low forties, turning the streets into a quagmire. Fortunately, Grace did not have to be concerned about whether a midwife or attendant could reach her on this dreary day; she had a bed at the Coeur d'Alene Hospital.

At five o'clock, under the glow of newly installed electric lights, Grace gave birth to a healthy ten-pound son. Delivery and recovery were evidently normal for both mother and child.

The next morning their tranquility was shattered by the alarm of two dire emergencies. The first patient was a railroad brakeman, who suffered broken bones and a severe head injury after falling from a freight car. Barely two hours later an ambulance arrived with Hans Ostensen, crushed beneath a pile of rubble when his haberdashery suddenly collapsed. Brought in on a stretcher, he died a few hours later.

The little boy's birth, overshadowed by the drama of injury and death, was announced on an inside column of the *Evening Press.* The baby was as yet unnamed. Grace later gave him her maiden name, Gregory, with or without Charles's participation.

What should have been a cheerful time was but a minor distraction for the couple's imploding marriage. Within three weeks of Grace's discharge from the hospital, Charles began spending his evenings away from home, rarely returning before midnight, if at all. In April, when Gregory was four months old, Charles accused his wife of "having intimate relations with other men," identifying them by name, and proclaimed that he was not the baby's father. Throughout the spring and summer of 1913 he did not physically abuse his wife, but that streak ended in November. Charles stumbled home drunk at three o'clock one morning, cursing with a tirade he repeated often, calling her a "damned bitch" and "damned whore." He grabbed her arms, squeezing until his fingers left bruises visible for weeks. Grace later named specific dates for other beatings, including a violent episode five days before Christmas when Charles knocked her down, pinned her to the floor with his knee, and slapped her. He was ashamed of her, she said, and never took her out in public. Often the baby's crying would elicit outbursts of rage against both mother and child. When she nursed Gregory, Charles called her a sow. He moved out of the house for good the following June, a small gesture since the couple had been separated for the better part of a year.

Gregory showed that he was already something of a climber during the summer of 1914. Playing in Grace's bedroom with some of her combs and brushes one day, he ended up on the sill of an open window. Looking down at the ground below, he decided that he "could make it in the air" and jumped out. "I hadn't learned the law of gravity yet," he later said of the experience. Grace found him lying in a flower bed, momentarily stunned, but he got back on his feet after she brushed him off.

The tumble might have been fondly remembered, but his parents' marriage was nowhere near as resilient as his head. On August 14, Charles visited each of the banks in Coeur d'Alene and arranged for them to refuse credit to Grace, then he contacted several in Spokane and relayed the same instructions. The following day, he went to the Foster Avenue house and tried to coerce her into packing her trunk and returning to South Dakota. She took the initiative instead, saying she had been "reliably informed" that Charles was associating with other women. One of them, in fact, was a neighbor, and Grace decided to call the woman into the yard. Charles became outraged, but Grace called the neighbor anyway. A loud row ensued in the yard separating the houses, with Charles screaming threats at his wife and the neighbor. Nothing more came of it, except that everyone realized the marriage was done for.

On the nineteenth Charles paid for a public announcement in the *Evening Press:* "I hereby notify all parties that from this date I will not be responsible for any debts contracted by my wife, Grace B. Boyington." The following day, she hired an attorney and filed a detailed complaint along with a request for divorce.

Charles hired his own lawyer, and, at the divorce proceedings, produced a love letter Grace had written (but apparently not mailed) to one Ellsworth Hallenbeck, a "young man of Spokane." Their affair had begun in the spring, claimed Charles, when they held "clandestine, lascivious, and lewd meetings" in Coeur d'Alene and other communities. Grace had also entertained different men in the Foster Avenue house in early June, during which they furnished "intoxicating liquors." His proof was her letter to Hallenbeck, written the day after, in which she described being "piffled" during the party.

We expected father [Charles] to walk in every minute and find us in our sad plight. The boys had their hats in hand ready to fly when they heard the latch key turn. But thanks to our luck, father didn't turn up until twelve, and his little "wuf" was sound asleep and snoring when he climbed in.

Whether or not she actually committed adultery, another portion of her letter to Hallenbeck left little doubt about her intentions. "One question I would ask of you loved one— have you feather beds and no bed bugs in your apartment? I'm used to one and not the other." In addition to the damning letter, Charles claimed that she subsequently visited Hallenbeck in his Spokane apartment. She mustered a weak excuse in court, calling the letter a joke written at the urging of a friend, but offered no other defense against the allegations.

The claims, complaints, and countercomplaints continued for months, until finally at ten o'clock on March 4, 1915, the judge presented the final decree. The marriage ended with a whack of his gavel, but the court appearance was only a formality. Days earlier, both parties had signed the judge's stipulations regarding disposition of property and custody of the baby. Grace was awarded custody of her son, the house on Foster Avenue, and its furniture. Charles kept everything else, including the house on Eleventh Street and the right to visit Gregory "at any time during reasonable hours." He paid fifty dollars to fulfill a temporary alimony award, after which he was under no further obligation to Grace or the boy. Evidently, his documentation of Grace's affair had the desired effect on the judge, who took a dim view of her behavior and refused to grant continued alimony.

In the meantime, Grace was already living with Ellsworth Hallenbeck in Spokane, and taking no pains to hide it. She was even listed beside his name in the 1915 city directory, issued months before the divorce. Considering all the trouble she had gone through with Charles, she did not make much of a change; Ellsworth was merely a younger version, but otherwise cut from similar cloth.

• • •

Born in Geneva, New York, on May 2, 1888, Ellsworth was raised in Wenatchee, Washington, along the Columbia River, where he developed a reputation for shenanigans with a gang calling themselves the Dirty Dozen. According to family lore, he had the number five tattooed on the inside of his thigh, putting him roughly in the middle of the gang's hierarchy. Described as "the type that wasn't afraid to try anything," he once took up a challenge from another youth to cross the Columbia. The bet was only fifty cents, but the conditions made it stimulating: the river was frozen, and Ellsworth had to cross it naked. Presumably his clothing remained on the near bank, meaning that he had to cross the ice in both directions before he could get dressed again. He did not have to swim it, just run across, and he pocketed the reward.

He may have been bold, but independent he was not. At the age of twenty-four he still lived with his mother and a sister when they moved to Spokane in 1912, his mother Maude by then a widow. Ellsworth's own life seemed none too exciting. Short, already balding, he was a bookkeeper by trade and led a bookkeeper's sedentary life. He appeared well dressed in photographs, but moved nary a muscle around his eyes or mouth, giving him an utterly flat, emotionless expression. According to his descendants, he was a heavy drinker and smoker. A common trait among alcoholics is a tendency to move frequently and change jobs, thereby attempting "geographic cures" for their lack of self-control. Ellsworth fit this pattern, changing locations and jobs on a regular basis.

The first apartment he shared with Maude and his sister was on Monroe Street, near the Spokane River. Within a year they moved to another on Second Avenue, presumably larger digs to accommodate a fourth person—Ellsworth's "wife," identified only as Josephine in the 1913 directory. He was employed by the Centennial Mill, a large lumber mill beside the river, while his sister Mildred worked as a dentist's assistant. Soon the Hallenbecks moved a few blocks to their third apartment in as many years, but Josephine was out of the picture. This was the year that a new "wife," Grace, appeared with Ellsworth in the 1915 directory.

For the next year and a half, Grace and little Gregory were crowded with Ellsworth, his mother, and his sister into an apartment on South Wall Street. The building was located near the elevated main line in a working-class neighborhood, surrounded by the booming downtown of industrial Spokane.

From one of the upstairs windows, Gregory made his second flight. "For some reason I became airborne again," he remembered later, calling his predilection for tumbling "a habit." Incredibly, he fell to the wooden sidewalk below without sustaining a life-threatening injury, though the force of the impact popped one of his eyes out of its socket. While his mother raced down the stairs, "all excited and hysterical," a nurse who lived in the building was summoned. She performed a neat piece of sidewalk surgery, using her fingers to stuff the eyeball back into its socket ("the cords weren't broken or anything"). His eye was bloodshot for six or seven months, but the condition eventually cleared with no permanent damage.

Gregory's adventures continued. During an outing to a lake one summer, before he learned to swim, he walked into the water until it was over his head. Looking up, he was intrigued by the surface, "like watching the whirling of the water going out of the bathtub," before Grace snatched him out. He sputtered and coughed while she scolded him for the fright she had received.

Ellsworth relocated yet again in 1916 (when Maude and Mildred departed from Spokane), to a five-story brick apartment house on Howard Street, still within a few blocks of the Centennial Mill. By this time, Ellsworth and Grace had been living a common law marriage for two years, and there is little evidence that they tried to legitimize the union. Much later, in a Seattle courtroom, Ellsworth would testify that he and Grace "were married at Spokane, Washington, in the year 1917," but there is no documentation to support this claim. A search of records in both Washington and Idaho failed to locate any record that Grace and Ellsworth applied for a license, let alone were married. There was, however, good reason for them to consider doing so.

Grace was pregnant, having conceived in late April or early May of 1917. Rather than making it legitimate, however, Ellsworth moved them again, this time across the state line into Idaho. If the lack of marriage documents is not convincing, the timing of the move certainly indicates a desire to avoid embarrassment. They went southeast to the small lumber town of St. Maries as husband and wife with virtually no paperwork or burden of proof required. For all practical purposes, Gregory had a new surname: he would henceforth be raised as a Hallenbeck, though nothing had been done legally to change his name.

The move covered less than fifty miles, but the contrast was striking. St. Maries (pronounced—and often misspelled—St. Mary's) was a beautiful small town nestled in a scenic valley. Majestic mountains sloped gracefully down to a plain at the confluence of two rivers, where the St. Maries emptied into the meandering St. Joe, the highest navigable river in the world. The town was defined by a small commercial district consisting of two banks, an opera house, a public library, and an electric power plant. Dominating the hillside above town, the three-story Lincoln School had originally looked pretentious with only a few clapboard houses in the neighborhood, but in seven years it had become overcrowded. Near the rivers, the Milwaukee Mill and a couple of smaller sawmills worked nonstop shifts, cutting up timber as fast as it could be brought from the surrounding forests.

One of Ellsworth's first official acts was to register in St. Maries for the selective service. Some nine million American males were compelled to sign up for the draft, instituted after the United States declared war on Germany. Records prove that Ellsworth did his duty, but the unanswered question is whether he registered as a married or an unmarried man. The deference rate for married men was almost seventy-five percent, much higher than for bachelors. He was not called up in any case, a relief for a twenty-nine-year-old bookkeeper who smoked heavily and drank just as much. Ellsworth did not shy from challenges, but he was more comfortable with ledgers and balance sheets than the rugged life of soldiering.

As an office employee of the Milwaukee Mill, he earned approximately one hundred dollars a month, enough to house his pregnant "wife" and Gregory east of town on a small rise known as Silk Socks Hill, where the residents were said to be the only ones who could afford silk stockings for their ladies. Mill owner Fred Herrick's large home commanded the best view, below which the elevation of each house in descending order signified the relative status of employees: bosses, foremen, and office help. Common laborers occupied the low ground in Milltown, purchasing their necessities at the company store at prices that were guaranteed (along with rent) to absorb the lion's share of their wages.

For miles around, lumberjacks toiled to harvest the seemingly inexhaustible white pine. The labor was grueling and hazardous, conditions were deplorable, and life in the slapdash camps scattered throughout the woods was rugged. In remote cutting areas, loggers often slept on the hard ground. Paydays and holidays brought them stomping into town, where saloons and brothels outnumbered churches by a hefty margin. The 'jacks blew their wages in bars along the muddy streets or down on the waterfront, where they dallied with prostitutes named "Boathouse Nellie" and "Giggles" aboard their rough-hewn shanties on cedar rafts.

Growing up among them, young Gregory saw the lumberjacks at their worst, when they came to town to do their drinking and whoring and fighting with the same vigor they applied to toppling trees. The calendar might have shown it to be the second decade of the twentieth century, but St. Maries could be as rowdy as the cow towns of the Old West. Gregory's perspective was close enough to the ground that he was more impressed by the lumberjacks' footwear than their behavior. "They were familiar sights in their calk boots, which they wore all the time," he later remembered. "Those were their prized possessions; the best piece of equipment they had."

Considering the prevailing environment, it is no wonder that Gregory developed a headstrong nature, partly inherited from Grace's independence, but equally absorbed from his surroundings. He was almost completely unfettered, especially after Grace gave birth to another son on February 2, 1918. She became occupied with caring for William DeWitt Hallenbeck, a situation that suited Gregory just fine. At just five years old, he hadn't a clue to his half-brother's different lineage, and would remain oblivious to it for years.

Gregory's infant sibling was certainly no playmate for him at this stage, but he had two young friends, John Theriault and Reed Elwell, both within a few months of his age. Together they roamed the unpaved streets of St. Maries, the meadows near the river, and the woods left uncut by the loggers. They covered a sizable region, sometimes hiking to a peak several hundred feet above town where they played at being lumberjacks. When it came to climbing trees, Gregory had no equal. "I seemed to have a penchant for climbing in high, dangerous places," he recalled, "like the tallest trees that were available. Some of them that I loved to climb especially well were situated right on the edge of a cliff, which made the height even more fantastic."

Another early development was a love of fisticuffs. Grace would later recall that Gregory "was always a fighter, always coming home with a bloody nose." The bloodletting was a result of his size. Heredity had seen to it that his legs were short (and by his fifth birthday they were chubby too), but his stature did not prevent him from being aggressive. He was obstinate, unconcerned with the possibility of pain or humiliation. The outcome of a fight was secondary—it was far better to fight and get whipped than not fight at all. Even if his opponents were bigger or stronger, Gregory learned to face them, and he gave as good as he got. He was "still a little kid" when he fought an antagonist fitting the bigger-and-stronger description in his own neighborhood. Kenneth

Fisher, several years older and about forty pounds heavier, lived a few doors away.

Their first encounter was brief. Kenneth "beat the living daylights" out of Gregory, who went home bleeding, his clothes torn. When Grace saw his condition she took pity and wiped away the blood, then helped him change clothes. Meanwhile, Mrs. Fisher called her son inside. Within twenty minutes Gregory returned to his opponent's house, knocked on the door, and asked, "Mrs. Fisher, is Kenneth home?" Again the fracas resumed, and again Gregory stumbled home, his clothing asunder and blood dripping from his nose. Grace, less patient as she ministered to this round of injuries, scolded, "Now, this is the last time—you stay away from Kenneth."

Gregory complied, but not before learning another valuable lesson. "I did go back for the third time," he later admitted, "and the same thing happened. I was all bloody and my clothes all torn up, but there was one thing different when I got [home] this time. My mother didn't clean up my clothing or my face; *she* beat the living daylights out of me."

Thus he established early the reputation that would echo throughout his life: of having a bulldog's tenacity despite being knocked down or hurt. Even when his enemies were not tangible, as Gregory learned was sometimes the case, he would never surrender.

2

A Trip Through the Air

By the spring of 1918, when doughboys of the American Expeditionary Force began their first serious fighting on French soil, Ellsworth Hallenbeck was keenly interested in the rapidly expanding air war. A bright and analytical man, he shared the dramatic accounts of aerial battles in magazines with his five-year-old "stepson," who was equally fascinated with flying.

For the past two years, American pilots had been shooting down airplanes as members of the Lafayette Escadrille, a volunteer unit attached to the French Flying Corps. The sometimes overzealous reporters loved to compare pilots to the knights of the Middle Ages, and the public ate it up. They thrilled to the tales of brightly decorated planes skidding and twisting through the sky as the heroes cheated death, using another modern invention, the machine gun, to duel with each other.

There was also a refreshing sort of etiquette in the sky. Stories were told, some of them true, of opponents who failed to gain a decisive advantage over each other, then exchanged salutes in mutual respect before heading back to their aerodromes. After years of indescribable bloodshed in the trenches, the deceptively clean nature of air warfare was welcome.

More realistically, especially as technology advanced, aerial combat frequently ended in violent death, the losing pilot perhaps horribly mangled in the wreckage of his plane or burned to a crisp in a fiery crash. The winners insisted they were shooting down the plane, not trying to kill the enemy, and most were genuinely glad to see their opponent survive. A triumphant pilot was rewarded with a "victory" rather than a "kill," and appropriately fêted for his bravery. Independent confirmation of a claim was required before credit was given, and pilots were known to brave shellfire at the front in order to locate the wreckage of a fallen enemy. When an individual reached five victories (initially ten for the French), he was deemed an "ace," a new word in the lexicon of warfare.

To keep up with the demand for stories of the valiant pilots and their encounters, publishers cranked out magazine articles, fictional serials, and pulp novels. Ellsworth read some of these to Gregory, who learned the lyrical names of dashing pilots such as Raoul Lufbery, America's first ace in the Lafayette Escadrille, and Frank Luke, an unruly, impossibly handsome loner who specialized in balloon-busting. Both died heroically in battle. The Germans had their own fascinating pilots. There was the arrogant Prussian, Manfred von Richthofen, and the gallant Oswald Boelke, and the colorful aristocrat Hermann Goering, later one of Adolf Hitler's top henchmen and commander of the Luftwaffe.

Even in little St. Maries, citizens didn't have to look far to find their own aviation hero. Clyde Pangborn was a flight student in the army air service, making him the town's first pilot. His widowed mother was a seamstress ("hem-stitcher," in Gregory's words) who lived in a clapboard house on the St. Joe floodplain. She kept the town informed of her son's training.

Gregory and his father followed another beloved American pilot, former race-car driver Eddie Rickenbacker, who emerged as the nation's most famous flyer when his score of Albatrosses and Fokkers began to mount. He accumulated twenty-six victories in a remarkably short span before returning at war's end to a whirlwind tour of parades, speeches, and keys to cities.* The reality was less glamorous for Rickenbacker. He learned (as did Charles Lindbergh less than a decade later) to despise invasive pressmen and greedy people who turned the tour into a circus.

Caught up in the romance of aviation, Gregory took a shine to airplane models "at a kindergarten age," fashioning his own from "bits of shingles and paper" in the days before commercial kits. Perhaps it helped to pass the time while he convalesced at home after a tonsillectomy in 1918. He spent three days in a hospital and never went back during his entire childhood.

Meanwhile, news of Clyde Pangborn's adventures made the rounds in western Idaho. He completed flight training in late 1918 and was commissioned a second lieutenant in the reserves, alas too late to participate in the war, so he remained in Texas as an instructor. After his unit was demobilized the following March, he made his way to Spokane, where aviation was just getting started. By the spring of 1919 he had associated himself with the Northwest Aircraft Company, fabricating what was said to be the first locally built aircraft. He would be its first pilot. He also purchased a surplus Curtiss JN-4 two-seat biplane, a forgiving machine known endearingly as the Jenny. While trying to fly it from California to eastern Washington, he encountered a series of mishaps, so the plane completed the trip on a railroad flatcar. While the Jenny was being rebuilt, he formed his own flying business.

The first half of 1919 was an equally interesting time for Gregory. He managed to fall into the river one day and was apparently in real danger of being swept away, but was saved, as he put it, by "a Jap farmer boy [who] snatched me from the spring floodwaters of the St. Joe River." Whatever led to the near drowning, the certainty is that Gregory was exercising his freedom to run loose and explore, probably

---

* In 1969 a U.S. Air Force review board reduced Rickenbacker's score to 24.33 after determining that several of his victories had been shared with other pilots.

with his pals Johnny and Reed. It was just another episode to them, a situation that turned out in Gregory's favor, soon forgotten as they played throughout the summer months.

Freedom ended in early September, when they began the daily walk to first grade in a small schoolhouse down by the lumber mill. Overcrowding at the Lincoln School had resulted in the opening of the Milwaukee School in the Herrick Building, names that sounded important, but the structure was indistinguishable from the nondescript houses in Milltown. The hike itself seemed long to Gregory, who described himself as looking "like the little boy . . . with fat, dimpled knees on a Campbell's tomato soup ad." But there were pleasant diversions along the way. Meadowlarks sang as he walked through the pastures between Silk Socks Hill and the school, and many years later he remained fond of their call. On warm days he made the trip barefoot, a Huckleberry Finn existence for a boy who loved the outdoors.

A break from the classroom came barely two weeks after school began. Wednesday, September 17, was set aside for the observance of Constitution Day, but the Tuesday edition of the *Gazette-Record* cautioned readers that the day was not for frolicking. Governor David Davis announced that he expected all citizens to gather at their community centers "for a day of study." In St. Maries, the Lincoln School auditorium would be the venue for patriotic music, followed by speeches in the afternoon. When the pontificating ended, Clyde Pangborn and an assistant (identified as Lieutenant Reed) would present the city's first aerial exhibition.

The *Gazette* article left little doubt that this would be one of the most thrilling and momentous occasions in St. Maries history, for not only was Pangborn going to "make airplane flights," he would also offer citizens an opportunity to fly. The idea of leaving the ground seemed so foreign that the newspaper described it quaintly: "All those who wish to make a trip through the air should make application to Lieutenant Pangborn and be on the field."

The "field" was simply a meadow down by the St. Joe,

toward which Pangborn and Reed pointed their biplane after taking off from Spokane that Tuesday afternoon. The nicest weather of the year frequently came in late summer, and September 16 was no exception, the mercury hovering near eighty as they followed the river to St. Maries.

Down below, Gregory and his schoolmates were at recess outside the Milwaukee School, playing in the shadow of pine-crested peaks. A column of steam, starkly white against the blue sky, rose from the sawmill, where the tone of the mill's big saw dropped as the blade bit into a huge pine, then rose again after the cut was done. The song of the saw reached the children clearly, a familiar rhythm of their day.

Faintly at first, a new sound came to the valley. It ebbed and flowed, then sharpened into a motor's distinctive throbbing that bounced off the mountains from high above. Children looked skyward, squinting against the sun, trying to locate the source of the noise that seemed to approach at a leisurely pace. Indeed it did, for the airplane piloted by Pangborn cruised at a mere sixty miles an hour. Its V-8 engine turned at low revolutions, creating a resonant exhaust note along with a secondary vibrato as its two-bladed propeller slapped the air—a sound as pleasant as a distant lawn mower on a lazy day. Suddenly there it was: two long, straight wings, the upper considerably longer and cantilevered ahead of the lower, a slender fuselage tapering to an elliptical stabilizer, a bright, tricolor rudder. The whole of it was symmetrically balanced, with colorful roundels on the bottom wing flashing red, white, and blue as the Jenny banked above St. Maries. In the aft cockpit Pangborn throttled back, slowing the Jenny as it glided earthward. He and Reed were visible now, cloth helmets atop their heads.

Galvanized into action, knowing instinctively that the Jenny was going to land, Gregory ran from the schoolyard toward the nearby meadows. Too late the teacher saw him and yelled, "Gregory, come back here! Recess is over!" Without slowing a bit he hollered over his shoulder, "Can't, teacher! There's an airplane gonna land down in the field, and I gotta be there when it lands!" Johnny Theriault ran after him, and together they made straight for the meadow as fast as their legs would go, racing toward the landing site while the Jenny burbled overhead. The two little truants did not see it touch down, but they heard the engine roar as Pangborn added power and taxied his airplane through the grass.

The boys were out of breath when they reached the plane, now parked at a jaunty angle on what looked like bicycle wheels, the wooden skid beneath its tail all but lost in the meadow grass. Up close, the boys could see the crisscrossed array of wires that braced the varnished struts supporting the wings. Forward of the wings the Jenny was all engine—an arched radiator, swept-back exhaust manifold, and cooling louvers in the metal cowling. Aft of the metalwork, the plane was covered entirely with fabric, stretched tight as a drum-head over wooden ribs by the application of highly flamma-ble "dope." In a few places, fresh repairs from Pangborn's recent mishaps smelled of lacquer. The Jenny had a special aura, ticking softly as her engine cooled.

Pangborn and Reed climbed down, perhaps not too sur-prised that a couple of boys were the first to reach the meadow. The aviators considered themselves "barnstorm-ers," members of that vagabond livelihood named after the practice of Old World actors who staged their performances in the barns of consenting landowners. At first it was enough to appear over a town where an airplane had never been seen up close, then land in a suitable pasture. Thrill-seekers and the curious would inevitably come, and some would pay for a ride. Eventually, barnstormers had to become creative to entice crowds, giving rise to the aerial circus. The slow, sta-ble Jennies were ideal platforms for daredevils to perform wing walking, parachute jumps, even transfers from one plane to another. Lieutenant Reed was a mechanic, but he hoped to draw crowds as a stuntman, and took the dramatic stage name of "El Diablo."

Boldly the boys approached and asked for a ride. Pangborn and Reed both laughed; the boys would hardly be able to see over the cockpit rim, even when standing on the seat. Instead of refusing, however, Pangborn declared that a ride was five dollars. It was the only motivation Gregory needed. "I tore off from the parked airplane," he recalled later, "and ran all the way to my dad's office."

Reaching the mill, Gregory burst through the door, jabbering about the biplane that had just landed and could he please go for a ride and it cost only five dollars. Ellsworth got almost as excited as Gregory and might have gone to see for himself, but he could not leave the office. There was no denying Gregory the opportunity, however, so Ellsworth fished in his pockets. Not enough. Five dollars, after all, represented more than a day's pay. As the story goes, Ellsworth punched keys on the cash register (Gregory called it "almost a reflex action"), and pulled five dollars out of the drawer. Gregory was out the door again in a flash. "I don't know whether I even said thanks," he later admitted, "but I grabbed that five and away I went with my little fat legs, back to that airplane. When I got there, I was exhausted."

After all that exercise, the boys were put off temporarily. The flight would have to wait until the following day. To offset their disappointment, Pangborn offered them money to stay with the plane while he and Reed went into town, a deal the boys were only too happy to accept. The men were gone several hours: When Gregory failed to return home for supper, his mother grew worried.

Years later she recalled that evening in a letter to radio correspondent and newspaper columnist Lowell Thomas, who was a friend of Pangborn's:

> About dusk [Gregory] came in all excited, saying that Pang had given him and his pal each a quarter for guarding the plane from souvenir hunters. He pleaded with me, begging to be allowed to go up, the next day. I remonstrated, saying it was pretty dangerous. Gregory said: "But, Mother, how will I ever learn to be a flier if I don't go up?"

In the morning Grace finally relented, and Gregory ran with Johnny Theriault across the meadows. The Jenny sat basking in the sun, the morning even more glorious than the previous day—a perfect example of Indian summer. Gregory held out five dollars, warm and crumpled, and the boys were hoisted into the front cockpit. It was cavernous and dark inside, under the shadow of the upper wing. Almost everything was made of wood, not unlike the interior of a boat, with exposed ribs and stringers. The varnished instrument panel held five simple gauges: water temperature, oil temperature, tachometer, airspeed indicator, and a huge altimeter, described by one pilot as "the size of a porthole on the *Queen Mary*." A crescent-shaped windscreen capped the fuselage, but the boys were too short to see through it, and the lower wing obstructed much of their downward view. They could see forward only by leaning their heads out. There were no helmets for their little skulls, nor did anyone strap them in.

Handing a stack of pamphlets to Gregory, Pangborn instructed him to toss them out when they were over the town, then climbed into the rear seat. Before he could start the Curtiss OX-5 engine, which had to be cranked by hand, the propeller was pulled through several revolutions with the ignition off to prime the cylinders—no easy chore considering the big engine's compression. This was Reed's job. When everything was ready, Pangborn checked that the propeller arc was clear, set the ignition, and hollered, "Contact!" With that timeless shout, Reed pulled down sharply on the propeller and jumped back as the engine kicked. The OX-5 was notoriously hard to start, and its propeller shaft was high, requiring Reed to stretch, off balance. Gruesome accidents were the result of failing to get out of the way soon enough. After several sputtering tries, the OX-5 caught and settled down to a steady roar. The noise that had seemed so sedate from the ground was now deafening, and the boys were buffeted by prop wash.

Pangborn opened the throttle to give the Jenny inertia. The plane began to bounce and sway over the uneven ground as he taxied to the end of the pasture, then the engine roared as he gave it full throttle to turn the long-winged plane into the wind. Suddenly the ship was surging ahead, rumbling loudly over the pasture. The boys gripped the cockpit rim fiercely, feeling the jolts through every bone. The tail came up and the grass seemed to race by, and at the incredible speed of forty-five miles an hour the pounding stopped abruptly. The boys' stomachs dropped as they felt the exquisite sensation of breaking free of the earth.

After that it was simultaneously the scariest and most exhilarating thing they had ever done. The Jenny was all wing and flat belly, giving them the world's greatest carnival ride as it smacked against pockets of warm air rising from the ground. Gregory would not think much of his cliff-side tree climbing after this. He could see far more of the wondrous details in the valley below: the railroad, meandering alongside the St. Joe, perhaps a steamboat that looked no bigger than a bathtub toy; there was the mill with its massive yards, and the Lincoln School on the hill. It was an experience that touched his soul.

Such perfection of circumstances—a gorgeous summer morning in the quintessential biplane with a dashing barnstormer—would have seemed too contrived were it not so well documented. The details from several accounts match. While they stood on the seat, the boys tossed leaflets advertising rides for Constitution Day, as if Pangborn needed the billing. Wind in their faces, splashed by warm droplets of water from the radiator, and being *told* to throw paper overboard, Gregory and Johnny were as close to heaven as any mortal six-year-olds could fathom. Even better, the ride lasted longer than the original bargain, simply because the Jenny climbed so slowly it took a good ten minutes just to reach leaflet-tossing altitude. Grace, having promised to come outside so that she could see Gregory wave, later commented, "I couldn't even see him, let alone his little hand waving."

The flight came to an end, of course, but there was good news. Pangborn promised he'd take them up again the next day for free if they would toss out more handbills. In the meantime, he and El Diablo spent the remainder of Wednesday flying passengers and performing stunts.

The boys tried to act nonchalant about their adventure when they got back on the ground, but little Julia Theriault saw right through them. "It scared them both," she remembered, "but they returned home full of bravado, saying, 'Oh, it was nothing.' It *was* a big deal, and both of the boys were so thrilled." Grace also wrote that Gregory talked in his sleep about airplanes throughout the night. The next morning, he confidently made an announcement before leaving the house. "He told me to be out in the backyard again," she wrote, "and he would throw a pamphlet down for me to read."

Together with Johnny, Gregory headed for the pasture again, where Pangborn honored his promise and helped the boys into the Jenny. Again they went aloft, and the youngsters dropped handbills while Pangborn maneuvered his machine above the valley. When he passed over Silk Socks Hill, Gregory failed to impress his mother. "He of course threw the slip of paper when he was directly over our house, and it landed a mile away." Nevertheless his second flight was just as exciting as the first, and the advertising paid dividends. The town's blacksmith plunked down thirty silver dollars for a half-hour ride.

From that day forward, Gregory's passion for airplanes and flying was insatiable. Unlike most boys, whose notion of what to do as adults changed whimsically throughout youth, he had met his heroes, shared an adventure with them, and knew what he wanted as though it was carved in stone. Grace later wrote, "Greg often said to me, 'Mother, you've always told me that if I wanted anything badly enough, to work for it and I could do it, and the only thing I want badly enough is to be a flier of the type that Clyde Pangborn is.'"

3

Deeds

After his dreams were carried about as high as they could go, Gregory's earthbound life seemed too tranquil. Passing the hours in school must have been agonizing, if eased somewhat by the status he and Johnny enjoyed briefly among their classmates. When the importance of his first flying feat diminished, further adventures became necessary.

Before he could dream up anything even remotely similar to the excitement of flying, another dashing visitor came to town. "When I was in first or second grade," he remembered, "my teacher's husband came home on leave and he was in his Marine Corps blues." It was an eye-catching uniform, with a bold red stripe down the trousers, a brass-buttoned tunic, and a fancy white hat. Gregory called it "the best looking getup . . . Sort of like Santa Claus."

His dream of becoming a pilot had now been romanced by the glamour of a military uniform, a perfectly ordinary progression. Patriotism was fervent nationwide in the aftermath of the war, as demonstrated by the turnout to observe Constitution Day. There was new pride in Old Glory. With Clyde Pangborn and the teacher's husband as his role models, Gregory decided early in life that he wanted to pilot military planes. A benefit of his ambition was that he worked hard at his studies, once claiming that he "never missed school." As a fourth-grader, he even wobbled into school one morning with a large knot on his forehead after being briefly knocked unconscious, the result of his first attempted horseback ride.

A Native American from the Coeur d'Alene federal reservation had come to town on a cayuse pony to sell huckleberries. The rider wore "a band around his forehead and regular Indian clothes," but Gregory had seen plenty of Coeur d'Alenes before. He was more interested in the pony. "I was fascinated by this little horse," he recalled, describing the typical cayuse as undersized but "real rugged."

To his delight, the Indian wanted to sell the horse. Gregory hoped he could borrow enough money from Ellsworth to buy it, and convinced the Indian to bring it around to O'Dwyer's Feed & Grain Company, where Ellsworth now kept the books. It might have been pure fantasy to think that "Dad" would loan the money, but Gregory had watched him pull a few dollars out of the Milwaukee Mill's cash drawer once; maybe the same would happen at O'Dwyer's.

Instead of making any such gesture, Ellsworth suggested that Gregory try the horse, probably wanting to see if the boy knew anything about riding. If so, the idea backfired. No sooner had Gregory swung his leg over the Western-style saddle than the Indian smacked the horse on the rump without handing up the reins. "Off the horse went," Gregory said, matter-of-factly. "I tried to reach the reins, but they were dangling way out of my reach, so there was nothing I could do but hold on to the saddle horn."

The pony raced along a side street that paralleled the river until it turned sharply at the wharf just a few blocks ahead. Gregory continually shouted "whoa" to stop the pony, but that only made it accelerate until its "little belly was only about two feet off the ground." Ellsworth ran inside the feed store and phoned the dock. Something—either his call or the shouts of onlookers—brought "a bunch of lumberjacks" to take position across a connecting road, where they lined up to intercept the pony when it turned the corner. But the animal had too much speed to negotiate the turn and skidded headlong into a building on the far side of the road. Gregory bounced off the building and landed on the ground, lying dazed while someone held a cold compress against his forehead. Despite the injury, he went to school wearing a lump on his forehead, and no doubt enthralled friends with his story. Getting knocked out was the Holy Grail of minor injuries.

His teacher, on the other hand, would not have shown sympathy. Mrs. Copenhoffer was "a tough old gal," the only teacher Gregory publicly recognized. In this case, it was a measure of his admiration for her. He learned the hard way that she was formidable—the type who would employ corporal punishment as often as necessary—and savvy too. "I forget what I had done that she didn't like," he began. "I knew she was going to belt me one, but at that age, in the fourth grade, I thought everybody was right-handed, so I was waiting to duck her right hand. Doggone if she didn't come around with a left hand and whack me smack on the jaw, and knock me right on my fanny."

In the same way his mother's tough love had taught him to heed reasonable advice, Mrs. Copenhoffer's boxing lesson lasted a lifetime. "From then on," he mused, "I observed whether people were right-handed or left-handed before I tangled with them."

Five years after Gregory's magical flight with Clyde Pangborn, another flier barnstormed into St. Maries. He was Nicholas Mamer, one of the first pilots in Spokane's new National Guard unit, the 116th Aviation Squadron. Officially credited with three aerial victories during World War I, he had been shot down once himself in flames. He survived by keeping calm, slipping his plane sideways to fan away the fire until he crash-landed in friendly territory.

As a lieutenant in the National Guard he flew plenty, but he liked to barnstorm throughout the region in his spare time using his own airplane. During his visit to St. Maries, he and an accomplice gave demonstration flights and took passengers on short rides. They used the same meadow Pangborn had flown from, now with an official-sounding name: Pangborn Field. Oddly, Gregory never mentioned Mamer's visit, but it is inconceivable that he missed it. Among the barn-stormer's thrilling stunts was a parachute jump from an altitude of fifteen hundred feet.

Gregory and Johnny, now eleven years old, sought their own aerial adventure. They dreamed up a good one. Starting with some pieces of lumber and a set of wheels from a child's wagon, they constructed what Gregory called an "airplane," though it was actually a coaster à la the Little Rascals, with a wing attached. There was no engine, meaning they had to push and drag their project up a hill in order to test it.

Gregory did not specify where the attempt took place, but described it as "near downtown." The logical site was Second Avenue, a favorite among sled riders due to its reputation as "the longest, steepest, most dangerous street in town." If the boys indeed pushed their contraption to the top, they started from high above St. Maries, with an unobstructed view down the street to its watery end at the river. A block from the riverbank, a railroad crossing promised a rough ride if the go-cart made it that far.

Gregory climbed aboard and was soon accelerating down the hill. He did not elaborate later about devices for controlling the coaster, and his description of the outcome indicates that there was nothing more than a pivoting front axle for steering. "I recall going down this hill pell-mell, getting plenty of speed," he stated. "About the time I got down to where the downtown buildings were, the front wheels of this little airplane got off the ground. The wing was up about two feet off the ground, just enough so that there was no more control over the wheels on this little airplane we made, and just high enough to go through [a] store's plate glass window when we went out of control."

His account, recorded in a California sound studio nearly five decades later, had all the earmarks of a fish story, and Gregory was a great one for embellishments. It is difficult to imagine, for example, the breaking of a plate glass window without serious injury. Before the advent of safety glass, plate glass splintered into lethal shards. It is also improbable that a heavy wooden go-cart gained enough lift to become airborne. But from Gregory's perspective, the sensation of careening out of control down a steep hill probably felt like flying. He also reached a wise conclusion about the go-cart: "Thank heavens it wasn't built any better and didn't get any higher."

Elements of his boyhood stories probably happened much as he told them, if only because of his reputation among his peers for stunts. He attempted them for a variety of reasons, including attention. Perhaps he had inherited what would later become known as the "extreme gene," in which a high level of the neurotransmitter dopamine causes people to enjoy pushing the limits of risk.

He certainly did not suffer from acrophobia. Near the train depot, a pair of grain elevators was connected by a beam that Gregory "especially liked" to walk across, holding his arms like a tightrope walker high above the tracks. "There was a little breeze up there," he added, "and [it was] quite precarious." One misstep would have meant certain death, but he believed he was invincible.

He was equally addicted to speed, revealed by his penchant for "borrowing" horseback rides. He also did his share of other mischief universal to young boys, such as teasing little girls. One, who remained in St. Maries nearly her whole life, remembered that Gregory showed her how to cross her eyes, telling her they would stick. She then demonstrated for her mother, who put a hasty stop to the practice.

There were other incidents, fondly recalled by John Theriault and Reed Elwell for the rest of their lives. As Reed's widow later put it, "They would laugh until they cried, having a couple of beers and talking about Greg. The kids were really daredevils in those days. The stories they would tell are unbelievable now, but at least some of it was true."

At the age of twelve Gregory witnessed a fatality, one that taught him a long-remembered lesson about human nature. In the late summer of 1925, advertisements for a "Gigantic Air Circus" in Spokane grabbed his attention. The event would feature the largest gathering of airplanes ever to visit the region, with army aircraft from as far away as Minneapolis and San Francisco, plus National Guard units from Portland, Seattle, and Spokane. The city's business community hoped the flight demonstrations and air races would draw huge crowds for a Liberty Bond drive.

The day before the event, scheduled for Sunday, September 20, Gregory and Johnny boarded a train at the St. Maries depot, intending to travel entirely on their own. The journey was not particularly long, but as Gregory put it, "At our age, going all by ourselves, it could have been a thousand miles." Grace and Ellsworth maintained little supervision, allowing Gregory to do as he wished (with Johnny as his willing accomplice), but it is still hard to imagine they let the two boys travel alone. Evidently the boys simply went on an unannounced adventure, pooling their money from summer jobs to cover the cost of the overnight trip.

Upon reaching the city they walked into the lobby of the Coeur d'Alene Hotel and told the desk clerk, "We'd like the cheapest room in the hotel." A nearby guest (who turned out to be an acquaintance of Grace's) burst out laughing, but the clerk honored the boys' request. "We *did* get the cheapest room in the house," Gregory explained. "I don't believe there was a bath in it, just a 'johnny,' but that's all we needed."

Unknown to the boys, tempers were flaring elsewhere in the city over a volatile mix of religion and politics, the outcome of which had a profound effect on the air show. The trouble began when the pastor of the Methodist church, one Reverend Magin, objected to the scheduling of the event on the Sabbath. Curiously, he had never complained before about the regular Sunday-morning aerial drills performed by the 116th Aviation Squadron; what set him off was the wording of the program as a circus. Without consulting the city's Ministerial Association—but freely using its name and political leverage—Magin sent telegrams to the governor of Washington and the War Department in Washington, D.C., claiming that the God-fearing citizens of Spokane did not want the show held on a Sunday.

Governor Roland Hartley wisely took no action, but the War Department issued a statement on Saturday afternoon grounding all regular army airplanes from the performance. A committee of Spokane businessmen pleaded with Reverend Magin to withdraw his protest, but he stubbornly refused. The same committee then stayed up most of Saturday night trying to reach political connections in Washington, while the National Guard pilots worked late to rescript aerial portions of the show. Their Jenny equipped squadrons and the Forest Service with its three De Havilland DH-4s would have to perform the entire program. As one guardsman later wrote, "I never flew so many different kinds of missions in my life."

At least the weather was cooperative. Clear skies and warm sunshine brought throngs of spectators out to Parkwater Field on Sunday. Trains shuttled many of the spectators to the airport, where the boys wandered through a crowd estimated at thirty thousand and gawked at more than two dozen biplanes parked wingtip-to-wingtip. The flight program got under way with a closed-course race between the three forestry service DH-4s, the most powerful aircraft to participate, with four-hundred-horsepower Liberty engines. Hometown hero Nick Mamer thrilled the crowd by flying one of the big ships during the race, but he lost to an army reservist, Lt. Schuyler Priestly.

Immediately after the race, the three pilots changed to Jennies for the next event—a dramatic demonstration of the "balloon-busting" techniques used by the late Frank Luke and others during the Great War. In his haste to change planes and missions, Priestly forgot to compensate for the fact that his Jenny had less than half the power of the De Havilland. Carrying an army private in the front cockpit, he reduced throttle and leveled off at four hundred feet, then entered a steep turn at the western boundary of the field. The underpowered Jenny promptly stalled and, in less than the time it took for the crowd to draw a collective breath, nosed over and plunged into a gravel pit. Gregory watched it fall. He was too short to see the plane crumple into the ground, but a column of steam from the Jenny's shattered radiator marked its location.

The pilots aloft maneuvered their planes in an attempt to distract the crowd, but spectators surged toward the crash site. The boys followed to the edge of the gravel pit and looked down, where they saw a twisted mass of broken spars and torn fabric. The impact had killed the private instantly; Priestly was alive when extricated from the wreckage, but he died while being lifted into a waiting ambulance.

As word spread that both aviators were dead, a bizarre reaction swept through the crowd. Gregory's most powerful memory of the tragedy was not of broken bodies, but of the crowd's behavior: "They just seemed to go wild. Before they could remove this poor pilot's body, they were hacking away at different parts of that fabric-and-wood airplane, getting souvenirs. Just pieces of it. They seemed to me like wild animals, like wolves, the way they tore that airplane literally to shreds in acquiring souvenirs."

His amazement over the crowd's pandemonium "never ceased over the years," particularly because the people were mostly adults. He discovered at the age of twelve that so-called civility had not taken bloodlust out of human nature. Perhaps the reverend had a point after all.

Gregory and Johnny endured a somber return to St. Maries but they had the satisfaction of knowing they had paid for the excursion with their own money. Gregory's share of the adventure was earned through at least two jobs. The first was a paper route with the *Gazette,* a small job with only two deliveries per week, but the second was "considered quite a plum." By the summer of 1925, Johnny Theriault's father, an employee of the U.S. Forest Service, had arranged summer jobs for the boys in one of the logging camps. They were "flunkies" in the cookhouse that served as both kitchen and dining room, setting tables and waiting on loggers, washing dishes and sweeping the floor. Camp life was rugged, but well suited to Gregory's independent nature. He worked long hours, ate simple meals, and breathed the fresh air of the piney woods.

There were pitfalls for a naive youngster, however. Having worshiped the hefty lumberjacks from a distance for practically his whole life, he was thrust into close quarters with these intimidating men. They needed little prompting to have some fun at his expense. On their first evening in camp, Gregory and Johnny were allowed to eat with the men before they started work the next day. The boys ate quietly, content to watch as the lumberjacks attacked dinner and bantered among themselves, but Gregory interrupted the conversation by dropping his fork on the floor. Johnny's sister Julia, who still vividly remembered the story, later revealed how the minor accident quickly snowballed into trauma: "Greg turned to the flunky and asked if he could 'have a clean fork, please.' Of course this brought forth guffaws from the seasoned guys and embarrassed Greg. John said the men kidded Greg because his face became so red."

Even worse than a random mishap with a piece of flatware, Gregory endured regular chiding in his own home. As Ellsworth's alcoholism progressed, he started to become acerbic, frequently derisive, creating an environment that was far from nurturing for Gregory and his younger half-brother, Bill. Grace, for all her periods of liveliness, was often indifferent and gave praise grudgingly. She, too, was drinking more.

Emotionally Gregory was in no-man's-land. His parents, particularly the person he knew as "Dad," did not measure up to the pilots and other heroes he worshiped. Ellsworth's drinking and cynicism had to have affected Gregory's outlook, and his own esteem. He compensated by continually trying to prove how tough he was, which in his mind was equated with bravery. His friends would later laugh about his adventures in their twilight years, but Reed's widow believed there was a troubled edge to Gregory's motives. "He would climb this peak outside of St. Maries," she said. "He would have fallen down a certain way, and would come home with all these scratches, or at least blood all over himself. Of course, the other kids with him knew he hadn't fallen. He had purposely abused his body so it would look like he had been a hero that day."

If it was acclaim Gregory sought, he realized partial success when Grace gave him his first nickname, "Deeds." It was certainly appropriate for a youngster who had flown in a barnstormer's airplane, sped recklessly down a hill on a homemade go-cart, crashed on horseback, and deliberately risked his neck on plenty of other occasions. She used "Deeds" as a pet name from time to time, otherwise it never got much notice. Twenty years hence the nickname would resurface unexpectedly, and with far greater impact. It was used just once—as a code word, no less—bringing incalculable comfort to a worried mother.

To the casual observer, Gregory led a charmed life. Participating in remarkable adventures for one so young, he had already escaped several potentially deadly mishaps with only minor injuries. As a result, he developed an unshakeable belief in his own indestructibility. Throughout his life, as an extension of this supreme confidence, he would continue to exhibit apparent fearlessness. It was his nature to charge into situations that were dangerous, then ask the "what-ifs" later.

Beneath the bravado, however, dwelled frustration. Here was a boy living under the same roof with a progressing alcoholic. Officially, Prohibition had been in effect since 1919, but in practice the Eighteenth Amendment merely made alcoholic beverages more difficult to obtain. No one understood the dynamics of alcoholism then, let alone realized that it was a disease; legislation did nothing but send drinkers underground. Instead of helping the Hallenbecks, Prohibition had a detrimental effect.

Ironically, Ellsworth did show some stability soon after Prohibition began. He worked for a few years at the

Milwaukee Mill, but resumed the pattern of moving and job changes. The first move came before 1920. Whether or not Ellsworth had been fired mattered little to Gregory, for their new residence at College and Seventh Avenues was just around the corner from Johnny's house. Gregory enjoyed some of the happiest years of his life while Ellsworth worked at O'Dwyer's feed store, but the good times were not to last. By the summer of 1926 the Hallenbecks were gone from St. Maries altogether, leaving Gregory's boyhood friends and the scenes of his fantastic adventures far behind.

As much as he loved to talk about life in St. Maries, Gregory never talked of his next home—an indication of how much the move disturbed him. Ellsworth had taken a job as a salesman with the Midland Lumber Manufacturing Company, and moved them to the industrial port city of Tacoma, Washington. Compared to the grandeur of western Idaho, the scenery around the basin of the Puget Sound was not nearly as lovely. Tacoma in the 1920s was a bleak landscape of malodorous factories and residential sprawl along the Puyallup River and Commencement Bay. The snow-capped majesty of Mount Rainier dominated the southeastern horizon on occasion, but it was frequently obscured by dreary weather, made worse in turn by the stinking clouds of smoke that belched from numerous pulp mills and a huge copper smelter. The "Tacoma aroma," as people called it, was no laughing matter.

Hallenbeck's move may not have been motivated solely by a geographic cure for his alcoholism this time. He knew the lumber business, and Tacoma had a rightful boast as the lumber capital of the world, but the industry was also booming in western Idaho and eastern Washington. It is doubtful, considering the family's move to a south-side apartment in a distinctly working-class neighborhood, that he sought a better standard of living. In all probability, Ellsworth was drawn not by Tacoma's employment opportunities, but by its other reputation during Prohibition, when it was known as "the sin spot of the Northwest" and "Seattle's dirty backyard."

Just about everything was legal: gambling rackets flourished, more than a hundred brothels did business around the clock, and countless speakeasies kept the liquor trade in high gear. On one street, scantily clad prostitutes stood in window displays and rapped on the glass, enticing passersby. The hospitals worked with the police to ensure a steady flow of booze, and deputies even used the department's paddy wagon to make bootleg deliveries. One of the largest stills in the city, captured by police during a raid, was "allowed" to be stolen from within the courthouse.

Ellsworth began to indulge in more than alcohol. Years later, describing his many infidelities, one of his own granddaughters characterized him as "not a very nice man." Surely Grace was aware of his activities, but she tolerated his lasciviousness to a degree, mindful of her own reputation for impropriety. In her younger days she had written, "What's life without spice—the dull monotony of it would kill us all don't you think." Still, she did not meekly acquiesce. The atmosphere in the Hallenbeck household was tense, frequently boiling over. "There was a lot of arguing," recalled one of William's daughters, who not only grew up hearing the stories of bitter quarreling, but witnessed it herself when Grace and Ellsworth were older.

Gregory wrote years later that the feuding spilled over to include relatives, making him and his brother especially miserable around the holidays.

Christmas Day was repulsive to me. Ever since my childhood, it had always been the same. Relatives were forever coming to our house and kissing my brother and me with those real wet kisses children dread so much, and making a number of well-wishing compliments that none of them ever seemed to believe.

And then it started after everybody had a snout full of firewater, fighting and speaking their true thoughts. All Christmases were alike, my brother Bill and I ending up by going to a movie.

Under the best of circumstances, Gregory's adjustment to life in the city would have been challenging, but given the turbulent conditions in the Hallenbeck household he must have felt lost—figuratively if not literally. The apartment on South Yakima Avenue provided no sense of attachment, no foundation for sentimental recollections as with St. Maries. Once, after visiting the neighborhood years later, he said it looked "as old as the hills" and could not remember the name of his street.

Fortunately, life in Tacoma was not entirely dismal. Despite the seedy underworld, some of the best of the Roaring Twenties and postwar modernization could be found in the cosmopolitan city, with its streetcars and theaters and shopping. Although there were no cliff-side trees to climb, Gregory had not lost his love of aviation or his passion for heights. And according to Grace, he discovered something just as exciting: "Greg was so fascinated with flying that when we moved to Tacoma we had to take him out to the flying field almost every Sunday. He'd climb the ladder to the blimp mooring mast, stand on top, and pretend he was flying."

The boy was becoming an adolescent, outgrowing his full name in favor of "Greg" now, a change that coincided with the family's move to Tacoma and the start of a new school year. Here was another advantage of moving to Tacoma— the city had a solid educational system. In the fall of 1926, Gregory enrolled as a ninth grader at Stewart Junior High, a classic turn-of-the-century school with an imposing brick edifice only a few blocks from his apartment. The efforts he had put forth in the little St. Maries schoolhouse were rewarded, earning him solid grades in English and Latin and even an A in algebra. Having inherited some of his mother's creativity, he also took an interest in music and mechanical drawing. At first he showed only moderate promise at drawing, but patience and an eye for symmetry helped him to improve.

The following spring, Charles Lindbergh forged his way across the Atlantic in the *Spirit of St. Louis*. Though Gregory never remarked on it publicly, he was surely as captivated as the rest of the world. Aviation was no longer an interesting means of travel, but a global passion from that moment on; unquestionably Lindbergh's achievement kept Gregory's dream of flying kindled.

In the fall he joined almost 450 sophomores at Lincoln High School, a striking Gothic-style building with complex rooflines and architectural details. There was nothing noteworthy about his first semester except for homeroom, where the teacher was cursed with the unfortunate name of Mr. Cockshoot. The second semester saw Gregory maintain a steady, if unremarkable, string of average grades, no small achievement considering the latest disruptions at home.

Ellsworth changed jobs again. Perhaps he was fired from the manufacturing job, for he made a distinct step backward in early 1928 to a neighborhood lumber store. The family moved again, to another apartment building on South Yakima Avenue, Greg's one consolation being that his walk to school was reduced from twelve blocks to three. Otherwise the situation at home was severely strained, with Ellsworth becoming moody and increasingly caustic. Gregory and his brother suffered for it. "Their growing-up years were full of a lot of cynicism," remarked Bill's daughter. "[Ellsworth] didn't build you up, he tore you down, and he did it with words."

In hindsight, more than alcoholic behavior was responsible for his erratic employment and constant moving. A particularly sinister sexual disorder had developed, leading Ellsworth to eventually become a pedophile. At the time of his latest job change, his son was ten; if Bill wasn't already being molested, he soon would be. Ellsworth's mental disorder became more advanced over the years, involving not only his son, but several of his grandchildren as well.

Naturally, the question arises as to whether Gregory was preyed upon, but there is nothing to indicate that he had any idea of his stepfather's mental illness. Years later, he put his own children at least partially under Ellsworth's guardianship, a seemingly unconscionable risk had he been aware of the aberration.

Nonetheless the environment in the Hallenbeck home was unsettled, secretive. During the last half of Greg's junior year at Lincoln, Ellsworth moved them yet again to the corner of Eighty-fourth and East D Streets, more than forty blocks from school. The situation at home would only get worse, with the onset of the Depression still to come. The present was grim enough already as Gregory began his senior year, adjusting to his third apartment in three years.

A busy schedule at Lincoln was the answer. Gregory was fortunate to be in a school system that allowed students to concentrate on chosen fields of study. He had improved his mechanical-drawing skill and was attracted to the engineering course, which required algebra, physics, and trigonometry in addition to the core classes in the liberal arts. He enjoyed sketching, particularly structures, and would later comment: "All the subjects I could take in high school were related to my becoming an architect."

If he sought an escape for frustration, or hoped to minimize his hours at home, he found the right outlets. After school, he occupied large chunks of time with participation in clubs and sports—a total of five his senior year. Undersized for squad sports, he was drawn to the individuality of wrestling. His torso supported well-defined pectorals and a thick neck, a physique that won bouts and earned a letter "L" for his school sweater. Swimming also interested him, though it was not recognized as a varsity sport. Nonetheless, Gregory was one of only twenty-five boys to pass the rigid tests required for membership in the Finned L Club.

Beyond sports, he spent extracurricular hours with the Spanish Club, and joined the yearbook staff that produced the *Lincolnian*. His crowning achievement was a request from the Knights of Lincoln to participate in their honors society. According to classmate Lamont Doty, the invitation-only club was "comprised of the most prominent boys in school."

Considering the challenges he had to overcome at home, perhaps Gregory could be forgiven for being seen as "kind of a cocky guy" in the opinion of Betty Smyth, a year behind him at Lincoln. He had a date or two with her next-door neighbor, popular Shirley Greening, giving him added confidence. "He was quiet," Betty remembered, "but he gave the impression of thinking he was pretty good. I guess he was."

Interestingly, when Gregory stood alongside his Lincoln teammates and club members for photographs, he generally looked dissatisfied. Furthermore, he displayed unique facial characteristics, which Betty could still picture almost seventy years after she last saw him in the hallways: "He wasn't tall, but he was stocky and had a round face."

His face was distinctive, so broad, and yet flat. The nose was wide, and his eyebrows provided little natural shade, causing him to perpetually narrow his eyelids, which in turn made his gaze seem menacing. The effect was enhanced by his heavy cheeks, which tugged the corners of his mouth into a natural scowl. There was an unmistakable hint of Native American heritage in his features, which Gregory later acknowledged was from his mother's side. Asked to define his bloodline, he once quipped, "Oh, Christ, I'm a mixture of alley cat, a little Scotch, and some Irish. There's even some Sioux Indian in there someplace."

Grace perpetuated the idea, telling stories about the Hunkpapa Sioux as though she had come from the tribe— which was indeed in the Dakotas—yet her grandchildren decided it was all part of a myth she wanted to cultivate. Her genealogy seems to support them. Grace's mother (if she was her natural mother, that is) was the offspring of two New York natives, while her father's parents came from New York and Quebec.

Thus, the origin of the Native American resemblance is a mystery. When Charles Boyington claimed he was not Gregory's father, perhaps he was correct. Somewhere in the interesting contours of Gregory's face, in the shadows that flickered behind his penetrating glare, the answer once lived.

•　　•　　•

The boy who had participated in enough wild adventures to earn the nickname of "Deeds" was gradually evolving into a studious young man. Not that his energies were suppressed—he was always physically inclined—but with the emergence of his artistic talents, he sought to improve his drawing skills beyond the course he took in school. He decided to take private art lessons, not a whimsical choice considering the family's economics. "I paid for these with money I earned doing odd jobs," he stated, adding that Grace and Ellsworth "were not able to afford anything like this."

His recollection came with hindsight. The Depression hit just two months after the beginning of his senior year at Lincoln, and though the financial shock wave did not reach Tacoma immediately, its effects were felt soon enough. Gregory decided to direct his plans more toward art than adventure. "As I passed through high school," he recalled, "my early daydream since first grade of becoming an aviator . . . had somewhat dimmed, simply because there was very little chance back in those times for a person to actually get into aviation."

Turning to architecture, he applied his typical doggedness. One teacher noted, "Whenever Gregory made up his mind to do something, there was no turning him aside until he had accomplished whatever it was he had set out to do." In the spring of 1930, with high school graduation approaching, he decided to apply for the architecture program at the University of Washington. He would have to work for a year first, he told his classmates, before he could afford to attend.

When he sat for his senior portrait, the flick of the shutter caught an intent stare, as if he were trying to discern his future. The overall effect was flattering. Backlighting created a masculine squareness to his jaw, adding depth to his features and enhancing the look of determination in his eyes.

On the last day of school an administrator calculated his grades and entered 85, a solid B average for his three years at Lincoln. "Greg wasn't a brilliant student," his mother later observed, "but he was thorough and whatever he learned he kept."

It was typical of Grace to give little praise. Gregory's classmates saw him differently, and managed in the 1930 *Lincolnian* to sum up his perseverance in just four words: "He can't be beat."

4

Slipping the Surly Bonds

Sooner than he thought, Gregory's wish to attend the University of Washington came true. In what can only be interpreted as a generous decision to shepherd him through college, Ellsworth and Grace moved the family north to Seattle. Perhaps their motive had as much to do with getting Ellsworth away from "the dirty backyard" of Tacoma, but at least Gregory could live at home while attending classes.

There were sacrifices all around. Grace started working, apparently for the first time since taking up residence with Ellsworth, as the manager of Plymouth House, where they lived on Seneca Street in the heart of the city. Her job allowed them to live in an apartment rent-free, while Ellsworth worked as an auditor.

Gregory officially began his college education on October 1, 1930, with a rigorous schedule of inorganic chemistry, trigonometry, and two courses in general engineering. One of the latter classes, Engineering Problems, gave him trouble and he received a D for his final grade that semester—the lone blip in his record. Every other grade he earned throughout college (and even back in high school) was at least a C, and there were few of those.

In addition to his engineering courses, two years of Reserve Officers' Training Corps or physical education classes were required. This was actually a welcome opportunity for Gregory, who immediately enrolled in ROTC and continued with the program every semester. Nor did he give up sports. During the fall of his sophomore year he entered the annual intramural wrestling tournament, a competition involving more than sixty grapplers distributed among six weight classes. Many of the young men represented fraternities, but Gregory wrestled as an independent at 145 pounds.

For a middleweight, his body mass was extraordinarily compact, making him appear to be one of the shortest men entered in the competition. The distance between his major flex points—ankles, knees, hips, and shoulders—was so truncated that his shoulders reached no higher than the average student's rib cage. The effect was deceptive. His enormous head and thick neck accounted for almost a fourth of his total height, resulting in an overall measurement of about five and half feet—and he was still growing.

His thickly muscled legs had the force of pile drivers, giving him great leverage for takedowns, after which his powerful chest, neck, and arms finished the job. One by one, Gregory polished off each entrant in his weight class to capture the tournament title. His victory got the attention of varsity wrestling coach Leonard Stevens, who saw to it that the intramural match was just the beginning of Gregory's wrestling career at Washington.

Involved as he was with engineering courses and wrestling, Gregory needed money for expenses and had to work. In 1931, Norm Hutchinson hired him at his downtown parking garage, where employees wore white overalls with an oval OLYMPIC GARAGE patch on the front. Constantly running for what amounted to pocket change, they parked and serviced vehicles for downtown customers. Gregory got along well with Hutchinson and the wiry manager, Al Abrahmson, who showed their appreciation by keeping him busy for the next three years whenever school was in session.

There were still a few ticks left on the clock for a social life, so he investigated the Greek houses on Fraternity Row. He found that some were geared toward academics, others toward sports, and eventually rushed Lambda Chi Alpha, a large fraternity adjacent to campus with about thirty full brothers. Accepted as a pledge, he was welcome to spend his available time there, an alternative to going back to his family's apartment. At times he was not even certain where that would be. Ellsworth, Grace, and Bill stayed at the Seneca Street apartment only through Gregory's sophomore year, then moved two more times in the next two years. The various apartment buildings downtown gave Gregory little sense of belonging, other than a place to sleep. The fraternity house—grander than the apartments and much closer to campus—provided continuity.

Lambda Chi was described by one of Gregory's contemporaries as a social fraternity. "We had some athletes," recalled Ronald Nelson, who also pledged in 1931. "One was an All-Coast tackle on the university football team; some were social butterflies. We had a nice house at 4509 Nineteenth Northeast, which is still there."

Nelson recalled Gregory's congenial personality, along with a quirk in his surname. "Greg was a great guy, and everybody at the house liked him. We knew him as Greg Hollenbeck, spelled with an *H-o*, I'm sure of it." Nelson's memory served him well. Due to an administrative oversight, probably caused by phonetic misunderstanding, Gregory's name was listed in campus publications as Hollenbeck, an error repeated each time his name appeared on a committee or sports roster or in the hardcover university annual. Whether he tried to correct the mistake without success, or merely brushed it off as not being important, the errant spelling persisted.

However his name was spelled, Gregory was well known around campus. He performed admirably in ROTC, had a reputation for his wrestling prowess, and even made the social scene through his involvement in Lambda Chi. Somewhat surprisingly, he later characterized his experience at the university as "fairly uneventful and rather dull."

As if presaging the observation, nearly all of the photographs of him in university publications showed him wearing a pinched, sullen expression. The lone exception was his smiling countenance after winning the 1931 intramural wrestling tournament; otherwise, he gave the impression of wishing he were somewhere else. Certainly the Depression created its pressures, including the strain of working in addition to going to school. Then there was the situation at home, where he felt less attached each time the Hallenbecks moved.

Rather than spend his summers with Grace and Ellsworth, he worked. Unable to find anything related to engineering in Seattle, he took a summer job in road construction with the Coeur d'Alene Fire Protection Association in Idaho, where he also stood fire lookout watches. For the long trek back and forth, he acquired a 1926 or '27 Ford (based on his recollection) sometime before the start of his junior year at Washington. Back in Seattle, he used it to drive between campus, his family's apartment, and his job at the Olympic Garage. Mobility came at a price, however. Owning a car meant he could not afford the room and board required for initiation at Lambda Chi. "I started out as a pledge," he later told a chapter representative, "and became a perennial pledge because I didn't have enough money to join."

The impact of the Depression affected not only Gregory's social life, but his outlook as an engineering student. Originally he planned to take engineering courses designed for structural and architectural applications, but his keen eye for what was happening in the wake of the struggling economy reshaped his ideas. "I soon discovered that even the top architects in the country were not getting any business," he said. "They got an occasional remodeling job. The same was true for the lesser architects. In fact architecture and building had just come to a complete standstill . . . It looked like this condition was going to exist for a long time to come."

Prior to the start of his junior year in the fall of 1932, he was in a dilemma over whether to switch majors. Unexpectedly, his mind was made up for him one Sunday afternoon in late summer when he decided to take his Model T for a drive. He ended up at an airfield along the Duwamish River, where a small factory had been producing commercial planes and a few military fighters for several years. Although it was a Sunday, Gregory could hear the rumble of an aircraft engine on the flight line. After parking near a hangar, he walked around to the front of the building and was captivated by the sight of "a beautiful little biplane."

Idling on the pavement was a single-seat aircraft, one of the small, colorful fighters that epitomized the Golden Age of aviation. Less than nine feet tall, the little biplane wore the bold graphics of naval aviation livery. The upper wing was a brilliant yellow, with two large disks bearing the national insignia at the wingtips; in the middle, a giant chevron pointed forward like an arrowhead. Well aft on the pale gray fuselage, nearly hidden in the shadow of the corrugated horizontal stabilizer, stenciled lettering identified the fighter's service: U.S. MARINES.

The spanking new fighter had been chained to tie-down points in the pavement while "slow time" was being put on the engine to break it in. The big radial engine was noisy even at idle, the deep, throaty barks from the exhaust ring giving just a hint of the five hundred horsepower that dwelled within. The polished aluminum propeller looked like a gleaming, translucent disk as it spun, its tips painted with red, yellow, and blue warning stripes that created distinctive rings of color.

No one else was in sight as the fighter sat there, trembling with latent power and buffeted by prop wash. Gregory felt something almost tangible pass between him and the biplane. "It seemed to me like it was a chained animal," he later said, "striving to get loose from its chains and take off into its natural habitat in the sky. I had an emotional feeling run through my body; I wanted to unchain this little airplane and take it on up, where it would be happy."

A few symbolic chains of his own seemed to break this day, as memories of his first flight and his dream of becoming a pilot came roaring back. He knew somehow that he could respond positively to the moment, rather than ignore it. Fortuitously, the man whose company built this little fighter had already laid the foundation for Gregory to fulfill his ambition.

Sixteen years earlier, William Boeing had built his first airplane in a boathouse along the Duwamish River. Shortly thereafter, needing proper facilities and a source of competent designers, he paid for a wind tunnel at the University of Washington. He even hired two promising seniors from the engineering school to work in his new company. Thanks to Boeing's continued cooperation, the university now offered a complete syllabus in aeronautical engineering.

After researching the degree, Gregory arranged the necessary administrative changes and, for the next two years, studied aircraft mechanics, aerodynamics, aircraft performance, and aerial propulsion. His major work was under the direction of Professor F. K. Kirsten, who described him as "an industrious worker and a dependable student."

Gregory also continued with the ROTC program beyond the minimum requirements, entering the advanced course for coastal artillery in the fall of 1932. It made financial sense—he could expect to receive a second lieutenant's commission in the reserves upon graduation—and his talent for engineering helped with military science courses. Praised by the unit commander as "an exceptional young man, of fine character [and] good habits," Gregory earned a 3.5 average in military science, was a captain in the cadet corps, and earned membership in Scabbard and Blade, the honorary fraternity for advanced students. He also put his studies into practice during the summer of 1933 when he attended "summer camp" for several weeks at Fort Worden, a coastal defense facility on a promontory of the Olympic Peninsula.

During his junior year, Gregory's social life took a turn for the better. He made time to work on the prom committee in the spring of 1933 and presumably attended; if not, he went to the dances sponsored regularly by the ROTC. These were semiformal affairs, held in Seattle's swank public venues. Prohibition was over, jazz ruled the big ballrooms, and cadets in dress uniforms jitterbugged the night away with young ladies in cocktail gowns.

One night when Ron Nelson's steady girlfriend was unavailable for a dance, he escorted a winsome teenager named Helene Clark. "I took her to an ROTC dance at the Olympic Hotel in Seattle one time," he recalled. "She was a real pretty girl who lived out in north Seattle on Twentieth Northeast." Those who knew Helene could not argue with Nelson's appraisal. One female friend who knew Helene a few years later described her as having "the face of a Boticelli angel." Bob Galer, an engineering student a year behind Gregory, recalled that Helene once entered a Miss Northwest pageant, hoping to earn a little extra cash. Another university student, upon meeting her for the first time, was "struck by what a beautiful woman she was."

Musically inclined, Helene sang in the glee club and took part in the school opera when she began her senior year at Roosevelt High School in the fall of 1933. It was sometime during that year that she met Gregory at an ROTC dance, perhaps the one she attended with Ron Nelson. She and Gregory shared more in common than they could have fathomed, for he did not yet know about his real father, and her own background was an even deeper mystery.

Originally from Oregon, Helene went by the last name of Clark in high school. Her only known relative was a sister, Constance Wickstrom, whose husband had a managerial position in Seattle. As one acquaintance remembered, "She was an orphan—she really didn't have a home. She was raised by people but I don't think they ever adopted her. It wasn't too pleasant."

In her senior portrait, Helene was notable as the girl *not* smiling. She gazed intently at the camera, a disdainful look clouding her features. Her hair, parted in the middle, was pulled back so severely that she might have passed for a boy were it not for the feminine collar on her simple blouse. Other photographs were equally unflattering, yet her beauty was etched in the memories of her friends and acquaintances. She began to date Gregory, who didn't have much time or money available for fun, during his senior year at Washington.

In addition to studies and work, he had chosen to devote more time to wrestling, resuming the sport with vigor. Everett McKellar, who wrestled at 118 pounds, admired Gregory's powerful physique and was grateful for his help. "He outweighed me [by] quite a bit and we didn't go at it real hard, but he knew wrestling and he helped me learn holds. That's the point of wrestling—you've got to learn how to get the other guy down."

The season was capped with a tournament in Seattle, the Minor Carnival, with several regional universities competing in eight weight classes. Washington won the title, taking four of eight bouts, including Gregory's victory at 155 pounds. He was declared the Pacific Northwest middleweight champion, while the diminutive McKellar earned the lightweight title.

Gregory pushed through an academically challenging senior year, carrying a full load of courses while continuing to work at the Olympic Garage. By the spring, he had the requisite 190 hours for graduation, but still needed a few essential classes. He would have to return for one more semester to complete his degree.

The army took his total hours into consideration along with his four years in ROTC, and on June 15 commissioned him as a second lieutenant in the Coast Artillery Reserve. That summer, Gregory went on active duty with the 630th Coast Artillery at Fort Worden, spending several weeks on the isolated, windswept eastern tip of the Olympic Peninsula, where the fort (along with its sister post, Fort Casey on Whidbey Island) guarded the Strait of Juan de Fuca and the entrance to Puget Sound. They were throwbacks to outdated theories of coastal defense, and in the ill-paid, poorly equipped army of the 1930s little training actually took place.

As soon as his active duty was over, Gregory hurried back to Seattle. He had plans with Helene.

• • •

On the last Saturday in July 1934, the King County auditor stamped the state of Washington's approval on a license for Gregory and Helene to marry. The next day, July 29, Pastor L. Wendell Tifield performed the ceremony in the Plymouth Congregational Church. Arnold Wickstrom and his wife, Helene's sister Constance, signed the marriage certificate as witnesses, after which the document was duly filed. But what a curious document it turned out to be. Gregory's surname was listed as Hollenbeck, not Hallenbeck, evidently another misunderstanding based on enunciation, but he did not bother to correct it before signing his name. Even more confusing, Helene's maiden name was recorded as Wickstrom. For some unknown motive, she used her sister's married name, obscuring the fact that just two months earlier, she had graduated from high school as Helene Clark. Virtually no identification was required to obtain a driver's or marriage license, allowing Gregory and Helene to be legally married as far as the state of Washington was concerned, despite their misleading identities.

Their next priority was finding a suitable place to live. At twenty-one, with a college degree to complete, Gregory's income consisted of a part-time job at the Olympic Garage; Helene was fresh out of high school and unemployed. Grace and Ellsworth, meanwhile, served as managers of the Ellenburt Apartments on East Harrison Street and were willing to accommodate the newlyweds, but would have to find more space. Bill, a student at Broadway High School, was still with them. They located two available units just a few blocks away, and all five Hallenbecks moved to apartments at 906 East John Street.

Within a month of the wedding, Helene was pregnant. Faced with this news, Gregory began the fall semester carrying an ambitious workload. The adjustment to married life did not hurt his final grades—equal to his previous best semester—which nudged his overall GPA up to a respectable 2.97. He received his diploma with a Bachelor of Science degree in Aeronautical Engineering on December 20, 1934, having never dropped any of the seventy-odd classes he started or taken an incomplete grade.

With a pregnant wife to support, he did not bother to wait until after the holidays before starting a full-time job. Immediately after receiving his diploma, he headed for the same factory where he had made the emotional connection with the little Marine Corps fighter plane. It was a logical place to start.

The depressed economy had throttled many industries around the country, but not the Boeing Aircraft Company. The military branches were pleased with the biplanes (predominantly fighters) that Boeing turned out, and the company's designers were at the cutting edge of monoplane development. The all-metal *Monomail* sired the Model 247, the first truly modern airliner, and the army air corps had recently ordered production of two new monoplanes: the slim B-9 bomber, and the stubby, wheel-panted P-26 "Peashooter" pursuit plane. Technology and developments were changing at a mind-boggling pace, such that a mere three years after the B-9's first flight, the army requested designs for a massive long-range experimental bomber. In response, Boeing began development of the XB-15, known as Model 294. When Gregory Hallenbeck appeared with his aeronautical engineering diploma, work had been under way on the new project for approximately eight months. There was room for a bright young man with solid educational credentials—especially someone with years of practice in mechanical drawing—and Gregory was hired as a draftsman.

The day after graduating from college, Gregory began his first full-time job with one of the world's premier aircraft builders, working on the most advanced bomber ever seen. The XB-15 would be the largest plane yet built in the United States, with a wingspan of nearly 150 feet and four powerful engines to carry it almost twenty thousand feet above the ground at a speed of two hundred miles per hour. Few fighter planes in existence could match its anticipated performance.

As it turned out, the XB-15 never went into production, but the experimental version did fly. It was an astonishing test platform for many features that appeared on Boeing's most famous warplane, the B-17 Flying Fortress, including the retractable main landing gear. Gregory was assigned to work on drawings for the beefy gear at a drafting station in the two-story brick engineering building.

Wages were so low during the Depression that his starting salary was approximately a hundred dollars per month, no more than Ellsworth had earned almost fifteen years earlier. But with the rarity of decent jobs, and a teenage wife already past the midpoint in her pregnancy, the position was a godsend. Their apartment rented for twenty-five dollars per month and groceries for two adults cost roughly the same; after accounting for incidentals, Gregory and Helene could get by, even have a little left over if they lived frugally. "I should have considered myself very fortunate indeed," he later said.

Unfortunately, trouble in the Hallenbeck camp took the luster off his fast start. Ellsworth and Grace were embroiled in a combative relationship, pushed to the limit by the strain of the Depression, the constant moves, and their own inner demons. They were drinking heavily.

In mid-March, Ellsworth walked out. He not only left the apartment, but moved some three hundred miles to the small town of Okanogan in central Washington. He took a book-keeping job with Charles Blackwell, an ambitious merchandiser who oversaw a small empire of department and grocery stores. Grace was left scrambling in Seattle for a meager income. A part-time job at the switchboard of the McKay Apartments helped, paying "the magnificent sum of $4.66 per week," but she wangled an apartment for herself and young Bill as part of the deal. Greg had been employed at Boeing for all of two months when this latest crisis arose, and had his own concerns. Helene was now seven months pregnant and did not work at all.

At this opportune moment, a confluence of politics and aviation intervened on Gregory's behalf. On April 15, 1935, Congress approved the Aviation Cadet Act, a program designed to save the financially strapped government some money while training a thousand new pilots. Headlines announced that qualified cadets would receive one year of flight instruction with pay, plus an allowance for uniforms and a premium-free government life-insurance policy. In return, successfully winged pilots would be obligated to serve three additional years of active duty (at cadet pay) before they would be eligible to receive a commission. The best part of the deal, which probably attracted as many men as the lure of flying itself, was that a bonus of fifteen hundred dollars would be paid at the end of the four years of combined service. Gregory learned about it through the *Seattle Post-Intelligencer.* "I read in the paper . . . that the navy and the air corps were starting up a tremendous drive for training aviators," he said. "They were going to enter five hundred cadets in the navy and Marine Corps flying school at Pensacola, Florida, and five hundred air corps cadets at Kelly Field in Texas. Somehow, watching that little plane [at Boeing] had made me decide on the Marine Corps."

Seattle happened to be home to a small Naval Reserve Air Base (NRAB) along a spit of land called Sand Point on Lake Washington. There, Gregory talked to a Marine Corps reserve pilot, whose response was rhetorical: "Why don't you go down to Pensacola and get yourself a pair of wings?" The reason, Gregory answered him, was that aviation cadets could not be married and had to remain single for the entire four-year obligation. He was not only married, but was about to become a father.

"You don't have to tell them you're married," the pilot suggested, but Gregory was skeptical. The services needed pilots, not more dependents. Still, the idea began to nag at him, affecting his work. Later he admitted, "As fortunate as I should have considered myself, I wasn't happy at all. I sat there at my desk in the Engineering Section of the Boeing Aircraft Company, and I would be looking out the window whenever a plane came by. Actually I was of very little use to the company. I don't think they really knew it, or maybe they did, but in any event, I was not happy."

A few weeks after the aviation cadet act was announced, Gregory picked up an application at Sand Point. Several additional documents were required, including a college diploma, five letters of recommendation, a résumé of at least fifty words describing his former experience, and a birth certificate. Obtaining the first items was not overly difficult, but the last requirement—a seemingly simple document— caused the shock of his life.

One of two things happened: Gregory asked Grace for a copy of his birth certificate, at which point she explained about his real father, or he questioned her after a response came back from Idaho that no record existed of a Gregory Hallenbeck born December 4, 1912. However the drama unfolded, his search for a birth certificate led to the stunning discovery that the name Hallenbeck had never been his. "He was dumbfounded," Grace acknowledged later. "He wouldn't believe [it] at first."

It must have felt to Grace as though her mistakes had come back to haunt her, especially now that Ellsworth had left. Deplorable as his behavior had been, he had always been "Dad" to Gregory, having raised him as his own. Gregory had gone to school as a Hallenbeck, served in the army as a Hallenbeck, worked for Boeing and even gotten married as a Hallenbeck. According to a paper trail going back twenty years, he *was* Gregory Hallenbeck. Suddenly, all of it rang false. "She started crying," he recalled.

Considering other current stresses, including Helene's pending childbirth and his mother's separation from Ellsworth, Gregory showed remarkable composure. Grace's emotional reaction probably helped him absorb the truth. Through her tears of shame, she described the circumstances of Gregory's birth and her subsequent divorce from his real father. She hadn't seen him for twenty years, leaving Gregory with unanswerable questions about the very core of his identity. Then there was Bill, whom he had thought of as a brother; suddenly he was viewed in a far different light. As for Ellsworth, he was no saint but at least he was a known person. Gregory tried but could not identify with a faceless stranger bearing an alien name: Boyington.

He buried his emotions somewhere deep inside, and did not outwardly agonize, at least not for long. The penalty for such repression would come later, but for now, as he had done many times before, he took the knockdown and regained his footing quickly. Almost immediately, he realized that the monumental discovery was actually a blessing in disguise. Gregory Hallenbeck was married, but nobody had ever heard of Gregory *Boyington*. There was no record that he was legally married.

He had a reason to feel upbeat, therefore, when he returned to NRAB Seattle on May 8 and submitted a one-page application for flight training with the Marine Corps Reserve. The form was primarily a series of promissory statements: The applicant agreed that he would consent to serve for a continuous period of four years on active duty, that he was unmarried, and that he would remain so until the termination of his active duty. A yeoman typed the name Gregory Boyington (no middle name) along with his address and birth information into the appropriate blanks at the top of the page. With neat, careful strokes—there had been little opportunity to practice—Gregory signed his name as Boyington, probably for the first time. Next he attached a 170-word résumé that accounted for his service with the coast artillery and various job experiences, including his employment at Boeing Aircraft Company.

The next step was to gather five letters of recommendation. Choosing not to tip his hand at Boeing that he planned to leave, he looked to former professors and ROTC staff for endorsements. It must have been embarrassing to explain to them why he was using a new name, but each man bent backward a little and lauded him as Gregory Boyington. The Navy Department would never know the difference.

While waiting for the recommendations, he reported to Sand Point on May 16 for a physical. The demands of flight physiology were well known by then, and the Bureau of Medicine and Surgery had set rigorous standards. Skeletal structure, vision, hearing, balance, heart function, respiration, blood pressure—all had to be essentially perfect. Even the applicant's teeth, in an era preceding fluoridation and routine dental care, had to meet strict standards. Missing teeth, holes, or poor fillings were potential causes of excruciating pain at high altitude. Doctor V. S. Armstrong, a lieutenant commander in the medical corps, did the honors. Boyington measured sixty-eight inches, about as tall as he would get, with a thirty-inch waist and a chest that expanded to forty. He had gained ten pounds since his wrestling days at Washington, his vision was excellent, and he responded normally to the standard hearing test using a ticking watch at forty inches, a coin click at twenty feet, and a whispered voice at fifteen feet. One after another he passed the standards, and finally Doctor Armstrong found him to be "physically qualified until aeronautically adapted for duty involving flying."

With so many diverse events in progress, nineteen-year-old Helene might almost have been overlooked, but the forces of nature would not allow it. At eight twenty-six on the morning of May 24, she delivered a healthy son at Swedish Hospital. His name had already been picked out: Gregory, for his father, and Helene's adopted name of Clark for his middle name. Consistent with the other spelling oddities, the newborn's last name was entered on the birth certificate as Hollenbeck, as were the parents' names. Despite the fact that Gregory had signed a government document as a Boyington more than two weeks earlier, the secret had to be preserved.

While Helene recovered in the hospital, the Marine Corps processed her husband's application for flight training. The results of his flight physical were forwarded to the Bureau of Medicine and Surgery, which eventually agreed with the original findings. In the meantime, Boyington returned to his drafting table at Boeing while awaiting the recommendations from his former professors. The emotional roller coaster of the past few weeks finally caught up with him. He was described as run-down in an unpublished manuscript written with his close supervision a decade later: "He never felt like doing anything when he came home. Occasionally he would go to a ten-cent movie across the street because it seemed to rest his eyes."

Three days after his son was born, Boyington collected the last of the recommendations and forwarded everything to Headquarters, Marine Corps (HMC), in Washington, D.C. The paperwork and results of his physical were routed along a chain of command that ultimately ended with the commandant, who rubber-stamped his approval in early June.

Having made it this far, Boyington was still not an aviation cadet. First he had to successfully complete ten hours of elimination flight training, thereby demonstrating his ability to cope mentally and physically with the three-dimensional world of flight. Sand Point was one of the few so-called "E-bases" around the country that provided the government with a practical means to eliminate those who couldn't hack it, of which there were many.

Events progressed quickly after Boyington received his orders to elimination training on June 13. When he reported four days later for indoctrination, he found the familiar face of Bob Galer, a fellow engineering student, along with Desmond Canavan, both of whom had just graduated from the university that spring. All three were sworn in as privates first class, after which they met their instructor, twenty-eight-year-old Richard Mangrum, an alumnus of the same university and a veteran of six years of active duty. A first lieutenant in the reserves, Mangrum had a stellar career ahead.*

After receiving a description of basic maneuvers and cockpit instruments, Boyington picked up a cloth helmet, a pair of goggles, and a parachute before following Mangrum to the flight line for the first of two indoctrination hops. They

---

* As commander of the first dive-bomber squadron during the defense of Guadalcanal early in World War II, Mangrum would earn a Navy Cross and a Distinguished Flying Cross. He eventually rose to assistant commandant, the highest position within the Marine Corps achieved by any aviator.

walked up to a silver-colored biplane, similar in overall size and appearance to the Curtiss "Jenny" that had captured Boyington's heart as a boy. This was the Consolidated NY-2, with a radial engine rated at nearly three times the Jenny's horsepower. The plane's fuselage-mounted wheels could be quickly detached and replaced with a centerline pontoon, transforming the land plane into a capable sea-plane. Boyington's first military flight was in the land con-figuration, designated NY-2(L).

Under Mangrum's guidance, he stepped onto the lower wing and climbed into the forward of two open cockpits. Settling into the seat, he scanned an instrument panel slightly more modern than the Jenny's, but with many of the same "steam gauges" he had previously seen. This time he had a better understanding of what they were for, and soon learned more as Mangrum strapped in behind him. Both men wore traditional cloth helmets connected by a "Gos-port," a one-way voice tube that allowed the instructor to talk to (or scream at) the student.

Mangrum described the procedures as he cranked the Wright "Whirlwind" engine, sending a blast of turbulence washing over them. After the engine warmed, Mangrum jazzed the throttle and taxied to the downwind end of the dirt field, then turned into the wind and shoved the throttle for-ward. The takeoff was much faster and louder than the last takeoff Boyington had experienced, and the field was smoother. In no time the "Husky" was off the ground and climbing at almost seven hundred feet per minute, giving the fliers a sweeping view of the countless bays and coves along the rugged coastline. It was a moment for Gregory to savor. Fifteen years and nine months after his flight with the barn-storming Clyde Pangborn, he was back in the air—but for the first time as a Boyington.

The indoctrination flight above Seattle lasted barely half an hour, enough time for Dick Mangrum to showcase basic maneuvers, after which he likely gave his student a chance to try for himself. Boyington's reaction to his first handling of the controls went unrecorded, but Mangrum later entered a comment about his good aptitude. More significantly, six tenths of an hour were logged in Boyington's navy flight record. The short hops were just as important as the long ones, and the hours added up during the course of a career.

Boyington flew twice the following day, the first being a mirror of the indoctrination flight, after which Mangrum took him skyward for his initial lessons. Throughout the rest of the week the schedule remained much the same—usually two flights per day of twenty to forty minutes' duration. The dynamics of flying, alien to human nature, had to be taught in small increments. Boyington struggled at first with simple procedures, eliciting written comments from Mangrum such as "Let plane get away from him" and "Slow in reaction." Soon Boyington was taxiing the plane and trying a few wobbly takeoffs. Like virtually all students, his first attempts to land were tentative—he leveled off well above the runway. "Hasn't found ground yet," wrote Mangrum early in the second week, but after five more hours of instruction, he determined that his student was "smoothing out nicely."

Several skill areas were graded, from taxiing and takeoffs to turns, spirals, landings, and emergencies. A grade of 4.0 was considered perfect in any segment, but it was an impossible mark to achieve because no instructor in his right mind would judge a student to be flawless. Boyington was labeled "a good, average student." By July 2, he was ready for the first of two check flights, each to be conducted by a pilot other than his instructor. He passed the first half-hour check ride with a navy lieutenant that afternoon, then flew with a naval reservist the next day and was rewarded with another thumbs-up. Each flight earned a respectable grade of 3.3, and Boyington was approved for a solo circuit around the field.

For any student pilot, that first moment of flying alone is unforgettable. There is no calming voice of an instructor, no umbilical cord of guidance. To this point, Boyington had completed twenty-three short hops totaling twelve hours of flight time, and had practiced a few dozen approaches. He

had witnessed a fatal accident at the Spokane air show, but
this was also the same Boyington who had been unafraid to
climb mooring masts, plummet down steep hills, or tightrope over railroad tracks. He was thrilled to be turned loose,
and later described the moment of truth.

I was so happy to have an instructor or check pilot out
of that plane, and to have that plane all to myself, that I
just couldn't contain myself. As I gave this little plane the
gun and started down the field (all they allowed us to do
was take off, do a circle around the field, and come in and
land) . . . I went, "Yeeeehoooooo!" I don't know whether
they could hear me over the noise of the engine, but I said
it so loud that I'm sure they could have. As I got airborne,
before I got to the end of the field, I stuck my hand out and
waved.

On that warm July 3, Boyington climbed in a turn to a few
hundred feet, completed the circle, and brought the plane
down for a three-point landing, the desirable method of
touching down with the tail wheel and two mains simultaneously. The entire hop, including taxiing out from the flight
line and back in, took five minutes.

A few days later, Dick Mangrum tallied Boyington's final
score—3.2 for flight training, 3.7 for his aptitude as officer
material—and recommended him for appointment as an aviation cadet in the flight training class scheduled to commence in mid-July. Des Canavan and Bob Galer received
similar recommendations, but the appointments for all three
would be dreadfully slow in coming.

As it turned out, a class at Naval Air Station (NAS)
Pensacola had just been filled with its quota of marine cadets. Always in a minority status, marine aviation was particularly stymied during the Depression and only a few
openings were available. Boyington and the others would
have to stay put until the next class that accepted marines
was announced.

Having taken a leave of absence from Boeing to undergo

his elimination training, Boyington now faced an uncertain future. He had enlisted as a private first class for the purpose of training, but was paid only for the actual duration of E-base. Therefore, he earned no more than thirty or forty dollars during his three weeks of training. Now that his cadet appointment was delayed, he had no choice but to go back to Boeing. Weeks turned to months while he waited to hear from the Marine Corps. At his drafting station in the engineering department, the days dragged by as he "settled back into the dull routine, hating every minute of it."

Matters took another turn for the worse when Grace and Ellsworth became locked in a bitter feud over custody of Bill. Ellsworth's emotional grip on his son was evidently strong despite the grim reality of his sexual deviation, and Bill joined him in Okanogan that summer. Midway through the vacation period, Ellsworth filed a formal complaint in Okanogan County in an attempt to gain custody of his teenage son. Claiming that Grace had "disregarded her marriage vows and denied . . . his marital rights," he stated that it was impossible for him to live with her as husband and wife. She had caused "great suffering and distress," he alleged, bold posturing from a man who was not even legally married in the first place.

Grace hired an attorney, who filed a motion for change of venue to King County, based on the financial distress Ellsworth had left her in, and argued convincingly for temporary alimony plus costs and legal fees. Long after their son moved back to Seattle to enter his final year at Broadway High School, Grace and Ellsworth continued their legal maneuvering. Grace's affidavits contained plenty of denials and counterarguments and were frankly stronger. In December a King County judge ordered Ellsworth to cough up support, adding to his decision a stipulation that all other proceedings be delayed until Ellsworth paid in full.

Boyington kept his frustrations to himself, at least in the presence of his Boeing associates, demonstrating this outwardly positive attitude in the form of practical jokes. He rode to work each day with Keith Schader, who also collected Dick Nelson and Bert Joseph. Inordinately proud of the Pierce Arrow coupe he drove, Schader invariably ran late and took corners recklessly in a madcap attempt to arrive on time. One morning, Boyington climbed into the rumble seat, concealing a heavy paper bag. He surreptitiously dumped the contents onto the pavement when Schader careened around yet another corner. "The clatter of the stuff," Nelson reported later, "pipe fittings, gears, bolts and nuts—was terrific." Schader skidded to a stop and cast an agonized look back along the road at the trail of scattered parts. From the rumble seat, a glib Boyington offered that "the rear end must have fallen out." Schader crawled under the car to investigate, found nothing conclusive, and gingerly resumed the trip, anticipating more disintegration. He didn't learn for two days that the trouble with his precious car was a gag.

Lighthearted moments at work were too few to brighten the atmosphere at the East John Street apartments. Christmas passed, then New Year's, almost six months after E-base with no word from the Marine Corps. Grace had been awarded a small settlement from Ellsworth, but the emotional cost weighed on the whole family. Helene was barely grown from a child herself while coping with a seven-month-old baby. Boyington fretted over swirling rumors about the cadet program—namely that he, Canavan, and Galer were the youngest, and that only twenty-five marines were going to be accepted from the entire country. He began to despair that his opportunity to train as a pilot was lost.

Finally, the logjam in Pensacola eased. The previous July, nine marine cadets had been accepted into Class 81-C, after which the next six classes were comprised of only navy cadets. Class 88-C was open to marines and would commence in late February, with Gregory Boyington ranked number three for appointment on the list of names forwarded by the secretary of the navy to the commandant. On January 11, the Marine Corps sent a package containing the commandant's endorsement along with several forms to Boyington's home address.

Boyington joined Canavan and Galer at Sand Point to be sworn in on January 27, 1936, after which the next step was quick in coming. Boyington received a letter dated February 8 assigning him to active duty, with orders to proceed to NAS Pensacola and report no later than the twentieth. Galer, Canavan, and Fred "Ray" Emerson (another cadet from Seattle who had passed through E-base after them) each received the same orders to begin their flight training.

The sky was a promising clear blue when they gathered a week later at Seattle's King Street Station. The temperature was just below freezing, causing thick steam to vent from the Northern Pacific locomotive waiting at the head of a passenger train bound for Chicago. Boyington took a slight risk and let Helene accompany him to the station, assuming correctly that the other cadets wouldn't blow the whistle about his marriage. Des Canavan's girlfriend, Marie O'Keefe, was there for the big send-off, anticipating a wait of several years before she could marry her marine. A quirk in the rules would shorten her wait dramatically.

Meanwhile, the minutes on the station platform seemed to race by. Too soon for the sweethearts, perhaps not soon enough for the cadets, the conductor gave the boarding call. With a farewell blast from its steam whistle, the train huffed slowly away from the platform, carrying four young men to a far corner of the country and a whole new way of life.

5

Rats

Almost four days after leaving Seattle, the rumpled would-be cadets stepped from a Louisville & Nashville train at the Pensacola depot. Mingling with other passengers on the platform, they appreciated the relatively balmy weather, a huge improvement over the past few days.

Boyington and his friends had suffered through a frigid winter storm while exploring Chicago during a full day's layover. Anticipating their move to Florida, they had brought only regular overcoats and were ill prepared for the arctic air that swept through the Midwest. The result was painful for Des Canavan when they decided to go sightseeing. "We had never seen a planetarium before," he recalled. "The planetarium was along Lake Michigan, and on the way out Greg looked at me and said, 'What's wrong with your ear?' He reached over and tweaked it; it was frozen. It remained sore for several months."

There had been other surprises. Coming from the small, provincial Seattle of the 1930s, the two cadets found themselves sharing a hotel room more sophisticated than either of them had ever known. Canavan later laughed about their naïveté: "What a couple of country rubes we were. Gregory took a shower and left the curtain outside of the tub. It flooded the whole bathroom and part of the other room—we had a real problem." The boys had to call for assistance, to the dismay of the hotel staff.

In Chicago they picked up another cadet from the University of Washington, handsome Jim Mueller of Michigan, before boarding the L & N passenger train that carried them into the Deep South. It steamed through the piney woods to Mobile, Alabama, then headed east toward the Florida panhandle, giving the passengers a view of the Gulf of Mexico as they crossed the marshlands at the top of Mobile Bay. Then the train reentered another long stretch of woods. There was nothing interesting about this part of the Gulf Coast if the newcomers expected the swaying palms and sandy beaches of the postcard version. It was mostly flat timberland, periodically interrupted with oddly named towns like Flomaton and Cantonment, barely a hill between them to break the monotony of the landscape. But a pleasant surprise awaited when the train finally hissed to a stop in the historic city of Pensacola.

Almost four hundred years earlier, Spanish expeditions had poked around the coastline, and except for a hurricane that blew the first encampment off the barrier islands in 1559, Pensacola might have supplanted St. Augustine as the oldest continuous settlement in the New World. The city was proud of its heritage, with moss-covered forts and various streets named after Spanish noblemen. The flags of Britain, France, and the Confederacy had also flown over Pensacola, which could rightfully claim that the first shots of the Civil War had been fired during a skirmish at nearby Fort Pickens, well before the bombardment of Fort Sumter in Charleston harbor.

For the last hundred years, Pensacola had been a navy town; now it catered to pilots as well. The emphasis had shifted after 1913, when the Chambers Board selected the Pensacola Navy Yard for training the first navy fliers. In the early years, naval aviation involved mostly floatplanes, making the Gulf Coast an ideal location because of the agreeable weather and large areas of protected water. In the years since, the airfield adjacent to the old navy yard had developed into the navy's sole training base for those who hoped to earn wings of gold.

Boyington and the other cadets had part of the day to explore. The buildings along Pensacola's main thoroughfare were lined with wrought-iron balustrades, imitating the French Quarter in New Orleans. A statue of Robert E. Lee anchored the north end of the business district, while to the south, Plaza Ferdinand with its ancient live oaks and manicured lawns served as a pleasant oasis. Halfway between, the modern San Carlos Hotel occupied a whole city block. South Palafox ended at the busy port on Santa Rosa Sound, a protected channel that served fishing boats and cargo vessels. Terrain and climate aside, Pensacola had much in common with Tacoma. Lumber—in this case yellow pine—kept the port in business.

On February 18, the new class of cadets from all over the country began to assemble at the air station. Most shared cabs, the ride from the city taking them through the new town of Warrington, with its typical beer joints and tattoo parlors lining the street. Off the main thoroughfare, peaceful neighborhoods of small bungalows were scattered beneath the oaks along Bayou Grande. The road bridged the bayou to the naval property, then meandered among more oaks festooned with Spanish moss, finally leading to a brick gatehouse. A navy sentry checked the cadets' orders and waved them through.

Class 88-C began its first days of in-processing by alternately sitting down and standing in line, enduring the timeworn adage of "hurry up and wait." Soon they moved into the Cadet Battalion, their mailing address for the next year if they were lucky and didn't fail. The cadets gathered in classrooms to listen to administrative lectures and fill out forms, after which the supply department gave them uniforms and the barber cut most of their hair. Flight surgeons conducted another battery of flight physicals, even more scrutinizing than the originals. For each new event, the cadets assembled and tried to march, moving everywhere in ragged cadence. If any of them labored under the illusion that they would soon take to the skies, the slow passage of the next several weeks would prove frustrating.

Before they could be taught to fly, the cadets had to be properly indoctrinated. This was simultaneously an individual issue and a collective one, impossible to accomplish overnight. Cadets had to be physiologically conditioned in stages, the most important derivative being to determine each individual's fortitude to accept the responsibilities of piloting an airplane. The few hours of training at E-base had been the first step in the weeding-out process, but E-bases could not, in ten hours, provide more than a preliminary separation of unqualified candidates. An additional forty percent of those who successfully reached Pensacola would fail to earn their wings.

There was no single formula for learning the military way. Instead, a slow acclimation took place over a period of weeks and months. It was necessary to acquire a level of conformity among the cadets, reducing individual personalities to a collection of common denominators that would respond automatically to situations. This was achieved through marching and close-order drill, which demanded teamwork in order to succeed. Individuals were pressured in a multitude of ways the moment training began, mostly through a culture of discipline.

An intense period of ground school accompanied the rigorous adjustment to military life. The first month of training consisted of classroom lectures in the fundamentals of naval service—customs and regulations, command and procedure, ordnance and seamanship—along with hours of drill. Floors, doors, and walls became decks, hatches, and bulkheads, and woe to the cadet who went to the bathroom instead of to the head. Cadets were virtually locked down, restricted to the station, until the privilege of off-base liberty was earned. They wore khaki uniforms, learned to keep their shoes and brass polished, prepared their racks (beds) and lockers for inspections, endured discipline as a group, and collected demerits for individual lapses. Almost without their realizing it, order grew out of chaos, and Class 88-C eventually began to think and act as a unit, developing along the way a sense of camaraderie.

Although the weather was usually moderate, it could be damp and raw in late winter, especially near the water. The cadets were particularly exposed to the elements during drill along the waterfront, and were always marching and studying in close proximity to each other. Three weeks after arriving in Pensacola, Boyington contracted a miserable cold and headed for the dispensary to seek relief. By the time he was examined, he had a fever. Preventing the spread of contagion was vital, so he was admitted to the naval hospital. He spent six nights in the large brick building that sprawled among shady oaks, but missed only three days of ground school and was able to make up for lost time.

The following week, the cadets entered progressively harder courses at the ground-school building near the pier. In rapid sequence they absorbed aerial navigation, aerodynamics, meteorology, photography, engine theory, aircraft assembly, and more. They sat at long benches with headphones clapped over their ears to learn Morse code; they gathered around the steel skeletons of fuselages to learn about structural design; they studied the naked framework of wings mounted on classroom walls and memorized the nomenclature of a hundred different parts; and they delved into the mechanics of radial and water-cooled engines. It was all part of the most comprehensive aviation training available anywhere.

Although ground school would continue for months, a half-day routine of flight instruction commenced at Squadron One in late March. Located along the vast concrete seawall, it was the first of five squadrons the cadets would encounter during their training. Squadron One operated the floatplane version of the Consolidated NY-2, the same aircraft Boyington had learned to fly the previous summer.

Closely tied as naval aviation was to floatplanes and flying boats, learning to fly off the water was the first step. Seaplane training was also relatively safe, for practical reasons. Pensacola Bay offered a large, calm body of water from which to take off and land, and as long as students properly gauged the wind, they could practice almost anywhere within the designated area. (Squadron Four, an advanced training unit equipped with larger flying boats, also operated in the bay.) Down on the surface, a racetrack pattern some twenty-five miles long was laid out with markers and could be circled three times in an hour's instruction.

The curriculum was designed as if the cadets had never flown before, a wise precaution since many of them (including Boyington) had not touched a plane for several months. Also, significant differences between the floatplane version of the NY-2 and its land-based sister dictated a fresh start. The waterborne model sat level on its pontoon, rather than nose-high as did the land version; and it was perched higher above the surface. An expert pilot switching between types would notice other characteristics, mainly the extra weight and drag of the floats, though the 250-horsepower Wright Whirlwind engine was more than capable of overcoming the penalty.

Boyington's inaugural flight, a twenty-minute warm-up with an instructor by the unlikely name of Coward, came on March 26. An enlisted pilot, C. G. Coward was one of the versatile breed of technical specialists who were qualified pilots. The designation of *naval aviator* was reserved for officers, therefore enlisted pilots were called naval aviation pilots, or NAPs. Coward was a qualified instructor, but as an enlisted instructor he could not conduct check flights.

The day after his warm-up flight, Boyington began the first of several instructional hours with Coward. His basic technique was rusty—he tended to skid through turns—but after a few hours he began to handle the NY-2 with confidence. After just eight hours instead of the usual ten, Boyington was deemed ready to solo, provided he passed a safe-for-solo check flight with a different instructor.

For some reason, perhaps a simple case of "checkitis," Boyington did the unthinkable and failed the flight on April 13. The lieutenant who conducted it determined that Boyington's spirals were not only unsatisfactory, they were "dangerously skidded." Worse, he recommended that Boyington should be dropped from the program. This turned out to be a routine comment and carried little weight (one

"down-check" was not enough to send a student packing),
but it went into Boyington's record.

The next day, he went aloft with Coward for a warm-up
flight, after which he flew a recheck with a different instructor and passed with little difficulty. Approved for a solo, and
with his confidence restored, he gunned his NY-2 off the water for his third hop of the day on April 14 and flew around
the pattern for a few minutes by himself.

From the cockpit he could look down upon Santa Rosa
Island, stretching for miles to the east, its pure silica sand
gleaming brilliantly against the emerald water. He had a fascinating bird's-eye view of Fort Pickens at the western end
of the island, with its time-bending combination of pre–Civil
War redoubts and modern concrete gun batteries. The army
still maintained coastal-defense guns in and around the fort,
and from personal experience Boyington could admire the
long-barreled "disappearing guns" in their reinforced pits.
On the mainland across from Fort Pickens, the brick escarp-
ments of historic Fort Barrancas kept their mute vigil over
the bay. Turning onto the final leg of his circuit, Boyington
judged the wind direction from the cats' paws darkening the
water, picked an open space, and brought the NY-2 down until its centerline float kissed the surface. At about forty-eight
miles per hour, it was like landing on soft grass.

Had he been the last in his class to solo, he might have expected a raucous group of instructors and fellow cadets to
throw him off the seawall into the bay. He never mentioned
such treatment, suggesting that he merely lost part of the tie
he wore with his khaki uniform. Tie cutting was traditional
and better (for the recipient) than a cold dunking.

During the next stage of training, Boyington accumulated
fourteen solo hours in the NY-2 for proficiency, punctuated
by occasional instruction with Petty Officer Coward in spirals and spins. Completion of the stage was measured by
another check flight, which he passed on May 1 with no
trouble. For the rest of the month he spent his flying time
above the picturesque bay, gradually mastering the techniques of precision landings and complex aerial maneuvers,

all of which would be judged later in a comprehensive check ride at the conclusion of the seaplane segment. Coward flew with him occasionally, logged as "dual instruction," otherwise Boyington was on his own.

Whatever confidence he acquired was severely tested on the first of June when he flew another major check flight. As with ground school, a variation of the four-point grading system was used to measure performance, but there was little margin between the good, the bad, and the ugly. A grade of 3.0 represented the low end of average, with anything below 2.5 considered failing. By the check pilot's standards, Boyington's performance was abysmal: eight of thirteen graded items were unsatisfactory and two others were well below average. The worst grade was for approaches, which bordered on inferior, probably because he made the mistake of landing in another squadron's operating area. More damaging, the instructor considered Boyington's aptitude unsatisfactory, and recommended dropping him.

At this stage of training, failed check rides were not uncommon. Fortunately for Boyington and the other cadets who suffered down-checks, there was an established procedure for determining whether they had suffered a temporary setback or were permanently flawed. By passing two rechecks in sequence, they could resume training. A failed recheck landed the student before a review board consisting of several instructors, who considered a number of factors before deciding whether to recommend extra training or drop the cadet from the program. If the latter was indicated, the ultimate decision lay with the commandant of training, upon whose carpet more than one cadet sweated out an appeal.

Boyington managed to avoid a review board by passing both rechecks the following day, receiving fair if slightly below-average marks during the two flights. His completion of the primary seaplane syllabus was signed off with a 2.9 flight grade, accompanied by a rudimentary fitness report, mostly a formality, which measured such qualities as his reliability, military manner, and devotion to duty.

With Squadron One behind him, Boyington boarded a

navy bus outside the cadet barrack early the next morning
for a ride to Squadron Two, some three miles north at Corry
Field. He spent that day and part of the next studying the
systems and basic operation of the Stearman N2S Kaydet, a
durable and forgiving biplane trainer, then had his first hop
on June 4. Naval aviation training was deliberately designed
to be a pressure cooker, with no breaks between stages, no
chances for a student to catch his breath.

Even more intimidating, Squadron Two was staffed with
"some of the toughest check-pilots who ever climbed into a
cockpit." Statistically, nearly one-third of the cadets would
wash out during this period. Those who got through the various stages received dual instruction in precision spins,
emergencies, and three-point landings (in a painted circle
measuring just one hundred feet across), then practiced
everything solo. Progress was measured by the "dreaded
twenty-five-hour check, the nemesis of many a would-be
naval aviator," followed by an advanced solo period of aerobatics. Students who made it that far would learn the intri-
cacies of loops, Immelmanns, cartwheels, figure-eight turns
around pylons, split-S turns, and more. Then came an intense phase of formation flying, including takeoffs and landings in three-plane sections, plus cross-country navigation
and night flying. In all, the course was programmed for
eighty hours of flying over four months, more than twice the
length of any other squadron.

For the first stage, Boyington had the fortune to be paired
with Lt.(jg) Lyle Koepke, an instructor famed for his grid-
iron prowess a few years earlier at the Naval Academy.
Despite measuring "five foot minus," Koepke captained the
1929 squad, which included such legendary aviators as "Indian Joe" Bauer and "Jumpin' Joe" Clifton. Under Koepke's
guidance, Boyington took quickly to the eye-catching
Stearmans. Painted bright, glossy yellow for the sake of vis-
ibility, they were nimble and well balanced, pulled through
the air by a Lycoming or Continental radial engine. The
sight of a formation of these yellow beauties sweeping between cottony clouds would stir the soul of even the most

jaded instructor. It was late spring, a period of blooming hibiscus and crepe myrtles in Pensacola. Corry Field with its still-new runways and hangars and classroom buildings was a beehive of activity.

Koepke saw from the first that Boyington had a "very good feel" for the Stearman, which continually improved as he logged additional hours. Ready to solo after six hours, Boyington earned better-than-average marks for general headwork and landings during his first check ride, confirming Koepke's assessment. He logged eleven more hours of solo time and passed the check ride for the next stage, then concentrated on the demanding challenge of circle shooting.

The technique of dropping a plane into a small area was a mainstay of naval aviation. Foremost was the premise that most navy pilots flew from carriers, and should know how to land aboard them. This required consummate skill in handling a plane, in knowing how to put it down with a relatively high sink rate within the confined area of a carrier's flight deck. Secondly, circle shooting taught a pilot how to cope with in-flight emergencies. Should the engine fail in midflight, training and confidence would enable him to react quickly and put the plane safely on the ground. The trick was in setting up the approach carefully, so that he rolled out on his final heading with the proper sink rate to make a three-point landing inside the circle. S-turns and sideslips controlled the descent but were dangerous if performed too close to the ground. The twenty-five-hour check required six circle landings, four of which had to be full-stall, three-point landings within the circle, plus the cadets had to perform all of the skills from the previous stages.

Through late June and into July, Boyington spent part of each increasingly hot, sticky day at Corry Field, accumulating hours of solo practice interspersed with instruction. He gained so much confidence that he even got into a heated argument with his instructor during one of their flights. Koepke was known at the Naval Academy for his "pleasant manner [and] willingness to help," but Boyington somehow pushed him into stepping out of character. Rather than assert his authority as an officer, Koepke decided to interrupt the flight and settle the matter with his fists. Afterward, the story raced through the cadet class. As Des Canavan heard it: "They were circle-shooting, had some altercation, and landed the plane. They got out and squared off, then pushed and shoved each other around. Boyington hung in there and Koepke apparently enjoyed it."

It was seen as a case of two young men letting their blood rise, nothing more. The behavior would never have been condoned—a cadet could be immediately discharged for fighting with an instructor—but no one of consequence was the wiser. The pair settled the disagreement on their own and got back to business, but Boyington discovered something useful about the established military system. If a person were careful, he could take some small satisfaction from occasionally stepping outside the boundary of acceptable conduct without getting burned.

This early hint of a maverick attitude was quickly dampened when he came up for his twenty-five-hour check. Koepke may have been amused by their little rhubarb, but C. F. Nieberle, a naval reserve lieutenant, was not impressed with Boyington's handling of aerial emergencies or his small-field work, and gave him a thumbs-down on July 17. Boyington was given the usual opportunity to make good by passing two rechecks in succession. The situation went from bad to worse, however, when his first recheck on July 20 was an even poorer attempt. With Lt. (jg) Lance "Lem" Massey grading his performance, he crowded the small field, overshot approaches, side-slipped ineffectively, and had trouble handling simulated emergencies.*

A review board convened the next day and decided to award three extra hours of instruction, after which Boying-

---

* Six years later, Massey was the commanding officer of Torpedo Squadron Three aboard USS *Yorktown* during the Battle of Midway. Like the ill-fated Torpedo 8, from which only Ens. George Gay emerged alive, Massey's squadron was decimated. Ten TBD Devastators were shot down and the remaining two ditched. Only three men survived, but Lt.Cdr. Lem Massey was not among them.

ton would have to pass two rechecks. Massey was assigned as his instructor for the extra period and took Boyington on a couple of flights, then rechecked him on Friday, July 24 with good results. Boyington took off again that afternoon with a different instructor for the second check, but a storm prevented them from completing all of the required segments. The entire flight would have to be repeated, forcing Boyington to worry over the weekend about his future. Monday, however, proved to be Christmas in July.

While certain instructors were known as cutthroats, others had reputations as being lenient, the kind of instructor the cadets called a "Santa." Boyington had the good fortune to encounter one of the latter for his second recheck on July 27, judging from the comments filed by Lt. Bruce Wright. Although Boyington managed to shoot only three landings in the circle instead of the requisite four, Wright entered a 2.5 and wrote, "Barely passing." It was a gift, probably because Boyington handled the emergency drills nicely at the end of the flight.

He was ready to move on to the advanced solo stage for his first taste of aerobatics. This was the fun part, where cadets spent hours in their snappy yellow Stearmans doing wingovers and loops and low-altitude turns around pylons. During the next month, the dog days of August, Boyington sweated profusely in his flying suit and cloth helmet, his vision distorted by the rippling heat waves that sizzled up from the runway, finding relief only in the slightly cooler slipstream aloft. He accumulated almost forty solo hours, accompanied periodically by Lem Massey, who made comments on his general improvement. Boyington passed the stunt checks successfully, then had a few hours of training in formation flying.

Here was a whole new bag of tricks to learn—using rudder to slide close to another plane, jockeying the throttle to match speeds, trying to maintain position while the lightweight planes bounced on pockets of rough air. Difficult enough in straight and level flight, turns and cross-unders and altitude changes made it infinitely harder to master without chopping off another cadet's tail.

After a couple of cross-country flights in formation to checkpoints in Alabama, Boyington flew four check rides in rapid succession, three of which were average, with one extremely shaky ride sandwiched in between. Another Santa let him slide. The last stage of Squadron Two was an hour's solo at night, followed by the final check flight on September 24 with no less than the squadron's commanding officer. Having failed four check rides previously, Boyington had been notably tense during the latest round of in-flight tests. Once again he struggled early in the check ride, but eventually smoothed out and even impressed the CO with his handling of emergencies and precision landings. Despite his struggles, he had made it through one of the most demanding phases of training, and could take comfort in the knowledge that failures among cadets who had made it past Squadron Two were rare.

If Boyington was ever in a mood to celebrate, this was the logical time. He and his fellow cadets in Class 88-C were finally able to enjoy some time in town on the weekends, though it was not guaranteed. Off-base privileges, difficult to earn, depended upon the class's performance during inspections and drill, while individuals simultaneously worried about their accumulated demerits.

Acquiring them was easy. An inspecting officer could find almost anything wrong, not only with a cadet's appearance but with his barrack-room, locker, or even community spaces such as heads. Demerits were assigned in increments of five to the guilty, and sometimes extended to his roommates or even the whole class. Flawed performance in close-order drill could lead to demerits; around the battalion spaces, cadets could be called upon to recite all sorts of promulgated information from memory, with failure to provide it promptly resulting in more demerits.

Conversely, they were hard to work off. An hour of extra duty would eliminate five demerits, but if too many were still on the ledger Saturday morning, the negligent cadet was restricted to base. There was a theater and a library and a "gedunk" store, but when the rest of the class was out on the town, staying on base was a jail sentence. No wonder they called the privilege of leaving the station "liberty." Looking back on the disciplinary environment, Des Canavan remembered the frustration shared by many cadets: "We were all graduates of university, and some had been working for one or two years during the Depression; we were solid people. Yet we weren't treated as officers and all the demerits and discipline didn't sit well with most of us, particularly with Greg. He was always caught up in petty regulations and assigned demerits."

Boyington usually managed to work off his demerits in time to join his fellow cadets for those precious hours away from military routine. Pensacola hopped after hours, with bars and casinos and restaurants of every description. Being a navy town, an atmosphere of tolerance prevailed, and aviators tended to enjoy high-octane fun.

There was good reason. It took machismo and intensity to belong to the elite fraternity of naval aviation—characteristics that pilots did not simply turn off at the end of the workday. Work hard, play hard, was their accepted motto, and the vast majority lived up to it. The cadets looked up to their instructors, nearly all of whom were veterans of the fleet. They were worldly in their ways, enjoyed swapping adventure stories, and the saltiest carried themselves with a practiced air of nonchalance, always ready with the right quip or a handy repartee. Their opposites—the loners and teetotalers and individuals who otherwise did not join in—were often viewed as outsiders. Camaraderie was everything.

Paradoxically, a distinct sense of competition existed in everything aviators did, weekend celebrations included. Egos were at stake. Squadrons competed also, for official recognition and specific awards and just for bragging rights. Thus, pilots constantly measured every facet of their lives against other pilots. Who was the best at formation flying, at bombing, gunnery, or dogfighting? It mattered a great deal.

Between flights, when they played acey-deucey or card games, someone was the winner; when they gathered at the bar to play drinking games, someone was the winner.

Even a pilot's ability to drink was measured. Reason dictated that if he could perform precision hammerheads and snap rolls and coolly overcome an engine failure, he should be able to hold his liquor. Not that it mattered if he became inebriated, for that was the anticipated outcome. Only during certain occasions—an introductory call at a senior officer's quarters or a full-dress affair—were officers expected to behave with restraint; otherwise no stigma was attached to being drunk. Getting "soaked" or "tight" was seen as amusing, even in navy publications. One pamphlet, given to all officers at NAS Pensacola to entice them to join the Mustin Beach Officers' Club, contained a chit for two free drinks. Inside the pamphlet was a cartoon caricature of a wobbling, bleary-eyed officer, tongue lolling to one side and liquor sloshing out of his glass.

The cadets were inevitably drawn into this complex culture of comradeship, drinking, and competitiveness. They emulated the savoir-faire of the pilots, copied their mannerisms, played their games. During liberty they congregated with other cadets to eat and drink, but instead of swapping sea stories they commiserated over tough exams and tougher instructors.

The marines of Class 88-C, tending like most of their service to be elitist, welcomed marines from other classes into their circle. One was Bill Millington, another graduate of the University of Washington (making at least five in the group), who had arrived in Pensacola several months behind the others. "We socialized quite a bit," he remembered. "People like Galer and Jim Mueller, Dick Baker, and a guy from Spokane named Winton Miller; we often gathered in downtown Pensacola, kicking it around, just relaxing, taking in a movie, having dinner or whatever. We even rented a house off base that we used to great advantage for poker games, beer-drinking sessions, and what have you."

The house was a matter of economics. Cadets earned only

$105 per month, from which $30 was deducted for mess-hall expenses. The balance left even the most frugal cadet with less than $20 per week to spend. The marines, therefore, pooled funds to rent a two-story house a few miles from the base. About ten others besides Boyington were involved, including Millington, Ray Emerson, Des Canavan, Bob Galer, and two marine cadets from California, Norm Anderson and Ralph Johnson.* The latter was a hot hand at the piano, so the cadets found a secondhand upright for him to bang on.

Boyington was a willing participant in the weekend festivities. As Galer put it, "He had a lot of competition when it came to partying. We were all bachelors and living in cadet barracks, and Saturday night was party night."

Except that Boyington wasn't a bachelor, and he struggled with burdens his classmates did not face. He almost certainly sent home some of his pay, meager as it was, to his wife and son. Always short of money, he began a habit of borrowing and buying on credit.

Then he became aware of major upheavals at home. First came the surprising news that his mother had moved from Seattle in the spring of 1937, taking young Bill with her to Okanogan after he graduated from high school. She had decided to reconcile with Ellsworth and make a new start in the little town on the Columbia River.

This was disastrous for Helene, who lacked skills, and was left on her own with a young child to care for. Possibly she looked to her sister Constance for help, but later events would indicate that their sibling relationship was less than supportive. Out of desperation (to give her the benefit of the doubt), Helene moved into another man's residence. The problem for her was that too many of Boyington's classmates were from Seattle. Bob Galer was still in training when he learned that she "was living with a man in a houseboat on Lake Union." Boyington inevitably learned about it, and as Norm Anderson later recalled, "was very upset and disap-

---

* From this small group of friends emerged three generals and two recipients of the Medal of Honor.

pointed with the fact that Helene let him down. She had been unfaithful to him, and that was a very disappointing fact roaming around in his head—because they had a child."

Worst of all, he was helpless to do anything if he wanted to earn his wings. "The Marine Corps," said Anderson, "would have terminated his career immediately, if it had been known that he was married." Boyington had two options: he could either give up flying and go back to Seattle, or stay in Pensacola and try to concentrate on flight school. There was probably no hesitation. In choosing to stay, however, Boyington must have realized that his marital problems would prove hugely distracting. Arguably, he had known what he was getting into before he left Seattle, and was willing then to set everything else aside.

That he would also face a completely different kind of challenge never occurred to him. Neither he nor his cadet classmates could have known that when he began to drink socially in Pensacola, he unleashed the first stage of a powerful disease.

Amazingly, considering that alcoholics raised him, Boyington arrived in Pensacola at the age of twenty-three with no personal drinking experience. Throughout his life he claimed to have never had a drink in high school or college due to Grace and Ellsworth's behavior. "They sure as heck ruined Christmases and other great occasions for the kids," he once said. Acquaintances from that time supported his claim. Knowing him as Gregory Hollenbeck at Lambda Chi, Ronald Nelson later wrote, "Studies came first with him and he did not enter into many fraternity activities." Likewise, a coastal artillery corps captain from Fort Worden described him as "sober, honest, a hard worker, intelligent, conscientious, and thoroughly reliable."

In Pensacola, something changed. Boyington was immersed in a culture unlike anything he had ever experienced, a social atmosphere that encouraged young men to drink. To this, Boyington added a growing list of personal worries about Helene and the baby, the struggle to provide for them, and the strain of flight school. It was a volatile recipe. He was under terrific pressure from several sides, not the least of which was the influence to participate in weekend merrymaking.

Thus, at one of the first cocktail parties he attended, Boyington cast aside the ugly memories of his family's drinking and tried hard liquor. Later he rationalized, "I figured I was at the opposite end of the United States, as far away as I could get from my relatives." It probably seemed an innocent matter of joining his classmates in what they were doing, but in one critical way, he was not like them.

Boyington was unable to control the body chemistry he had already inherited from his parents, both of whom drank (and according to their divorce transcript, Grace drank during pregnancy). Another strong factor influencing alcoholism, ethnic heritage, can only be presumed in his case, but Boyington himself later remarked, "The fact that there's Irish and Indian mixed in didn't make me an alcoholic, but it helped, probably."

From the moment alcohol first entered his bloodstream, he experienced an affinity for it. "At this first cocktail party," he admitted, "I made a statement: 'I don't know why I stayed away from this stuff for so long, because this was made for me.'" Alcohol had an increasingly pleasant effect on his outlook, and as the evening progressed, each trip to the restroom brought renewed appreciation: "While I was washing my hands I looked in the mirror and I became more handsome. And I was taller; I always wanted to be taller. I was a little bashful around women, but liquor fixed that. Being a blackout artist from the start, I got the tale the next day that I didn't care whose garter I snapped that night."

The blackout he referred to dramatically illustrated his predisposition to the chemical impact of alcohol.* At first,

---

* As one clinical psychologist described them, "Blackouts are a very distinctive feature of alcoholism, and one symptom that clearly distinguishes alcoholics from nonalcoholics. The events which occur during an alcoholic blackout are not forgotten, they are simply not stored or are imperfectly stored in the brain."

the stimulating effect seemed wonderfully liberating. As his blood-alcohol level rose, functioning improved, even beyond the point where most people would have been reduced to clumsiness and slurred speech. Soon, however, his tolerance changed, not as a measure of how much he could consume without passing out (a common misconception), but as a factor of what he needed to function at a "normal" level. For him, that definition constantly evolved as his liver enzymes and brain cells adapted abnormally to the presence of alcohol.

The initial changes in his personality were deceptively positive. He loosened up, feeling congenial while under the influence, and was fun company for his friends. Thus, he was encouraged to drink more. When he drank to excess, which happened more frequently as his system continued its errant adjustment to alcohol, he began to exceed the standards of acceptable behavior, loose as they were in the aviation community. A cadet could not afford that sort of attention, as Boyington later described: "There were some people who were trying to help me. They didn't know how. They would tell me in a friendly way to slow down the drinking, just have a few like everybody else and have a good time. I thought at first they were trying to ruin my fun [by] lying to me about what I did. Right off the bat—in a matter of a few weeks—I started telling myself, 'Well, I'm not going to have another drink until Saturday night.' I always did this where somebody could hear me, because I wanted them to know that I was giving forth, doing something for other people."

Unfortunately, such promises soon became familiar mantras that no one, including him, took seriously. By the time his classmates gathered at the cadets' club on base, or made plans for a party at their house in town, Boyington had convinced himself that he was strong enough to "take a few beers with the rest of the boys." After drinking one or two, however, he would exclaim to his pals, "This stuff bloats me," thereby excusing himself to switch to his favorite, bourbon and soda. Beer simply wasn't strong enough, and its alcoholic absorption was relatively slow. The soda he pre-ferred to mix with hard liquor contained plenty of carbon dioxide, which accelerated his stomach's breakdown of al-cohol and thus its absorption.

Although he probably drank only on weekends at first, Boyington continually stretched the limits of his adaptation to alcohol. This made it harder for his central nervous sys-tem to recover after each night of drinking. "I remember having a good time," he would later say about those days in Pensacola. "Sometimes I'd even remember some nice fights. And then I wouldn't remember. I would wonder what in the heck I'd done, the next day, when I unglued the first sticky eye and started thinking."

Bill Millington had no trouble remembering, and later ac-knowledged that Boyington was the instigator for a fair share of the roughhousing. "He was a hell of a wrestler. He . . . could wrestle anybody at any time, and often did when he took on a load of alcohol and became a little pugnacious. If anyone got out of line, he was flattened by Boyington."

Early in his military career, therefore, Boyington firmly established his legendary definition as a hard-drinking, brawling marine. He would always be remembered for his behavior while under the influence, a sad irony considering that he was generally pleasant when he wasn't drinking—which was actually most of the time. And even when he was drinking, he did not always turn belligerent. "He looked like a tough guy but he had a good heart," vouched Des Canavan, "and he was fun for us to be around." Other classmates echoed Canavan's assertion: Boyington was a likable guy.

Soon after Class 88-C entered Squadron Three, when the cadets first used two-way radios for communication, the classmates began to hail each other with nicknames. These were practical—pilots prided themselves in economizing their words over the radio, using monosyllabic names for identification as much as possible—as well as fun. There was one rule: no one could choose his own handle. For bet-ter or worse, a call sign was earned, often from common sources such as a surname ("Buzz" Sawyer), distinguishing characteristic ("Slim"), or geographic roots ("Tex"), but also by way of derring-do or misdeed.

Boyington's nickname was born of coincidence rather than the usual sources, for he happened to strongly resemble Gregory Ratoff, a character actor in contemporary movies. Born in Czarist Russia, Ratoff fled the Bolshevik revolution and performed in French theaters before an American producer discovered him in the early 1920s. After starting out on Broadway, he made his Hollywood debut in 1932 and within five years had performed in a dozen films. Sometimes cast as a villain, he was known for punctuated expressions in his thick Russian accent. A classmate made light of the similarities between Ratoff's swarthy appearance and Boyington's bellicose moments (not to mention their shared first names), and applied an abbreviated nickname. Laughter surely accompanied the first tag of "Rats" Boyington. Being nicknamed for a movie star was one thing, but association with unsavory rodents was hardly appealing, which of course made it all the more fun to use. Unlike his boyhood nickname, known only to Grace and a couple of chums, "Rats" was widely used and would stick with him for years.

Despite all the fun he enjoyed with his friends, the challenges Boyington faced resulted in discernable changes. Between his struggle with alcohol, the demands of flight school, and the rumors about his wife's behavior, it is little wonder that Boyington's instructors began to notice his moody disposition. "Has a rather sullen appearance which is against him," wrote one in early 1937, when Boyington was all but finished with flight training. By that time, the workload in the last three training squadrons had made a degree of burnout predictable.

Squadron Three was a challenging combination of new planes and new skills. First came several warm-up flights in powerful Vought O2U biplanes, the first aircraft the cadets flew that were concurrently used in the fleet. A check ride after eight solo hours was followed by intensive practice in section and division formations. The good news was that no student had been dropped from the program after passing that eight-hour check; the bad news was that Boyington managed to give the record a serious challenge.

Boyington's check flight, in mid-October, proved almost too much. He failed the first attempt miserably, receiving the lowest possible unsatisfactory score in three crucial areas. Any lower, and he could have been arbitrarily dropped from training. The following day he flubbed the recheck, compelling his instructor to write that Boyington was "not sure of himself in any phase." A review board awarded Boyington several hours of instruction, meaning that almost a week elapsed before he attempted the two compulsory rechecks. He passed the first by the slimmest margin, then managed to complete the second with better results. Once beyond that hurdle, his work improved.

In the next phase of Squadron Three, he learned to handle another legitimate fleet aircraft, the 620-horsepower Vought SU-1, a larger scouting biplane. The training became more realistic, too, with practice in cross-country navigation and formation radio work. Even better, he received his first training in aerial gunnery. Individually, cadets had already peppered targets at the rifle range, first using revolvers, then rifles, and finally Lewis machine guns, fired from aircraft ring mounts bolted to tables.

Before he was turned loose with a machine gun in the air, Boyington learned the techniques using a camera. Compact gun cameras had been developed that "shot" film instead of bullets when a trigger was squeezed on the pilot's control stick. The lens of the camera, mounted on the biplane's upper wing, was marked with a sighting reticle so that students and instructors could evaluate the "shooter's" performance. After two days of camera gunnery, cadets manned the rear gunner's seat for free-gun practice. Working in a remote area over the Gulf of Mexico, they fired at a sleeve target towed on a long cable behind another aircraft. The variables of hitting a moving target and the lack of experience many cadets had with firearms virtually guaranteed some wild shooting. Occasionally the towline was severed or a few bullets came close to the tow plane, which the cadets took turns flying. It was an unwanted assignment, and the towline never seemed long enough.

Boyington completed his camera and free gunnery on December 7, a conspicuously unpleasant flight because of his disagreeable instructor. It was his first encounter with Capt. Joe Smoak, who bore little resemblance to the rugged marines in recruiting posters. Described by Boyington as a "fat son of a bitch," Smoak was indeed heavy-looking in a contemporary group photograph, with a small mouth and dainty chin that seemed out of place in his large face. Of the check ride, Boyington later wrote, "He had rattled me so much by screaming at me I had no idea what he expected me to do, so I don't know how I could have flown properly." He correctly identified the event as a check flight in Squadron Three, but erred in claiming Smoak gave him a down (he actually scored a 2.95). No matter, the young cadet and the portly instructor evidently developed a mutual animosity that would fester for years. The Marine Corps was too small a service for their paths not to cross again. Fortunately, Boyington's flight with Smoak was practically his last event in Squadron Three, and he soon moved on to the next stage of training.

Ground school finally ended at about the same time, allowing Boyington to devote his workdays to flying. Squadron Four found him back at the seawall at the main base, where he began instruction in Martin T4M torpedo planes on floats. He made his first hop on December 17 and enjoyed good progress for the next week, which included the most thrilling segment of the syllabus to date: four takeoffs from a stationary steam catapult mounted on the seawall. Afterward, the cadets prepared for a quiet holiday break, but Boyington faced a medical situation that created an even longer delay in his training.

For the past several months, he had tried to ignore a painfully ingrown nail on his left great toe. Topical treatments and even a visit to the dispensary in September had failed to help, and the toe became infected. Rather than risk being grounded, he decided to wait until the Christmas break before seeking further treatment. His instructor, Lt. Phillip Allen, admired Boyington's determination and later gave him high marks for devotion to duty, but in the long run the delay caused an increased loss of training days. By the time Boyington finally went to the dispensary the day after Christmas, his toe had become so inflamed that he was sent straight to the naval hospital for admission. Three days later he underwent surgery, during which a doctor excised a large portion of the nail and a chunk of the toe. Because of the risk of infection—antibiotics were still years in the future—Boyington was kept as a patient for more than a week until the cavity filled in.

He returned to duty on January 8, but had to wait for three days until his next scheduled flight. By then, nearly three weeks had elapsed since his last flight. Nonetheless, Lieutenant Allen found him "much improved after rest," and cleared Boyington to solo in the T4M. He performed well on his solo check that same day, but ran into more trouble just two days later.

The check pilot he drew for his torpedo-plane final was also the CO of Squadron Four, a navy lieutenant with the tongue-twisting name of Troy Thweatt. In addition to failing him for spirals, Lieutenant Thweatt remarked that Boyington constantly oversped the engine and flew too fast, reflecting a case of the jitters. Rather than being given an opportunity to settle down, Boyington was sent back out with another instructor. Now completely rattled, he failed the taxi phase before he even got airborne. The instructor decided to complete the flight anyway, but every segment of Boyington's performance was graded below average.

Once again he went before a review board of instructors, including Allen and Thweatt. Allen got the board to consider Boyington's delay due to hospitalization as a factor, resulting in a minor penalty of extra instruction. Fortuitously, an entire week of bad weather prevented anyone from flying and gave Boyington an opportunity to refocus. With no fur-

ther setbacks he finally completed the torpedo-plane stage in
late January.

Immediately he moved into the patrol-plane syllabus,
where students got their first taste of multiengine aircraft.
These were the "big boats," ungainly-looking Douglas
PD-1s with dual controls. The pilots sat in an open cockpit
at the bow of the boat-shaped hull; behind them were two radial engines suspended between the enormous main wings.
To make the most of the flying boat's endurance, an additional student usually manned the observer station behind
the cockpit, enabling him to "hot-scat" with the first student
after an hour. The passenger benefited from watching the
cadet and instructor in the front cockpit, though sometimes
he saw more happening than expected.

Des Canavan flew one day with Boyington and "Jumpin'
Joe" Clifton, the noted Naval Academy football player. After
a fleet tour in scouts, the assignment to patrol boats in a
training squadron was probably frustrating for Clifton, who
showed no patience when Boyington argued with him during the flight. As Canavan later described their disagreement: "Greg met his match. Joe was tough as nails and
wouldn't take any stuff from Boyington. It was fun for me to
watch them going at each other while they were flying the
airplane. They were side by side in the cockpit, just arguing
back and forth. The two of them were pretty active, verbally.
Most of us would listen to our instructors and just say 'Yes,
sir,' but Greg had a way of testing them."

This was at least the second time Boyington had con-
fronted an instructor. Was he being bold and independent,
like the lad who had run free in the Idaho mountains, or was
he irritable, his nerves raw? Probably a combination of both,
but he was clearly frustrated. He had accumulated seven
down-checks, bore the aforementioned concerns regarding
his wife, and probably experienced behavioral changes
linked to his drinking. The latter could certainly make a person's actions unpredictable. Boyington's disillusionment was
evidenced by a remark he made some years later: "This regular commission that I told myself I wanted all through

training, before I took the examination: I apparently didn't want it at all, because I abused it something frightful."

Fortunately for him, the instructors he argued with probably cared little about the nuances of rank at their level. To question their aviation experience was another matter, and a dangerous precedent, but most instructors grudgingly admired a cadet who wouldn't be cowed. In any case, no real harm came of Boyington's confrontations with Lyle Koepke or Joe Clifton, but he had nearly crossed the line. As graduates of the Naval Academy in good standing—and beloved because they were football heroes—either or both of them could have made his life miserable. To their credit, they simply chose to let the incidents pass.

If anything, the last half of Boyington's flight training was more hectic than the first. Within two weeks of learning to fly patrol boats, he passed his checks in night flying, navigation, and level bombing. The culmination of his training in the big biplanes was a cross-country navigation flight that included a stop at Maxwell Field in Montgomery, Alabama. Until recently, it had been home to a famous army air corps demonstration team called the Three Men on a Flying Trapeze, led by a hatchet-faced fighter pilot named Claire Chennault, but the team had disbanded. (During the same month that Boyington visited Maxwell, the army recommended the forty-three-year-old Chennault for retirement, prompting him to accept a lucrative offer as a consultant for the Chinese Air Force. Had Boyington been told he would follow Chennault to the Far East in just a few years, he would have been astounded.)

His navigation check flight completed, Boyington departed temporarily from Squadron Four to begin his final phase of training in fighters at Squadron Five. Cadets who made it this far were usually ecstatic about the opportunity to fly a legitimate fighter; in Boyington's case the reward was especially sweet, for the squadron flew the same little Boeing biplane he had found idling near a hangar one long-ago Sunday in Seattle. Four and a half years had elapsed, but his urge to set that biplane free would finally come full circle when he flew an F4B-4. The thrill of handling one was vividly described in the 1937 *Flight Jacket*. "After two months at the beach, kicking the T4Ms around the course and lugging the Big Boats off the water . . . they launch you all by your lonesome in a tiny ship with controls so sensitive that they turn cartwheels if you sneeze. But if you like to fly, and like to feel yourself part of the airplane you are flying, this is your squadron, and you will agree that they have saved the dessert for the last course."

It was no exaggeration. At just over twenty feet long and less than nine feet high, the Boeing fighter was so small that most pilots felt they were strapping it on rather than climbing into it. Fully loaded, it weighed less than a compact car, but its Pratt & Whitney "Wasp" engine had five hundred gut-wrenching horsepower. Said a navy pilot of the beautifully balanced fighters: "They made you feel like you literally had wings."

Because they were single-seat fighters, there was no place for an instructor to sit, so Boyington got his first taste of soloing after a simple cockpit orientation. For check rides, grading was done from the ground (the instructors were experts at judging aerobatics), or from another plane during the formation flying stage. Fewer instructors were required; therefore the squadron was staffed with only seven.

Starting in the first week of March, Boyington flew practically nonstop to satisfy the syllabus requirement of some sixty hours in a matter of weeks. In a mind-boggling test of fortitude and adaptability, the stages included practice carrier landings, aerobatics, fixed gunnery, bombing, formation tactics, night flying, even a ceiling test (a timed ascent at the Boeing's maximum rate of climb to eighteen thousand feet). The check flight for aerobatics involved several violent new maneuvers, all of which had to be completed within a time limit. There were plenty of thrills too. Boyington fired the nose-mounted machine guns and dropped practice bombs against ground targets, then learned fighter tactics in mock combat against the instructors.

At the end of the first week, he began switching back and forth between different types of aircraft in the most challenging segment of his entire training. The syllabus wasn't planned that way, but he was compelled to spend half of each day at Squadron Five advancing through the fighter syllabus, and the other half at Squadron Four learning instrument flying. Nearly all of the latter was done "under the hood" in a float-equipped O3U Corsair biplane. After taking off, Boyington pulled a heavy canvas drape over the cockpit to block his view of the outside world, then flew the prescribed course using only the instruments in the cockpit for navigation while the instructor kept a safe lookout from the rear seat. The few land-based navigation aids in use during the 1930s were radio-beam stations, tricky even for experienced pilots, so the training Boyington received was rudimentary at best.

Most of the instrument flights were devoted to learning how to recover from "unusual attitudes." It was like a child's game: Boyington closed his eyes while the instructor maneuvered the plane into an abnormal situation. When he opened his eyes, Boyington had to quickly assess the plane's attitude using the instruments, then apply the proper controls to bring the plane level. The lessons were serious, designed to save his neck in a violent storm or on a moonless night with no natural horizon.

Between instrument hops, Boyington climbed into a Boeing every day for fighter training, and by March 12 was ready to face an instructor in mock aerial combat. He went up against Lt. Charlie Crommelin, one of five navy brothers from Alabama and a fleet hotshot, in a lopsided engagement. They twisted and zoomed and corkscrewed through the air, Crommelin occasionally holding back to see if his student-opponent recognized moments of vulnerability, but Boyington did not take advantage of the opportunities. Several times he lost control of his sensitive fighter, tumbling into unplanned spins. Crommelin gave him a passing score, with a slightly below-average grade. (Whether or not he realized it, Boyington's first real taste of combat maneuvering was against one of the best. Several years later, as the CO of VF-10 aboard the second carrier named *Yorktown* (CV-10), Charlie Crommelin would have the honor of leading his squadron into the first aerial combat engagement for the new F6F Hellcat. He was not destined to survive the war, but he did score 3.5 aerial victories before he lost his life in an operational accident.)

On March 12, as Boyington neared the end of the syllabus, a message was sent to headquarters advising that he would be available for fleet orders on April 9. His first and second choices for assignment were included, though it was widely regarded as an exercise in futility. Marine pilots received initial orders to one of two locales: Aircraft One in Quantico, Virginia, or Aircraft Two in San Diego, California. The choice, therefore, boiled down to a preference for the East or West coast. It hardly mattered, for headquarters sent pilots where they were needed with little regard for personal preferences. Boyington requested duty with Aircraft Two, probably because it was closer to his family, which naturally left Aircraft One as his second choice.

Meanwhile, as he continued to juggle his days between the sluggish Vought biplanes and the snappy Boeings, he stumbled again on March 17 when Lt. A. S. Heyward Jr., observing from the ground, gave him an unsatisfactory grade during his advanced aerobatics check. One of the trickiest maneuvers was to perform a snap roll at the top of a loop, the hard part being to stop the roll at the proper heading with wings level. Boyington could not keep his fighter pointed in the right direction. A review board of instructors met to ponder the situation, and quickly decided to grant a few hours of extra instruction. Immediately Boyington wrung out his fighter for the prescribed hours, then was allowed another opportunity that afternoon to perform the aerobatics check. This time he passed, though his total score was actually lower than before.

By coincidence, headquarters sent a message to Pensacola the same day, stating that Boyington was designated Naval Aviator No. 5160 pursuant to successful completion of the syllabus, effective March 11, 1937. The squadron was obviously notified not to unduly slow his progress, because he was allowed to proceed in the syllabus without flying a second recheck of the failed stage. There was little doubt now that he would get his wings, short of having a complete meltdown.

Later that week he finished the instrument flight syllabus at Squadron Four, after which he concentrated solely on the remaining fighter stages. The pace was furious: twelve hours of formation and division tactics, a couple of hours each for carrier familiarization and a night cross-country, six hours of night formation flying, twenty hours of bombing and gunnery. The weeks blurred together and suddenly it was Friday, the ninth of April.

He still wasn't finished. One final check ride was required that day, a test of skill at the target range. As it turned out, he was considerably more accurate with his two practice bombs than with his guns, but he did well enough to pass with an overall average mark. There was no time to calculate his total grade that day or to finish the necessary administrative work, but he made it to a simple winging ceremony with Des Canavan that afternoon. Because the two of them had finished the syllabus randomly, there was no grand winging event before sending them on their way. If the ceremony was anticlimactic, nothing could diminish the intense pride Boyington surely felt at wearing a pair of gold wings over his heart.

Not surprisingly, he learned that he had received his second choice for assignment: Aircraft One with the fleet marine force in Quantico, with thirty days' leave authorized en route. He simultaneously received confirmation from headquarters that he had officially been selected for a regular commission, though it would not become official until July 1. Thus, he could anticipate a monthly pay raise while the probationary period for his "unmarried" status would be cut in half. If there was any chance of fixing the situation with Helene, it was far better to anticipate just two years of hiding her and Greg junior than the four years they had started with. (Earlier, the Marine Corps had decided to make several regular commissions potentially available to Class 88-C based on competitive examinations. No doubt his prior army experience and background in aeronautical engineering helped him score high enough to earn one of the coveted spots.)

Now that he would soon be wearing the gold bars of a second lieutenant, Boyington needed to acquire the proper assortment of officer's uniforms. His generic cadet uniforms, provided by the navy, would never do for a commissioned marine. There was a downside: He was obligated to purchase a full range of working and dress uniforms for all possible seasons and occasions, which added up to an expensive stack of clothing. Several shops in Pensacola, well prepared for this eventuality, did a brisk business selling "tailor-made" uniforms, actually made in northeast factories. The tailors charged what the market would bear, allowing cadets to purchase everything on credit to soften the sticker shock. Naturally the shop owners then tacked hefty interest rates onto their profits. By the time Boyington was done choosing uniforms and accessories, he had acquired hundreds of dollars' worth of clothing.

Just before he left Pensacola, Boyington received his final aviation training report. As with the earlier competitive exams, his ground school grade reflected his experience in aeronautical engineering, while his cumulative flight grade was somewhat below average—not surprising considering he failed nine check flights and faced three review boards. A remark in his fitness report summed up his progress succinctly: "A little slow to learn, but works hard." It was as if his mother had spoken: *"Greg wasn't a brilliant student, but he was thorough and whatever he learned he kept."*

With thirty days at hand before he had to report to Quantico, there was no question but that Boyington wanted to get to Seattle somehow. A train trip would be too costly on his limited budget, but Des Canavan learned that a

"Coastie" was driving to Seattle and would gladly take passengers to share expenses.

Boyington brought along his collection of new uniforms, eager to wear them at home and everywhere else he could think of. He was fully aware that every youngster he encountered (and most adults as well) would look upon his uniform and gold wings with the same deep admiration he had once given Clyde Pangborn and his teacher's husband. The youngster from the lumber town had seen his dream to fly come true, without special treatment from anyone.

But the price. For more than a year he had virtually abandoned his wife and son, who were now living God only knew where. At the same time, he had unleashed his own malevolent genie in a bottle. There can be no doubt, however, that Boyington was ready to enjoy being a pilot, a Marine Corps pilot at that.

If he decided to wear every piece of uniform in his inventory during the next thirty days, regardless of the occasion, he had earned the right.

6

Adventures in Uniform

When Gregory Boyington reported to the marine barracks at Quantico on May 17, he might have experienced a touch of déjà vu. The streets on the base were lined with buildings nearly the same as those at Pensacola, down to the red clay bricks. The landscape was familiar, too, with its low-lying tidal basin, sandy soil, and clusters of pines. In yet another similarity, Quantico fronted a protected body of water, the Potomac River. The biggest difference between the two locales was the northern latitude and subsequently colder winter weather at Quantico—nothing to scoff at for pilots who flew year-round in open-cockpit biplanes.

At the barrack, Boyington closed out his allotted thirty days of leave. After adding them to the travel time he was authorized to use en route, a total of five weeks had elapsed since he left Pensacola. It had not been much of a vacation. First came the arduous trip of nearly twenty-five hundred miles to Washington, no small accomplishment on the roads of the 1930s. He was dropped off in Okanogan, having prearranged for Helene to meet him there with "Bobby," their nickname for Gregory junior. Nothing else is known about Helene's "arrangement" in Seattle while her husband was in Pensacola, but they did reach some sort of reconciliation: she became pregnant during their reunion.

Eager to learn more about his real father, Boyington used part of his leave for a trip to Idaho. By coincidence, Charles

Boyington had moved with his own family to St. Maries in 1934. He had kept his dental practice going in Coeur d'Alene for almost twenty years after divorcing Grace, but remarried in 1920 to Rosena Kvern, who gave birth to Keith two years later. If Boyington knew about Keith before he visited, it was a complete surprise to his half-brother. With a touch of rancor, Keith later recalled, "I never knew he even existed until I was a junior in high school. I did meet him, but he hadn't come to see me; he came to see his father." Rosena Boyington was even more resentful. When Gregory became well known years later, she minimized her acknowledgment of him, claiming that "she did not keep clippings of news accounts . . . because her husband never told her he had a son."

Boyington's visit to St. Maries was not a long one. His former friends were grown and gone—Reed Elwell to California, John Theriault to Montana—giving him no reason to stay. He wasn't much interested in hanging around Okanogan either. The house on Seventh Avenue was unfamiliar, part of the Hallenbeck household. Bill worked for the Blackwell chain of department stores; Ellsworth had gotten into small-time politics, assisting the Okanogan County auditor. In Boyington's eyes, Ellsworth had lost virtually all status as a parent, and would henceforth remain in Grace's shadow. His alcoholic behavior was objectionable, too, despite the fact that Boyington now drank. "There was lots of conversation about the drinking on the Hallenbeck side, drinking to the point that Greg didn't even want to go home," recalled Keith. "There was too much of it."

Boyington was still unaware of Ellsworth's vile sexual attractions, else he would not have brought his own family anywhere near him, but in the community, Ellsworth had already begun to develop "a very bad reputation" for his infidelities. His granddaughter Ramona heard "over and over" about his infamy, so widespread that the local Native American women displayed a bizarre ritual whenever he walked past. They scooped a handful of dust, then threw it on their own crotch as a sign of disgust. The Coleville Indian

Reservation was just across the Columbia River from Okanogan, giving credence to the story. Because of Ellsworth's notoriety and his pedophiliac behavior, the Hallenbecks were said to be "a family filled with loners."

Instead of hanging around Okanogan, Boyington used much of his available leave to establish his young family and their belongings far enough from Quantico to maintain the secrecy of his marriage. The village of Quantico, surrounded on three sides by the marine base and on the fourth by the Potomac, offered no place to hide a family, nor did the hamlets of Triangle or Dumfries nearby. The nearest viable place was Fredericksburg, twenty-three miles south of Quantico, where homeowners commonly rented rooms during the Depression. Helene and "Bobby" lived there, recalled Des Canavan, while Boyington diligently maintained the charade of being a bachelor, though as Canavan pointed out, "All through his cadet training program and the time at Quantico, all of us knew he was married."

After stashing his family far enough out of sight to avoid scrutiny, Boyington began his first fleet duty immediately upon his arrival. Awaiting him was a set of orders to Fighting Squadron 9M—the *M* was for *marines*—located about a mile south of the main base at Brown Field.

Nothing could have suited him better. VF-9M was not just any fighter squadron, but the premier squadron in the entire corps and currently one of the most famous aviation units in the country. Established twelve years earlier, the outfit was renowned for its formation stunts at the biggest air shows across the country. With its brightly painted Boeing fighters and flamboyant pilots enjoying wide media coverage, the outfit was a flying advertisement for marine aviation. Boyington already knew of the squadron's exploits; to become part of it was extraordinary.

Considering that he was known as "Rats," with a reputation as a fun-loving aviation cadet and a capacity to drink long into the night, the squadron's legacy of boisterous activity was well suited to Boyington's personality. VF-9M was synonymous with colorful pilots, including Lawson

H. M. Sanderson, the unit's first CO beginning in 1925. Ordered back for a second stint in 1930, he nicknamed the squadron *Rojos Diablos,* the Red Devils, and took VF-9M to the National Air Races. That summer, Sanderson's pilots entertained more than five hundred thousand spectators, flying their machines so close together that the crew chiefs routinely had to patch damaged wingtips.

By the spring of 1937, when Boyington joined the squadron, Capt. Ford "Tex" Rogers had commanded VF-9M for almost three years, establishing a reputation nearly as spectacular as Sanderson's. Rogers was scheduled to turn it over on July 1 to Capt. William "Skeeter" McKittrick, nicknamed for his diminutive size. On the same date, the squadron would be redesignated VMF-1 in order to alleviate some of the confusion between similarly labeled navy and marine units.*

In the meantime, the squadron prepared an aerial demonstration program for a scheduled VIP review on Saturday, May 22. No less a personality than President Roosevelt, accompanied by the National Press Club, would be on hand to observe all the squadrons of Aircraft One. Just one week after joining the squadron, Boyington had an incredible opportunity to perform before one of the world's most famous people.

It did not work out that way. Blame it on poor judgment, or a hasty decision gone bad, but just three days after joining the squadron, Boyington found himself in trouble with his superiors. In an act reminiscent of his youth in St. Maries, he decided to perform a spectacular deed, only this one went sour.

The trouble began when he and cadet Freeman Williams decided to demonstrate their worthiness of the *Rojos Diablos* legacy. Described alternately as "a jolly fellow" and

---

* Early in the history of naval aviation, the Bureau of Aeronautics settled on the letter V to designate fixed-wing aircraft. M represented the Marine Corps, and the last letter denoted the unit's primary mission: F for fighting squadron, B for bombing squadron, S for scouting squadron, and so forth.

"spoiled," Williams was Boyington's equal when it came to high jinks, and the two may well have goaded each other into borrowing two F4B-4 fighters on May 20 for a mock dogfight. No one had briefed them on the assigned operating area (or they deliberately chose to ignore it), for the young pilots gleefully staged their aerial drama right over the main base. The snarl of powerful engines at full throttle reverberated loudly off brick buildings, bringing onlookers outside. Among them was Canavan, who observed, "They just tore up the whole countryside." Exacerbating the problem, the cadets remained engaged far longer than they should have. A little flat-hatting was one thing, but the dogfight went on for nearly an hour, raising the blood pressure of the brass on the ground. "The post was not appreciative of their performance," added Canavan in a calculated understatement.

Still, the young men might have avoided serious retribution but for the fact that they fought until dangerously low on gas. At the last moment they raced for Brown Field, Williams making it before his engine conked out, but Boyington's engine sputtered as he entered the landing pattern. Too late he remembered to switch to the reserve tank. His attempts to restart the engine at low altitude failed, and the distraction of the attempted restarts carried him downwind of the field too far to glide back for a landing. Hoping to make the most of a rapidly deteriorating situation, he decided to land on the only flat terrain nearby—the Quantico rifle range. Reports that he plopped down dead-stick in the middle of firing practice might be exaggerated, but land he did, confirmed by a photograph. If he was not superstitious before the flight—a large 13 adorned the Boeing's fuselage—afterward he might have reconsidered.

Retribution was swift. The air group commander, Lt. Col. Francis Mulcahy, a veteran of World War I and recipient of the Distinguished Service Medal (superior at that time to the Navy Cross), gave the wayward pilots a severe dressing down for their unauthorized flight. He also issued an official slap on the wrist, writing letters of admonition that went to headquarters for entry into their service records. The third element of their punishment was the harshest. Both were confined to quarters for several days—"placed in hack" in military vernacular—preventing their participation in the aerial review for President Roosevelt.

For the next several weeks Boyington maintained a low profile, with no particular ground duties to perform due to the forthcoming squadron reorganization. On July 1, all hands gathered in ranks on the flight line for twin cere-monies—the change of command between Tex Rogers and Skeeter McKittrick, and the squadron redesignation—after which Boyington was discharged from the reserves in order to accept his appointment as a second lieutenant in the regu-lar Marine Corps. Concurrently with the squadron's reorga-nization, he was given an assignment as assistant engineering and propeller officer, a nominal ground job. "We had duties," quipped Des Canavan, "but they were pretty low on the totem pole. We'd be the assistant engineering officer or the assistant something; mostly we just played."

The departing CO, Rogers, had been low keyed, a kindred spirit to Sandy Sanderson and one of the best-liked pilots in the Marine Corps; McKittrick wielded more military bear-ing in order to build the new VMF-1 to its previous glory. The squadron was passed over in favor of the dive-bombing squadron, VMB-1, to represent the marines at the National Air Races that summer, so McKittrick (forthwith called "Mac," a more suitable nickname for a commander than "Skeeter") got down to business.

Executive officer Bill Brice, a veteran from the Sanderson years, worked with a couple of the seasoned pilots to mold the new lieutenants, while McKittrick kept close watch on a pair of troublemakers named Williams and Boyington. No one got into mischief for two months. In early September, McKittrick received permission to take his squadron to Parris Island, South Carolina, for gunnery and bombing training. For the next six weeks, VMF-1 conducted morning gunnery hops and bomb-dropping exercises, followed by formation flying in the afternoon, but if McKittrick thought his junior aviators were too preoccupied during this isolated training session to stray, he hadn't counted on Boyington's nose for trouble. "We were all sitting down at a meal one evening," remembered Canavan, "and heard this car engine turning up at a high rate. It was Boyington, who kept coming closer and closer, and faster and faster, then went by us in a blur. The next thing we knew, he had gone through a tennis court."

Leaving a certain amount of damage to government property in its wake, a vastly improved fighter squadron returned to Quantico in mid-October. A month later, VMF-1 staged McKittrick's first air show in front of the Quantico brass and Washington guests. Its success was rewarded the next day with an exciting announcement: all of the Quantico squadrons would participate in the Miami Air Races in December, with VMF-1 as the featured unit. For Boyington and the rest, the trip promised to be an unforgettable experience. They would be the star attraction in a warm, sun-dappled cosmopolitan city, with throngs of spectators watching them perform. Anticipation ran high, as an unofficial squadron chronicler explained: "Mac warned his men to watch their conduct, especially the young hell-raisers, but he didn't expect it to do any good."

Billed as the 1937 All-American Air Maneuvers, the spectacle commenced on Friday, December 3. For the next three days Boyington was an integral part of the squadron's formation stunts. Between demonstrations he was free to mingle with the crowd and observe the other exhibitions, including the latest innovations in aviation design. His attention was drawn to an aluminum-skinned army air corps fighter, a monoplane with sleek lines that made Boyington's aging biplane look pint-sized and frumpy. This was one of the early appearances of the Seversky P-35, the first all-metal pursuit aircraft with an enclosed canopy and retractable landing gear to enter service with the army. Alexander Seversky, a Russian-born designer who had lost a leg in World War I, was there in person to demonstrate it, having specially rigged the P-35's rudder and brake pedals.

Besides performing and spectating, Boyington enjoyed a Saturday-night celebration of his twenty-fifth birthday in Miami. Indeed, he partied every night, as did the rest of the squadron. VMF-1 was scheduled to depart Monday morning, but unexpectedly the pilots were rewarded with an extra day's visit because of their success in the air show. After a fourth night of carousing, a few pilots arrived late for the departure briefing on Tuesday. Williams and Boyington, two of the culprits, claimed they were ready for another night on the town after they ingested some coffee.

Enough was enough, and McKittrick knew it was time to leave before something happened. Summing up the four-day party, historian Jess Barrow wrote, "Mac was very proud of all his boys. None had caused any serious trouble. Of course there were the usual reports of a few wild beach parties and swimming in the nude with girlfriends, but nothing that caused any real concern to the city officials."

Considering the squadron's legacy, Boyington did not stand out from other pilots when it came to hard drinking. The Marine Corps was a melting pot of ethnic backgrounds, with the greatest percentage being Irish, Scots, and Welsh (or a combination thereof). For most marines, esprit de corps was not founded on the globe-and-anchor emblem they wore, but on the camaraderie they developed from drinking and fighting and singing together, not necessarily in that order. Boyington, who enjoyed all three, was particularly good at the first two. Just as in Pensacola, his world revolved around flying and boozing and not much else. There were few rules, fewer taboos.

Even the perceptions about his unauthorized dogfight with Willy Williams began to change. It became an accolade, a tale passed around at happy hour. Instead of being described as dangerous fools, the two of them were just hell-raising pilots with the *cojones* to have buzzed Quantico in the first place. There was a sense of approval about the whole event, augmented by the general consensus that a commander seeking pilots with fighting spirit would remember such men first.

The remainder of Boyington's first operational assignment elapsed with just a few comparatively minor mishaps. One night, he somehow managed to demolish a De Soto within a week of buying it, but escaped unhurt from the accident. Subsequently, a pilot who had been with him ever since Seattle decided to make a special presentation. Ray Emerson—on the train with Boyington at the King Street station, at Pensacola when he failed nine check rides, in VMF-1 when he landed on the rifle range, and now amazed at his friend's fortune in a car wreck—paid a tribute. "I would like to toast to the luckiest unlucky man I know," he was quoted as saying. "Here's to Rats, may his luck continue forever."*

It was probably sometime in November that Helene took Bobby back to Seattle. She was by then into the last trimester of her pregnancy, this during an era when obstetricians frowned on travel or excessive activity. Boyington could provide little assistance without exposing their marriage, and his squadron was scheduled to be deployed on a fleet exercise when the baby arrived. In Seattle, she relied partly on help from Canavan's girlfriend, Marie O'Keefe. Helene did not drive and evidently received little support from her adoptive or foster family, so Marie was often her chauffeur. "I used to take her to the doctor for checkups," the future Mrs. Canavan recalled. "In fact, I took her to the hospital so that she could have the baby."

The New Year began quietly for Boyington, who left Quantico with the rest of Aircraft One for San Juan, Puerto Rico, on January 23. Just five days later, Helene gave birth to a daughter, Janet Sue. With virtually no resources of her own to cover medical expenses, Helene relied on the generosity of Dr. O. H. Christofferson, who rendered three hundred dollars' worth of services with the vague hope that the woman's far-off marine husband would reimburse him.

Boyington was busy with Fleet Landing Exercise IV,

---

* Emerson himself was not so fortunate. He later was killed in a dive-bombing accident.

which lasted seven weeks. It was no hardship to fly and play in the balmy Caribbean. There was work, if flying to support war games could be called that, but at night the rum flowed freely. Somehow, McKittrick kept his pilots focused on the war games and VMF-1 earned a letter of commendation from the chief of naval operations.

Boyington may have been anxious to see Helene and his new baby when FleetEx IV concluded, but he was no less enthusiastic about the delivery of brand-new Grumman F3F-2 fighters scheduled for the first of March. Although somewhat outdated already—the Grumman was still a biplane in an era when low-wing fighters were becoming more commonplace—technologically it was a quantum leap ahead of the old Boeings. The Grumman was descended from a line of fat-bellied, rugged biplanes with retractable landing gear and fully enclosed cockpits. No more unbearable flights exposed to bitter cold or lashing rain; no more douses of eighty-octane gasoline and oil in the face when inverted. Purists might have mourned the passing of the open-cockpit mystique, but most of them had not been compelled to fly year-round.

Boyington and his comrades were undoubtedly familiar with some of the F3F's properties. The inside scoop: the newest Grumman flew like a dream, was the quintessential dogfighter with plenty of wing area and horsepower, was agile yet rugged. But it also had a short, thick fuselage and narrow landing gear, resulting in less favorable reports of the fighter's behavior on the ground. Pilots likened it to a "beer barrel on roller skates."

When VMF-1 returned from San Juan on the weekend of March 12, the pilots swarmed over the ten brand-new F3F-2s that had already been delivered. On Monday, Grumman representatives briefed the marines on the F3F's features and characteristics. The Dash-2 model had been upgraded to a Wright "Cyclone" engine of 950 horsepower—nearly double the power of the F4B-4—yet the Grumman weighed only thirty-five hundred pounds fully loaded, about the same as a common sedan. On the front of the big radial engine, a three-bladed propeller gave the Grumman a sixty-mile-per-hour speed advantage over the Boeing.

Qualification flights commenced that afternoon. Right away the marines discovered the worst aspect of the retractable-landing-gear design. The wheels were raised manually, using a small crank beside the pilot's right leg. In order to free his right hand to raise the wheels after takeoff, the pilot had to move his left hand from the throttle to the control stick, an awkward adjustment for pilots accustomed to left-hand throttle, right-hand-stick after hundreds or even thousands of flight hours. It took thirty-three and one-third turns of the crank to fully raise the gear, during which the pumping motion in the pilot's right arm invariably transferred across his body into the control stick. The sensitive biplane bobbed happily in response. Formation takeoffs magnified the cockpit gymnastics and "Tail-end Charlies" bounded like gazelles, but everyone got the hang of the procedure.

Soon after VMF-1 completed its qualifications, the roster swelled with the arrival of eleven new pilots, including seven cadets from Pensacola. One of the experienced newcomers was 1st Lt. John Condon, twenty-six, a graduate of the Naval Academy. Popular, highly respected, and destined to achieve the rank of major general, Condon became friends with Boyington during this transitional period. Their paths would later cross at several junctures that were important to Boyington. "I always liked him in many ways and there was never a question about his ability in the cockpit," wrote Condon. "He was fun to be around until he got too 're-laxed,' and then 'Katie, bar the door'!"

A few months after qualifying in the new aircraft, Boyington and several other junior officers received orders to attend the Basic School in Philadelphia. Heretofore, they had received little credible instruction in the profession of arms. That they were aviators was irrelevant. The Marine Corps's heritage as a sea-based force required that officers receive a thorough education in a broad range of war-fighting specialties, including amphibious landings, artillery, demolitions, infantry tactics, and more. Students spent almost a year in the program.

Shortly before departing, Boyington had the opportunity to meet two officers who would have a future impact on his life. One was Lt. Col. James "Nuts" Moore, who reported to Quantico after completing a stint at the Naval War College; the other was Sandy Sanderson, ordered to Quantico after serving with Aircraft Two on the West Coast. It is not certain how much Boyington visited with the legendary fighter pilot, but Sanderson's presence at Quantico made an impression. Also arriving at this time, Capt. Joe Smoak had been ordered for a tour of duty with VMB-1. Boyington was all too glad to put some distance between himself and the overweight former instructor, but they were destined to spend considerable time in close proximity later on.

Still keeping his family a secret, Boyington reported to the marine barracks at the Philadelphia Navy Yard, his new home for the next year, on July 5, 1938. Joining him were several old friends and plenty of new faces, seventy-three lieutenants in all. Virtually everyone grumbled about having to sit in classrooms. After the thrill of flying, the study of military campaigns and lectures on naval gunfire or landing operations seemed inordinately dull. Occasionally the students trained with mortars, machine guns, and antitank weapons, but much of the time they endured such dry topics as constitutional law.

Boyington became frustrated again, caused in part by financial strain. Whether Helene and the two children tried to live off base in Philadelphia, or he sent them money in Seattle, he fell behind on his bills. In early February and again in March, he purchased additional clothing and accessories from a Philadelphia uniform merchant, then left an unpaid balance of forty dollars. A specialty tailor over in Annapolis fitted him with almost two hundred dollars' worth of new uniforms on credit, a balance likewise unpaid. A trend had started that would eventually become insurmountable.

Mounting pressures caused Boyington to become temperamental, according to Bob Galer, who didn't realize his fuse was short. Three locals learned the hard way.

We were assigned to go somewhere on a Saturday morning, and we could take a guest. Boyington and I left the BOQ in our uniforms and I parked near a little bar while I picked up my date. He hadn't had a drink when I last saw him, and I was only gone about fifteen or twenty minutes. By the time I got back, he was a mess. I asked the bartender what the hell had happened.

He said, "The lieutenant was sitting at the bar. Three guys came in and sat at the little booth behind him. After a couple of minutes, one of them says, 'This guy ought to have a yellow stripe down his back rather than a red stripe down his side.' The lieutenant didn't pay any attention but they kept up the same program. All of a sudden the lieutenant rolled around and pinned all three of them in the booth with the table. He hit all of them and they ran out. He kept hitting them from the running board of their car, and fell off when they went around the corner."

For a change, the incident didn't directly involve alcohol, as the fight happened well before lunch. "He hadn't finished his first beer," Galer stated. "He wasn't drunk." But Boyington may have been struggling with a severe imbalance from the previous night. He loved to fight, and there was the issue of defending his service's honor, yet his explosive reaction was suggestive of unpredictable behavior caused by alcoholism. He had been drinking for close to three years, and the effects were beginning to show.

Perhaps the most telling result was his performance in the Basic School. He passed all subjects satisfactorily, but drifted through the courses with little regard for the outcome. He graduated on May 1, 1939, ranked seventy-one out of seventy-three students, a surprising underachievement for someone who had excelled in ROTC, received high praise from officers in the army coastal artillery, and gained professional experience in engineering.

Having dug himself into a hole professionally, Boyington discovered that a career in the Marine Corps was not just about flying. Furthermore, his graduation near the bottom of his Basic School class was only the beginning: there was lots more room for his reputation to descend.

7

Conduct Unbecoming

If there was a redeeming outcome to Boyington's ten months at the Basic School, it was the new friends he made. One was lanky Charles "Chick" Quilter, a six-foot-four-inch Irish Catholic who scrunched down in the seat of open-cockpit airplanes to keep his head out of the slipstream. He was younger than Boyington by a couple of years, but the two pilots got along well and had fun with their nicknames, Chick and Rats. They flew an O3U-3 in early April 1939 to renew their instrument qualifications, the last of several dual flights they enjoyed together in Philadelphia.

A few days after their flight, both received orders to the 2d Marine Aircraft Group for duty. Freeman Williams and another new friend, Charlie Endweiss, would also be going to San Diego. Having squeaked through the Basic School, Boyington could look forward to flying fighters again, this time in southern California, but he arrived in San Diego to learn he'd been assigned to the scouting squadron, VMS-2. Endweiss, Galer, and Williams had been the fortunate ones, going to VMF-2, the fighter squadron. It was common practice to shuffle pilots between scouting, bombing, and fighter squadrons to broaden their experience (the various types of aircraft were all single-engine biplanes), so switching was not particularly challenging for Boyington. The scouting mission was simply dull. VMS-2 was equipped with Curtiss SOC-3 Seagulls, the last of that company's operational biplanes. A capable scouting and observation aircraft, the Seagull drove like a truck compared to fighters.

Boyington could hardly complain about his new surroundings. The marines flew from North Island, not really an island but a bean-shaped landmass protruding into San Diego Bay on the end of an isthmus. Several navy and marine squadrons, flying from a huge, circular landing mat, shared the western two thirds of North Island. The city of Coronado with its quaint, colorful bungalows and palm-lined boulevards occupied the eastern portion. Vehicles could reach Coronado by taking a ferry across the "Hellespont," the narrow channel between North Island and San Diego, or by driving some twenty miles around the bay and up the isthmus, a strip of sand known as the Silver Strand.

Helene and the two children moved to Coronado and established a semblance of family life in a small rented house on Seventh Street. Although the probationary period ended on July 1, Boyington could not promptly jump up and announce that he was married. He already had two children, including a four-year-old, and by midsummer his wife was pregnant for a third time. Boyington decided to wait until late November before reporting his "new" family to the Marine Corps, then listed the youngsters as stepchildren, implying that he had married a widow or divorcée. Gregory junior was recorded as Robert Roy Boyington. By this time, Helene was already four months pregnant and probably starting to show it; most people knew the truth anyway.

Boyington took two weeks' leave over the Christmas holiday, one of the first extended periods he'd spent with his family. (He had spent ten unhappy days at home in September, grounded after a head cold developed into sinusitis—a hazard of constant air-pressure changes while flying.) The Boyingtons enjoyed a period of domesticity, though fault lines were beginning to develop.

Many of their friends were settling down. Freeman Williams married Eva Theodora Lilley, a socialite from Waterbury, Connecticut. Her bloodlines may have been blue, but she had brilliant red hair and the personality to go with it. The marines dubbed her "Torch." Charlie Endweiss was likewise married, and so was Bill Millington. The Depression was easing, and though the pilots were not highly paid, they lived relatively well on the Coronado economy. It was a little easier for Galer and Quilter, who lived in the breezy, Spanish-style bachelor officers' quarters on base. Without a family to feed, Quilter drove a flashy yellow Pontiac Phaeton convertible everyone called the "Yellow Peril."

The young couples had their own kind of sophistication. The social scene was the liveliest yet, with top jazz acts and dance bands at the incomparable Hotel Del Coronado, and dances every Saturday night at the North Island Officers' Club. "Each lady wore an evening gown," one of the wives remembered, "and had two or three more hanging in her closet." Whenever they socialized, the marines (and their women) consumed ample amounts of liquor. Bar tabs often exceeded rent, at a time when bungalows in town cost fifty-five dollars a month.

With a loan from a San Diego bank, the Boyingtons bought a new car, a 1940 De Soto Tudor sedan. Helene acquired a wardrobe from Coronado's trendy shops, where merchants such as Charlotte Hats and the Lelah Elgin Dress Shop were happy to extend credit. Unfortunately she was no better than Gregory was at keeping track of bills. He splurged by having his uniforms cleaned and pressed at the Hotel Del Coronado laundry, and both of them used credit plans at furniture stores and grocers and drugstores throughout Coronado and San Diego. Meanwhile, Helene's third pregnancy resulted in mounting bills. One of their friends later said, "They were basically two naive creatures. I don't think either of them had been exposed to the sort of life they would lead when they got into the Marine Corps."

Despite the gap between the money he was making and the money he spent, Boyington had good reason to celebrate the holidays in 1939 thanks to a new set of orders. On the first workday of the New Year he joined VMF-2, commanded by another smallish Irishman, Maj. Vernon Megee. Boyington found several familiar faces in the fighter squadron, including his former department head from VMF-1, Capt. Boeker Batterton, who promptly arranged for him to become the assistant engineering officer. Endweiss and Williams were still in the squadron, the only second lieutenants besides Boyington. Small as marine aviation was in those days, Megee surely had heard of Rats from Quantico, both as a flier and a potential troublemaker. Boyington created sequels to the legacy in each category.

Within a month of joining the squadron, he was involved in an incident that became legendary. It was probably February 23, the last Friday of the month, when he took the ferry to San Diego and made his way to the marine training depot on the north shore of the bay. He had been invited as an officer sponsor for an enlisted men's dance, ostensibly to make certain no booze entered the building, but by the time the dance ended he was inebriated. Worse, he had missed the last ferry to Coronado. He phoned Helene and told her of his plight, but she hung up with the words "If you got over there, you can swim home."

He decided to try just that, later telling an interviewer that his only alternative was "a helluva long and expensive cab ride." Gauging the channel to be about three-fourths of a mile across, he thought it was a manageable distance: "I was a good swimmer who was feeling no pain, and I figured I could get my uniform dry-cleaned the next day. So I dove off the dock and started to swim."

Using a light off to his left as a guide, he struck out for the opposite shore. The weight of his waterlogged uniform became a problem, so he shed his blue jacket and left it behind. Soon his shoes, socks, and red-striped trousers went to the bottom or drifted away. After an exhausting swim, he gained the shore and crawled out of the water in his skivvies, then started climbing the rough embankment. Halfway up, he tumbled painfully back down to the shoreline, shredding his shorts. Now he was completely naked as he struggled at last to the top, where he made an awful discovery: he was still on the San Diego side of the bay. The light he had guided by was actually a midchannel marker or was mounted on an anchored vessel. By keeping it to his left, he had merely circled it and landed south of his original starting point.

By this time Boyington was a tired drunk, living a nightmare. He had no clothing, no means of getting home, and needed to seek cover. To be discovered by the civilian police would mean a night in jail, more damaging professionally than the embarrassment of nakedness. His best bet was to reach the shore-patrol office, located in a narrow alley not far away.

Boyington made it without being intercepted, but as he approached he saw several women—the wives and girl-friends of servicemen who had been rounded up—sitting on benches near the duty office. With every ounce of bravado he could muster, he strode up to the chief petty officer on duty. Looking up, the chief muttered, "I don't know whether you're crazy or not, but I'll bet you're a marine."

Gratefully, Boyington covered himself with a navy blanket, but from there the tale of his eventual rescue diverges. One account had him picked up by "a married lady friend" (Torch Williams), who provided him with a ride home. Bob Galer, an unassuming man who later achieved his own legacy as a Medal of Honor recipient and brigadier general, gave a different account: "I was a bachelor living at the BOQ, and I got a call from the shore patrol. They had Greg, all wet and out of uniform, and could I come and get him. I drove down the strand to where there was a bridge across the inlet, about twenty miles at midnight, to bring him home. He was a fellow marine, in trouble."

Boyington missed work on Monday, February 26, and was sick in quarters for two days. The timing of his illness is circumstantial, but seems too coincidental to be anything else but a result of his chilly dip in the "Hellespont."

In another coincidence, Torch Williams's best friend Elizabeth Howe arrived in Coronado within a day or two of Boyington's escapade. As young ladies, Liz and Torch had been friends at the Ethel Walker School for Girls with classmates named Ford and Zimbalist and DuPont. A graduate of Smith College, Liz and her divorced mother decided to make a break for sunny California. When the former Mrs. Howe heard about Boyington's attempted swim across the channel, she scoffed at the marines (her own father, brother, and nephew were naval officers), calling them "the people who wear those vulgar blue trousers with the red stripes." To her dismay, Liz began a whirlwind romance with Chick Quilter. Four months later they were married.

During her courtship in the spring of 1940, Liz observed that Gregory was not the only Boyington with a drinking problem: "The doctor had told Helene not to drink during this particular pregnancy, meaning the hard stuff, so she would go to the parties with this *huge* jug of port wine slung over her shoulder, mountain-man style, and glug away."

There was other trouble in the Boyington camp. Gregory had strayed at least once, and was also careless. In what Liz Quilter later referred to as "a shameful thing," Boyington had found it necessary to borrow Chick's car in order to correct the situation. His benefactor may have felt more guilty than he, according to Liz's account: "My husband was a very proper Irish-Catholic type. One of his great sins was to loan his 'Yellow Peril' 1937 Pontiac Phaeton to Rats, who took his current amour down to Mexico to get her an abortion. That grieved Chick, who said, 'I don't think I did the right thing.' Apparently this happened right before Mother and I got there in February 1940."

Boyington was soon able to put some distance between himself and his troublesome private life. In February, VMF-2 qualified aboard the aircraft carrier USS *Yorktown* during work-ups for an April deployment. The state-of-the-art flattop, commissioned three years earlier, had come through the Panama Canal in 1939 to operate in the Pacific. The whispers of war were already being heard now that Hitler had invaded Poland and the Japanese were killing Chinese by the tens of thousands. In a large-scale exercise,

Yorktown would sail from its San Diego base and train with other fleet units en route to Hawaii.

Marine aviation customarily worked closely with the fleet but did not often join their navy counterparts aboard; thus marine pilots' carrier qualifications were often out of date. Boyington had never landed aboard ship, and nearly three years had passed since he learned the basic techniques in F4B-4s at Pensacola. Thus, he had to start from the beginning, with field carrier landing practice (FCLP) on the landing mat at North Island.

Although no specific flight log for this period of his career is known to exist, Boyington spent hours in the landing pattern making repetitive approaches to a small area marked to represent a carrier's deck. To the left of the box stood a landing signal officer (LSO) whose job was to help him align his approach, which was steep and rapid, with a glide slope designed to plant the aircraft firmly on the deck. The F3F Boyington flew was designed to absorb the punishment of a hard landing, which increased the likelihood that the plane's tailhook would engage one of the dozen arresting cables stretched across the landing area of contemporary carriers. To prepare for the real thing, he rehearsed every aspect again and again with an LSO on dry land. It was common to shoot twenty or more approaches during a single session, and FCLP went on for days prior to the onboard qualifications.

On April Fools' Day, Boyington departed with the squadron aboard *Yorktown,* leaving Helene to face the uncertainties of childbirth without his support. She had done it alone before, but could not have been pleased that he would be absent a second time. Meanwhile, he learned how the navy lived—superbly by military standards, particularly aboard a carrier that displaced nearly twenty thousand tons. Junior officers had small but efficient space in staterooms, cleaned for them by stewards who also saw to their laundry. Meals were served in the aviators' wardroom, also attended by mess boys. Snacks and incidentals were available in the ship's store; there was a barbershop, a library, and other amenities. When not engaged in flying, eating, or sleeping, the pilots congregated in the squadron's ready room, where they sat for briefings, lounged, chatted, played cards.

Boyington favored cribbage and poker, but betting on cards was not condoned in the naval service, so he had to find a quiet place to play. He found an ally in Jim Condit, whose bunkroom was the perfect locale. Although he had earned his wings in 1938 and flew torpedo bombers for VT-5, Condit was still a cadet, an advantage in this case: "I had a room down in the double bottom—as an aviation cadet I didn't rate much—and it was way down by the anchor chains. That's where we'd play poker. God, it was so far down."

Boyington participated in a variety of flight operations as *Yorktown* and her accompanying ships trained for the war that many suspected was coming. During Fleet Problem XXI the force rehearsed tactics and strategies, some of them prophetic. The determination that navy and army units must coordinate their defense of the Hawaiian Islands, for example, went largely unheeded but became a stark reality just nineteen months later.

After the exercise, *Yorktown* paused at Pearl Harbor, affording some much-anticipated liberty. Having spent several weeks at sea in "dry" conditions (alcohol was banned aboard naval vessels), the marines were no doubt warned to watch their behavior. Boyington did nothing outrageous, recalled Bill Millington: "I joined him on several occasions for shore parties, and he always managed to recover all right and report when he was supposed to."

When VMF-2 flew off *Yorktown* and landed at North Island on June 1, Boyington went home to meet his third child, Gloria Joyce. Born in Coronado on April 24, she was already five weeks old.

Settling back into domestic routine, the Boyingtons spent the southern California summer in the company of friends. They took part in the Quilters' wedding in late July, Gregory an usher and Helene a bridesmaid, both of them remaining nervously sober throughout the ceremony. "Helene was shaking up a storm," recalled Liz. "Even her bouquet shook, but both she and Rats stayed sober before the wedding and

waited until the reception at the O'Club before imbibing."
They were not alone, prompting Liz's father to exclaim:
"I've never seen people drink like this in my life!"

Trying to be a proper service wife, Helene attempted a
turn at hosting a luncheon. But the pressures of social etiquette were too great, resulting in a wife's worst nightmare.
"Helene invited us all to lunch—practically the whole
squadron—and then panicked," recalled Liz Quilter. "She
took to the O'Club and drank herself silly, leaving all of us
waiting for her to show up. She never did, so we turned to
and cooked our own lunch over at Helene's house."

Boyington could also be unpredictable, according to Bill
Millington, who occasionally played bridge with Gregory and
Helene until the fun stopped. "He was kind of mean to play
with, and invariably he'd drink too much. Helene would end
up having an all-out argument with him, and they'd use language that was pretty offensive to my wife. Finally she said,
'No more of that,' and we quit playing bridge with them."

Another memorable evening developed unexpectedly
when several of the husbands were away. Liz Quilter had
joined Shirley Endweiss at Torch Williams's house, and all
three were well into their second cocktail when Boyington
rang the doorbell. "Putting up a good front, aren't you?" he
asked, an intentional pun that eventually led to the topic of
female endowment. Years later, Liz was straightforward
about the result.

> Rats joined us in spirits and in spirit. We challenged his
> assertion that even if he were blindfolded he could tell
> which of us were which by simply feeling our boobs. So
> natch, three tipsy females stood in a row before the blind-
> folded Rats and dared him. He took his job seriously and
> slowly manipulated his way through the line. We were all
> flabbergasted when he came up with the names of the
> right owners.

For the pilots, the workdays grew more serious, their con-
centration being on the art of warfare. The regimen for

VMF-2 included gunnery and bombing practice, the former conducted with a towed canvas sleeve. Several F3Fs would rendezvous with the tow plane, then take turns making runs on the sleeve from different deflection angles. Individual results were scored by counting colored holes, each plane's ammunition having been tipped with a different color of paint. As an alternative to live gunnery, which used up ammunition during those poorly funded days, camera gunnery was inexpensive and had the added benefit of capturing the results of high-energy dogfights on film. Early models of gun cameras, mounted on the top wing, fogged during temperature changes induced by climbing and diving, but a new heated model improved the results dramatically.

As a result of such training, Boyington earned a reputation for being a gifted dogfighter. If he had an advantage, it was in his stout, muscular torso and powerful neck. The best fighter pilots have always been those in excellent condition, for dogfighting exerts tremendous physical forces upon the body. During combat, pilots do not "turn" their fighter left or right in one dimension, like a car; they flick the control stick in the direction of the turn, then pull back mightily, as if making the plane climb while lying on its side. The result is an instantaneous onset of centrifugal force, often many times the normal pull of gravity. At one "g," earth gravity, the average human head weighs about seventeen pounds; at five g's it suddenly weighs eighty-five pounds, yet the pilot must still be able to move his head to track his opposition. All the while, that same centrifugal force is pulling his blood toward his feet. It literally flows from his head, causing the brain to lose oxygen. Vision is the first to go. A "grayout" comes as peripheral details disappear in a milky haze. As the g's increase, blackout follows and the pilot relaxes, momentarily unconscious. The g's decrease because he is no longer pulling on the stick, and alertness returns when the brain gets enough oxygen.

Boyington found he could increase his g-tolerance by tightening his abdominal muscles, grunting to force some of the blood to stay in his upper body. Until the advent of the g-suit about five years later, which automatically squeezed the legs and abdomen to achieve the same result, there was a limit to how much a pilot could withstand and still maintain the vision to fight effectively. The nimble biplane fighters of the era were capable of withstanding many g's beyond the blackout region, giving Boyington a small advantage over many of his opponents. The 1940 annual gun-camera competition, in which VMF-2 faced the navy fighter squadrons at North Island, showcased his ability. By the time the contest was over, he had earned acclaim as a fighter pilot rivaling his reputation for trouble.

The crowning moment came when he squared off against a member of VF-2, the "Flying Chiefs," renowned because the pilots were all NAPs. Boyington's challenger was forty-two-year-old Louis Hoffman, a crusty chief petty officer known as "Cokey." Nobody gave much of a chance to Boyington, who had been three when Cokey joined the navy, but when the two biplanes landed after the showdown it was Hoffman who walked off muttering, "That's it, no more fights with Boyington."

Years later, Charles Quilter II, himself a retired marine fighter pilot, drew from his father's letters to describe what the gun camera film revealed: "Hoffman's film showed nothing significant, and at first, neither did Boyington's. As the film rolled on, the judges were astonished to see tiny wings appear to grow from the aiming cross which developed into a head-on view of a Grumman F3F-2 fighter that rapidly filled the screen, with the cross remaining resolutely on its propeller hub. The ensuing shots showed close-ups of the cross resting on Hoffman's cloth-helmeted head."

Boyington had simply gotten the veteran enlisted pilot to blink first during a deadly serious game of "chicken."

Shooting of the Hollywood variety likewise occurred during the summer of 1940. Boyington flew in some of the aerial scenes when Metro-Goldwyn-Mayer used North Island as the setting of *Flight Command,* the story of a shunned replacement fighter pilot (Robert Taylor) in a fictional squadron. Originally, the navy's VF-6 provided the planes and pilots for the aerial sequences, but in the middle of the production the squadron was suddenly ordered aboard USS *Enterprise* for maneuvers. A camera crew accompanied VF-6 to capture at-sea footage, but another squadron was needed for the "home field" sequences. VMF-2 flew identical F3F-2s and got the nod, but there was one technical obstacle: the markings on the Marine Corps fighters were different.

Swallowing their pride in the interest of celluloid fame, the marines let their planes be repainted. In early August, MGM artists used watercolors to turn VMF-2's Grummans into navy fighters, complete with a pouncing tiger "Hellcat" insignia on the fuselage. That month and the next, Boyington participated in several flying sequences, mostly involving formation flying. It was delicate, as the squadron's eighteen planes had to be packed tightly together to fit in the camera frame.

At one point during the production, Boyington and nineteen other VMF-2 pilots posed for a photograph in front of their fighters, which clearly show the Hellcat insignia. Remarkably, three of those present would earn the Medal of Honor; another recipient, a contemporary member of the squadron, did not make the picture. Between them, they earned four of the twenty-nine Medals of Honor awarded to naval aviators for aerial action in *all* wars.*

While the movie production continued, Williams and Endweiss were promoted, leaving Boyington as the sole second lieutenant in VMF-2. A board had convened in Washington, D.C. to consider the selection of eligible second lieutenants, including Boyington, but the officers found his service record to be less than exemplary. As Bill Millington later commented, "Flying for him was a pleasure, but if he had to do any paperwork, forget it. He loved to live 'off base,' so to speak, as far as anything military was involved. It's a wonder to me that he passed inspections or

---

* Harold Bauer, Gregory Boyington, Robert Galer, and Henry Elrod.

could march in parades, because none of that meant anything to him. He just loved to fly."

Millington's assessment was accurate. Boyington indeed failed the subject of drill during a promotion examination in early August, and the board found him "not professionally qualified." A document to that effect was entered into his service record, but the news wasn't all bad: if he passed a re-examination, he would suffer no loss of lineal ranking, as though the failure had never happened.

In the meantime, work on *Flight Command* and a short deployment aboard USS *Saratoga* provided some distraction. When the squadron flew out to the "*Sara*" on August 28 to conduct a three-day exercise, Bob Galer provided the squadron with a reminder that carrier operations were fraught with dangers. On the first day out, his F3F's engine failed due to fuel-line blockage while he approached the ship for a landing. Forced to ditch in the carrier's wake, he swam free before the Grumman sank in eighteen hundred feet of water.*

Boyington did pass his reexamination for first lieutenant and was officially promoted on October 26, but made the cut by only a tiny margin: of forty-seven officers promoted, he was next to last. A month and a half later, he received new orders for aviation duty at NAS Pensacola, which translated into a job as a flight instructor. He and Helene packed the De Soto for a cross-country journey, then bid farewell to southern California on December 15. They drove east, leaving several friends and plenty of unpaid bills behind. Before long, some of the former and all of the latter would catch up with them.

Saving some of his authorized leave in transit, Boyington reported to the marine barracks in Pensacola on January 3,

---

*On April 4, 1990, the wreckage of the F3F-2 was raised from the ocean floor, and Bob Galer was on hand to greet the salvage vessel at a San Diego pier. His aircraft—the only original F3F-2 remaining—was fully restored and is now on display at the National Museum of Naval Aviation in Pensacola, Florida.

1941. There were no quarters available for married officers, so he and Helene rented a bungalow under the live oaks in the Bayshore neighborhood, across the inlet from the naval property. The grass was sparse, struggling to exist in the sandy earth, but there was a picket fence around the big yard, a good place for the children to play. With his extra pay as a first lieutenant, Boyington took advantage of the dismal job market among underprivileged blacks in the Deep South and hired a maid to help Helene. Knowing it would seem an unheard of luxury to the folks in central Washington, he had the maid pose with the family for a snapshot. The woman's eighty-six-year-old mother joined them, the first time in her life she had been photographed.

Assigned as an instructor at Corry Field in primary trainers, Boyington reported January 6 to instructor's school. He spent the next three weeks under training in the newly formed school, which brought much-needed standardization by teaching every instructor the same methods and grading policies.

The training program had changed greatly in the years since Boyington was a cadet, with new squadrons, different training syllabi, and dozens more planes crowding the airspace. The primary training squadron no longer flew floatplanes, and had been increased to three independent squadrons (with a fourth in the works), each using an identical syllabus either at Corry Field or brand-new Saufley Field. The huge influx of students caused by the mobilization of the country's armed forces dictated the need for extra squadrons. Quality standards remained high, but the risks were greater for instructors and students alike. The one constant in primary training was the parade of wide-eyed kids, the vast majority of whom arrived with no more than ten hours of flight experience after E-base. It was Boyington's job to prepare them to solo safely, then perform more complex instructional flights as they progressed, and finally conduct check-flights at the appropriate stages.

After completing the training course on January 27, he reported to Squadron 1-B, commanded by Lt. Cmdr. Charles Lee, better known as "Chink." Several times each weekday during decent weather, Boyington took to the skies above the air station, which reverberated with the swarming noise of N2S Stearmans and N3N "Yellow Perils." For self-preservation, he had to develop a blend of patience and vigilance— the former to cope with vastly different talents and tendencies, the latter because the neophytes in other trainers, let alone the one in his own airplane, could be wildly unpredictable.

Coming from the fighter community, he no doubt enjoyed the aerobatic syllabus the most. Pity the students with weak stomachs whose names were chalked on the board opposite G. Boyington; with his innate ability to withstand high-g maneuvering, he could perform loops and spins and cartwheels until many of them were green and heaving, hopefully over the side. Those blessed with fortitude and fine inner-ear balance just as surely earned his admiration.

The training schedule called for a five-day workweek unless it was necessary to make up lost time. Otherwise, weekends were wide open, and Boyington was already familiar with the popular bars and restaurants. Liz Quilter, who had come with Chick to Pensacola at about the same time as the Boyingtons, recalled that he ran up a sizable debt at Carpenter's, a favorite establishment. Then there was the night at the Mustin Beach Officers' Club when the Boyingtons arrived in disarray: "The car he was driving ran off the side of the road into the sand, and [rolled over] several times. It turned upright again, so, undaunted but covered with dust and slightly ruffled, he and Helene continued on to the O'Club and very casually mentioned what had happened."

The Boyingtons' reputation became widely known in Pensacola, and before long, even new arrivals heard the stories. Second Lieutenant Pat Weiland, having earned his wings in Miami in advanced fighters, returned to Pensacola that spring as an instructor. Raised on a farm in South Dakota, the twenty-three-year-old shared a house in Pensacola with several other instructors, including 1st Lt. Stan

Bailey. Both of them came to know Boyington to varying degrees. "He was a typical old renegade, really, that was our impression," remembered Weiland. "But he laughed it off; he was a real character. Later, the rumor was that he could kill a fifth of whiskey before ten o'clock in the morning." Bailey would get to know Boyington even better, two years hence.

California native Dick Rossi, twenty-six, was also a "re-tread" instructor. He was assigned to Squadron 1-C at Saufley Field after getting his wings and, for a short period, shared a ten-dollar-a-week room in a boardinghouse with another South Dakota farm boy, Joe Foss, a marine cadet at Corry Field. Foss knew of Boyington mostly by reputation during this period, but later their lives would become permanently intertwined after Foss earned a Medal of Honor and established an incredible record of aerial victories.

Rossi stated that not all of the negative publicity regarding Boyington was accurate. "People talked about Greg being drunk all the time. He wasn't much different than all the rest of us, as far as that went. He was unreliable at times. He had a bad reputation around town for the simple reason that his wife was an alcoholic and was running up all kinds of bills around town."

Between the debts, drinking, and infidelities, the Boyingtons' marriage began to implode. There is ample evidence that he strayed almost immediately in Pensacola, leading to speculation about a girlfriend from his cadet days. On February 9, just two weeks after he started at Squadron 1-B, Boyington was involved in a high-profile incident at the Mustin Beach Officers' Club. In a tussle over an unnamed female, Boyington slugged the commanding officer from one of the satellite fields. "Greg had a date, and she was playing the piano and he was sitting on the bench next to her," explained Bob Galer. "The CO got on the other side of her and bumped Boyington to the floor. People separated them, but when Boyington started to take his date home, the skipper came out and grabbed her by the arm and said, 'I'll take you home,' or words to that effect. Boyington decked him."

A report of the incident went through the bureaucratic levels of various commands. Boyington had struck a senior officer, a navy three-striper, a court-martial offense. As it was, the commander's complicity probably saved Boyington's career, but his behavior could not go unpunished. A review went as far as the commandant of NAS Pensacola (not to be confused with the Marine Corps leader), Capt. A. C. Read, who suspended Boyington for "unofficerlike conduct" for a period of five days. It was the second time Boyington had been placed in hack, and once again the incident was recorded in his service record.

Though the official punishment was relatively light, the evening in question might have been the proverbial last straw for Helene. She took the three children back to Seattle in March, and he moved into the BOQ on base, leaving the marine barracks as his forwarding address. Their seemingly extravagant lifestyle near the water, with the big yard and the maid, had lasted two months. Years later Boyington blamed the breakup on alcohol: "We figured that if we got rid of each other, it would end the drinking. Well . . . it didn't do me any good, because I drank more than ever."

The end of their relationship was only the beginning of a chain reaction. Thus far, Boyington's skill as a pilot had kept his notorious off-duty reputation in check, but less than a month after the temporary suspension, his career began to disintegrate. For at least two years, he had been staying one step ahead of creditors from several states. They found him in Pensacola.

The first claim was the most damaging, not only in its dollar amount, but because it was issued by a large and powerful corporation. On May 2, The Great Atlantic & Pacific Tea Company notified the commandant that Boyington owed a debt of three hundred dollars for groceries purchased in Coronado. Headquarters responded to A & P, assuring the firm that the matter would be brought to Boyington's attention. It was, and swiftly. A veritable storm of messages came down through the chain of command, requiring an endorsement at each level. Compelled to answer in writing, Boyington stated, "This is just indebtedness my wife assumed while I was on the cruise in Honolulu last year. I am now making $10.00 (ten dollars) per month payments to liquidate this indebtedness."

His blithe response, forwarded by headquarters to A & P, prompted another volley of letters. The debt would take more than two years to pay off at that rate, complained an attorney, who added tersely, "If he were very sincere in liquidating his obligation, he would have . . . at least been courteous enough to answer the many statements and letters we have sent him."

Fresh on the heels of A & P's complaint, a letter from a Pensacola attorney representing an appliance company arrived at headquarters. Boyington had not paid his heating bill after leaving the rented house, where the Boyingtons had used almost thirty dollars' worth of butane gas in the span of two months. Next, a claim was filed by a uniform company for a debt going back two years, then one from a credit bureau in San Diego seeking liquidation on behalf of several creditors. The volume of letters increased until a thick stack of claims, responses, and counterclaims had crossed the desk of the commandant, Maj. Gen. Thomas Holcomb. Each new report was forwarded to the marine barracks in Pensacola for Boyington to answer. He was wearing a path on the CO's carpet. In the case of the gas bill, he answered that he was paying one dollar a month. Headquarters responded, "Your method of payment is not considered satisfactory and tends to bring discredit on the Marine Corps."

Holcomb fired a separate "rocket" on July 1, ordering a statement on the current status of every debt. Boyington later described how he handled it: "I was instructed by the commandant to write him a letter each month. On the first one he wanted [a list of] every firm I owed money, and opposite them, how much. Each and every month thereafter, I was to put down how much I was paying on each one of these. Now, previous to that I never found it difficult to lie verbally, because I figured most people never remembered; but I found out it was just as easy to lie in writing."

The compilation of creditors that he forwarded on July 15 must have boggled Holcomb's mind. Boyington listed twenty-eight individual debts spread across five states, totaling more than thirteen hundred dollars. Most of the figures were in whole increments of five or ten dollars, estimates of what he *thought* he owed. Furthermore, he had revealed only about one-third of his actual debt: papers filed in a Seattle courtroom a year later showed the amount to be nearer four thousand dollars, including a balance on the De Soto.

He had taken a terrific risk, hoping the Marine Corps would not learn more. There was little else he could do. Earning perhaps $350 per month, he was barely getting from one payday to the next. Headquarters forwarded to him a copy of each complaint that would be entered into his service record, every one labeled with the damning instruction: "File in Selection Board Case." Boyington knew he would be passed over at the next promotion opportunity. Shortly thereafter his service with the Marine Corps would terminate. If he managed to stay in uniform beyond his current assignment, his next job would be flying a desk somewhere no one had ever heard of.

His future looked grim indeed, but someone forgot to tell the Fates. They seemed to favor Boyington, especially when he needed rescuing. Either that, or he simply had a knack for being in the right place at the right time, as the accidental discovery of his real last name at an opportune moment attests. Other coincidences, some of them inexplicable, provided similar lifelines throughout the years. The summer of 1941 proved no exception. This time, saving grace came all the way from China.

8

Slow Boat to Burma

Pat Weiland had the foresight to keep a diary of his activities as a marine pilot, including his stint as a flight instructor in Pensacola during the summer of 1941. His entry for August 6 was cryptic, mostly reflecting a normal workaday routine: *Flew another five hours today. My third student got an UP today. Went to Spanish tonight.* But his last sentence that night revealed an unusual detour. *Afterward, went to town and interviewed agent on Burma Road deal.*

The interview Weiland attended after language class took place at the San Carlos Hotel, where he met with a recruiter hiring pilots to go overseas. The "agent" was a vice president of the Central Aircraft Manufacturing Company, part of a multinational corporation headquartered in New York City with offices throughout the Far East. CAMCO's primary purpose was assembling military planes in China under license, a lucrative industry for its owner, William Pawley, who took advantage of coolie labor to build factories and move equipment. In addition to building aircraft, CAMCO provided instructors for the Chinese Air Force (CAF), at the time a Third World assortment of inexperienced pilots and obsolete planes. The company also served as a convenient cover for a U.S. government–sanctioned program, begun in late 1940, that circumvented the China Trade Act to provide war materials to the Chinese.

China and the ongoing Sino-Japanese war were little understood by most Americans, primarily because the region was mysterious, always in a state of change. China's strongest leader, a self-proclaimed "generalissimo" named Chiang Kai-shek, controlled the military after reaching a shaky allegiance with the Communist Chinese. Much of what Americans knew about the country came from his wife, the graceful, Wellesley-educated Soong Mei-ling, a darling of the media described as "China's Joan of Arc."

In 1937, she had helped convince a former U.S. Army pursuit pilot to leave his retirement in Louisiana and go to China to build the CAF into a formidable service. Claire Chennault, the erstwhile leader of the "Flying Trapeze" stunt team from Maxwell Field, was paid handsomely as a civilian advisor. To give his position authority he adopted the title of colonel, though as an outspoken advocate of fighter doctrine in the early thirties, he had been retired from the army as a captain after rubbing wrong his bomber-minded superiors.

He found a measure of redemption for his theories in China, where the CAF scored remarkable early successes with biplane fighters and old Boeing P-26s. The Japanese made adjustments, however, rendering the CAF's outdated hardware ineffective against their advancing juggernaut. Consequently, the aerial destruction of China's cities was virtually unopposed. If Japan was to be stopped, Chennault and the Chiangs needed modern warplanes—and skilled American pilots to fly them.

In the spring of 1941, with President Roosevelt's approval (backed by the army and navy secretaries), the Chinese negotiated massive loans from U.S. banks to quietly purchase warplanes and recruit military pilots in a deal arranged through a murky network of businessmen, politicians, and military leaders. The airplanes would be shipped circuitously as crated cargo, while the pilots would resign voluntarily from their respective branches of service and enter a contract of employment with CAMCO.

In actuality, the pilots were volunteers only in the sense that they willingly quit their peacetime job with the military; otherwise, they were handsomely paid through CAMCO.

Pilots earned $600 a month, flight leaders $675, plus a fat bonus for each Japanese plane destroyed. This was double or even triple the current military salary for pilots. The dozens of armorers, mechanics, clerks, and other specialists needed to support the little air force were likewise well paid by contemporary standards.

In March, several representatives of CAMCO began actively recruiting military pilots for what would later become the American Volunteer Group (AVG). The goal was a hundred pilots to go with an equal number of Curtiss P-40 fighters, some of which were already at sea in the hold of a freighter. The recruiters traveled from base to base, pitching the pilot-for-hire deal to just about anyone who would listen. They painted it as defending the Burma Road, a twisting, treacherous truck path that went from the Rangoon docks into China—the country's only remaining lifeline now that the treaty ports had been overrun by the Japanese.

Favoring naval air stations for his recruiting chores, a retired navy three-striper named Rutledge Irvine set up an interview room at the San Carlos in early August. It was a clever idea: the hotel had one of the few air-conditioned bars. During the dog days of summer, when the temperature at night dropped only a few degrees from the sweltering heat of afternoon, it was a popular watering hole for pilots.

The night of August 4 was no exception for Greg Boyington, who found himself down on Palafox Street simply "looking for an answer." Payday had been just a few days earlier, but already he was broke. Physically he was in poor shape as well, thirty pounds heavier than when he was a cadet. It showed in his fleshy cheeks and nose, making him resemble Babe Ruth. He had smoked heavily for years, supporting the commonly held notion that "smokers drink and drinkers smoke." His wife and children were gone, he was deeply in debt, and many of his superiors were breathing down his neck.

He carried his checkbook, but his bank account had been wiped out to pay the "nasty people" who were hounding him for unpaid bills. Lack of money couldn't stop his craving for alcohol, however, so he went inside the hotel. Later he described his rationale.

> I knew darn well [the money] was gone but I wrote out a check for twenty bucks and they cashed it. By the time they got hold of me, I knew it would be payday and I'd tell them it was an oversight and they'd have their money. That was my routine.
> I knew my answer was inside that air-conditioned bar.
> Somebody said, "Boy, aren't you lucky. They're recruiting pilots to go over with Chiang." I said, "Well, how can you get out of the service? But don't tell me; I've got to have a couple or three doubles before I can think."
> The guy talked on, and I said, "Where is this recruiting man?"

Whether it was fate or merely an accident, Boyington stumbled upon the answer he had been looking for. After learning the room number, he knocked on the door, entered Rutledge Irvine's suite, and told "the story about the most fantastic pilot in the world."

The recruiter Boyington talked with was not Irvine, however, based on his description. "He was a retired air corps boy, and he was in the Lafayette Escadrille, and he wore his wings around on his civilian clothes. I can see that face today: looked like a rubber sponge being massaged in the hands."

This was Richard Aldworth, also a CAMCO employee, who claimed he had been a member of the famed World War I fighter squadron and often postured in uniform. The Escadrille connection was a sham, but it probably made an effective analogy. Just like the American pilots in France during World War I, the AVG pilots would have the honor of fighting for another country's freedom.

Boyington was attracted by Aldworth's sales pitch. "He said we'd be flying against people who wore thick lenses and were not mechanical, like we boys were. . . . He said we'd be getting five hundred bucks besides a good salary—twice what we were getting in the service—for knocking down Japanese planes. . . . These would be unarmed transports, nine out of ten of them. Well, I wasn't above picking up money like that to pay off bills."

The contract with CAMCO called for a year's employment beginning upon arrival in China. Boyington was promised that when the year was up, he could return to the Marine Corps at his current rank with no loss of lineal number. He was further assured that the program had the approval of the president and the secretary of the navy, and that his resignation paperwork would be locked in a secret safe until he returned. Even better, he could sign now as a flight leader for an extra seventy-five dollars a month, and would become a squadron leader when he reached Burma.* Even if the deal sounded too good to be true, Boyington's dire financial situation left him with no other options. He signed immediately.

He mentioned the interview to fellow instructors, resulting in Weiland's decision to visit the San Carlos after language lessons. As word spread, Dick Rossi also heard about the deal. By the time he got to the San Carlos, Irvine was interviewing pilots two at a time. Though not long a pilot, Rossi had traveled the world in the merchant marine to earn money for college, and Irvine accepted his application.

The recruiters were having a tough time finding a hundred pilots—let alone fighter pilots—willing to give up their current job for a far-flung adventure. Some of the pilots CAMCO accepted were bomber and patrol pilots, including Lt. Joe Rosbert, who had gone through a shortened training syllabus before his assignment to a navy patrol squadron in California. He loved the idea of flying fighters, but was ini-

---

* About six weeks later, Aldworth wrote Chennault regarding Boyington and Curtis Smith, another marine: "I urge your particular attention to these two pilots, especially Gregory Boyington. Boyington was an officer in the regular Marine Corps. He was skipped on the promotion list, really due to a most unfortunate state of affairs in his family. I investigated him thoroughly, and the more I got to know him the better I liked him. . . . Smith's record speaks for itself. I feel you will be doing yourself a favor if you make them both Squadron Commanders."

tially turned away. Later, when CAMCO recruiters saw that pilots weren't tripping over each other to get in line (he was the only one from his squadron to apply), he got a position. Ultimately two thirds of CAMCO's pilots wore naval-aviator wings, including several from carrier-based squadrons.

Pensacola was a mother lode for Irvine, who eventually accepted three dozen applications from navy and marine pilots. However, they could not enter a contract until their resignations were approved, a process Boyington had already set in motion. He addressed a brief, two-paragraph letter to the commandant on August 8:

1. I hereby tender my resignation from the U.S. Marine Corps.
2. Immediately upon acceptance of the resignation I will accept a position with the Central Aircraft Manufacturing Company.

His resignation was forwarded along a prescribed chain of command, first to Lieutenant Commander Lee at Squadron 1-B, then to the CO of the marine barracks, followed by Captain Read at Pensacola. Because of Boyington's sullied reputation, no one had any reservations about sending him on his way. The paperwork reached the director of aviation at headquarters a week later, where the process paused briefly while Col. Ralph Mitchell reviewed Boyington's record. His approval was finally forwarded with a strongly worded endorsement.

Acceptance of resignations at this time, of well-trained Naval Aviators, will delay attainment of the number of pilots required by the greatly expanded aviation program. However, due to the apparent inability of Lieutenant Boyington to handle his financial and personal affairs in a manner becoming an officer, his early separation from the Marine Corps is considered to be for the best interests of the service.

It is further recommended that Lieutenant Boyington

not be reappointed at a future date in either the regular Marine Corps or Marine Corps Reserve.

Boyington was unaware that his promised reinstatement was already in jeopardy. After his file was screened to determine whether he owed any money to the government, it went to the commandant, Major General Holcomb, who forwarded his endorsement to Frank Knox, secretary of the navy, on August 21. Knox gave his approval "by direction of the President," and Holcomb forwarded the appropriate orders to Boyington. His resignation became official when he signed the paperwork on August 26.

The Marine Corps made no secret of its willingness to let Boyington go, thereby ridding themselves of what they perceived as a bad apple. Of the hundred pilots recruited to fly P-40s, he stood out as the only pilot who held a regular commission; the other ninety-nine were all reservists.

Meanwhile, Captain Read went ballistic when he saw thirty-five more resignations: his training command would be virtually paralyzed by the sudden departure of three dozen instructors. Frank Knox told him to pare the number to eighteen, which still left him smarting. Dick Rossi made the CAMCO half; Pat Weiland did not.

Boyington's new employers directed him to check into a San Francisco hotel by September 12. The CAMCO contract provided him with first-class rail fare, three dollars per diem travel allowance, hotel accommodations upon arrival, and one hundred dollars cash for incidental expenses, but he pocketed whatever cash he was given and drove his De Soto to Okanogan, Washington.

The Marine Corps was aware of his home of record but his creditors were not, and Boyington had left plenty of loose ends in several cities across the country. Rather than deliberately dodge them, he arranged for an attorney to act on his behalf. Joseph Wicks, an eloquent veteran of World War I, would pay creditors as funds allowed from a portion of Boyington's CAMCO salary deposited in an Okanogan bank. Wicks sent instructions to each of the creditors and also informed headquarters of the arrangement in case claims continued to arrive.

From Okanogan, Boyington made a side trip to Seattle, presumably to see his children before going overseas, and while there was handed a summons to appear in King County superior court. Opening the attached complaint, he read that Helene was seeking a divorce, having accused him of cruelty and abuse. She also wanted custody of the children along with financial support. The summons was dated September 9, and he was to answer the complaint within twenty days. Whether or not Helene's timing was deliberate, there was not enough time for Boyington to appear in court before he left for San Francisco. The divorce would have to be uncontested.

Arriving at either the St. Francis Hotel or the Bellevue Hotel in San Francisco, Boyington registered at the desk with the occupation he'd been told to use—laughably, a missionary. CAMCO employees were registered under a variety of civilian jobs while waiting to board the ship that would take them overseas, from clerk to circus performer to radio announcer, covers that no one took seriously.

On September 13, they gathered with company representatives for their first official meeting. Former marine captain Curtis Smith (who had also served with the army air corps) had the most experience and was placed in de facto charge of the group. Another who had been on inactive reserve—indeed had not even flown a plane since 1939—was former navy flying-boat pilot Robert Keeton, nicknamed "Buster" after the movie comedian Buster Keaton. Dick Rossi had also joined this variegated bunch, which represented experience in everything from basic trainers to B-17s, from all three aviation branches at bases scattered around the country. The group—the third contingent to sail for the Orient—consisted of twenty-six pilots, including a CAF instructor.

At the meeting they received travel pay and were informed that their ship would not depart before the twentieth. Then, on the nineteenth, they learned that departure was yet another five days off. Boyington marveled that the press "never got the early scoop" on their true mission, writing, "There must have been a minimum of ten bars in each square block in downtown San Francisco, and each of us was in every one of them." He was unaware that *Time* magazine had already reported the unloading of one hundred P-40s on the docks at Rangoon and revealed that American pilots were going to fly them. The program wasn't much of a secret.

In the early afternoon of September 24, the Dutch motor vessel *Boschfontein* of the Java Line cast off from Pier 23 and worked her way out of San Francisco Bay. Four hundred seventy-two feet long, sixty feet by the beam, she reached her fifteen-knot cruising speed and steamed under the Golden Gate Bridge. In addition to the twenty-six employees of CAMCO, a handful of *real* American missionaries were aboard, along with dozens of British, Indian, and Chinese passengers—slightly over a hundred in all. Only seven were women, including four of the missionaries. For their own good, the women had a block of staterooms near the nurses' station.

Hull space aboard *Boschfontein,* as with the other ships of her line, was given over to cargo. Built in 1928 with a classic steamer profile, she had a raised forecastle, a large superstructure amidships, and a smaller superstructure at the stern. On the cargo decks, four derricks towered above an equal number of hatches, one of which converted into a swimming pool when the cover was removed. (A canvas liner, fitted into the open hatch, was filled with seawater.) Accommodations for 112 passengers were located in the large white superstructure amidships. Though *Boschfontein* was no luxury liner, staterooms and amenities were comfortable, including a large dining room, a well-stocked bar, and two smoking rooms. Malaysian stewards wearing white uniforms with a red sash and a turban moved quietly on bare feet, serving first-rate meals. The ship's officers, stolid

Dutchmen, tried with only partial success to understand the full-throttle antics of the American pilots.

The sea remained calm as *Boschfontein* steamed toward Honolulu, a relief, as all passengers received batteries of shots over a period of days to ward off tropical diseases, and some drank too much in the ship's bar. The constant throb of *Boschfontein*'s machinery did nothing to ease aching muscles or sore heads. The pilots brightened when they learned that *Boschfontein* would be making stops at Surabaya and Batavia after crossing the Pacific, and they scrambled to look at the ship's atlas while planning excursions.

After *Boschfontein* docked at Honolulu and cleared a customs check on the morning of September 30, the passengers were permitted a few hours ashore, but everyone was warned to be back aboard by 3:30. Having just been paid, Boyington and several others went straight to the Alexander Young Hotel. *Boschfontein*'s departure was pushed back while she waited to receive harbor clearance, a fortunate delay as several CAMCO pilots did not stagger aboard until six. Boyington, "plastered to the gills," kept on drinking. He didn't stop when *Boschfontein* departed Hawaii—the last landmass any of them would see for more than a week—nor for a couple of days after. He shared a bottle he had smuggled aboard (to avoid paying at the ship's bar) with Bus Keeton, Bob Layher, and Curtis Smith. Later that night, he and Keeton decided to investigate the hostess and nurses' area, but found other CAMCO men already there. Later still, Boyington nearly came to blows with Smith, who took his job as officer-in-charge too seriously in Boyington's opinion. Something of a martinet, Smith mustered the CAMCO detachment in formation every morning; his military enthusiasm—and Boyington's lack thereof—eventually led to the altercation.

The next day, the canvas pool was installed and filled with warm saltwater. Boyington, still drunk, collected rope burns across his back when he fell in that afternoon. After climbing out he kept on drinking. Keeton didn't see him again until lunch the following day, but thought he looked pretty good for someone who had been drinking nonstop for two days.

Boyington had company when it came to excesses. Many of the CAMCO employees were left groaning after several long days of steaming west by south with nothing to see but an endless expanse of ocean. They took turns standing two-hour watches in the crow's nest on the forward derrick, but otherwise there was no work, and little to do other than eat, drink, and play poker or blackjack far into the night. They spent nine bacchanalian days at sea before sighting land, and even that provided only a brief distraction from the endless hours of steaming.

In the predawn hours of their eighth day out of Honolulu, they encountered the first high seas of the voyage. All that day and into the next, *Boschfontein* pitched up and down "like a busy elevator," and by the second day of it even the ship's captain fell victim to seasickness. George Burgard, an ex-army bomber pilot out of MacDill Field, found him sitting at the bar "getting stewed." It was the best medicine, the captain told him.

Earlier that day, October 9, they had briefly sighted the Santa Cruz Islands before *Boschfontein* continued into the Coral Sea toward Australia. The next day, the Chinese passengers took over the bar and drank to their Independence Day. Some of the pilots were put out, but Burgard thought most of the Chinese "were pretty good eggs, so let 'em celebrate."

Three days later, after sailing nearly eight thousand miles from San Francisco, *Boschfontein* reached a point just east of the Great Barrier Reef and slowed to a stop. The engines were cut and the ship drifted quietly, waiting for the next day before picking up a pilot to guide them through the heavily mined Torres Strait. *Boschfontein*'s passengers found the sudden silence and lack of vibration disquieting, "as though there was something seriously wrong."

Perhaps the quietude that Sunday inspired Boyington and some of the others to attend the missionaries' weekly service. They sang "Rock of Ages," then listened to what sev-

eral agreed was an interesting sermon. Boyington, who sat
in the front row, later wrote of the young American missionary: "He seemed to direct the entire sermon at me and at the
group I represented. His point was how horrible it was for
people to fight for money."

After picking up a pilot, *Boschfontein* hugged the eastern
coast of Australia until she reached the northern tip of the
continent, then steamed through the Torres Strait and into
the Arafura Sea. The passengers enjoyed the view of the
coastline, but soon *Boschfontein* was back into open sea,
with two thousand miles yet to go before reaching Surabaya.
Another four days of drinking and eating and card games
passed as her blunt bow shoved aside the warm tropical waters. The nearer she got to port, the more everyone's tension
from idle time and alcohol seemed to slow *Boschfontein*'s
progress.

On Saturday the eighteenth, with the ship positioned for a
final night at sea, the crew outdid themselves with a traditional captain's dinner. Passengers and crew dressed in their
best clothes, an excellent meal was served, and there was
"much good wine." The drinking caused more trouble.
George Burgard and another pilot got into a scrap until
Boyington waded in and pulled them apart, but soon the
scuffle resumed. This time, Curtis Smith collected a punch
in the mouth when he tried to separate them. Boyington
would later write that the initial fight was staged in order to
plant the real blow on Smith, but in the process he ran his
own hand through a plate glass window, receiving several
cuts.

When he explored Surabaya the next day, he found a
bustling city of some four hundred thousand, the streets
filled with an odd assortment of ox-drawn carts, small "dog
carts" on bicycle wheels drawn by Shetland-size ponies, and
motor vehicles. He had visited San Juan and Honolulu, but
those territories did not seem particularly exotic compared
to Java. Here the CAMCO employees spent the day "gawking at the combined modern magnificence and medieval

primitiveness" of the city, and learned the art of haggling with the chattering Javanese over just about everything.

On their second day in port they met two CAMCO pilots returning from Burma to the United States. Both had decided to quit. George Burgard thought their stories were "pretty thin," adding, "We do not place much credence in them." But the two pilots were actually part of a bigger problem. A total of seven pilots and a crew chief had already quit the AVG by this time; another two pilots had been killed in accidents (and a third was destined to die just five days hence). A few others had remained, but refused to fly; they would serve as staff officers. Deeply disturbed by the fatalities and early departures, Chennault had been compelled to communicate with CAMCO in New York, requesting that the recruiters paint a more accurate picture of the actual conditions employees would encounter. Boyington later said the real reasons they quit were "the lack of planes and the shitty weather."

The *Boschfontein* pilots didn't dwell for long on the stories they heard, turning instead to the opportunity to be tourists during their layover. Boyington joined the others in an excursion to the island of Bali, a fabled tropical paradise where the young women went bare breasted. The pilots traveled in small groups, using different means of transportation, but in every case the trip was hair-raising. The journey by car involved nearly two hundred miles of narrow roads around the coastline to Banyuwangi, where a ferry crossed a five-mile strait to Bali, then another drive of about seventy miles to the town of Denpasar. Their ultimate destination was the Kuta Beach Hotel, run by an American named Bob Koke. The Dutch drove like madmen, squealing the tires around hairpin turns, blasting through towns, killing chickens. One pilot, completely shaken by the time he reached the ferry, considered it the wildest trip in his memory. The alternate method was to go by train through the mountains to the ferry, then by bus to Denpasar. The railroad wound through the jungle valleys between tall mountains—some of which were semiactive volcanoes rising ten thousand feet or more above sea level. The bus trip around the coast of Bali was a different story. It stopped at every little village along the road, disgorging and picking up natives carrying baskets and babies or even livestock.

No matter how they got there, all of the CAMCO pilots agreed the strenuous journey was worthwhile once they reached the Kuta Beach Hotel. The beachfront at Bali-Bali was every bit as lovely as they had imagined, an idyllic spot for swimming and romping in the surf. The hotel consisted of a clubhouse surrounded by small cabanas made of bamboo and palm fronds, open to the balmy breeze, delightfully comfortable. Bob Koke's staff served hearty American meals, including maple syrup for the pancakes at breakfast.

Everyone was intrigued by the Balinese practice of tooth filing, a coming-of-age ritual performed on boys and girls upon reaching the age of sixteen. The pilots hiked or rode bicycles to a nearby kampong to watch as a youth, stretched across a table and covered with a bright sarong, bit down on several small blocks of wood separating the jaws while an old man filed the four front upper teeth down to nubs with a common file. Some seventeen years after seeing it performed on "a beautiful Balinese girl," Boyington wrote, "Even now, today, I can still hear the sound of that file. I had to scurry away. The rest of the scenery, though, I highly approved of. No brassieres and so forth."

When they weren't watching a native ritual or a traditional dance, the pilots spent hours wandering along the beach, visiting native villages and taking photographs with cameras purchased in San Francisco. They explored the shops of Denpasar, swam, and tried surfing on heavy, primitive boards. Mostly they soaked up the quiet bliss of island life, lounging, eating good food, admiring the young women. Whether or not anyone mentioned it aloud, all could sense that this was their last opportunity to savor a place of beauty and peace.

Boschfontein loaded and disgorged cargo for several days in her home waters of the Dutch East Indies, then returned to Surabaya on October 29. By then, the Americans had lolled for ten days on Java and Bali. The Dutch had their work to do, so the passengers waited another few days while *Boschfontein*'s last cargo was loaded, during which a pair of three-inch guns was mounted on the bow. No one doubted they were heading into a war zone.

During the layover, the "CAMCOers," as they had started calling themselves, encountered John Young, NBC correspondent for the Far East, whom they would see again in Singapore several days hence. By now there was no secret about the American Volunteer Group's purpose. Boyington even made the news in his native state. The Okanogan *Independent* ran a story based on letters he posted to his mother, but erroneously reported his arrival "in China" on October 21.

The pilots were excited to at last be nearing the end of their journey, but when *Boschfontein* steamed slowly into Singapore at midday on November 4, a hush fell over the ship. Only two entrances into the harbor were free of mines; passengers lined the rail to gaze at the camouflaged pillboxes and fortifications dotting the hillsides, at the fighter planes crisscrossing the sky.

Once docked, they went ashore to visit a city that assailed their senses even more than Surabaya. Burgard called it "a town the likes of which I've never seen . . . a combination of trash and beauty that is hard to reconcile." The pilots hopped a bus to the Raffles, an old but distinguished hotel in the cosmopolitan heart of the city, where they met John Young again for drinks and "quite a chat." It seemed that everyone was in uniform: Scots in kilts, Indian Punjab troops, Royal Air Force pilots, Australians, and New Zealanders.

At night the pilots drank at one of three different dance halls, aptly named the Old World, the New World, and the Great World, where the barmaids were of mixed Oriental and European nationalities. Boyington found them beautiful, later waxing poetic about how "the whiteness of the whites blended into the symmetrical features of that part of the world." If he found it strange that there were so many barmaids, he soon realized the girls were prostitutes, available for the evening after a "bar fine" was paid to the establishment. At least once, he took a girl by taxi to her flat, where she bathed him with hot compresses after "each effort of physical exertion" throughout the night.

The ship was due to sail on November 8, but a day's delay was announced. Many of the pilots, low on money or just plain tired, stayed aboard. They were rewarded when several AVG members appeared and briefed them on what was happening at the group's airfield in Toungoo, Burma. Leading the group was Harvey Greenlaw, Chennault's second-in-command, who had come to Singapore for supplies. A junior officer in the army air corps ten years earlier, Greenlaw had resigned his commission (so said his wife) in 1933 to join the aviation mission to China. The Greenlaws left China after three years, then returned again in the winter of 1937–38 when Harvey worked with North American Aviation selling trainers. Not much had gone right. He and his wife were in Hong Kong, packing their bags to return Stateside, when Chennault offered him the position of AVG chief of staff and executive officer.

Boschfontein left Singapore's busy harbor on November 9, then turned northwest to pass through the Strait of Malacca and begin a three-day voyage to Rangoon. John Young was aboard, and spent much of his time talking with the pilots about the situation in the Far East. He thought the Japanese were good fliers and should not be underestimated, but didn't believe Japan was going to give the U.S. much trouble. Conversely, he "did not conceal his contempt for our AVG gang," wrote former army bomber pilot Charlie Bond, who thought the correspondent was simply opinionated. Young was not above drinking with the CAMCO pilots, and took part in a large champagne party in the ship's bar during their last night at sea.

After steaming up the Rangoon River past the coastal plains of Burma, *Boschfontein* docked shortly after dawn on November 12 with the last large contingent of pilots for the AVG. (Four more pilots, including crusty old Cokey Hoffman, arrived two weeks later.) Ed Pawley, brother of wealthy, flamboyant CAMCO owner Bill Pawley, met the pilots aboard the ship. Straightaway he took them to the company office in Rangoon and paid them in rupees for the month of October. Some of the pilots had to pay tabs at the ship's bar before they were cleared to leave. As Dick Rossi later recalled, "The skipper said they had never sold more booze on any trip than the one we were on."

There were several hours to kill before the pilots reported to the train station, where they were to depart at four that afternoon on the narrow-gauge "Up Mail" for the final, overland leg of their journey to Toungoo. During a brief exploration, Boyington found Rangoon hotter, dirtier, and smellier than previous ports. "I wandered about in a daze," he wrote, "my lips remaining clamped tightly together for fear that the stench that hung in the air would get into my mouth." That changed when he reached the Silver Grill, Rangoon's main watering hole, where he had no qualms about parting his lips to down a few drinks with the other pilots.

Everyone made the train on time, "although some were well stewed up," reported Burgard. For the next six hours the train chugged up the valley of the Sittang River, stopping regularly for water and once for the passengers to eat. The cars were fairly comfortable, with cubicles that could be opened to the outside air. Boyington later claimed that some of the pilots entertained themselves with their sidearms: "We took the liberty of shooting the insulators off the wires that ran along the railroad."

One hundred and seventy-five miles north of Rangoon, the train finally stopped at the brick railroad station in Toungoo. Kyedaw Airfield, several miles away, was the pilots' ultimate destination, though it had not been Claire Chennault's first choice for the AVG's base. He had intended to start in China at Wu Chia Ba Airport near Kunming, high in the mountains of the Yunnan Province, until summer monsoons and Japanese bombs made that place untenable. Kyedaw was subsequently leased from the RAF, but conducting a training program in Burma had its drawbacks: in trying not to provoke Japan, the British initially refused permission for live gunnery practice.

Some AVG members were waiting at the platform when the train hissed to a stop. "The gang met us at the station and, man, they looked good," wrote Burgard. They were feeling good, too, thought Keeton, who observed that "several were quite plastered." After a raucous welcome, everyone piled into Studebaker station wagons and headed to the airfield. It was well after dark, preventing the newcomers from seeing much of Toungoo or the surrounding valley during the seven-mile ride. Arriving at Kyedaw, the caravan stopped at the pilots' mess. The rest of the AVG pilots were assembled to greet the new arrivals while disposing of a midnight ration of coffee and doughnuts.

Joe Rosbert, who had arrived earlier on *Klipfontein,* was among the veterans interested in meeting the newcomers, especially those with a reputation. "Outside of 'Cokey' Hoffman . . . Greg Boyington caused the most comment among us," he recalled. "That he had been a Marine Corps fighter pilot and a permanently commissioned officer, we knew. He was the only one in the entire group to enjoy the distinction of having resigned a permanent commission. . . . Naturally we were curious." Upon meeting him that first night, Rosbert discovered that he had stereotyped Boyington's image. "I expected that he would have a rough, booming voice and an overbearing nature, but I was wrong. Boyington's voice was soft, his manner pleasant. There was something in his personality which made me like him immediately."

The new arrivals were dead tired, but one more surprise was in store. When they reached their quarters, they found the barracks to be nothing more than teakwood frames covered with flimsy walls of woven bamboo and thatched roofs. Inside each building, the dim glow of kerosene lanterns revealed a rough wood floor with twin rows of stout wooden army beds fitted with lumpy mattresses. Overhead, shrouds of mosquito netting hung from the rafters like so many ghosts in a Halloween fun house. There was a latrine around

back, with urinal cans emptied occasionally by the Burmese
help; unheated water flowed to three open shower stalls and
a primitive washstand. "Little wonder some of the earlier arrivals . . . went home in disgust," Boyington later wrote.

There was some good news. The P-40s were out there
somewhere, in the darkness. Daybreak would bring the first
opportunity to look over the planes and the surrounding airdrome—the beginning of the next phase of Boyington's
overseas adventure.

For the present, however, his lone concern was finding an
empty bunk. Crawling onto his hard bed, he tucked mosquito netting around the edges and listened as swarming insects tried to locate weak points in the material. As he put it,
"Their work was serious until sunup the next morning."

9

The Sharks of Toungoo

Reveille would normally have come at 5:30 A.M. on November 13, but someone decided the late arrival of the *Boschfontein* contingent warranted extra sleep. Boyington and his fellow newcomers arose early anyway, eager for the adventure to begin. After all, this was what they had come halfway around the world for. They began with breakfast at six o'clock in the mess reserved for "officers." (The AVG was supposedly a civilian organization, but ground-support personnel were treated as "enlisted men.") The dining facility contained tables for each of the three squadrons along with a small cluster of tables for the staff. At one end of the room stood a makeshift bar, where a screen was set up periodically for movies.

After an American-style breakfast, better than expected, the new arrivals set off to investigate. The airfield sat in a broad, flat valley, most of which was cultivated for paddy fields though there was still plenty of rough jungle. Some fifteen miles to the east, a ridgeline of dark mountains rose from the valley floor, defining the border of Thailand. The airstrip itself, originally built by the Royal Air Force, was four thousand feet of asphalt, suitable for the hot-landing P-40. There were two corrugated hangars with thatched roofs, large enough to house several aircraft, and a collection of tin-roofed supply and maintenance buildings. One low metal building served as headquarters. The control

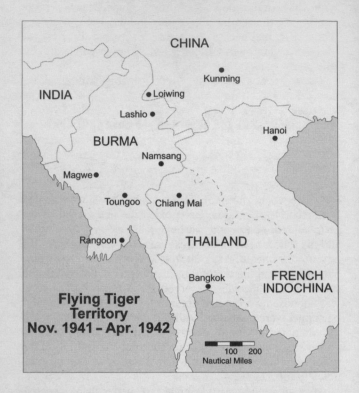

CHINA

Kunming

INDIA   • Loiwing

Lashio •

Hanoi

BURMA

Namsang

Magwe •

Toungoo •   Chiang Mai •

Rangoon •

THAILAND

Bangkok •

FRENCH
INDOCHINA

**Flying Tiger
Territory
Nov. 1941 – Apr. 1942**

100   200
Nautical Miles

tower, an open-sided hut, was perched on heavy poles. All of
the structures, including the barracks and mess halls, were
prime examples of British practicality, built with native materials that served their intended purpose, nothing more. The
barracks atmosphere reminded one pilot of Boy Scout camp,
the hard, slat-boarded British army bed disturbing his sleep
not a wink.

The food had been poorly prepared when Kyedaw was
first settled by the AVG, but a near-revolt resulted in several
improvements in time for the *Boschfontein* contingent to
appreciate them. In another stroke of relative luck, the mon-

soon season had ended. The morning temperature was pleasantly cool, though by afternoon it would become stifling. Those who had been at Kyedaw for the past three months had suffered through miserably hot, steamy weather and frequent downpours.

One element of nature that did not change with the season was bugs. They were legion. From tiny, biting ants to giant cockroaches and rattling beetles, they crawled over everything (including food) and dropped unexpectedly from walls and rafters. Unless there was a breeze, bloodthirsty mosquitoes and disease-carrying flies swarmed in the air. The barracks were constructed to allow as much air movement as possible, but everything that crawled, slithered, or flew had easy access too. Sometimes the insects were more than a nuisance, as when Boyington forgot to shake out his shirt one morning and received a nasty surprise from a scorpion. The bite on his back swelled to "the size of a cantaloupe," a painful reminder that lasted for two days. Some pilots placed the legs of their beds into cans filled with water, which kept most of the ants and other crawlers out of the beds, a small victory.

As the *Boschfontein* pilots looked around that first morning, they discovered that their number had already been divided among the three fighter units comprising the AVG, the 1st, 2d, and 3d Pursuit Squadrons, pending successful qualification in the P-40. The first contingent of pilots had yielded the squadron leaders and vice squadron leaders, chosen by staff member "Butch" Carney. Boyington, told by Richard Aldworth that he would become a squadron leader, perceived this as a slap in the face.

Chennault had backed the choices. The 1st Squadron's leader, Robert "Sandy" Sandell, was a former army P-40 pilot from Maxwell Field, where Chennault had served in the thirties. The 2d Squadron was given to John "Jack" Newkirk, whose most recent service in the navy had been flying Brewster F2A Buffaloes with VF-5 aboard *Yorktown*. The 3d Squadron went to a P-40 pilot with the lyrical name of Arvid Olson, otherwise known as Oley.

Looking over the names, Boyington found himself assigned to the 1st Squadron at the position he was being paid for, flight leader. The majority of pilots were hired as wingmen, making him one of the few to start at the higher pay level during the early part of the AVG effort, but the flight-leader position soon became watered down.

Eager to get a close-up look at the P-40s, Boyington spent part of that first morning admiring the Tomahawks dispersed around the field. By this time the AVG had received nearly all of the one hundred fighters delivered to Rangoon by freighter, although a sizable number were subsequently destroyed or damaged in operational accidents. The fighters, culled from an order originally placed by the RAF for Tomahawk export models, were taken randomly from the Curtiss assembly line in Buffalo, New York. Virtually identical externally to the P-40B in U.S. Army service (there were minor internal differences), the AVG's Tomahawks had been slated for service in North Africa and wore a camouflage scheme of dark green and light brown on all upper surfaces, with light gray on the belly and undersides of wings. Off-loaded at the Rangoon docks, the crated planes were trucked a short distance to Mingaladon Airport, where they were assembled in a CAMCO factory. Wings, tail, and propeller from one crate were mated to the fuselage and engine from a crate stamped with matching serial numbers. Once assembled, the Tomahawks were flight-tested and delivered to Kyedaw.

Boyington had never flown anything except biplanes, and had probably not been this close to a low-wing monoplane fighter since the Miami air races, when he admired a Seversky P-35. Having last flown trainers at Pensacola and a chunky F3F before that, he could not help but be impressed with the sleek Curtiss fighter.

At nearly thirty-two feet in length, it was almost half again as long as the old F3F; it also had a considerably longer wingspan, though less total wing area than the F3F. This was an important matter. The P-40's size, weight, and wing area equated to a much larger turn radius than the Grumman enjoyed; otherwise, the monoplane would out-class the biplane in virtually every category.

This was evident simply from the fighter's slim profile. Where the F3F had a huge, round body, the P-40's slender fuselage flowed gracefully from the conical tip of its spinner to its small elliptical tail. Only a small supercharger intake and the muzzles of two .50-caliber machine guns protruded from atop the nose. Underneath the chin, a shark-jawed scoop served the oil cooler and two ethylene/glycol coolers for the engine. Although the liquid cooling system was a potential Achilles' heel (a single bullet or piece of shrapnel could shut down the engine within minutes), the Curtiss fighter was big and ruggedly built. The fuel tanks had self-sealing liners and the pilot's back was protected by heavy armor plate. Even sitting on the ground, the P-40 promised to be a fast, capable fighter. The only problem as far as Boyington was concerned: he wasn't scheduled to get his hands on one for a few more days.

Surprisingly, the new arrivals had yet to see the man in charge, Claire Chennault. But he had seen them, and was none too pleased with their physical condition. The drinking and eating they'd done aboard *Boschfontein* was evident. Word came down that the pilots were to get bikes for their primary transportation, so they loaded into station wagons for a ride to Toungoo. Browsing through open-air market stalls and shops, they refined the art of haggling learned in Surabaya. At first Toungoo seemed loud and colorful, a fascinating blend of the old Orient and the British-flavored Burma of Rudyard Kipling, but that soon wore thin. "Probably the dirtiest town I ever seen in my life," Keeton wrote after his first visit.

He would get no argument from Harvey Greenlaw's wife, Olga, one of the few American women living in town. To her, Toungoo was "miles from nowhere at the edge of the jungle," and she was no stranger to life in foreign countries. Raised in Mexico, where her father was a mining engineer, she had spent six of the past eight years in the Orient, most of it in China with Harvey. They had reached Toungoo in August and settled into a small house at 124 Steel Road, but boredom tempted her into nearly quitting on several occasions. As she later put it, "After the first novelty of this disgusting little Burmese whistle-stop wore off, which didn't take very long, there was nothing to do."

It didn't take the *Boschfontein* pilots long to discover that the train station offered the only restaurant and drinking establishment. There was a small commercial district, a few brothels, and little else in the way of entertainment. After concluding their tour and haggling for bikes, the pilots rode the seven miles back to Kyedaw. Subsequently, most turned in early that night.

The next day, Boyington and the other newcomers received a formal welcome from their new boss. They made the usual banter and small talk while waiting, but when Claire Chennault strode to the front of the room, the buzz fell quiet. He wore a khaki bush jacket against the cool air of morning, a British pith helmet atop thick black hair that was graying at the temples. His physique was trim and muscular on a five-foot, ten-inch frame. On this day, he was just two months past his forty-eighth birthday, but his deeply chiseled face made him look ten years older. He spoke slowly in his native Louisiana accent, a southern gentleman's voice. He chain-smoked, so chances are better than good that he held a lighted Camel while he introduced himself to the spellbound pilots; if his hands were busy he dangled the cigarette from the corner of his mouth and kept right on talking. As soon as one cigarette was finished, he lit another, three packs a day, with only an occasional break for a pipe. After more than thirty years of this—puckering to inhale, squinting to keep the smoke out of his eyes—his face was so deeply etched that people started calling him "Old Leatherface" behind his back.

He hid well the hearing loss that had ended his career in army fighters, partially caused by the long hours of exposure to the elements, but mostly from the countless power dives he did with the Three Men in a Flying Trapeze. His bearing was tough, determined, with a distinctly military aura that greatly impressed Boyington and the other new pilots. Chennault's knowledge of Japanese aviation was unparalleled, and in the days to come he would impart as much of it as possible.

Following his welcome-aboard, the pilots remained for lectures on the P-40's operating procedures. Former navy pilot Ed Goyette was in charge of checking out the new pilots, and began of necessity with basic lectures: everything from starting the Allison engine to the location of items on the electrical panels, the instrumentation, and how to operate various controls. Another pilot described the local regulations and "course rules," the particulars for the landing patterns, tower signals, and radio protocol. Among the newcomers, none had flown for at least three months; Bus Keeton, having been on inactive reserve, had not flown for two years. The chalkboard talks were essential before anyone got back in the air, with the first flight checks scheduled for Monday, November 17.

In the meantime, Boyington had a cockpit check with an experienced pilot, who stood on the wing and guided him through a review of the instrument panel, side panels, controls, levers, and switches. It was a new sensation for Boyington to see that long hood stretching out in front of the armor-glass windscreen. For the bomber and flying-boat pilots, the feel of a single-seat, single-engine plane would be a major adjustment, and some would never adapt.

November 15 proved to be a notable day in the history of the AVG. The newcomers spent the morning at the field, getting fitted for a parachute and visiting with the dozens of other members. That evening, several *Boschfontein* pilots were invited to dinner at the home of Baptist missionaries Robert Klein and his wife, who served a Saturday-night meal of Boston baked beans and brown bread. The company had retired to the living room to talk of the war when Charlie Bond spied a magazine on the rattan coffee table, picked it up, and was fascinated by a color photograph of a Tomahawk in the RAF's 112 Squadron, based in North Africa.

He was looking at essentially the same aircraft he would fly in just two days, but the striking feature of this photograph was the Tomahawk's nonregulation paint scheme. The open jaws and vicious teeth of a shark had been applied stylistically around the chin scoop and cowling of the Tomahawk, with an evil-looking eye between the spinner and the exhaust manifold. From the viewer's perspective, below the nose, the effect was stunning: very much like a lunging great white. Bond announced immediately that the shark face was just what his own plane needed.

The next morning, having received permission from Mrs. Klein to take the magazine, Bond pedaled his bike into Toungoo and brought back several colors of paint "to jazz up the planes." His legs ached after the fourteen-mile round trip, but he worked the soreness out later that day when the 1st Squadron engaged in games of softball and volleyball. There was a movie after supper, a pleasant conclusion to an active, satisfying weekend. As the new pilots prepared to turn in, George Burgard penned a thought that surely echoed what was on everyone's mind: "Tomorrow, gals, we fly the P-40. I wonder just what it will be like."

Boyington learned exactly what it was like, and he had an audience. His inaugural flight was in serial number P-8116, sixteenth of the one hundred planes sent to China. (A special sequence of serial numbers for the CAF/AVG was assigned, from P-8101 to P-8200.) He donned a leather helmet and buckled a lap belt for the first time in three months, then started an in-line aircraft engine for the first time in his life. Once the three-bladed propeller became a transparent disk, he had a clearer view through his windscreen than he'd ever experienced, with no bulbous radial engine protruding above the hood. But the length of the nose and its canted angle prevented him from seeing directly ahead, so he used the steerable tail wheel to swing the nose from side to side while he taxied to the end of the runway. He parked at a slight angle in order to see down the asphalt strip, then held the brakes and advanced the throttle while he checked the magnetos and scanned the engine instruments. There was no such thing as a muffler on the six exhaust outlets protruding from each side of the engine; they simply collected into a manifold, from which the blue-hot flaming gases of more than a thousand collective horsepower howled past the cockpit.

Buffeted by noise and the propeller's blast, Boyington completed the checklist, then released the brakes and aligned the nose with the runway. The Tomahawk surged forward, its tail coming up quickly. Virtually all of the first-time pilots reported that they became airborne surprisingly fast, as the P-40 seemed to fly itself off the ground.

Boyington flew for approximately forty minutes, getting a feel for the fighter's handling characteristics. It was technically far ahead of anything he'd piloted, with no awkward crank for the landing gear—he just selected the gear handle position, and hydraulics took care of the rest. He put the Tomahawk through its paces, measuring its rate of roll, its awesome speed in a power dive, pulling out above the patchwork quilt of fields, and then zooming toward heaven.

When it was time to land he reduced speed in the landing pattern, fingering a button on the stick for the hydraulic flaps, then lowered the gear before turning onto his approach. Because of its sleek profile, the P-40 didn't want to slow down. Even with flaps, its landing speed was a good thirty miles per hour faster than anything Boyington had ever flown, and it would naturally stall and lose control sooner than he was accustomed to. Therefore, he had been instructed—probably by Goyette—to watch his landing speed carefully and touch down on the main wheels with the tail in the air. The three-point technique favored by naval aviators was unsuitable for the fast characteristics of the Curtiss.

Boyington was evidently cautious on his first landing and followed the advice. His technique was within acceptable limits, else he would not have been signed off as successfully checked after the first flight, which lasted a total of forty-five minutes.

Now that he was qualified, he took another fighter, P-8102, almost immediately for a second flight of the same duration. When he returned to Kyedaw this time, however, he ignored the warning about three-point landings, perhaps intending to impress the observers in the gallery with how things were done the marine way. He must have dragged it in carrier-style, for the P-40 landed hard and almost immediately started to ground-loop. As he later described it: "I bounced to high heaven as a result of my stubbornness, and I started to swerve off the runway. So I slammed the throttle on, making a go-around. In my nervousness I had put on so many inches of mercury so quickly that the glass covering the manifold pressure gauge cracked into a thousand pieces."

That Boyington was able to cob on so much power and still keep the plane in the air—the sudden torque would have spun most new pilots into the ground—was a testament to his flying skill, but his plane-saving reflexes were not enough to overcome first impressions. Olga Greenlaw, something of a gossip in her writing style, later described a slightly differing version of what happened.

> With all the boys watching to see if he was as good as advertised, [he] wound up in a ground loop which damaged a wing—a bad start for a reputedly crack pilot. He jumped out of the cockpit to be greeted by one of the youngsters with a significant "What's the matter, Captain? Lil' old shark get away from you?" Boyington's answer was a dirty look.

Although she had accorded Boyington a rank that was not used by the group, the essence of her story was plausible. If Boyington did scrape a wing, it did not cause enough external damage to prevent newcomer Jim Cross from flying the same plane later that morning.

What Cross and the mechanics didn't know, couldn't see, was that Boyington had evidently overrevved the engine, causing internal damage. Some minutes after Cross took off, a young native ran up to say that a P-40 had crash-landed in a field. When everyone realized it was Cross, making his first flight in a P-40, few believed he could have survived the mishap. Two hours later he walked into the mess hall in time for lunch, looking little worse for the wear. The engine, he reported, had thrown a rod and started burning, so he made a hasty wheels-up landing in the nearest flat place he could find. Boyington realized that his earlier rough handling of the plane led to the accident. "Even though Jim wasn't hurt," he later wrote, "I felt very bad about it, as they were forced to use this P-40 for spare parts."

Training resumed the next morning and started off well. Boyington logged more than an hour and a half on an early flight, and Charlie Bond managed to check out in P-40s while George Burgard completed his third flight. But at approximately 11:00 another pilot suffered a landing mishap. Freeman Ricketts was unhurt, but his P-40 was badly damaged when he plopped onto the asphalt with his gear lowered only partway. Chennault called a temporary halt to training for the newcomers, unable to afford the cost at the current rate of a plane per day. "The brass hats were peeved," wrote Burgard. About half of the new arrivals had not flown a P-40 yet, and would have to wait while those who had already checked out used the available aircraft.

Meanwhile, shark faces were being painted on the P-40s. Within a day or two of the baked-bean supper, pilot Erik Shilling had approached Chennault about using the shark face on the 2d Squadron airplanes. The Old Man denied the request to use it as a squadron symbol, and instead directed that the design be painted on all of the airworthy Tomahawks. Thus, pilots and ground crew drew the necessary outlines with chalk, then began to paint the P-40s. The design was consistently smaller than the RAF version, blending more aesthetically with the opening of the chin scoop. In time, the toothy shark faces applied to the aircraft during the last two weeks of November would become synonymous with the AVG, even though the idea was copied.

At about this same time, the crews also added the CAF roundel (a twelve-pointed white star on a blue disk) and settled on unique insignia for the three different pursuit squadrons. Charlie Bond was credited with the logo of the 1st Squadron. Drawing with chalk, he superimposed two running stick figures over the outline of an apple—Eve chasing Adam in the Garden of Eden—a play on the "first pursuit." He had painted the design and was touching up the shark face on his P-40 when Chennault stopped to observe. He made no immediate comment, but would later inform Bond that the big red apple looked too much like the "meatball" on Japanese planes. Bond solved the problem by repainting the apple green. The 1st Pursuit Squadron became the Adam & Eves; the 2d adopted the name of China's seemingly cuddly Panda Bears; and the 3d borrowed theirs from a movie about World War I aviators, *Hell's Angels*.

Boyington began courting trouble soon after he reached Toungoo, a result of his attraction to Harvey Greenlaw's wife. In this he was not alone; plenty of other AVG men, Claire Chennault included, vied continuously for Olga's attention. It was understandable, for there were few females within the AVG, besides which she was attractive, intriguing, and bold. "I think the two most serious problems we had at Toungoo," she wrote, "were the lack of mail and the lack of girls. The average American young man past voting age occasionally craves the companionship of an American—or at least approximately American—girl."

Olga made herself visible around the airfield, occasionally dining at the officers' mess, which gave everyone ample opportunity to appraise her. Easily as tall as most men, she was well proportioned, with a handsome if not necessarily beautiful face and a mane of dark hair. More striking even than her long legs were her exotic green eyes, enhancing a myth that she was a mix of White Russian and Mexican. (She was neither, though she was raised in Mexico.) Olga was careful about her appearance, carrying a small Elizabeth Arden makeup kit wherever she went, and wore slacks or dresses that accentuated her slender shape.

When she arrived with Harvey at Toungoo in August, several young pilots greeted her at the station with approving stares and whistles. "They were all grinning and giving me the once-over, drawing their snap conclusions about the chief of staff's wife," she noted with obvious pleasure. "I wished I'd tidied up a bit more before leaving the train—and was my lipstick on straight? I was looking them over too—knowing instinctively I was going to like them."

She was glad to have the attention, for she received little from Harvey. Theirs was clearly a marriage of convenience. Harvey was forty-three but looked considerably older, especially when he removed his hat, revealing a large bald patch on the back of his head. He called himself Major Greenlaw in the AVG, yet he had served as a junior officer in the army, having graduated from a two-year West Point program in the bottom ten percent of his class (and on his second attempt, at that). He found his niche in the Orient, where Americans and Europeans lived like royalty on the local economies.

Olga looked half his age but was probably in her late thirties. She was fully aware of the perks and mystique of living in the Far East, wielding considerable power over the maids and servants in her own household. As for her relationship with Harvey, she plumped the importance of his work with China's aviation program, but much can be read into her statement, "Harvey is a man who must occasionally be screamed at."

Olga made no secret of her attraction to several individuals in the AVG, most of them being considerably younger than her husband. In her 1943 book, *The Lady and the Tigers*, she described several romantic interludes with different individuals, though the conventions of the time prevented her from openly admitting she had sex with any of them. Between her upbringing in Mexico and her years in the Far East, she had acquired worldliness—a lust for life uncommon in a woman of that period—and often shared her wiles beyond the bounds of matrimony. As one pilot described Olga's reputation: "There used to be a running gag: 'There's only two guys who didn't sleep with Olga, and I don't know who the other one is.' She had all kinds of men, as you can tell by reading her book. Someone once said that if your name was in there more than twice, you were one of them."

Because she made herself available around Kyedaw on a regular basis, Boyington surely knew about her within a short time of his arrival. They probably met for the first time at her Steel Road residence during the weekend of November 22–23, by which time she had heard of him and knew him by sight as "the Bulldog." Two other pilots from the Adam & Eves, Bob Prescott and Bob Little, were also at her house "one rainy afternoon," waiting for Boyington to arrive. They had invited him to be a fourth for bridge, but were not certain he'd show. He did, as Olga later described with breathless sensuality.

> The patter of rain was interrupted by a cheerful whistle, the opening bars of "The Halls of Montezuma," and a figure framed the doorway. Not too tall, dressed in rain-soaked khaki shorts and unbuttoned shirt which exposed a barrel chest and bull neck supporting a square-cut face with powerful jaws, thick lips, flattish nose, broad forehead, and protruding, heavy-lidded eyes. His waist and hips seemed much too slender for his massive torso and shoulders and his curly hair was wet. . . .

Their first encounter resulted in nothing more than a quiet afternoon of cards, but that smoldering, mutual appeal soon led to private meetings. "He became a frequent caller after that first visit," she acknowledged, "popping in at odd times for coffee or whatever. He was restless and lonesome." There can be little doubt about her meaning of *whatever,* although Olga was simultaneously attracted to several others, including Little ("his eyes were large and dreamy"), Chennault ("muscular and supple"), and even the chaplain,

Paul Frillman (quite young, about thirty-three, "unmarried and handsome").

Some twenty years later, Boyington would author a steamy novel about a married seductress in Burma, a self-described nymphomaniac among a group of pilots called the Fighting Sharks. As a measure of how thinly his femme fatale was disguised, the character's name was Tonya Brownfield. Everything else was pure Olga Greenlaw.

Throughout the rest of November, training intensified as qualified pilots were integrated with their respective squadrons. Because of his experience, Boyington figured prominently in the organization of the Adam & Eves, though he bucked against some of the pilots who had gotten there ahead of him. Squadron leader Sandy Sandell, a former army P-40 pilot from Missouri, was short and wiry, with a mousy face that suited his intense, domineering personality—a young General Montgomery. Vice squadron leader Bob Neale was a good counterbalance. A former dive-bomber pilot from VB-3 aboard *Saratoga,* he had a broad Charlton Heston smile and a quaint Irishman's way of describing small things as "wee." There were several other pilots ahead of Boyington in the pecking order, including Ed Leibolt (the engineering officer), Frank Schiel (operations), and Little, a fighter pilot formerly assigned to Langley Field, Virginia.

By the end of Boyington's first week at Toungoo, talk circulated of repositioning the 1st Pursuit to Kunming, China, which had withstood numerous bombing attacks by the Japanese Army Air Force (JAAF). The flight schedule was filled with formation flying and pursuit tactics, complemented by several classroom lectures. It was familiar work to Boyington, who simply needed to overcome the rustiness of his layoff and apply his experience to the unique characteristics of the P-40, but for the former bomber pilots the airplane's performance and the tight formations were thrilling. It was hard work at first, trying to hold position in a six-plane formation as the leader twisted and corkscrewed through the sky, and Charlie Bond nearly gave up in disgust at his early mistakes. Soon he and Burgard were able to hold their own in mock dogfights. On the morning of November 25 they practiced their first ground gunnery, after which twelve P-40s from the Adam & Eves mixed in mock combat with an equal number of Pandas over the airfield, providing a spectacular show.

Later that same evening, the last contingent of pilots to join the AVG arrived in Toungoo. Only a handful had sailed aboard the Dutch ship *Zaandam,* but one of them had plenty of experience. Former enlisted pilot "Cokey" Hoffman, whom Boyington had beaten during the camera gunnery competition at North Island, joined the 1st Pursuit. The newest arrivals were welcomed with a late-night party at the bar in the mess hall. Maybe it was Hoffman's presence that led to a bit of wildness. According to Bus Keeton, Boyington "got to talking about how tough he was and threw his fist through the bamboo wall."

Chennault's role in the training process was to lecture on the fighter tactics he had been advocating for twenty years. He was as expert as any American alive on the capabilities and weaknesses of the Japanese aerial machine—knew the aircraft, the pilots' fearlessness, their discipline. Having witnessed the incredible maneuverability of the Japanese fighters, he drummed into his men the notion that they must never try to dogfight them. The AVG pilots were impressed with Chennault's knowledge, though not even he could say for certain how the P-40s would do in combat against formations of bombers or the nimble fighters. His lectures, therefore, were sometimes speculative. In one of them, Boyington thought he recognized a flaw. No slouch himself when it came to fighter tactics, Boyington had logged hundreds of flight hours practicing the methods of the period, which were based on the three-plane element then in vogue.

Explaining his recommended method for attacking Japanese bomber formations, Chennault maintained that the defenders should single out a bomber and open fire in three-plane formations, thereby concentrating the firepower of eighteen machine guns. Listening to this, Boyington thought the idea of massed firepower was good, but in mentally calculating the firing problem based on the boresighting distance for the machine guns, he realized Chennault's idea was clumsy. He decided to speak up, but either by design or mistake he was tactless when interrupting the Old Man.

I said, "Mr. Chennault . . ." He looked at me and said, "You will refer to me as Colonel Chennault." There were several yes-men standing beside him, and they all nodded in unison that he would be called Colonel.

"On the way over here," I said, "I dropped by the line where they were boresighting a P-40, and they told me the guns were being boresighted at 250 yards. Is that correct, sir?" He nodded yes. "Well, then, the thing that bothers me: if [we] fly in formation to this distance of 250 yards to open up on a bomber, how in the world do I keep my wingman's wingtips out of my cockpit?"

Boyington was referring to the fact that the three attackers would be converging toward a collision with each other if they all tried to hit the same target at that distance. At normal closure speeds, 250 yards was almost point blank. Chennault was livid. Boyington had made an accurate point, but blundered badly in causing Chennault to lose face. The faux pas was not something the Old Man was likely to forget, and Boyington claimed he "never got to officially ask a question of the gentleman again."

With the city of Kunming under repeated bombing attacks, too much was at stake to let personality clashes interfere with training. A full morning schedule of training was even held on Thanksgiving, November 27, though the group took the afternoon off. A softball game between the pilots and "enlisted men" went in favor of the ground troops, who generously shared the winner's prize of Java beer. There were no breaks the next day or the following morning, when a few more hours of flight training were squeezed in, but on

Saturday afternoon the Adam & Eves got away from Kyedaw for a picnic.

All of the 1st Squadron pilots rode a truck packed with
food and beer to the mountains east of the field. They
stopped at a promising stream and worked their way into the
jungle, where they found a swimming hole beneath massive
teaks and lush tropical undergrowth. They ate, talked aviation, swam in the stream, and drank beer. "Everyone got
tighter than a tick," Charlie Bond wrote in his diary. The picnic was a success, but several people had lost shoes, so the
whole truckload headed for Toungoo.

With few exceptions, the pilots were already juiced when
they rode into town like wild cowboys. The drinking resumed, and eventually a few of the Adam & Eves turned
Toungoo upside down. Boyington started the uproar when
he walked over to a cow standing in the street, then grabbed
the beast and began wrestling it to the ground. John
Hennessy and Bob Prescott got into the act, refereeing Boyington "to the great delight and entertainment of the gathering crowd of natives."

An even drunker Prescott and some others went berserk
later that night. One pilot noted that they were "chasing natives and scaring half the population to death . . . going into
restaurants, jerking table cloths off tables, breaking glass,
and threatening to beat hell out of the door . . . a very absurd
thing to do." The local police were generally tolerant, but
they reported the incident to Chennault, who was "very put
out about the whole affair."

It was probably during this same night that Boyington
hired a rickshaw driver to trot him back to Kyedaw. Halfway
from town, he "began to feel like a heel letting that poor,
scrawny, underfed native pull a big husky guy," so he convinced the runner to change places. Boyington was still
drunk (and by Charlie Bond's account, so was the "coolie")
when he charged up the road to Kyedaw at a gallop, pulling
the grinning native. Hearing the tale the next day, Olga
Greenlaw worried that "the British residents of the district
would be horrified."

Expecting to sleep in on Sunday morning, November 30, the hungover revelers were summarily roused at 6:00 A.M. Word came that Kunming had received another aerial pasting, resulting in an order from Chennault that everyone needed to pack, ready to leave for the northern city on three hours' notice. Most of the AVG pilots looked forward to it: Kunming sounded like a much nicer place than Toungoo, with pristine lakes on a mountain plateau six thousand feet above sea level, where the air would be cool and dry. The following week was tense as everyone waited for the order to move out, but the departure kept getting postponed.

While waiting, the pilots squeezed in all the flight training they could—high-altitude indoctrination, gunnery, formation tactics, dogfighting. Between hops the ground crews endeavored to put aircraft into combat readiness. The Adam & Eves were to take twenty P-40s to Kunming, with the untrained pilots following in a transport when the time came.

Some of the planes, fitted with a rudimentary optical sight mounted in the cockpit, were towed to the "gun butts" where their tails were hoisted to level the wings, and the two .50-caliber nose guns and four rifle-caliber wing guns were sighted in. Oddly enough, they were now harmonized at five hundred yards, twice the original distance Boyington had noted. Apparently, his challenge of Chennault's pet tactics had been taken seriously.

On December 4, while a Japanese landing force set out from the island of Hainan bound for Malaya, Boyington celebrated his twenty-ninth birthday with his longest flight yet in a P-40. After nearly two hours of formation flying, the hop concluded with "a grand windup, a rat race involving twenty-four aircraft," wrote Bond. For the first time Boyington flew serial number P-8130, a Tomahawk that he would fly almost exclusively for the next two months. Its side number is unknown, but later he was reportedly assigned P-8182, believed to wear number twenty-one.

December 5 was another busy day of training, as was Saturday the sixth, though Sandell let the Adam & Eves sleep in. He might have done it in the interest of morale, which some pilots thought was beginning to suffer. Sunday was quiet around Kyedaw and Toungoo. Hard rains fell, and most everyone "loafed the day away," content to enjoy their first full day off in the past few weeks. Despite the wind that sometimes blew the rain almost horizontally, Bond was pleased to note that the barracks remained dry.

For a small band of Americans living among the jungles and rice fields of Burma, their last hours of peacetime were spent relaxing to the sound of rain cascading off thatched roofs. Throughout the day and all that night, they remained completely oblivious to another kind of storm being unleashed in several places at once.

While the AVG slept into the early hours of Monday morning, Japan commenced a multipronged "breakout" across an enormous expanse of the Pacific basin, from the Malay Peninsula to the Philippines to Wake Island to the Territory of Hawaii. Various attacks had been under way for several hours when reveille sounded at Kyedaw, yet a normal day began with no one the wiser. Having finished breakfast, AVG personnel were almost two hours into their workday routine when someone finally heard the news.

Early reports that battleships were afire and three hundred people had been killed in Honolulu, where it was still December 7, stunned those at Toungoo. Gradually the news sank in, and it got much worse as the damage and casualty reports became more accurate. Olga Greenlaw tuned a shortwave radio to a San Francisco call sign for the frightening details, then packed essential things for herself and Harvey, closed the house, and took her dog Lucy to the airfield. Chennault added her to the AVG staff as keeper of the Group War Diary.

Chennault set the entire group on twenty-four-hour alert, then designated Oley Olson as the group commander in the air with Jack Newkirk as deputy commander. The 3d and 2d Squadrons stood the ready alerts as the "assault" and "support" echelons respectively, with the Adam & Eves in reserve. Strangely, after naming Olson as senior pilot, Chennault sent him to Rangoon to inquire about a supply of "tin hat" helmets and gas masks, a fairly menial task that one of the other pilots could have accomplished.

The Tomahawks—warmed up periodically, and ready with full loads of fuel and ammunition—were parked south of the unfinished portion of the runway. An alarm system was created using a siren and light signals from the control tower: three steady blasts for "yellow" alert, a continuous rise-and-fall siren for "red" alert, and a continuous steady tone with a white light for all clear.

As more details of the widespread Japanese attacks began to arrive, reactions among personnel were predictably warlike. As one pilot put it, "My plane is ready and so am I— and it is my dearest wish that I get my sights on one of those Jap bastards. They killed a lot of fine men with that rotten attack at Honolulu."

Chennault was particularly nervous about the proximity of Chiang Mai Aerodrome in Thailand, 170 miles east, or less than an hour's flight for the Japanese. "Many of us scan the eastern skies continuously," wrote Bond, "as if we would have a chance to scramble if we caught sight of an incoming Jap raid."

The day eventually gave way to a long night of tension, and before the following dawn the AVG put up a continuous patrol of the Thai border. Boyington patrolled for two hours, his first flight since his birthday. Late that afternoon a high-flying plane was spotted, presumably Japanese reconnaissance, but it was too high for anyone to catch. Pilots not on patrol sat in their planes, itching to hear the sirens. The alarm sounded twice and engines were started, but both cases proved false.

At 3:10 the next morning the siren sounded again. Everyone spilled out of his bunk, jumped into clothing, and stumbled through the darkness to the flight line. Olga Greenlaw sought cover in a shelter with her two most important possessions: her dog Lucy, wrapped in a blanket, and the Elizabeth Arden makeup box that she seemed to pick up out of habit "in every emergency." Air raid sirens evidently qualified.

The manned alert planes were already aloft by the time the off-duty pilots found their P-40s in the dark. In the excitement, some tried to start cold engines without waiting for a line chief to pull the prop through to prime the cylinders first. After a while, when no attack came, pulses began to recede to normal. Why the alarm? Then, flashes on the horizon. "The Japs were off on their navigation and bombed a field about thirty-five miles south of us," offered one pilot, but it turned out to be only a distant thunderstorm.

The six patrolling planes were called back, but the lanterns placed down each side of the four-thousand-foot runway were almost useless. The field was in the middle of an underdeveloped valley, where there were few lights in the native villages to begin with, and Kyedaw was under a blackout. As Boyington put it, "You can't imagine how dark it is . . . like being in a coal mine." Sure enough, the fourth pilot down, lanky David "Tex" Hill, landed long and piled his P-40 up in the darkness off the end of the runway. He was only dazed, but the airplane was reduced to spare parts. To bring down the last two planes, the available vehicles were lined up with their headlights illuminating the landing area.

After that inauspicious beginning, the Adam & Eves and Panda Bears flew constant patrols during the first week of the war, with several reconnaissance forays over the border into Thailand to check on the existing fields. Chiang Mai remained empty, but the Japanese were in force to the south in Bangkok.

In the meantime, most of the 3d Squadron's pilots repositioned to Mingaladon airport near Rangoon on December 12, supplemented by three pilots culled from the other two units. The move was the result of another compromise, a hallmark of the AVG's paramilitary status. The sinking of the British battleships *Repulse* and *Prince of Wales* off the Malayan coast the previous day sent shock waves through the command structure, leading to bickering over who should control the AVG. The RAF insisted that the AVG should serve under its umbrella for the defense of Burma, particularly Rangoon; Chiang Kai-shek was still footing the bill, and desperately needed help in China. Chennault split his team, sending Oley Olson and seventeen others in their P-40s to Rangoon, while the other two units completed their preparations to move to Kunming.

The 1st Pursuit planned to navigate the nearly seven-hundred-mile flight nonstop, which would put them over Kunming with little fuel remaining. More than one pilot voiced concern about getting jumped by the Japanese at that inopportune time. Chennault's answer was to have the Panda Bears stop at Lashio in northern Burma and refuel, allowing them to loiter over Kunming while the Adam & Eves landed; that way, at least half the planes would be prepared for a fight.

Kunming's civilian population was bombed again at approximately 11:00 Thursday morning, December 18, even as Boyington and the other Adam & Eves launched for the cross-country flight. Two P-40s were badly damaged in separate departure accidents, and a third disaster was narrowly avoided when a pilot's oxygen hose came loose after he reached twenty-one thousand feet. John Dean passed out from hypoxia and his P-40 nosed over, but he regained consciousness upon reaching denser air, remedied the problem, and climbed back to the formation.

The Adam & Eves droned on, each pilot listening closely to the sounds of his engine, knowing that everyone's plane had already seen a lot of wear, that anyone who lost power over this remote territory was as good as dead. Even Boyington, raised in the Rockies, was impressed: "As we continued to fly northward, the mountains became higher, and the terrain was by far the most rugged I had ever witnessed. At that time the maps of this territory we were forced to use, for lack of anything better, happened to be very inaccurate indeed. We found that points of reference, in some cases, were off a hundred miles or so."

He and the others were in aerial limbo, not quite sure of where they were, and wholly uncertain of what they would find when they reached their destination. They only knew that Kunming was where the Japanese had been dropping bombs, and that sooner or later they would be back.

10

Fighting Tigers

After glancing nervously at their fuel gauges for two and a half hours, the Adam & Eves welcomed the sight of the ancient, mile-high city of Kunming in the province of Yunnan. "I had to give Sandy all the credit in the world," Boyington later wrote. "He found the six-thousand-foot-high valley, and the three lakes nestled within, amid the surrounding high mountains and the layers of stratus that covered them."

Locating the Wu Chia Ba Airport seven miles southeast of Kunming was comparatively easy: a seven-thousand-foot runway had been under construction for years and was still unfinished. Thousands of coolies swarmed over it, hauling rock in wicker baskets, spreading it on the surface, and crushing it with a massive roller pulled by harnessed workers. There was evidence of recent damage around the field, including a bombed-out hangar.

The site of a CAF flying school for several years, Kunming was one of Chennault's favorite locales, and the Chinese were well prepared for the AVG's arrival. The Adam & Eves were housed a mile or so from the airfield in a cluster of buildings known as Hostel Number Two, a vast improvement over the Kyedaw barracks. "We are happy as children," wrote George Burgard in his diary. By the next day, his opinion was even stronger: "With every passing hour I find it harder and harder to believe that Kunming is such a tremendous improvement over Burma. This is really

great. The quarters are splendid—soft cots, furniture, showers, good food, nice bar, excellent reception at the hands of
the Chinese, and a good field to operate out of for a change."

Burgard also enjoyed the cold weather, which reminded
him of winter in Pennsylvania. Kunming's high altitude and
crisp mountain air made all the difference, for it was situated, surprisingly enough, at the same latitude as the Florida
Everglades. It was plenty cold at night, so each of the quarters was equipped with a charcoal brazier. They were none
too safe, remembered Joe Rosbert, who was nearly asphyx-
iated by the fumes.

Not everyone approved of the hostel. Boyington dis-
missed it as a collection of old mud buildings with worn,
loose-fitting floorboards, his attitude no doubt influenced by
the discovery that the Panda Bears and AVG staff members
were housed in a large, lovely structure in the city. Hostel
Number One had originally been a university residence hall,
commandeered in the 1930s by the CAF flying school and
now made available to the AVG. The central building in the
three-sided compound featured an arched entryway covered
by an elegant pagoda-style portico. From the two-story central hall, main wings with private rooms stretched to the
sides. The steeply pitched roofs, with traditional upswept
eves, were covered with heavy clay tiles. The rear courtyard
had a baseball diamond, basketball and tennis courts; indoor
facilities included a large dining hall that doubled as an auditorium, a bar, even a game room with a Ping-Pong table
and record player.

Boyington began to see the way things were run in the
AVG. "The name of our quarters, and everything else,
seemed to stand for second best," he later wrote. "In fact I
gathered that the entire attitude was one of first come first
served. As far as I could determine, this applied to squadron
commanders, staff, and to women."

He was referring, of course, to Olga Greenlaw, who lived
with Harvey in a comfortable apartment made from two adjoining rooms, decorated with items hauled from Toungoo.
Not much changed as far as she was concerned, and she

made no pretense about her multiple relationships. "As soon as I got our quarters comfortably furnished, they became the same transient hotel they had been in Toungoo," she boldly wrote. "Boys in the afternoon, boys for dinner, boys all hours of the night."

Differences between the hostels seemed less important after Boyington and several others explored Kunming that first afternoon. The surrounding countryside was beautiful, but much of the city was like a grimy floodplain for an overflowing river—in this case, refugees retreating along the Burma Road. Kunming's population had swollen to an estimated three hundred thousand, and the carved blocks of stone lining the narrow streets were all but invisible under accumulated filth. The city was choked with Chinese soldiers in drab uniforms, ragged civilians with their carts and wagons, and a few decrepit vehicles. Most sections of town were overcrowded, the buildings shabby and neglected like the people who lived in them.

Boyington, Rosbert, and another pilot toured an area that had been bombed that morning by the Japanese. Unimpeded by any sort of defense, the air strike had devastated the neighborhood, killing hundreds of civilians. The cleanup was far from over. Gazing at the sickening scene of ruin and gore, Rosbert heard Boyington growl, "I can't wait until I get my gunsights on those dirty bastards!" With visions of shattered corpses etched firmly in their minds, each of them sensed his purpose far more urgently, realizing that the opportunity to engage the Japanese was looming near.

Beginning the next day, a rotating schedule of day-on, day-off alert duty was shared between the 1st and 2d Squadrons, with more pilots available than the thirty-four fighters on hand. Routine patrols and scouting missions were also sent out while pilots waited on standby at the field. Boyington was presumably on duty during the nineteenth, but there was nothing more interesting than two false alarms and he did not fly.

Luck of the draw, therefore, found him sleeping in on the blustery, cloudy morning of December 20, when he and

George Burgard were roused by the cries of *Gin bao!* An air raid was in progress. They raced to the airfield—Boyington wearing only his trousers, an undershirt, and slippers—but by the time they got there Sandy Sandell was already aloft with fourteen P-40s of the 1st Squadron, and Jack Newkirk had followed with three Panda Bears. The eighteen fighters had been given advanced warning by the Chinese net of watchers, which had reported ten enemy bombers approaching from the southeast at 9:30 that morning. Burgard later noted in his diary, "This was one of the most miserable days I have ever spent. The Japs came over at 10:00 with ten airplanes. Boyington and myself enjoying the day off, damn it—rushed over to the field but couldn't find a spare airplane so had to stay on the ground."

Not a single P-40 was ready to fly out of sixteen still on the ground at Wu Chia Ba. Boyington and Burgard did the next best thing and went into the operations building to follow the radio exchanges. They could only picture the developing scenario as Jack Newkirk's flight made the first contact, sighting a V formation of bombers boring in from the northwest at thirteen thousand feet.

The JAAF twin-engine bombers (*Ki*-48s) had come from Hanoi, about 350 miles southeast, then curved around Kunming to attack from the opposite direction. Newkirk's fighters opened fire from beyond maximum range and didn't hit anything, but the bombers dumped their ordnance over the countryside and scurried away toward Indochina. Curiously, Newkirk's flight did not give chase, but Sandell's pilots saw the *Ki*-48s racing toward them.

The squadron leader began dictating an attack plan, dividing his planes into smaller groups and holding one in reserve before he initiated attacks against the well-disciplined bomber formation. After several minutes of a running battle, the reserve group grew impatient and jumped in. Three of the Kawasaki bombers were felled, but the formation moved fast and the battle soon carried them 175 miles from Wu Chia Ba. With three bombers down and several others smoking, Sandell called his fighters together and returned to Kunming.

The only damage suffered by the AVG in its first combat against the Japanese had been a few bullet holes, none in vital places, though one P-40 crash-landed due to fuel starvation. Later, the Chinese determined that another bomber had exploded in the air sometime after 11:25 A.M., when the last reporting net counted seven enemy planes still airborne. Therefore, the *Ki*-48 formation returned to Hanoi minus forty percent of its planes, and with dead or dying gunners in ones that did make it back. The JAAF unit, the 21st Hikotai, never attempted to hit Kunming again. Naturally there was great rejoicing in the Chinese city and throughout the province. As if scripted, the AVG had put a stop to the Japanese menace within two days of arriving.

Pleased as the Adam & Eves were with their initial success, morale in the squadron was already poor. Ostensibly it had nothing to do with those who had missed out on the AVG's first action, but with Sandy Sandell. Many of the pilots and even the ground crew disliked his methods and overbearing personality. The problem was bad enough that Boyington visited Charlie Bond that night to discuss it. They were soon joined by George Burgard and Matt Kuykendall, and together the foursome drove over to the airfield to see Frank Schiel, the operations officer. "We asked him what should be done," wrote Bond later that night. "We expressed a lot of dissatisfaction about organization and leadership." Schiel prepared a harshly worded memorandum for Chennault, which the other pilots approved.

The next day Boyington and Burgard were scrambled to intercept a contact suspected to be a Japanese observation plane. After missing the action the day before, they were doubly anxious to do something positive, but the Japanese plane turned back short of Kunming. Burgard later noted that "it was no consolation just to scare him away."

Boyington was already frustrated, therefore, when he met Sandell that evening with Bond and Schiel to discuss the unit's poor morale. Not unexpectedly, Sandell "flew off the handle," and childishly refused to cooperate or talk with them. Finally he got over his pique, agreeing to an all-hands meeting the following day, during which Bond, appointed adjutant of the 1st Squadron, was given the authority to enforce discipline.

Coming fast on the heels of this turmoil, Oley Olson sent a radio message to Kunming on December 23 stating that Rangoon had been bombed that morning. The Hell's Angels had been in a rough battle, with six enemy bombers downed for the loss of two pilots; a third was shot down and strafed in his chute (he reached the ground safely); and a fourth P-40 was destroyed when the pilot hit a bomb crater in the runway at full landing speed. The city had been hit heavily, with huge loss of life, and the field itself had sustained considerable damage.

In Kunming that afternoon, the pilots who had participated in Saturday's air battle were decorated by Chinese dignitaries in a special ceremony at the airfield. Boyington's reaction can only be imagined as he watched the governor of Yunnan give a speech on behalf of Chiang Kai-shek, after which the pilots each received a red sash, followed by "really attractive young belles" presenting bouquets of flowers. He felt envy, no doubt; more than half the Adam & Eves were decorated, making it difficult for the ones left out.

Chennault left Kunming that afternoon in a Chinese National Aviation Corporation (CNAC) transport, bound for a meeting with Chiang Kai-shek. The airplane also carried the ranking British general in the China-Burma-India theater, Sir Archibald Wavell, along with his U.S. Army deputy, Maj. Gen. George Brett. Rumor had it that the meeting in Chungking was about the army's desire to induct all of the AVG pilots into the air corps. Chennault was dead set against it, and the majority of the pilots hoped he would prevail. A few former army pilots favored regular commissions, but Boyington and his fellow navy and marine pilots had no desire whatsoever to become army lieutenants. There was also the issue of the lucrative CAMCO pay. Anxiety over the status of the AVG would prevail for months.

Even worse from Boyington's viewpoint, Harvey Greenlaw assumed command of the AVG during Chennault's absence. As much as he liked Olga, Boyington despised Harvey's officious behavior. "The self-made executive officer," he wrote, "called himself Lieutenant Colonel Greenlaw, although no one else would. The manner in which Harvey was forever talking courts-martial to threaten a group of civilians gave me the impression that he must have been at least one jump ahead of a few himself in his military days. The poor guy gave the impression that he hated everybody."

Boyington's opinion was backed by the senior member of the U.S. military mission to China, Brig. Gen. John Magruder, who disapproved of most of Chennault's staff and considered Greenlaw an amateur. Boyington aimed a little lower, calling Chennault's staff "Asiatic bums of the first order."

While Boyington dealt with Greenlaw's leadership, he encountered still more frustration. At 10:00 A.M. on December 24, another scramble sent the squadron aloft to intercept almost two dozen inbound Japanese bombers. According to his flight record, Boyington participated in this one, but the P-40s patrolled for two hours and found nothing.

Then came Christmas Day, when the screws of frustration were tightened yet another turn. Down in Rangoon, the Hell's Angels countered another heavy attack with just twelve serviceable P-40s. Though two pilots were shot down (they turned up alive), the squadron was credited with thirteen Japanese fighters and four bombers.

The pilots at Kunming were chafing. After one fight against a small force of enemy bombers, they had done nothing but fly dull patrols or launch against false alarms. Meanwhile, Olson's squadron was getting all it could handle and more. He made it sound "like shooting ducks" in one message, though he did not actually feel so exuberant. The reality was that he had nearly run out of resources. The tension was nerve-wracking, prompting him to include in his Christmas Day radio message: "HAVE FEW SHIPS LEFT. . . . AWAITING INSTRUCTIONS."

On December 27 orders were issued to relieve Olson's beleaguered outfit with Jack Newkirk's 2d Squadron. Olson was to keep four volunteer pilots and an equal number of ground crew at Rangoon until the Panda Bears could get into Mingaladon, after which the Hell's Angels would get a breather in Kunming. As he watched Newkirk's squadron take off on the morning of December 29, Boyington felt he'd been shafted yet again. "How I envied the Panda Bears as they, too, left to join the battle at Rangoon," he later wrote.

For the Adam & Eves, the atmosphere of discontent worsened, and again the squadron leader was the cause. Burgard indicated in his diary that he liked Sandy Sandell well enough as a person, but conceded, "He is a terribly inefficient squadron head. Boyington would be the man for the job. Bond would be a dandy if he only had the pursuit experience."

Several of the pilots were recommended as flight leaders, including Bond, Burgard, Cross, and Hoffman. Boyington and Bond tried to arrange a meeting with Chennault, but he was reportedly down with the flu, after which they got nowhere trying to talk with Harvey Greenlaw. They ended up meeting with Skip Adair, who was considered the chief of staff. Within a few days, Chennault decided to promote only Bond, which caused more strife within the squadron. Now others could see what Boyington had been complaining about: politicking and power struggles were ruining the organization's morale.

Further affecting the malaise among the Adam & Eves over the lack of action at Kunming, Newkirk and the Panda Bears were getting plenty in Burma. When the Japanese stopped coming to Rangoon for a while, the AVG took the fight to them, crossing Martaban Bay to strafe airfields in Thailand with considerable success. Wrote Boyington, "Our Adam & Evers might just as well have been back in the United States blowing bubbles in the bathtub, for nothing came over Kunming or even near it. Damn it to hell. Stuck here. Our First Pursuit seemed to be worse than second best, maybe third best."

This sort of frustration was the worst possible thing for an alcoholic, especially with booze readily available in "Adobe City," as the pilots called Hostel Number Two. During the first week and a half of January, he flew only four local hops totaling three hours. His behavior became more erratic as well as inflammatory, according to Joe Rosbert.

Boyington, being a wrestler, and with nothing else to do, would sit around in what served as the dining room in one of the mud buildings. People would be drinking, and Boyington would get in a pretty good state. The first thing he'd do is get in his wrestler's stance and try to get someone to wrestle with him. He may have been a couple of years older than some of us, but we would just say, "Greg, you're drunk. Go to bed." Well, he proceeded to do that. He'd go to his little cubicle and flop down on his bed, pull out his gun, and shoot the light out. He was always obstreperous in some way, always pulling some sort of crazy stunt—wrestling, or shooting, or whatever.

If there was one bright spot, the AVG had started to earn recognition back in the States. A story about the raid on Kunming appeared on an inside page of *The New York Times,* after which the national magazines got into the act. In its last issue of 1941, *Time* printed the first known usage of the "Flying Tigers" name in the United States, which had an immediate impact on the public. Ironically, the name was a classic publicity gimmick concocted by employees of China Defense Supplies, who had commissioned Walt Disney to design a caricature of a flying tiger back in October. The war-weary citizens of China, meanwhile, began referring to the pilots as *fei hu,* "flying tigers," with a sort of reverence. Whether the Chinese picked it up from Stateside publicity, or used the same term by coincidence, the name became famous on both continents.

The discontent in Kunming finally eased for Boyington and several other Adam & Eves near the middle of January. By that time, Newkirk's squadron at Rangoon had been whittled away until it could offer little resistance to the Japanese. Eleven planes had been shot down or badly damaged, several pilots were hospitalized, one had been killed, and another captured.

On January 12, Chennault decided to augment the Panda Bears with eight pilots from the 1st Squadron. To avoid more accusations about favoritism, the process of choosing the pilots was diplomatic: the eligible pilots' names went into a hat. When the drawing was done, Bob Neale, Bob Little, Greg Boyington, Dick Rossi, Jack Croft, Frank Schiel, Bill Bartling, and Bill "Black Mac" McGarry headed for their rooms to pack for the journey.

Before leaving, Boyington stopped to visit Olga Greenlaw at her apartment. She was busy at her typewriter, presumably smoothing the previous day's entries in the Group War Diary. Later, she described in her book how Boyington sat in silence for a few minutes while she worked. Finally he made small talk, then asked whether she had known he was divorced. Olga said she hadn't. "It's kind of tough, I guess, for a young, attractive woman to be married to a marine," he admitted. "I was no bargain to get along with."

If the dialogue happened as she portrayed—and her book proved consistently accurate regarding numerous events—then Boyington was edgy that day. He walked over to the Greenlaws' radio, picked up a framed photograph of two children that stood atop the cabinet, and asked Olga if they were hers. "My sister's," she explained.

"My kids are as pretty as these," he said, "although maybe you wouldn't believe it." He was deprecating again, feeling sorry for himself. While he gazed at the picture, Olga noticed that his face reflected the inner turmoil eating at him, but she decided to keep quiet. She offered tea. He sat to sip it, lost in thought. When the cup was empty he said, "I am going tomorrow with a flight to join Jack's squadron. I wish to say a parting word—you won't take it wrong? You are the only bright star in this place—does a man's heart good to look at you."

He left without giving her a chance to respond, leaving her to question why he had come to China, wondering what he had run from.

The Adam & Eves actually departed that afternoon, Boyington flying P-8130, the Tomahawk he'd had since the beginning of December. After bucking strong headwinds, they remained overnight at Lashio, then reached Rangoon after a late start the next morning.

The large, dusty field at Mingaladon was pockmarked with bomb damage from the raids that had been coming since before Christmas (coolie labor had filled the holes in the runways), and a damaged barrack with holes in the roof served as the alert shack. The AVG shared it with the RAF 67th Squadron, equipped with lend-lease Brewster Buffalo fighters, known to the U.S. Navy and Marine Corps as the F2A. Around the field, most of the buildings that were not already destroyed had been damaged, and the wreckage of several burned aircraft had not been moved. Two of the hulks still lay in the middle of the field, between the runways that crossed like a giant A.

After getting reacquainted with some of his 2d Squadron friends at the RAF bar, Boyington got another glimpse of the war's proximity: "After drinking all the scotch I dared I was shown to the RAF barracks, where I was to sleep for the next few nights. Surely, if the mess looked like no-man's-land, the barracks were worse. In addition to the machine-gun ventilation an unexploded bomb had gone through the roof, down through the two-story wooden building, and finally come to rest in the earth beneath the ground floor. We slept there even though a sign said: BEWARE UNEXPLODED BOMB."

He was accurate about sleeping only a few nights in the ventilated barracks, for he was sent back to Kunming soon after arriving. During his short stay, he logged just two local flights of an hour each (presumably in response to false alarms), plus several short hops to and from the outlying field where the Tomahawks were dispersed at night.

It turned out that more than enough Adam & Eves had come from Kunming. As Bob Neale put it in his diary on January 17: "I am going to have to send two pilots back to Kunming as Newkirk's squadron has about 20 planes in commission. Nobody wants to go so we are going to have to draw straws." Boyington and Croft were the losers.

The next day, they were sent on their way—either by train or CNAC transport—and arrived at Kyedaw field at 6:00 P.M. They were evidently supposed to ferry P-40s to Lashio, but as it was too late in the day to continue, they felt free to enjoy themselves. "They both got well soaked and went to town," wrote Bus Keeton, who had remained at Kyedaw to do postrepair check flights and build experience in P-40s.

He was just getting to work the next morning when Boyington and Croft staggered back to the base. "They [drank] all night and were still planning on going to Lashio," he noted. "I don't know how they do it." He sent two crew chiefs to preflight the P-40s while the pilots went to clean up. Later, he found Croft passed out and Boyington heading for the shower, having decided to delay their departure until after lunch. But when Keeton arrived at the mess hall for lunch, Boyington was drunk again, and Croft had started drinking. Keeton described the outcome in his diary:

> Eddie [Goyette] told Greg they could not take off in the condition they were in. Greg said he would take off and to hell with Eddie. I tried to talk them out of taking off, but no soap, they were going regardless. Eddie had [Harold] Walker and [Daniel] Keller take the fuse[s] and disconnect the batteries on their planes. They arrived at the field about 2:15 P.M. with baggage and tried to start the planes. Did everything they could, but no success. Greg asked me what the hell was going on and I told him. After talking to him awhile he saw his mistake and was swell about the whole thing. I took [him] and Jack back to the barracks and they went to bed.

The next day, when a more sober pair of pilots started their planes for the trip to Lashio, Boyington discovered a glycol leak. Quite possibly, getting too drunk to fly the day before had saved his life. After repairs were made, he and Croft flew on to Lashio for fuel, then continued to Kunming, arriving on January 20.

Boyington next participated in what one pilot called "the most ambitious mission of the war thus far." Earlier, Chennault had worked out a coordinated effort with the Chinese to strike Hanoi, deep in French Indochina. Twenty-three SB bombers of the CAF landed at Changyi on January 21 and remained overnight, while the Adam & Eves worked out the details for an escort mission. The next morning at 8:30, Sandy Sandell led six P-40s aloft, followed an hour later by Boyington leading a flight of four, all of which landed for fuel at Mengzi, near the Indochina border. They took off again and rendezvoused with two divisions of the Russian-built twin-engine bombers.

So far, so good, but the CAF flight leader headed on a course for Hanoi without correcting for winds aloft. Sandell tried to shepherd the bombers onto the proper course, but as Burgard later noted, the effort was "spoiled purely by the hardheaded stupidness of a Chinese captain." Navigation was compounded by a solid undercast, which left just the mountaintops visible. To Boyington they resembled "tiny islands in a large ocean of snow-white water," and he worried about his engine failing deep in enemy territory. Flak came up at one point, causing one bomber to turn back after getting hit. According to others, it went down slowly and disappeared into the cloud layer. The Chinese finally dropped their bombs, ineffectively, and the P-40s squeaked back into Mengzi with only a few minutes of fuel remaining, "a very narrow call" in Burgard's opinion. While they refueled, a flight of Hell's Angels provided top cover in case the Japanese decided to retaliate.

Although the results were negligible, the raid was hailed in the United States as a huge success, the propaganda machine claiming that heavy damage had been inflicted. In retrospect, it was providential that the overcast prevented Japanese fighter resistance. Had the P-40s been involved in even a few minutes' worth of aerial combat, they would have crashed from fuel starvation short of Mengzi.

For Boyington, getting back in one piece from the long Hanoi mission was a small consolation. Since his departure from Rangoon, the pilots there had been involved in several huge encounters with the Japanese. To date, the AVG had been credited with sixty-two aerial victories and eleven planes destroyed on the ground, while losing three killed in action and one captured. The Chinese paid for confirmed Japanese planes regardless of how they were destroyed, giving some twenty-five Flying Tigers a share of $36,500 in the bonus account. Jack Newkirk had singularly accounted for $4,000. No wonder Charlie Bond wrote, "I began to feel bitter about us just sitting here with the guys down in Rangoon fighting their hearts out." Boyington no doubt felt exactly the same way. He had not even seen a Japanese plane, and his debts back home were not getting any smaller.

But on the evening of January 24, Sandell appeared "all in a dither" with the news that a dozen more Adam & Eves would leave in the morning to help protect Rangoon. Once again the names were drawn diplomatically, and Boyington's luck was good. Among the others picked were Cokey Hoffman, Charlie Bond, George Burgard, Bob Prescott, Albert "Red" Probst, and Joe Rosbert.

The next morning, Sandell took off just before ten o'clock with a flight of six Tomahawks, followed forty minutes later by Boyington leading another six. Years later, he gave a literary finger to the staff and ground crew who waved goodbye: "On most of them I had interpreted this wave to mean, 'I hope you get back alive.' I assumed that a few were thinking: 'I hope you never get back.' But to hell with them. To hell with them all."

Boyington led his six P-40s into Lashio, where a long delay for gas enabled the pilots to enjoy a good meal and a beer at the hostel run by the Chinese National Aviation Corporation. Then it was on to Rangoon, where they hoped to land just before dusk and avoid a raid. The trick was in the timing, else they'd find themselves landing in complete darkness. As Boyington put it, "In the lower latitudes there is no such thing as twilight. As the sun sets, you get the impression that someone has suddenly put a bucket over it." He brought his flight in right at dusk, and everyone made it down with nothing worse than a blown tire.

The newcomers had been at Rangoon for barely twelve hours when the first alarm sounded. Pilots ran to their planes and roared off, climbing to twenty thousand feet as they headed east toward Thailand to search for the enemy, but there was no raid after all. A ground operator broadcast "free beer" over the radio, the signal to return to base. Twice more the alarm sounded and the pilots climbed to altitude, returning each time when the alarms proved false. By the time they were back on the ground after the third alarm, some were feeling miserable: the constant pressure and temperature changes were hell on sinuses.

When the fourth alarm came at 10:45 that morning, eleven P-40s took off in a confused scramble. Jack Newkirk of the Panda Bears got off with a flight of three, then was joined by Probst, Hoffman, Boyington, and Prescott from the Adam & Eves. Probst was a designated flight leader, but like Boyington he had never seen combat, so he followed Newkirk's lead.

Bob Neale, racing into the air a few minutes later with three other Adam & Eves, spotted a large (by AVG standards) formation of about twenty fighters that resembled "a bunch of buzzards milling around." They were Nakajima *Ki*-27 "Nates" of the 50th Sentai out of Bangkok, performing a favorite Japanese tactic derived from the World War I-era Lufbery Circle, from which several fighters could quickly pounce on an enemy if he tried to get behind one of their own. To make it even more effective, the Japanese frequently used a decoy as bait.

Newkirk's radio failed as he climbed from Mingaladon

field, so he signaled by hand for Red Probst to take over the lead. He pulled aside, followed by his two wingmen.

Just like that, Probst was leading the defenders, down to four now as they climbed toward the Nates. His tour with the AVG, characterized as "one damn-fool adventure after another" thus far, wasn't about to improve this day as he climbed his flight straight toward the sun. Boyington, able to see very little, hoped "the guy who was leading knew what he was doing," but Probst apparently didn't have a clue.

Boyington squinted ahead, could see the Nates moving like shadowy wraiths against the sun's glare; they had every advantage while the P-40s strained for altitude. Still, Probst never deviated from his straight-ahead climb. "Couldn't that jerk see where he was taking us?" wondered Boyington, but he was soon too worried about his own preservation. The Nates had tipped over and started their runs.

Ahead of him, Cokey Hoffman's P-40 "gave all the appearance of a fish writhing in agony out of the water." It was an apt description of the way an airplane flops and tumbles when it has lost a wing. Eyewitnesses on the ground saw Hoffman's plane come spinning down, shedding a wing before it smashed inverted in a cloud of dust. Probst had dived away at the last second, leaving Hoffman to bear the full brunt of the Japanese attack. Some theorized that he collided with a *Ki*-27, but there was no account of a corresponding enemy loss. Just as likely, he was a victim of Probst's ignorance, his P-40 so riddled by gunfire that it began to disintegrate.

Boyington, too, found himself suddenly alone as tracer rounds reached out from the Nates. Prescott admitted later that when he saw a Nate diving from behind his left shoulder, he crossed to the other side to put Boyington between him and the Japanese fighter. Boyington saw the Nate and split-S'ed, pointing his P-40 earthward and using his heavy fighter's superior speed to dive away. To that end, he followed the doctrine that he had been infused with over the years, but he forgot the rest when he spotted a pair of *Ki*-27s to one side. Pulling level and adding power to close with them from behind, he was caught in the classic trap.

In the blink of an eye, one of the Nates looped over the top and came down from behind, even as Boyington squeezed the trigger button on his control stick—for the first time ever in anger—at the other fighter. Worse, Boyington ignored Chennault's mantra about not dogfighting with the enemy, and tried in vain to pull around on the Nate that had jumped him. His famous ability to withstand high g's was no help now, not against these mercurial Japanese fighters, and even though he pulled himself "plumb woozy," their tracer rounds kept cutting inside his turn radius. He eased up, only to stare at the fat radial engine of another Nate boring in head-on, and finally got wise. "Frig this racket," he told himself, and dived out.

Once burned, twice shy, the old saying goes, but Boyington tried to engage the *Ki*-27s a second time, thinking that a thousand-foot perch and more speed would work to his advantage. "As I approached this Nip fighter," he wrote, "he also permitted me to get close enough to where my tracers were sailing about him. Then I witnessed this little plane perform one of the most delightful split-S's I had ever seen, and then I discovered that I was turning again with some of his playmates."

He had been sucked in again, chasing a decoy while others jumped from up-sun. This time, he dived under and pointed his P-40 toward Mingaladon field, knowing the day was done. He later described himself as "[a] complete picture of dejection and disillusion" as he flew back to base. Along the way he supposedly discovered a minor injury: a spent incendiary round was stuck in the skin on the inside of his upper left arm.*

The ineffective result of his first opportunity to engage the enemy wasn't directly Boyington's fault. Probst probably had no business being in the fight, let alone as a section

---

* In subsequent medical examinations, no mention of such a wound was made by either Boyington or the physicians.

leader. Throughout his service with the AVG, he never earned so much as a fraction of a credit for an enemy aircraft, while sixty-seven other pilots—virtually all who were involved—scored at least a partial claim. His singularly barren record is suspicious.

Probst was inept, but Prescott had actually run from the fight, leaving his flight leader unprotected. He later offered some excuses, claiming that early in the melee he forgot basic things, such as throttle control. He zoomed up, he explained, just as Boyington went by in the opposite direction with a Nate on his tail. Later still, he confessed that he had lost his nerve and could not make himself reverse course to aid Boyington. He flew away to a safe distance, waited until he heard "Free beer," and then scooted back to Mingaladon. He planned to cop a quiet bargain with Boyington when he got back—and would quit the AVG if Boyington promised silence about the craven act—but he didn't have to go through with it. When Boyington taxied in, Prescott jumped onto the wing beside the cockpit, ready to apologize, but Boyington simply smiled and said, "We didn't do so hot, did we, podner?"

Boyington was too disgusted with his own performance to worry about Prescott. "I hated myself so badly, I didn't even bother to write up my first combat report, for this could have happened to others—but not to me," he wrote. Little information was forwarded to Kunming about the fight. Besides Hoffman, Robert "Moose" Moss had been shot down, though he received only minor scrapes, meaning that the fight had been essentially a draw. Three Nates were claimed by the AVG at the cost of Hoffman's life and two P-40s. It had been an expensive day.

The first twenty-four hours in Rangoon had been exhausting ones, but the day took a decided turn for the better after the P-40s were parked at the satellite field for the night. Boyington received new quarters for the duration of his stay in Rangoon, an experience that left a lasting impression.

Due to a lack of suitable housing at Mingaladon field, the

RAF had implored the British and European citizens of Rangoon to open their doors to the pilots. (In return, the homeowners were reimbursed for the cost of food.) On the night of the air battle, Boyington and Joe Rosbert were among several pilots pleasantly surprised to be met at the field by two wealthy Scots.

Jim Adams and Bill Tweedy, veterans of the Great War and both still bachelors, had made a fortune in the oil fields north of Rangoon that the Japanese now desired to possess. They billeted half a dozen AVG pilots in their lavish homes ("dream estates," Boyington called them), some four miles from the field. Rosbert was impressed with Adams's collection of art, which included "carved Chinese chests, ivory figurines, shell pictures, intricate woven prints, and Chinese paintings."

Boyington marveled at the life he suddenly found himself free to indulge in. He had a private bedroom with a bath, was waited on by servants who kept his *chota peg* (whiskey-and-soda) or *burra peg* (double the whiskey) conveniently topped off. After a late dinner, he and the other well-fed pilots gathered with their hosts on the landscaped patio to await the Japanese bombers. With a view of the city, they relaxed on lawn chairs, drinking and chatting until the sirens sounded and the show began. Soon came the throbbing sound of engines, then the flash of explosives that looked like lightning off low-hanging clouds, followed by the flat, drumming *crumph* of detonations. When the fireworks ended, the chatting and drinking resumed until it was time for bed.

In the morning, Boyington woke to "the delightful aroma of freshly brewed tea," already poured and waiting on the bedside table. He enjoyed it with a cigarette, went into the bathroom to shave, then returned to find a hot breakfast tray had been brought. After eating, he dressed in his flying clothes and joined the other pilots for a ride down to the satellite field, where the P-40s were started, flown to Mingaladon, and parked in the alert positions at the ends of the runways. This was the way to fight a war.

There were alerts and Boyington logged more than two hours of flight time, but nothing came of them. The evening routine was a repeat of the previous night: bath, drinks, an excellent dinner. This time during the nightly raid, a Japanese bomber was shot down in flames by an RAF night fighter in full view of the luxurious homes. After the bomber hit the ground, galleries of neighbors up and down the street could be heard "clapping their hands in glee." Many more nights would be just like this one in Rangoon. Life had become surreal.

When Cokey Hoffman was buried the next morning at the church of Edward the Martyr, Boyington was unsteady. "I became nervous and perspiring, looking down into the open grave with Cokey's coffin beside it," he later wrote. His reaction was understandable. Hoffman's mangled corpse hadn't been recovered until the day before, nor had it been embalmed. After two days in the sun his remains were already rotting, and even through the flag-draped casket "the stench was sickening." Then, as the casket was being lowered, it jammed—the grave was too small. The minister excused the distraught pilots, who immediately lit cigarettes to cover the odor. Walking away, Boyington imagined he could hear the crusty old chief yelling, "You bastards. You were doing great. Why did you have to leave me fouled up—halfway down?"

The day's dramatics were not yet over. Just after he got out to Mingaladon field, Boyington witnessed the amazing conclusion to a fighter sweep by Nates of the 50th and 77th Sentais. Sandy Sandell had already downed two of the Ki-27s when his Tomahawk suffered hits in the coolant and oil systems, and he turned toward the field. Any farther from home base and he would have been shot down, but he reaped the benefit of defending friendly territory and got close enough before the engine seized to land dead-stick at Mingaladon.

He was not yet out of harm's way, for a pilot of the JAAF was also gliding overhead, his Nate out of commission. A lieutenant named Yamamoto aimed his stricken fighter at

Sandell's plane while it coasted to a stop, clearly intending to take it out with his last mortal act. Somehow the diminutive Sandell realized what was happening and took cover in a ditch.

Yamamoto's *Ki*-27 clipped the P-40's tail before shattering into pieces against the hard, dusty runway. A flash fire or the force of the impact seared the fabric from the rudder and elevators of Sandell's number eleven, though the rest of the P-40 seemed relatively unscathed. It appeared as though the Japanese pilot's suicide had been in vain, for the damage was repairable, but as time would prove, Yamamoto accomplished his intended deed.

In the meantime, Boyington investigated the results of the sensational crash. There was not much left of the Nate or the suicide diver. As Boyington later put it, "The largest part of the pilot I could recognize was a tiny hand with the severed tendons sticking out."

Once again he had missed a fight, and he missed an even better opportunity the next day, January 29, when AVG pilots claimed sixteen victories following another Japanese raid. Curiously, he wrote of this engagement in his memoir as though he scored two of the victories. He did not date the event, hedging instead that it occurred "two days after [the] first flubdub," which put the date slightly off. In a subsequent magazine interview, he recalled more accurately that the event was *three* days after his first fight on January 26. But this was not Boyington's day. His name did not appear among the victory credits, and his own flight record shows that he was not on the alert crew when the Japanese attack came.

Oddly enough, January 29 was highlighted by another Japanese suicide dive. An enlisted pilot, Sergeant Nagashima of the 77th Sentai, tried to hit an RAF Blenheim bomber parked in a revetment. As Boyington described it in his book, "This Nip had committed hara-kiri [sic] in that revetment without placing so much as a scratch on the parked aircraft. It was unbelievable that this I-97 could have fitted into the unused space at any angle except the one it did—straight down."*

During the first week of February there was virtually no daylight activity from the JAAF. Their recent heavy losses—significantly less than the Allies claimed, but costly all the same—had convinced them to try night bombing for a spell. The moon was bright that week, resulting in as many as three or four raids each night. Many came in the early hours of morning, and the pilots grew accustomed to the sirens. Boyington probably slept through most of it. He put away so many *burra pegs* that Jim Adams decided the name should be changed to "the American drink."

On their days off, the pilots toured Rangoon's shops, visited the gold-plated Shwe Dagaon pagoda, or sported at the posh Kokine Club, a genteel swimming establishment where they enjoyed honorary membership. Boyington occasionally tore himself away from the luxuries of Jim Adams's estate when he had a "craving for excitement and women." The answer was the Silver Grill, a nightclub where patrons could get everything from strawberries and ice cream to mixed-nationality prostitutes.

The lull ended on February 6, a Friday. Boyington was on duty with five other Adam & Eves and two RAF pilots when a fighter sweep of thirty-five Nates was identified. The defenders scrambled at 10:30, Bob Neale off first accompanied by Boyington, Charlie Bond, Bill McGarry, Bob Little, and Bob Prescott. After gaining altitude, Bond waggled his wings to get Boyington's attention, having spotted the incoming Nates. "His flight followed me," Bond noted later, "and we tore into them." Bond was disappointed to end up with only a probable after the engagement, but most of the

---

* The Japanese identified their planes by the year of entry into service based on the ancient Koki calendar, thus the *Ki-*27 was Army Fighter Type 97 (introduced in 1937). The Allies used the contraction I-97 for that fighter until late 1942, when male nicknames for fighters and female nicknames for bombers were introduced.

others earned credit for kills, including Neale, who shot a Nate off Bond's tail. Bob Little earned credit for two, while McGarry and Prescott scored one apiece.

Finally it was Boyington's turn as well. By the time of the scramble that morning, a total of forty-five other pilots in the AVG had been credited with 110 aircraft destroyed, sharing fifty-five thousand dollars in bonus money. Even Bus Keeton had claimed a bomber over Toungoo. Boyington could only be considered a victim of remarkable bad luck that in two months of war, he had fired his guns twice at the enemy. This time, his effort resulted in credit for two *Ki*-27s, but his account of the engagement was brief.

> I caught a Jap flying along not paying attention, which is a dangerous thing to do, so I got up behind him and put a burst or two into his fuselage. Seconds later he burst into flames and went down. A minute or two later I found another safe bet. I followed this guy along and put a steady burst into him at point-blank range. Pieces of aircraft started to fall off and hit my plane. He rolled over and headed for the ground on fire and twisting crazily.

Later that day, Sandy Sandell sent a cryptic radiogram to Kunming detailing the day's action: "FIRST SQUADRON UNASSISTED BAGGED SEVEN ENEMY FIGHTERS AND FIVE PROBABLES. RAF GOT THREE. ONE BULLET HOLE IN ONE WING." The claim of ten kills and five probably destroyed represented almost half of the force of 50th and 77th Sentai Nates that had attacked, a wild exaggeration, but the Japanese had certainly been stung. That night they retaliated with four bombing raids.

A worse blow came later in the morning. The damage caused by Lieutenant Yamamoto's suicide dive to the empennage of Sandell's P-40 had finally been repaired, but an earlier flight check evidently revealed a lingering problem. "He had been having some trouble with the controls of his ship and was checking it out thoroughly," wrote Bond. That Saturday morning, he watched as Sandell performed more flight checks. "On one pass near the field he went into what looked like the start of a slow roll, but he was awful low—some five hundred feet. He rolled all the way over on his back and that was as far as he got. He lost altitude very quickly and went right in. We don't know whether he had control problems or what."

Just as Yamamoto's dive set in motion the events that killed Sandell, so did Sandell's death start a ripple that spread outward, ultimately affecting several people. Jack Newkirk radioed a simple but stunning message to Kunming: "SANDELL SPUN IN AND KILLED TESTING PLANE WITH REPAIRED TAIL." A flurry of radio traffic followed, including orders for Newkirk's Panda Bears to return to Kunming, and another addressing the loss of the Adam & Eves' leader. "FOR NEALE. TERRIBLE SORRY LEARN SANDY'S DEATH. ENTIRE GROUP SENDS DEEPEST SYMPATHY TO FIRST SQUADRON. YOU ARE APPOINTED SQUADRON LEADER EFFECTIVE THIS DATE. CARRY OUT INSTRUCTIONS ALREADY ISSUED FOR SANDELL. RECOMMEND DEPUTY LEADER FOR APPOINTMENT. CHENNAULT."

The news was especially hard on Neale, already given to fretting before this responsibility was unexpectedly thrust upon him. He was one of the few people in the squadron who had actually liked Sandell. "No one will ever know the mental anxiety I am going [through] here on top of losing a very close friend," he wrote that night in his diary. Some of the anxiety doubtless had to do with choosing a new executive officer. In a separate message to Chennault he responded: "HAVE APPOINTED BOYINGTON VICE SQUADRON LEADER SUBJECT YOUR APPROVAL."

In Kunming, Olga Greenlaw heard Chennault say: "I want to see what Bob Neale can do—now that he took Sandy's place. I am interested in Boyington too. I want everybody to have a chance. Neale is a good boy. I think he will do all right. Too bad about Sandy. He was a fine fellow."

Sandell's body was buried on Sunday morning in the familiar Rangoon churchyard. Later, a couple of escort missions for RAF Blenheims went out to try to hit the Japanese at Pa-an, north of Moulmein. Boyington flew twice that day, both flights too short in duration to have been part of the bomber escort. No enemy aircraft were encountered or even mentioned in any other AVG records, yet he claimed in his memoir to have shot down a Japanese fighter on the day of Sandell's funeral.

The Panda Bears cleared out later that day, and remarkably, so did the Japanese—at least from the skies over Rangoon. After the raids on the night of the sixth, the fighter and bomber units of the JAAF were diverted to other areas or sent home for refitting, giving the Adam & Eves another lull. The only air activity for the next week or so was what the Allies generated themselves, bombing and strafing the Japanese to stem their advance. Boyington stood his share of alerts and did fly two escorts to Pa-an, but in the two weeks following Sandell's death he logged few hours. Retrieving the planes from the dispersal field each morning and flying them back at night occupied more flight time than anything else.

With the sky suddenly empty of Japanese planes, the pilots began to wonder what was happening. "We are all very deeply puzzled," wrote Burgard, who assumed the Japanese were preparing for a big push. "Probably they are waiting until forces can be relieved from the Singapore area and then they will hit this place like a typhoon." Bond chafed at the lack of action and surely Boyington did, too, with only two planes to his credit after so much action had swirled above the city.

As the pilots began to relax a bit, there was a natural tendency to stay up later and drink harder, resulting in some memorable evenings. During one wild night at the Silver Grill, Boyington "had a terrific load aboard" when he and several others got into an argument with the proprietor. They refused to leave during an air raid, so the owner tried to have them bounced. The well-armed Yanks got their way after shooting the chandeliers from the nightclub's ceiling. That they wore sidearms in town was no accident: There was a strong consensus that Anglos were not entirely safe now that Rangoon was in a state of anarchy.

The night of February 12 found a good number of the Adam & Eves in a mood to "drink the RAF under the table." Boyington, evidently a part of the action and more than capable of serving the AVG cause, was off duty the next day. Charlie Bond hadn't the stomach for such imbibing. "I finally lost my cookies in the men's room," he admitted, lamenting his miserable hangover the next day.

An even bigger party was arranged on Saint Valentine's Day at the home where some of the pilots were billeted. It was a balmy Saturday night, there was music and dancing with local girls under the stars, but mostly the pilots drank, and this night many of them got "really stewed." Boyington was among the many, even though he was scheduled for alert duty the next day.

In the morning, Bond, Rossi, and Burgard went out to the field to begin the familiar routine. When the other five pilots who were supposed to be on duty failed to show, Bob Neale was outraged. "Can't say that I blamed him," Burgard sympathized. "He is really trying hard and doing a good job." Designated the senior AVG officer in Burma by Chennault, Neale had fewer than twenty P-40s with which to defend Rangoon. Meanwhile, the enemy had not appeared overhead in eight days and everyone expected a huge raid at any moment. Now, his pilots were late for alert duty, and were in rough shape when they eventually appeared. In the face of such negligence, Neale lost his temper when Boyington showed up, still drunk. The result was a very public and vehement argument between Neale and his new vice squadron leader.

Boyington did fly later that day (a bomber escort to Thaton and back, more than two hours in all), but from then on, the relationship between the two men was strained. Neale was likable, normally jovial, and had a difficult job to do. Many of the pilots backed him unquestioningly. At the same time, opinions of how Boyington conducted himself began to change. Charlie Bond, for one, admired Boyington's ability as a fighter pilot and recognized his accumulated experience, but noted, "He does not seem to care to do anything on the ground."

The unfortunate reality was that Boyington had started losing control of his own situation. No one understood that a disease controlled *him*. Had he been able to meet with a modern-day clinical psychologist, in all probability he would have been diagnosed as a "middle-stage" alcoholic.

Ever since his boyhood, Boyington had been independent, capable of fighting his own battles and overcoming obstacles in his way, but he could not control his drinking. This not only bewildered him, it caused a jumble of emotions: shame, loss of self-respect, guilt over his inability to manage his life. To be reproached by his fellow pilots only compounded the problem, as did the physical effects of alcohol. He was literally poisoning his body. Hangovers were torturous, his emotions raw.

He made great efforts to improve. Joe Rosbert once characterized him as having "an incessant, frantic desire to achieve success in his work. It was almost a mania with him." But when those attempts came up short—sometimes due to bad luck, as with his lack of aerial engagements—the psychological fall was that much harder. Invariably he began to rationalize his role, blaming others for what was going wrong, taking little interest in anything except for his own opportunities to fly. Jim Adams's home had become a sanctuary, where luxury and servants were a balm for his battered ego.

The fifteenth of February brought word that Singapore had fallen. Just five days later, forty-eight-hour evacuation notices were posted throughout Rangoon. Residents began to leave by the thousands, hoping to get north before the Japanese cut off the last overland escape routes. The flow of pedestrians hindered the pilots as they drove brand-new jeeps, recently "liberated" from the docks, to the dispersal field each morning. (With tons of unclaimed material piling up on the docks, the pilots had taken to helping themselves to truckloads of goods.) After parking their Tomahawks at Mingaladon for the alert duty, they lounged in the shade of their fighters' wings and watched the unending line of refugees plodding past on the perimeter road. They called the exodus "the alligator."

Within a few days, all administrative and civil order had collapsed in the city. Looting was rampant despite the fact that soldiers shot dozens of thieves nightly. The inmates of asylums, jails, and leper colonies were turned loose on the streets. Wild rumors became the norm rather than the exception. Thousands of American shock troops were coming; Japanese paratroopers were about to encircle Rangoon; the road north had been cut.

Evacuation orders for the AVG were published as Neale prepared to send most of the ground personnel north in convoys. Some of the wealthy Europeans piled their belongings into cars, but Jim Adams and Bill Tweedy supposedly set off on foot, leaving practically everything behind. "The most pitiful sight I ever saw," Boyington later wrote. He also related that Adams begged him to torch his house and shoot his Great Dane, Angus, when it was the Americans' turn to leave. Boyington couldn't go through with it and sent another pilot in his place. That may well have been, but probably not for the sentimental reasons he described. Neale put the whole squadron on a one-hour evacuation notice beginning February 22, after which the pilots brought their belongings with them to the field. During the jeep ride to Mingaladon from the ownerless billets, they passed a city now deserted, the streets eerily silent. When their former hosts' domestics fled, the pilots began to eat with the ground personnel, billeted out of town at the appropriately named "Eighteen-Mile Ranch."

A large convoy, many of its trucks loaded with contraband, started off for Magwe to begin the evacuation of AVG personnel. Protection was arranged by staging six P-40s out of Magwe, from which they would conduct patrols for a few days until the column got farther north, then leapfrog ahead to the next field.

Thus did Neale find a solution for Boyington. Having virtually ignored him since the day of their public row, he sent Boyington to Magwe on February 23, thereby putting plenty of extra distance between them. Boyington's AVG flight record confirmed the assignment. He made the 280-mile leg to Magwe that day, then flew twice the next for a total of almost four hours, evidently patrolling over the convoy as it headed north. He also flew on the twenty-fifth, stopping at Lashio before proceeding due north to Loiwing, just inside the Chinese border. The day after, according to Bus Keeton's diary, Boyington and four others flew to Toungoo from Magwe with five war-weary P-40s, then took off with refurbished ones. Boyington's flight record doesn't show this detour, but reveals that he did finish his work in Burma that day and landed at Kunming.

Because he was in Central Burma and not Rangoon in late February, Boyington missed out on another huge opportunity. For the first time in almost three weeks, the Japanese attacked Rangoon during daylight. After several engagements on February 25 and 26, the Tomahawk pilots at Rangoon were credited with an astounding forty-three victories. How it must have frustrated Boyington to learn that another $21,500 would be paid to bonus accounts from those actions, just days after he departed.

How surprising also that he claimed in his memoirs to have shot down three fighters during the battle. Vague about the date (he described it only as "[one] of the last alerts of any size . . . around the middle of February"), it could only have happened during those two days, the first daylight raids over Rangoon since February 6. The truth of the matter, based on his own flight record, is that he was hundreds of miles to the north, flying lazy circles above a convoy of trucks in the vicinity of Lashio.

Misadventures continued to plague Boyington, almost from the moment he returned to Kunming. On February 28,

Generalissimo and Madame Chiang Kai-shek announced
that they were hosting a special dinner that evening in honor
of the AVG. A gala banquet was planned in the large dining
hall in Hostel Number One, and the pilots were ordered to
look and behave their best. Most were enchanted by the
madame, as was Olga Greenlaw, but Boyington had no intention of attending the dinner. "I was positive the madame
was a number-one con artist if I had ever seen one," he
would later write. He put in an appearance, but held back
with pilot Percy Bartelt when the crowd filed from the bar
into the dining room. Chennault had ordered the bar closed,
but they managed to scare up a bottle from somewhere. As
Boyington later explained, "[We] decided to remain in the
bar while the madame was blowing smoke like she always
had before, so we didn't go to dinner at all."

On empty stomachs, they drank while the others sat
through dinner, a Chinese play, and speeches. If Chennault,
sitting at the head table, noticed the absence of the two pilots, he did nothing about it. Olga realized two seats were
empty and "hoped that the missing boys were not getting
into any mischief," but her hopes were in vain. Boyington
and Bartelt were doing a performance of their own in the
bar, taking turns mimicking the madame between bursts of
applause from the banquet. At first they were out of eyesight,
but Olga recalled that they appeared drunk a little later, and
behaved embarrassingly.

The Chiangs departed the next morning for a conference
in Lashio, but stopped at Kunming three days later on their
way back to Chungking. Another dinner was held for the
AVG at the hostel, recalled Bob Layher of the Panda Bears.
"We had a wonderful banquet that the generalissimo and the
madame hosted for us. That was the time she called us 'her
angels with or without wings.' They gave us our silk flying
scarves with the generalissimo's chop."

The next morning, March 5, Boyington and Layher were
on duty with four other pilots when Harvey Greenlaw found
them in the alert shack and said, "I want you to fly a little
farewell routine for the generalissimo and the madame while

they're getting aboard the plane." The Chiangs, Greenlaw informed them, were scheduled to return to Chungking. He instructed the pilots to escort them to Chanyi, some eighty miles to the east, where the DC-3 would turn north toward Chungking. At that point, the generalissimo would be out of reach of potential Japanese interception, and the P-40s could return to Kunming.

The instructions were easily understood, if given only verbally, and the pilots manned their planes for the demonstration. As Layher recalled, it was about 9:00 A.M. by the time the generalissimo's party gathered near the Douglas airliner. Frank Lawlor led the P-40s through several low passes in formation, then signaled for the pilots to take intervals and form a string. They now went down in a high-speed pass, rolling inverted over the runway threshold in a spectacular game of follow-the-leader. Boyington was the second to flip his P-40 on its back, then came Gil Bright, Red Probst, Hank Geselbracht, and finally Bob Layher.

As tail-end Charlie, Layher had been "hanging it on the prop" in aviator lingo, trying to slow his P-40 enough to get the proper interval behind Geselbracht. Thus, he was well below the recommended speed for slow-rolling a fully loaded Tomahawk. He hated to be the one to spoil the show, however, so he entered a roll. Instantly he realized that it was a terrible mistake. The P-40's controls went sloppy and the fighter began to settle toward the ground, tail pointing downward; Layher lost sight of Geselbracht up ahead, his visual reference.

Down below, the stunned spectators standing beside the DC-3 watched as Layher's P-40 appeared to struggle upright before disappearing behind trees. (Some versions of the story have Layher coming in so low that the dignitaries threw themselves flat on their faces—just as any Hollywood director would have arranged it). Chiang Kai-shek, who had been preparing to board the plane, reportedly sent an aide to learn the condition of "the pilot that just crashed." Later, counting only five P-40s when his plane reached altitude, the generalissimo must have assumed that a crash had indeed occurred.

But the missing man was the flight leader, Frank Lawlor, who had signaled Boyington to take the lead after discovering the baggage door on his P-40 had popped open. Layher had miraculously saved his own neck by relying on his navy instrument training. After righting his plane and nearly scraping the ground, he mushed through the air for several agonizing moments, wrestling to keep control of the airplane until it built enough airspeed to safely climb away.

Boyington's trouble was just beginning. To this point he had been along for the ride, copying whatever Lawlor did. When the leader had a problem and turned back, Boyington suddenly became responsible for two of the most important people in China, and five P-40s. He was ill prepared. For starters, his radio wasn't working, a problem so common in the P-40s that the pilots had learned to cope without them. As Layher said of the commercial radio's reliability, "Very seldom were more than one or two of us in contact in the air." Communicating by hand signals accomplished most needs, and Boyington had been well trained during his Marine Corps career.

The biggest problem, according to Boyington, was lack of knowledge about the route. "I just simply did not know [where we were going]," he later wrote, "and neither did the other escorts." But Layher was adamant that all had received adequate instructions. He speculated that Boyington merely hadn't listened. Perhaps it had something to do with taking orders from Harvey Greenlaw, but the instructions had not registered with Boyington. Therefore, he followed the DC-3 in what Layher described as "a lazy escort" until it reached Chanyi, and continued to follow it north, unaware that their part of the mission was over.

Unknown to Boyington, an invisible problem was already affecting the situation. At this time of year, powerful monsoon winds swept eastward from the Himalayas at jet-stream velocities, even down at the relatively low altitude where the formation flew. The DC-3 pilots compensated correctly when they turned north, "crabbing" into the wind at a drift angle estimated to be almost twenty degrees west to maintain the proper track. Boyington, following blindly, did not recognize the crosswind component. Gil Bright tried to get Boyington's attention, signaling that it was time to head back to base, but was only partially successful as Layher explained later:

We probably went halfway to Chungking, and finally they got him turned around—the ones who were closest to him—but instead of taking into account the drift angle we had been flying, he turned around and flew a reciprocal course to the south. Well, that just doubled our drift. We tried and tried, getting as far to the west as we could, to entice him over, but he just kept going. There's a cardinal rule: you don't leave your leader, you stick with him, right or wrong.

Boyington eventually figured out what had happened, but too late to correct the situation. He had simply made a series of compounding errors, and the whole flight was too far east to make it back to Kunming.

Layher, also with an inoperative radio, was the first to go down. He had drained both wing tanks and was practically on fumes in the main tank, so he eased alongside Geselbracht and pointed down. Geselbracht understood, and the two waved good-bye.

Boyington and the other three pilots managed to get as far as Wenshan, still 150 miles southeast of the Chanyi turn point, before they had to put their Tomahawks down. All of them ground-looped in a cemetery. Layher was sixty miles behind them, having climbed unhurt from his P-40 after crash-landing it in a field. He was met by armed militia who appeared ready to execute him, but when he showed them the Chinese writing on his parachute, they took him to a hamlet where one of the villagers had an old hand-cranked field telephone from World War I. After the natives talked

and made a connection, Layher was handed the receiver. He
was incredulous to find Hank Geselbracht at the other end.
Geselbracht said they had located an army vehicle and
would meet Layher in two days at a larger village; the
Chinese then used the phone to work out the logistics.

Treated as royalty from then on, Layher spent the night on
a straw bed, then was taken by donkey, sedan chair, and
stretcher on a memorable two-day journey over mountainous
terrain to rendezvous with the other pilots. He found Boyington, Bright, Geselbracht, and Probst already waiting as
promised with a Chinese driver and an American-made six-
by-six cargo truck. Reunited at last, the five pilots set out the
next morning, March 7, for a distant town where a narrow-
gauge train to Kunming stopped for passengers two or three
times per week.

The truck ride proved to be the most torturous part of the
odyssey. Boyington took the seat up front, but the other four
withstood a miserable pounding. No one could sit as the
truck bounced over rocky paths and trails. Boyington tried to
take over the driving, but was stymied, according to Layher.

> The Chinese driver only knew one speed, and that was
> about twenty-five miles an hour over stones or whatever.
> We went over bamboo bridges that wouldn't have held us
> if he hadn't been going that fast. Boyington got mad at
> him and wanted to drive. We saw an argument going on
> up front, and finally the truck stopped. Boyington took out
> his sidearm and was threatening this guy. But a Chinese,
> when he's given duty with a truck, he's not going to let
> anybody else manipulate anything. We told Boyington to
> back off, because that Chinese soldier was not going to
> give up the wheel of that truck.

Boyington finally acquiesced, and eventually the exhausted group arrived at the train station. The next train was
due the following day, so the pilots took a couple of one-
room huts for the night. Like the railroad itself, the accommodations reflected a strong French influence, for inside

were the first bidets any of them had ever seen. Layher laughed about discovering an unintended use for it: "Gil Bright found some rice wine somewhere, and as you can image, we got right with that. We'd been in the hut about an hour when all at once Gil jumped up, took his clothes off, turned on the bidet, and stood up in it. Of course that water shot up about five feet or so, and he took a shower. Well naturally, every one of us did, after that."

On Sunday, March 9, somewhat cleaner but no less bedraggled, the stranded pilots finally reached Kunming. They were tired from the train ride itself. The old engine had no grit spreaders, and all the passengers had been compelled to get out and push at least a dozen times on the steepest grades.

The next evening, Chennault met with the five wayward pilots over dinner. "He wanted to find out how this thing got so fouled up," recalled Layher. "I think at this point we had less than ten aircraft left at Kunming. He wasn't happy, by any means. Chennault was the type of guy that didn't get on somebody in front of other people. He listened, and I'm sure he thought it over, and later he talked to us individually."

The next week passed quickly for the chagrined Boyington, who naturally tried to downplay his complicity in the event (calling it "my apparent blunder"), while recovering at least one P-40 from Wenshan. After some repairs were made, just enough fuel was put in the plane to fly it to Mengzi, sixty-seven miles to the west. All other nonessential equipment was stripped to lighten the load, and Boyington made a successful takeoff.

Fortunately for him, if not for others, a different kind of redemption came two days after he returned to Kunming. Another group of five pilots, led by Duke Hedman, the AVG's first ace, made forced landings en route to Loiwing; a sixth P-40 attempting to drop supplies to the first bunch also crash-landed. In the span of a week, a not-so-laughable comedy of errors had cost the AVG eleven planes, temporarily at least. "The colonel will die," George Burgard wrote after hearing of the latest fiasco.

Boyington remained unhappy despite having the heat diverted elsewhere. His mishap had hurt his standing in the Adam & Eves, most of whom had been flying out of Magwe after finally evacuating from Rangoon at the end of February. Just before the squadron returned to Kunming for a much-needed rest, Bob Neale indicated to Charlie Bond that he wanted him as vice squadron leader. Bond worried about how Boyington would react. "He's built like a bull," he observed, knowing that when Boyington was drunk, he was a ticking bomb.

There were indeed hard feelings when the Adam & Eves arrived in Kunming on March 13, but the lid didn't blow until a week later. Bond returned to his room from a Kunming movie theater to find Boyington and several others sitting there, "stewed to the gills" after helping themselves to his booze. All of them were scheduled for alert duty first thing in the morning, so Bond tried to shoo them out.

At this point, obviously trying to draw Bond into a fight, Boyington challenged Bill Bartling, who stood firm and told Boyington to swing first. He did. Blood from Bartling's chin splattered on Bond, who then grabbed Boyington and pulled him away. This was what Boyington had wanted all along—once contact was made, the rules of engagement were wide open. "It took all the persuasion I ever had to keep [Greg] from powdering me, but I was sober and he wasn't," Bond wrote in his diary. "[He] wants to fight me more than any other guy in the Flying Tigers. It didn't register at the time, but I guess the vice squadron leader replacement deal was at the core of the problem. I did a lot of talking and his belligerence finally subsided."

Not surprisingly, Boyington was late for duty the following morning, as were several others. Bob Neale "raised hell," according to Bond, venting most of his wrath on Boyington. It was the second time in as many months that Neale had severely chastised Boyington in front of the other pilots.

Considering Boyington's frustration over failing to get into action and his continuing struggle with alcohol, he was surprisingly resilient. As much as he got into trouble with others, he was punishing himself more, aware of the remarks about his being an "enemy ace" for losing five Tomahawks, while his own score of Japanese planes stood at two.

Despite all the misfortune, he remained in China long after many pilots and ground personnel had given up and gone home. To him, it was just like facing Kenneth Fisher on the dirt street in front of his house in St. Maries. This time, he was getting a psychological beating (some of it self-inflicted), instead of a bloody nose. Still, Boyington refused to quit. The idea had probably crossed his mind, but the word *quit* had not yet been past his lips.

11

For the Good
of the Service

After the fall of Rangoon on March 7, the Japanese began an unprecedented buildup of aerial strength at Mingaladon Field and its surrounding satellite bases. They prepared deliberately for two weeks, then launched a massive attack on the afternoon of Saturday, March 21, against the AVG and RAF planes that had escaped to Magwe. Swarms of Japanese bombers and escorting fighters hit the Allied base in several waves, but the RAF's pitifully inept warning system allowed only a handful of Tomahawks and Hurricanes to rise against them, with predictably lopsided results.

On the ground, an AVG crew chief was mortally wounded, a pilot received serious shrapnel wounds (he later died of complications), and few aircraft were left in flyable condition. The Japanese returned the next day to mop up, after which the Allies were forced to quit Magwe altogether. Only a dozen hastily repaired fighters were flown out; everybody else went by convoy across the border into China.

Taking this sledgehammer blow personally, Claire Chennault plotted almost immediate retribution, though he lacked the assets for anything except a small hit-and-run effort. He called Neale and Newkirk into a meeting at 8:00 Sunday morning, even before the second round of Japanese attacks at Magwe, to work out the details for a strafing attack inside Thailand. "The result of the talk was that at 1200 this date I am to take ten P-40s to Chiang-mai via Loiwing &

Namsang and strafe the Jap airport there," Neale wrote in his diary. "Hell of a nice mission as Chiang Mai is 165 mi. inside Jap lines."

In the span of five hours, Chennault's plan for revenge progressed from concept to having planes in the air. The hastily arranged mission called for Newkirk, Geselbracht, Keeton, and Lawler to strafe the bomber base at Lampang at dawn on Monday, while Boyington would go with Bob Neale, Charlie Bond, Bill Bartling, "Black Mac" McGarry, and Ed Rector to hit Chiang Mai. Fuel stops would be made Sunday at Loiwing and Namsang.

The whole evolution had been planned so quickly that no one remembered to notify the ground crew at Loiwing. Thus the facility was unprepared when the P-40s landed on Sunday afternoon. Bond blew the tire on his tail wheel, so Neale decided to slide the mission twenty-four hours. This was no hardship for the pilots, who spent the night in the American Club near the Pawley brothers' CAMCO factory. It had all the comforts a pilot needed: good food, cold beer, and nicely furnished quarters with real Simmons mattresses.

On Monday, the raiders delayed taking off until afternoon, so as to slip into the RAF base at Namsang undetected at dusk. While waiting, several stragglers from the attacks at Magwe arrived and told of the horrific bombing. "They almost scared us out of going on our mission," Keeton wrote, but the raiders left Loiwing that afternoon and landed at the small base in the Shan Province, 170 miles northwest of Chiang Mai. After dinner in the RAF mess, they headed for the barracks and a few hours' sleep. Boyington was standing at the typical Burma washbasin with several others when a sergeant came up and warned, "It's all right to use that water to wash your face and hands in, but don't drink it or brush your teeth with it because it's polluted." Newkirk brushed his teeth anyway. "Well, after tomorrow," he said, "I don't think it will make any difference."

A Burmese number-one boy woke them a few minutes past four the next morning. Pilots shivered as they dressed by lamplight, guts in knots from nerves and the chilly highland air. They jumped when an RAF officer burst in bellowing, "All right, you curly headed fellows, it's time!" Laughing away their tension, they joked and grab-assed on the way to breakfast.

It was still dark when they climbed into their P-40s and cranked the Allisons, letting them warm while their eyes adjusted to the red backlighting of the instruments. Pulling out from the dispersal area, they taxied carefully, feeling their way to the ends of the two runways. A mist lay on the ground, morning fog thickened by smoke from scattered fires across war-torn Burma. They began taking off using alternate runways at approximately 6:00 A.M., concentrating on the dim reference points provided by truck lights and a few lanterns. Bystanders could see only the exhaust flames, streaming blue-hot as the fighters lifted into the air. It took several minutes for all ten to get airborne and rendezvous, but contrary to the plan, Jack Newkirk turned toward Thailand as soon as Keeton, Lawlor, and Geselbracht had joined on him.

His impatience was one of several mistakes. Chennault had intended for the Panda Bears to strafe Lampang, a bomber field fifty miles southeast of Chiang Mai. Somehow, this was construed as *Lamphun,* a village located fifteen miles south of Chiang Mai. Nothing of military importance existed there, but Newkirk set off for it anyway.

Meanwhile, Bob Neale's formation got sorted out, with Bond, having flown a reconnaissance mission over Chiang Mai in December, on his wing as a guide. Boyington was next, then Bartling, constituting the four shooters, while Rector and McGarry would serve as roving top cover.

Neale orbited for twenty minutes, waiting in vain for Newkirk's flight, before turning his six P-40s southeast toward Chiang Mai. Boyington watched the leader's exhaust flame as they winged through the darkness into Thailand. "What was passing by in the jungle below us, or how close we came to any mountains," he later recalled, "was in my imagination only." At a few minutes past seven, Bond recognized their location from the terrain as the sky began to lighten. Easing up beside Neale's P-40, he waggled his wings, made a diving turn to the left, and triggered a short burst after arming his guns.

McGarry and Rector leveled off at five thousand feet as the shooters continued their descending turn. Finding themselves south of Chiang Mai, the raiders pulled more sharply to the left, able to make out the dirt landing area off their shoulders. Boyington watched the target "take shape in the semidarkness" as the formation swooped around in echelon. Goggles lowered, the pilots dropped to two thousand feet and strung out one behind another, holding their fire until they got closer. Adrenaline pumping, pulses racing, each held a gloved index finger just off the spring-loaded trigger in the control stick.

Newkirk almost ruined it. "We intended to strafe any enemy planes found in Lambhun [sic] area," wrote Hank Geselbracht in his combat report. But of course there were no enemy planes there; the only ones nearby were at Chiang Mai. Inexplicably, Newkirk decided to shoot up the town itself. His flight followed a river until they reached the city, whereupon Newkirk dived and strafed the train depot. The other three held their fire, but subsequently several made a pass at a large barrack, and finally all four of them opened fire at a row of storage buildings lining the road south of Chiang Mai. Farther down the road, Newkirk spotted a couple of military vehicles and maneuvered into position to strafe them.

Newkirk's strafing attacks had alerted the airbase at Chiang Mai. Fighters were being warmed up and pilots had already manned some of the planes when Charlie Bond swept across the field first, triggering his guns as he raced down a row of parked aircraft. Neale spotted "a line of planes two and three deep on the east side of the field" and opened fire; Bartling saw "a very closely packed line of fighters with three twin-engine ships in the center"; Boyington noticed the same cluster of transports, could see that Bond and Neale had already commenced firing, and noticed tracers from Japanese machine guns reaching blindly into the sky.

Lining up on the transports, he fired into them and saw "blurred forms jumping off wings, out of cockpits, and scurrying all over the field like ants." It took just ten seconds to streak along the row of planes while he held the trigger down. Hundreds of his slugs shredded thin aluminum, found fuel tanks, tore the earth; if a .50-caliber round hit a person anywhere near the torso, the shock of the impact itself was usually lethal. By the conclusion of his first pass, the three transports blazed into "one large fire 1000 ft. high," illuminating the rest of the field.

Skimming low, jockeying, he somehow missed the other P-40s as he pulled a high-g wingover and came back over the field for another run. He fired into a row of fighters, packed so tightly they reminded him of the flight line at Pensacola. Forty to fifty planes were reportedly parked on the field, the majority identified as "I-97s" and "Model 'O's," though there were no Mitsubishi A6M Zeros in the JAAF. The raiders had seen Nakajima *Ki*-43s, later called the Oscar, which looked virtually identical to the Zero in the blur of a high-speed pass. Their neat alignment made aiming easy as the P-40s swept back and forth.

Six minutes was all it took. Boyington completed two passes, but by then the Japanese gunners made it too hot to stay around. Neale rolled his wings as a signal, then scooted five miles southwest of the field and climbed to five thousand feet. Boyington joined him a few minutes later, and they watched eight or nine fires burn brightly at the field before they steered for Namsang.

The antiaircraft gunners shifted to Rector and McGarry. Several shells burst "uncomfortably close," so the pilots jinked their P-40s as Charlie Bond and Bill Bartling raced up to join them, then warped around to the northwest toward Thailand.

South of Chiang Mai, Keeton completed his run on the storage buildings just as Newkirk and Geselbracht swung around to engage two camouflaged vehicles on the road to Lamphun. Newkirk dived first, opened fire, then cleared out of the way. Geselbracht made his pass and pulled up, saw a bright flash of fire beyond the target. Keeton also witnessed it as he pulled up from his strafing run—a burst of flames in a nearby field.

It was Newkirk. According to later speculation, the two camouflaged vehicles were armored cars that might have scored a lucky shot. Just as plausibly, he didn't allow himself enough room to pull out. Whatever the cause, his P-40 struck the ground at a shallow angle, traveling at upwards of 250 miles per hour. Inertia threw burning fuel, Newkirk, and pieces of his plane for 150 yards across the field.

Black Mac's number also came up. The others noticed he was waggling his wings, saw his airspeed falling rapidly, circled back to see what was wrong. Smoke poured from his engine: a late burst of AA had ruined his hope of reaching Burma. The others flew protectively around him for several minutes, willing him to stay in the air just long enough to make it across the Salween River, but the P-40 could carry him no farther. Thirty miles from the border, he slid the canopy back and bailed out successfully. Bond and Bartling tossed down maps, Rector dropped a candy bar, then they returned to Namsang and found Boyington and Neale already there. (Black Mac was fortunate. Captured by Thai militia, he was interrogated by the Japanese, then was remanded to a Bangkok jail rather than taken into the dreaded POW camps. He was released in early 1945.)

The five Adam & Eves pressed on, wanting to put as many miles as they could between themselves and the Japanese air force. Rector stopped at Lashio to inform British army headquarters about McGarry, then continued to Loiwing, where Lawlor, Keeton, and Geselbracht waited with the news that Newkirk was dead. He and McGarry were eulogized at the American Club bar, after which the survivors drank to their success, calculating that at least half of the planes parked at Chiang Mai had been destroyed. Bartling claimed ten, Boyington seven, Neale five; Bond's combat report was evidently lost but his diary confirms the general assessment. Two days after the raid, Neale indicated that their estimate had not been lowered: "After looking over combat reports find that the four planes that hit Chiang Mai destroyed about 25–30 Jap fighters."

If the four shooters anticipated large sums in their bonus accounts, they had good reason. Six days earlier, Ken Jernstedt and Bill Reed of the Hell's Angels were credited with fifteen planes after strafing two fields. Reed earned four thousand dollars, a record for a single mission, and Jernstedt received the balance. But when the Chiang Mai raiders returned to Kunming for a debriefing with Harvey Greenlaw, they were credited with fifteen aircraft—half their initial estimate. Someone, perhaps Chennault, made an arbitrary decision to divide the bonus money equally. Boyington probably agreed to this in principle, believing he would be paid for almost four planes (3.75 to be exact, or $1,875), but instead, all six Adam & Eves were given an equal share. The cutting didn't stop. A few weeks later, when Chennault was away from Kunming, Skip Adair wrote to China Defense Supplies (as acting commander of the AVG) requesting payment to the bonus account on behalf of *all ten* participating pilots. Boyington, like all the rest, got credit for 1.5 planes.

The decision to divide credit equally had a precedent (the December 20 raid on Kunming), though it contradicted a statement by Hell's Angels pilot Jim Howard, who presided over a confirmation board in the spring of 1942. In his memoir, *Roar of the Tiger,* he wrote: "Since each approved victory was worth five hundred bucks to the claimant, our board had a great deal of responsibility. Our decisions were fair but exacting—we always required proof beyond a doubt that a pilot's claim was valid."

Boyington, who at one point probably envisioned a payment of $3,500 for claiming seven planes on the ground, was paid $750. Bitterly frustrated by the outcome of the raid, he was galled that his efforts and his bonus account were at the mercy of nonflying staff members, people he considered

"Asiatic bums." Whereas he had never turned his back on a fight or failed to volunteer for combat, other pilots had quit. After running from the Christmas Day fight over Rangoon, Curtis Smith had been transferred to Chennault's staff as the adjutant. Boyington despised cowards and malingerers and others of their ilk—not just in China but for the rest of his life. Weakness in others fed a simmering rage that exacerbated his struggle with alcoholism.

As if things weren't bad enough already, Chennault called a meeting in the Hostel Number One auditorium the day after the raiders returned to Kunming. He asked for a show of support for induction into the army; instead many pilots said they would resign, or agreed to remain only until their contract ended. Chennault backed down for the time being, but the AVG was not going to remain a quasi-military group for long. Too much was at stake for a number of career army officers with enormous egos—Chennault included—which put the "civilians" of the AVG in the middle of a classic power struggle.

Upon learning that induction into the army was imminent, Boyington queried Chennault about the "written agreement back in Washington." Chennault's response was a snub—complete indifference. Having counted heavily on the promise that he could be reinstated in the Marine Corps at his old rank, and truly believing there were "secret papers lying in Admiral Nimitz's safe," Boyington was outraged. From the very beginning, his rationale for joining the AVG had been money; he wanted to erase his debt and clear his sullied name in the corps.

Still, he was not ready to give up, and when a call went out for volunteers to help the 3d Pursuit at Loiwing, he raised his hand. It was just what he needed. Out of favor with the Adam & Eves, denied his fair share of bonus money after risking his neck at Chiang Mai, Boyington felt there was nothing more for him in Kunming. He wanted to go where the fighting was, though he harbored no illusions about what he would find there: "When I flew to Loiwing on this trip, I figured that I was going to stay for a while. This time I was nothing special . . . and I wasn't invited to bunk in the American hostel either."

Unfortunately, his run of bad luck did not end with the Hell's Angels. On the last day of March, just three days after his arrival, he was attempting to take off in a P-40 when he overran the runway and came to an abrupt stop in a rice paddy. Most everyone familiar with the incident believed that the engine had lost power, but at least two sources, one of them an eyewitness, claimed that the mishap occurred because Boyington was drunk.

The eyewitness was Leo Schramm, number ninety-two's crew chief. Having been called on an errand, he arrived at the field after Boyington had taxied out. Right away he saw that something wasn't right.

> I noticed that it was not tracking on a straight line and asked a mechanic who was at the controls. "Boyington," he answered.
>
> "What's his problem?" I asked.
>
> "Gee, Leo," another mechanic replied, "all I know is that I saw him drunker than a skunk about a half hour ago. He probably shouldn't be flying."
>
> Well, there was nothing that any of us could do at that moment but stand there and watch an inebriated pilot attempt to roll my plane down the runway for takeoff. As he approached the position on the field where his wheels should have been lifting off, it wasn't happening. There was still time to get the bird in the air, but he continued off the end of the runway. He hit a ditch, and belly-flopped into a rice paddy. We all started to run toward the plane, but even before we reached the edge of the field Boyington had already emerged from the wreckage. He ran straight for a water truck that was parked nearby, started it up, and raced away from the base.

Boyington did not get far. The water truck was found where he had abandoned it—wrecked at the base of a tree. He showed up a few hours later claiming he had crashed the

P-40 because it lacked sufficient power. The next day, squadron leader Oley Olson included a sentence about the accident in his daily status report to Kunming: "BOYINGTON CUT SLIGHTLY WHEN SHIP CUT OUT ON TAKE-OFF YESTERDAY."

Boyington later claimed that he sustained injuries to both knees after striking the bottom edge of the instrument panel, and cut his head on the gunsight. The P-40 was heavily damaged, he alleged, but Schramm disagreed. "It just ran into a rice paddy filled with water and crap. We pulled it out, changed the prop, and washed if off. Ed Stiles got in and cranked it, and the engine ran fine."

According to the rest of Boyington's story, his knees were too swollen for him to wear slacks at the wedding of Fred Hodges and Helen Anderson on April 2, so he attended in a bathrobe. He got "full of whiskey" at the celebration in the American Club, then stumbled by accident over a steep hillside when an air-raid warning sounded. The fall knocked him dizzy and caused more injuries.

Boyington was indeed hurt at Loiwing, with a deep gash on his head and both knees banged up, but the culprit was the ignominious fall after a night of drinking. The injuries were serious enough that he was evacuated to Kunming, where he was placed in the small AVG hospital adjacent to the Hostel Number One. Easter Sunday and the better part of two weeks passed while he recuperated. Learning that Harvey Greenlaw was away on a trip, he sent a note to Olga: "Dear Mrs. G., Why don't you bring a guy American cigarettes when he is in the hospital?"

Bringing a pack of Camels from her apartment, Olga found him with his head wrapped in bandages, his two knees covered with tape. "Hello, handsome," she said, lighting a cigarette for him. He explained his version of the P-40 accident, then asked if she had any clean pajamas. "I haven't been to my quarters yet," he said, "and I feel pretty dirty with what I have on." On her next visit, Olga brought a pair of Harvey's silk pajamas, which Boyington then wore under a bathrobe when he hobbled up to her apartment for tea the following afternoon. He despised Harvey Greenlaw, but he wasn't above wearing the man's pajamas while playing with his wife.

On April 10, he was again at Olga's apartment (as were Erik Shilling and Tom Jones) when a knock came at the door. In walked Clare Booth Luce, playwright, correspondent, part owner of *Life* and *Time,* and wife of *Time* magazine's editor-in-chief. Having no idea of her fame, Boyington blurted, "And who the hell are you?" Olga thought it funny, caring little for Luce herself. (She gave the correspondent some vague background information, which Luce subsequently used to describe her as a "White Russian" and the wife of the paymaster.)

When it was time for Boyington to return to the hospital, Olga and Jones helped him back to his bed, then returned to her apartment. Jones probably anticipated a pleasant night with Olga, but they found Skip Adair waiting on the top step. "Someone broke into the bar," he informed them, "and one of the men told me it was Boyington."

Olga refused to believe it. Boyington had been at her party, she explained. Unconvinced, Adair asked if anyone had noticed Boyington absent, and Jones mentioned that he had seen Boyington leave to go to the bathroom. "That's the time he did it, then," said Adair. "We'll have to try him for that."

Olga suggested that the guilty person was just trying to put the blame on Boyington, but Adair disagreed. "The man who did it twisted the lock off the door with his bare hands," he said. "Only one guy in the group can do that, and that's Boyington." Olga steadfastly refused to cooperate and the threat was eventually dropped, but for Boyington it was the last straw. Adair had been the one to cut his bonus account after the Chiang Mai raid, and now he insulted Boyington with his petty threat of a trial.

Two days later, Boyington went to a telegraph office in Kunming and sent a message to Marine Corps headquarters: "CONTEMPLATING RESIGNATION AVG CHINA WIRE MY STATUS IN MARINE CORPS UPON RETURN BOX

104 KUNMING CHINA. (SIGNED) GREGORY BOYING-
TON SQUADRON COMMANDER." Realizing the situation in Kunming was never going to improve, he had no
qualms about inflating his AVG status if it would help to get
him back into the marines.

He was anxious to get home for another reason. The first
and only letter from his mother had recently arrived, and the
news had not been good. Seattle's juvenile court, responding
to complaints from family and neighbors, had taken the children from Helene in early March. (Boyington's divorce had
proceeded by default since he was out of the country. The
judge awarded Helene $150 per month for alimony and child
support, paid as an allotment from Boyington's CAMCO account. The divorce decree was signed on November 7, but
would not become final for at least six months.)

Immediately after the preliminary hearing in September,
Helene had brought the children to Okanogan and left them
there. The family heard nothing from her, nor did she provide any compensation from her allotment, so the Hallenbecks petitioned the court for an amendment to the decree.
Now it was Helene's turn to be summoned. Prior to the dead-
line, she picked up the children and took them back to
Seattle, where she habitually left them in the care of others
for long periods—sometimes weeks. Thus, in early March
the juvenile court stepped in and removed them from her
care. Gloria, a toddler, went to live with Helene's sister, Constance Wickstrom; the two older children returned to Okanogan with the Hallenbecks.

Having indicated in his message that he was merely contemplating his resignation, Boyington made up his mind
when he heard that Olga Greenlaw was traveling to Loiwing
to meet Harvey. She was almost aboard the CNAC plane
when he caught up with her at the airfield. "There are a lot
of things a guy can't take," he said, "but I took them, on the
chin. But now that you are going—I don't know." She took
his hand and urged him to keep his chin up. "They're gang-

ing up on me, Olga," he added. "Next time I'll fool 'em—
I'll resign. To hell with it."

"No, Greg Boyington, you can't do that," she answered
firmly, reminding him that those who left early were given a
dishonorable discharge, but Boyington wasn't listening.

After she departed, he went on a bender that lasted for
days. He reported late—and still drunk—for the alert one
night, and was chewed out by Bob Neale. In the midst of the
tongue-lashing he calmly asked for the keys to the AVG station wagon. Caught off-guard by the irrelevant question,
Neal handed the keys over. "Good-bye," Boyington said to
the people in the alert shack. "I'm going over to the adjutant's office and turn in my resignation. . . . Guess that's what
you all want."

Claire Chennault and Harvey Greenlaw were both at
Loiwing, leaving Skip Adair in charge. Boyington resigned
on April 21, after which Adair named Charlie Bond as vice
squadron commander of the 1st Pursuit. That evening Bond
wrote, "At dinner I saw [Greg] come in completely looped
and staggering. Bob Neale said he had been that way for six
days and nights."

As Olga had warned, Boyington did receive a dishonorable discharge from the AVG. Curtis Smith wrote the "official" declaration by virtue of being the group adjutant:
"Having terminated his contract with the Central Aircraft
Manufacturing Company and his services with the American Volunteer Group in time of war and with the Group in
contact with the enemy, Vice Squadron Leader GREGORY
BOYINGTON, First Pursuit Squadron, is hereby dishonor-
ably discharged from the American Volunteer Group." Thus,
in the most laughable irony of all, Boyington received his
dishonorable discharge from a pilot who had turned in his
wings after running from combat.

One of the last Flying Tigers to see Boyington in
Kunming was not a fellow pilot or one of the despised staff,
but a crew chief, one of the regular guys. Irving Stolet, sent
to the hospital to recover from a broken ankle sustained
while jumping from a P-40's wing, later wrote, "After I got

to hobbling around, I was in the bar in Hostel Number One one evening, sitting next to Greg Boyington. He was loaded, and mumbling in his drinks. After a while, he turned to me and said, 'Piss on this outfit, I'm shoving off.' I thought he was going to try for his sack, and offered to help him, but he snorted and said he'd 'make his own way.' Next morning I heard he blew town, took off, and was gone from Kunming."

It was true. Boyington had walked into the CNAC office at Wu Chia Ba Airport and exchanged a few thousand Chinese dollars for a ticket to Calcutta.

Before he left, he stopped by the headquarters office and asked Doreen Davis, a friend of Olga's, to hold a note for her. Olga did not return for several weeks, but Davis was true to her word and handed over Boyington's short, sincere message:

Dear Olga,
By the time you get here, I shall be gone. I have resigned because I think it was the best thing to do. "For the good of the service," shall we say? I want you to know that I am not a coward, but I don't have to tell you that. Best of luck to you, and here's hoping we meet again.

There is no evidence that they ever met again, but Olga burned a candle for Boyington for a long time to come. Years later, so the story goes, after she had divorced Harvey Greenlaw and was living alone in California, one of the Flying Tigers visited her apartment. Of all the former Tigers she had known—in every way imaginable—she displayed a photograph of just one: Greg Boyington.

12

About Face

The trip home proved far more expensive and time consuming than Boyington could have imagined. The routes to the south and east were cut off—civilians could not get back to the States by crossing the Pacific—so he had to go west, the long way around. The first challenge was to reach India. He left Kunming on April 26 aboard a CNAC DC-3 bound for Calcutta, but heavy turbulence forced the plane to turn back. The next day's attempt was hardly better, but after an extremely bumpy flight he arrived at Dum Dum Airport.

From Calcutta, he planned to go on to Karachi, Pakistan, and hop a Tenth Air Force transport to Africa, but getting out of the hot, filthy city proved difficult. Several AVG pilots on their way to pick up new fighters were put up at the Great Eastern Hotel on expense accounts, then took a British Overseas Airways Company flying boat to Pakistan, but Boyington had no such privileges. He spent an entire week in Calcutta before finally getting a BOAC flight, which took off from the Hooghly River for the fourteen-hundred-mile flight to the Arabian Sea, with a refueling stop on a lake in central India. Reaching Pakistan on May 4, he found Karachi much like Calcutta. The indigents lived in utter poverty while the whites enjoyed a life of luxury—movies, fine dining, nightclubs, sailing clubs. The city was a regular stop for Pan Am Clippers, and several AVG pilots were offered jobs on the spot at eight hundred dollars a month.

Boyington never mentioned such a tantalizing prospect. If the offer was made, he turned it down—he was on a mission to get home.

Unfortunately, he was stymied by army regulations. Official authorization was required for a seat on a transport headed west, so he telegrammed Kunming to request approval. Chennault not only denied the request, but allegedly replied to the army, "AM UNABLE TO GRANT PERMISSION FOR BOYINGTON. SUGGEST YOU DRAFT BOYINGTON INTO TENTH AIR FORCE AS SECOND LIEUTENANT."

Of his own reaction, Boyington later wrote that it was "the closest I ever came to out-and-out murder." He did travel to Tenth Air Force headquarters in New Delhi, but was not inducted; some weeks later, during a trip to India, Olga Greenlaw heard that the army "shared the general opinion that he was no damn good and never would be."

Halfway around the world, attorney Joseph Wicks learned of Boyington's resignation in a message from CAMCO, which stated that his "full salary settlement would be made . . . in the Orient," indicating no further allotments. The settlement explains why Boyington had purchased his CNAC ticket at Kunming with a "briefcase full of paper money." Having burned his bridges, it wasn't long before he went broke trying to get out of Pakistan and was compelled to send a telegram to Grace and Ellsworth in early May. They informed Wicks that Boyington was stranded in Karachi and needed funds, which he apparently arranged by wire.

Seething over his predicament, Boyington focused his anger on Chennault, sarcastically referring to him as "Laughing Boy" because of his inability to display emotion. Boyington was particularly incensed at the suggestion that he be drafted. "This tyrant had to be taught a lesson," he later wrote, "even if it meant my swimming back to the corps and shooting down a thousand Japs." For months to come, Boyington would be motivated by an intense, bitter desire to prove Chennault wrong.

He didn't have to swim, but he did leave Karachi by way

of the sea. After learning that the steamship SS *Brazil* was to leave shortly for New York, he "simmered down, forgetting the past somewhat, and enjoyed the nightlife in Karachi." Although Wicks might have wired him enough funds to party and buy passage on the ship, Olga Greenlaw provided another plausible explanation: "[In] Karachi something happened—don't ask me what. My guess is that he finally hit bottom with a crash that brought him to his senses. Whatever it was, he met some sailors from the SS *Brazil,* which was about to sail for the States, and shipped on as a deckhand."

Perhaps he did not stoop quite that low, for he claimed he had a stateroom, but however he managed it, Boyington was aboard *Brazil* when she sailed down the coast and docked at Bombay. Here, in India's largest city, he met another attractive woman cast from the same mold as Olga—a tall brunette with green eyes and a husband.

She used the stage name of "Dora Lee" as a high-kicking showgirl in the late 1920s, and claimed to have danced on Broadway in a production of *The Street Singer.* When her star faded, Lucile Rogers headed to foreign shores, working her way from the Riviera to Cairo and then to Bombay. She was still young, just twenty, when she hooked a wealthy man sixteen years her senior. Her husband, a production manager for General Motors, gave her a life of privilege far beyond anything she had known.

But now that the British were rapidly losing ground to the Japanese, Stewart Malcolmson sent his wife to the States, ostensibly for her safety. Unintentionally, he threw her to the wolves. When *Brazil* departed Bombay around the first of June, Lucy Malcolmson was among "any number of export wives returning without their husbands," according to Boyington. He and the women were joined by servicemen and even some of the missionaries he had met aboard *Boschfontein.* The latter, he explained, were "able to keep their morale and morals up, the same as before, but the rest appeared to have morals that suited my own. For many an orgy took place during the six weeks it was to take the SS *Brazil* to reach New York without an escort."

Lucy, now thirty-one and still alluring, intended to have a good time. Boyington was hosting a party in his stateroom, having somehow squirreled two cases of scotch aboard, when they met. As he told it, the ship lurched, causing him to stumble while carrying drinks in both hands. He ended up kneeling "in front of two very attractive gams." By the time *Brazil* reached Cape Town, South Africa, he and Lucy had become "pretty friendly," his euphemism for sharing a hotel room during the stopover.

Lucy apparently had refused his early advances, but her feelings changed after he took care of her during a bout of malaria. He brought food and even washed her clothes. "Gosh, he was good to me," she later said, as though surprised to find a hard-drinking fighter pilot capable of compassion.

Boyington relied equally on her. She was evidently a good listener as he vented his outrage over Chennault and explained the difficult situation at home. He knew that his kids were no longer with Helene; beyond that, little was certain except that he owed $150 a month in alimony and child support, and he had no income. At some point, Lucy became involved beyond listening, and promised to help.

Boyington's goal was to restore his name in the Marine Corps. The only way to accomplish such a resurrection, he thought, was to get his commission back and shoot down lots of planes, which would mean leaving his children behind again. With few options available to him, he decided to accept Lucy's offer to help. "I was worried about my children after the divorce and all," he later explained. "[Lucy and I] got to talking and she suggested that she was pretty good at business. She said she'd be glad to handle my money while I was out in the Pacific fighting. I knew my mother wasn't any too good at finances. It seemed like a good idea . . ."

Thus, he decided to let Lucy become enormously influential regarding his anticipated service pay. If she had ulterior motives, they remained inscrutable. Perhaps she had really fallen in love with him, or was bored and looking for a worthwhile cause. Boyington was young, rugged, and muscular, with a magnetism that appealed to many women, and was a fighter pilot in the bargain. He had everything going for him *except* money. If Lucy was a gold digger, she stood to gain very little at this juncture, and there was no assurance that he would even get his commission back. In the meantime, they decided to enjoy themselves during the long trip across the Atlantic.

Boyington was unaware that the telegram he'd sent to headquarters from Kunming two months earlier had received considerable attention. His message had arrived on April 13, then traveled up the chain of command to reach the director of aviation ten days later. This was the same individual who had recommended that he "not be reappointed at a future date in either the regular Marine Corps or Marine Corps Reserve," but Col. Ralph Mitchell had since experienced a change of heart. He recommended that Boyington be commissioned in the reserves "with the same precedence he held in the regular service at the time of resignation." Between his lines of military rhetoric, he practically chortled over the prospect of getting a combat veteran, expressing his opinion that Boyington's "value to the service" would be enhanced by his "very active combat experience."

He was only too right in implying that combat-experienced pilots were a commodity. As of his April 23 correspondence, not a single combat veteran was available in the Marine Corps fighter community due to devastating losses since the opening of the war. No marine fighters had gotten off the ground at Pearl Harbor on December 7 (hence, none of the pilots there had aerial combat experience), and the squadron at Wake Atoll did only slightly better, holding out for two weeks before every pilot was killed or captured.

Mitchell was compelled to remind the commandant about Boyington's earlier fall from grace, the Marine Corps being too small for former debts and embarrassments to be overlooked. "It is hoped," he wrote, "that the sizable monetary remuneration he has received during his duty with CAMCO will have permitted him to place his personal finances in order."

Boyington would have laughed out loud.

When SS *Brazil* glided past the Statue of Liberty on July 13, Boyington did not regard the sight of the green lady as a welcome home. Instead, she was "a prelude to being able to go out again." The statue could not tell him what the future held, but CAMCO's main office was in New York; maybe someone there could help. After the ship docked, he met with Bill Pawley regarding the status of his marine commission. Pawley proved a powerful ally and dictated a letter to Capt. Frank Beatty, USN, an aide to Frank Knox, reminding him of "the arrangements."

Two days later, Boyington reached Washington, D.C., and submitted a letter to the commandant, requesting that he be recommissioned "as agreed to by the secretary of the navy." He added: "I am available for immediate service and further request that I be assigned to active duty as soon as possible." Having learned that recommissioning in the regular marines would be a long and convoluted process due to current law, he requested a temporary commission in the reserves, then went home to await orders for duty.

Most of Okanogan knew he was coming. He had phoned Grace from New York on his first night there, after which she evidently told the Okanogan *Independent* about his return home. Although he had never lived in the little town, the paper announced, "Okanogan's 'Flying Tiger' to Pay Visit." He went by train to Chicago, where Lucy joined him for the remainder of the trip to central Washington.

In the meantime, Colonel Mitchell endorsed Boyington's official request for reappointment. He indicated that Boyington should be commissioned in the reserves "with the precedence that he would have had," but added that his record in the AVG was being investigated "prior to any recommendation regarding his request." Major General Holcomb agreed with Mitchell's endorsement and sent a letter to the secretary of the navy, requesting that Knox propose legislation in Congress that would permit Boyington's reappointment in the *regular* Marine Corps without loss of precedence. Remarkably, Boyington's case had gone straight to the top within a few days of his arrival in the States.

Lucy stayed in Okanogan for a week before moving on to San Francisco. In sharp contrast with the humble agricultural town, her new residence fronted the Marina Boulevard yacht basin, one of San Francisco's most luxurious neighborhoods. It would be several months before Boyington saw her again, but their plans remained intact.

Soon after she left, Boyington received a telegram from headquarters, ordering him to report for a physical examination with the nearest navy medical officer. That he was going to get back into the service now seemed assured; the only question was when. The nearest flight surgeon was in Seattle, so he decided to make the trip after first taking advantage of his local popularity. He spoke at several venues, beginning with the Okanogan Kiwanis Club, where he presented himself as Captain Boyington. Making a few embellishments during his speech, he claimed the AVG never had more than eight planes in the air at any given time while facing as many as 150 enemy attackers, and said he had been "severely injured in a forced landing," but he gave due respect to the Japanese pilots and their aircraft—and to Claire Chennault's tactics. Curiously, he did not mention aerial victories, though he did talk about the raid on Chiang Mai, joking that it took more nerve to speak at the luncheon than it did to strafe the airdrome. The next night he lectured at a school auditorium, and was reportedly in demand as a speaker throughout central Washington and even in California.

Leaving the limelight temporarily, he drove to Seattle and underwent a flight physical on August 10. The same flight surgeon was still at Sand Point, and found that Boyington had grown in the past seven years: a half-inch gain in height, an inch bigger around the chest, two at the waist. As a consequence he weighed more, though not as much as the summer of '41. Bloated then at 190 pounds, he had slimmed down to 174.

Boyington also handled family matters during his trip to Seattle. He went downtown to the courthouse and filed a motion to gain custody of his children, basing his charge on Helene's conduct, especially her addiction to "the excessive use of intoxicating liquors." The *Seattle Post-Intelligencer* sniffed out the details of their divorce and pending custody battle, and published an account with a large picture of Helene in pajamas and a disheveled robe. Her unflattering appearance was said to be due to illness, but was attributable to acute alcoholism. In the accompanying story, Boyington's former income as a Flying Tiger and even his projected pay as a marine were revealed to the public, along with other personal details.

On the appointed date, Helene appeared in court and explained to the judge that she was destitute, too ill to work, had lost her rented home, and had had no choice but to move in with one Mr. Hart. She denied living with him improperly, claiming the arrangement was only temporary. The judge was unsympathetic. On September 1, amending the decree he had signed ten months earlier, he awarded custody of the children to Boyington but ordered that they remain in their current environment: Greg junior and Janet with the Hallenbecks in Okanogan, Gloria with the Wickstroms in Seattle. Noting that Boyington was still two thousand dollars in debt, and that his anticipated lieutenant's pay would provide only half of what he had earned with CAMCO, the judge reduced child support to a hundred dollars a month, payable directly to the juvenile court. Helene would get whatever funds were left at the end of the month, as supervised by the juvenile courts, but it's doubtful that she received more than a pittance.

She ended up marrying Mr. Hart, but later divorced him. The remainder of her life was obscure and alcoholic.

•   •   •

Boyington was not at the courthouse when he was awarded custody of the children, but in Okanogan, anxious to know what was happening with his commission. In Washington, the Marine Corps had received a less than glowing report on Boyington from Claire Chennault, who had indicated that Boyington was a "capable flyer and would have been of valuable service were it not for his excessive drinking." Colonel Mitchell sent General Holcomb a memorandum recommending that the steps to recommission Boyington in the regular Marine Corps be stopped. The commandant decided to pursue the regular commission anyway, but agreed in the interim to appoint Boyington as a first lieutenant in the reserves.

A "mailgram" Boyington received on September 3 was only partially helpful: "REAPPOINTMENT TO COMMISSIONED RANK APPROVED. YOU WILL BE INFORMED WHEN FINAL ACTION IS TAKEN." He misunderstood it to mean a regular commission. There was no indication as to when he could take the oath of office, after which he could be paid.

Out of money, he went back to Seattle during this period of limbo and visited Norm Hutchinson at the Olympic Garage. Eight years had passed since Boyington worked there, but Hutchinson and Al Abrahmson were still going strong. The crew was now made up of teenagers, since older boys were training or fighting in the war. Boyington said he needed a job.

"You don't mean it. You're kidding," responded Hutchinson, but Boyington assured his old boss he was broke, at least until his marine pay started. Hutchinson gave him a pair of overalls. Thus, while his country neared the end of its first full year of war, Boyington was parking cars for seventy-five cents an hour.

Another two weeks passed with no further word from Washington, so he bugged headquarters with another message. His appointment as a first lieutenant in the reserves came two days later along with correspondence from headquarters, stating that he would be "assigned to active duty in the near future." First, headquarters needed to know the earliest date he would be available. Inexplicably, Boyington's response was October 15, which delayed his pay for another month. He was sworn in as a first lieutenant on Tuesday, September 29, and orders were issued for him to proceed on October 15 to Pasco, Washington, for a final physical. Suddenly, his orders were canceled.

The delay might have been caused by an interoffice memorandum sent to Frank Knox's aide, Captain Beatty. Going through Boyington's service record, a staff member noted that Boyington's career had been dismal prior to his resignation in August 1941. "It is extremely doubtful," wrote the assistant, "that Boyington would have been temporarily promoted with his class in view of his military record."

Unable to draw pay until he reported for duty, Boyington became exasperated when weeks passed with no further word from Washington. He blamed the delay on an unnamed antagonist at headquarters, calling him "a renowned son of a bitch who attained his promotions by other than endangering his own life." On November 8, he peevishly cabled headquarters: "HAVE BEEN STANDING BY FOR FOUR MONTHS PATIENCE EXHAUSTED WOULD LIKE TO BE ENLIGHTENED IMMEDIATELY PLEASE."

Theatrical though it was, his telegram later evolved into a three-page letter, which he claimed was wired to "the assistant secretary of the navy." In his memoirs he explained, "Owing to the length of this night letter, I had consumed a fifth of bourbon while I was composing the masterpiece, so there was no pain in reading it off over the telephone to Western Union." No trace of such a letter exists. Almost certainly his one-line telegram of November 8 grew proportionally every time he told the story, like many of his anecdotes. He also claimed that his orders to active duty came within three days. That much was true: his orders were published November 10, just two days after his telegram, which means the original telegram got the desired response.

Headquarters ordered him to report for a follow-up physical on November 16, after which he was to continue to San

Diego for aviation duty. Upon arrival he would receive a temporary promotion to major. That was the best news he had heard in a long time, for it meant a significant increase in pay.

During his last days in Okanogan, Boyington sat for a studio photograph with "Bobby" and Janet Sue. They made a handsome trio, freshly scrubbed and neatly combed, but none of them smiled. Their expressions were wooden, as though they realized the picture would not be a true reflection of their family. The children had just gotten their heroic daddy back after a miserable year, and now he was leaving again. Janet, only four years old, had the most resigned look of all.

Boyington reported for his physical on the appointed date, then arrived at North Island seven days later. The trip did not require a week, implying that he visited Lucy in San Francisco along the way. At North Island he was assigned to Air Regulating Squadron 2, a sort of warehousing unit for Marine Corps pilots, where he received the promised promotion to major. Less than two weeks later he celebrated his thirtieth birthday, which happened to fall on a Friday night.

Lucy joined him in San Diego later that month and got more deeply involved in his legal affairs. The idea was to have her manage a portion of his income, with which she would pay off his remaining debts and take care of his children's needs—the same thing Joseph Wicks had been doing. The attorney didn't work for free, however, and Lucy evidently promised to do it out of the kindness of her heart. Furthermore, she was accustomed to handling money, she was beautiful, and she was sleeping with Boyington. No doubt he viewed the arrangement as a great bargain all the way around.

The financial picture had improved now that he was earning a major's income, with a monthly base pay and allowances totaling more than six hundred dollars. Boyington figured he could get by on two hundred a month. Three days before Christmas, he went to the San Diego County Courthouse and filed a petition to make Lucy the legal guardian of the two older children (they actually remained in the care of Grace and Ellsworth), then made out a new will naming Lucy as the beneficiary and executrix of his estate. Back at the base, he submitted an allotment form to have $420 deposited in a San Diego bank account every month. If he spent a year overseas, Lucy would receive more than enough to settle his debts and pay the monthly child support ordered by the courts. Amazingly, his name was not on the account, only Lucy's, who was under no legal obligation to spend the money on Boyington's debts or his children. She had risked nothing, whereas Boyington had just placed two thirds of his pay in the hands of a woman who was unfaithful to her husband, and whom he had known for only a few months.

Perhaps the tenets of common sense did not apply to a divorced man when he was about to leave dependent children during wartime. Whether his decision to put most of his pay in Lucy's care was bold or naïve, it was made by a man who said his own mother wasn't much good at handling money.

While he waited for an overseas assignment, there was little for Boyington to do in ARS-2. He had occasional duties, but otherwise was only required to report in from time to time that he was alive, after which he disappeared to horse around and party. There were many new faces—marine aviation had mushroomed since the beginning of the war—but a few familiar ones as well. Bob Galer, a veteran of the fighting at Guadalcanal with a Medal of Honor pending, currently had a staff job at North Island. John Condon, formerly with VMF-1 at Quantico, was getting ready to ship over to Guadalcanal as the operations officer of a new air group. Captain Stan Bailey, a fellow instructor from Pensacola, was also getting ready to sail to the South Pacific. A stoic Vermont native with a large brow and square jaw, Bailey was a former member of the Marine Corps's equestrian team and was known to carry a riding crop.

During one of his periodic duties as officer of the day, Boyington picked up where he left off with the Marine

Corps. He was supposed to be standing night duty at Miramar, an airfield several miles north of San Diego, when he wrecked a government vehicle down in the city. Like the old days, he phoned a friend for help.

"Were you hurt?" Bob Galer asked first.

"No," Boyington answered, "but my problem is, I'm the officer of the day at Miramar. I'm not supposed to be in San Diego; I'm not supposed to be driving an official vehicle in an unauthorized area."

Galer helped him get the vehicle back to Miramar, and the matter went away quietly. There was probably more tolerance in the corps than had existed in prewar days, especially for a combat-experienced fighter pilot. Boyington made it through the rest of his stay in San Diego without any other known mishaps.

In early January 1943, he received overseas movement orders to join a group of approximately twenty replacement pilots, and went aboard a converted liner carrying a marine raider battalion to New Caledonia. Without a squadron assignment, he could only hope to fill an available opening in a combat outfit. He would be obligated to serve three combat tours, each lasting about six weeks with a month or so between tours, before he could return to the States. Thus, as he bid good-bye to Lucy on January 7 and stepped onto the gangway of SS *Lurline,* he could reasonably expect that if he didn't die in combat, he might return to the States in as little as nine months. As it turned out, almost three years would pass before he set foot again on U.S. soil.

Lurline, former passenger liner and flagship of the Matson Line, had been converted into a fast transport capable of carrying many times her original passenger capacity. During the war she made numerous unescorted runs from the West Coast to the South Pacific and back, her sole defense being an effective one: speed. Comfort was not a consideration. Staterooms that had once accommodated two people in luxury had been gutted; tiers of bunks for a dozen or more men were now crammed into the same space. The ship still retained its civilian crew, however, and meals were good. "They had to practice to keep their proficiency up," recalled Condon. "The food was in cold storage, and we ate pretty well. It made me nervous, like they were filling me up to go to the slaughter."

True to form, Boyington provided his own entertainment by bringing aboard whiskey, telling people it was a gift, though his intention was to strain it through his own kidneys. One of the replacement pilots, twenty-one-year-old Henry Bourgeois of New Orleans, later recalled, "He'd brought a case of scotch that he was taking for his friend, a general. We weren't out at sea for a day when he said, 'Oh, God, I've gotta have a drink!' He started sampling the scotch, and by the time we reached New Caledonia it was all gone."

Whether he shared it or drank most of it himself, the scotch disappeared at the rate of almost a bottle a day, based on speedy *Lurline*'s two-week crossing of the Pacific. She docked on January 21 at Noumea, New Caledonia, the primary terminal for war matériel and personnel coming from the States. Upon arrival, Boyington was officially attached to Marine Air Group (MAG)-11, based 450 miles to the north on Espíritu Santo. Curiously, when the rest of the pilots continued their journey north, he remained stuck at New Caledonia for another week. He finally boarded USS *Henry T. Allen,* an aging transport that took another three days to steam along the New Hebrides chain before reaching the anchorage at Espíritu Santo. From there, the last few miles of the journey brought him to the Turtle Bay fighter strip on the southeast end of the island.

Justifiably labeled "one of the great bases of the Pacific," the island had been the sleepy tropical home of coffee and copra plantations until July 1942, when Seabees bulldozed a coconut grove and laid a fighter strip near a picturesque inlet, then followed that feat by building two bomber fields and a seaplane base. Turtle Bay was an all-marine airstrip, from which MAG-11 funneled aviators and aircraft to the combat area.

By the time Boyington arrived on February 1, the command area on the west shore was well developed, but the fighter strip still had a temporary, transient air about it. Pilots, staff, and enlisted men lived in tent cities among groves of deep, green grass and stately coconut palms. Appearances were deceivingly idyllic. The grass hid trash and heaps of rotted husks, a breeding ground for mosquitoes and flies, which in turn swarmed over the typical GI food in the mess tents. On the positive side, MAG-11's commanding officer was none other than "Sandy" Sanderson, the popular, fun-loving stunt pilot from the golden days of the air-show circuit. That he and Boyington were birds of a feather and did a bit of drinking off-duty is beyond question.

But Boyington was frustrated with his assignment as MAG-11's assistant operations officer, a ground job that gave him "the say of nothing." Considering his combat experience, the job was a gross underemployment. "All I did was count the planes when they went out for training flights, and count them again when they returned," he later wrote. At least he wasn't missing out on combat action, for the air war in the region had temporarily fizzled.

He encountered several acquaintances who earlier had endured the brutal conditions at Guadalcanal, including Joe Foss, "truly a gaunt specimen." Suffering from malaria and gastroenteritis, Foss was on the verge of collapse when he reached Turtle Bay, but had recently tied Eddie Rickenbacker's all-time American record of twenty-six victories. On his way back to the States when he crossed paths with Boyington, Foss would wear a Medal of Honor by the middle of May. Neither man could have guessed that by the end of the year, both of them would be sharing the same headlines.

At about the same time, another acquaintance from Pensacola arrived at Turtle Bay after a tour on Guadalcanal. Captain Pat Weiland had been temporarily transferred from his regular outfit, which flew the photoreconnaissance version of the Grumman Wildcat, to fly the fighter version, and had downed a Zero over New Georgia two days after Christmas. He was back at Turtle Bay as the operations officer of VMO-251 when Boyington dropped in to see him. "He had just checked in, and said it was good to renew old acquaintances," recalled Weiland. "He said, 'Hey, I need some flight time. You got an airplane I could fly?' I said, 'Sure. Let me look at my board. How 'bout old number seven here.'"

Boyington asked Weiland to give him a cockpit check, saying, "you'd better come out with me and refresh my memory a little bit." While he sat in the airplane, Weiland teased him, pointing to the stick, rudder pedals, and instruments common to any plane of the era. "I was really joking around with him," continued Weiland. "Well, he took off and flew it around for about two hours. Then I found out he'd never flown a Wildcat before."

Boyington's disappointment over his current assignment turned to envy when a fighter squadron arrived to finish its combat training with the new, technologically advanced Vought F4U-1 Corsair. Just to gawk at the new plane on the ground must have thrilled the aeronautical engineer in him. With its long, cylindrical cowling, enormous propeller, and unique inverted gull wing, the Corsair exuded speed and power. The fuselage had been designed to fit like a glove around the most powerful radial engine available, an eighteen-cylinder, two-thousand-horsepower Pratt & Whitney monster that gave the Corsair a legitimate top speed of more than four hundred miles per hour at sea level. The cowling was wrapped so tightly around the engine that no space existed for oil-cooler intakes, which were mounted instead at the forward edge of the wing roots. Because of their location and shape, the intakes emitted an eerie whistle during high-speed dives.

Meanwhile, the "months seemed to drag on" as other combat units staged through Turtle Bay on their way to the 'Canal. In reality, Boyington served less than six weeks in the operations department before wangling a spot in a fighter squadron, thanks to his association with Sandy Sanderson. The problem was, he didn't actually go anywhere. He was assigned as executive officer of VMF-122 on

March 11, but the squadron's flight echelon was in the midst of training and would remain at Turtle Bay throughout the spring of 1943.

Boyington could rejoice in the freedom of flying again after months of inactivity (VMF-122 was equipped with the venerable Wildcat), but it came at a price. Major Elmer Brackett Jr., tall and heavyset, was an odious commanding officer. Widely regarded as a martinet, he possessed a mean streak and few subordinates could tolerate him. As one put it, "He was always bitching and complaining. We stayed away from him as much as possible."

The squadron had arrived on Espíritu Santo the previous November with a typical complement of approximately 250 officers and men, but shortly thereafter the nonflying personnel were sent to Guadalcanal as an autonomous servicing unit. For Boyington and the rest of the flight echelon at Turtle Bay, there was little to look forward to except more training. The air war in the South Pacific had slowed dramatically after the battle for Guadalcanal, during which the Imperial Japanese Navy's 11th Air Fleet, based at Rabaul, had lost hundreds of aircraft and well over a thousand trained aviators. The lull lasted for weeks, and Boyington was frustrated to find himself on the fringes of activity again, far from any action. Henry Bourgeois, also assigned to the squadron, later recalled, "There was a lot of drinking going on, every night. I don't even remember him flying at that time. I'm sure he was getting some time in F4Fs, but I never flew with him there."

In early April, the Japanese launched two desperate air attacks against Guadalcanal and the nearby Russell Island group. Fighters and dive bombers from four Japanese carriers, augmenting the battered 11th Air Fleet, struck on April 1 and again six days later. The second attack, by a force of 177 planes, was the largest raid to date by the Japanese. Aichi D3A "Val" dive bombers sank a few ships, but marine fighter squadrons were credited with twenty-nine victories at the cost of several Wildcats. All of the marine pilots were recovered.

Setting the standard for generations of fighter pilots, Pappy Boyington epitomized the qualities that separate the quick from the dead: fearlessness, aggression, originality, tenacity, leadership—and a measure of blind luck. (Frank Walton collection)

Gregory with his mother in Coeur d'Alene, 1914. Grace was free spirited and racy as a teen, but her life had become complicated. She was 26 years old, with a lover in Spokane and a failing marriage to dentist Charles Boyington. (Granath collection)

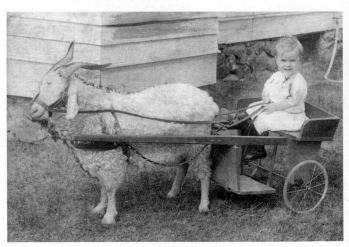

On the go before the age of two, Gregory posed in Coeur d'Alene—probably in the fall of 1914, a few months prior to his parents' divorce. He would not discover for 21 years that his real name was Boyington. (Keith Boyington collection)

Ellsworth Hallenbeck's seemingly pleasant demeanor was deceiving. Said one of his granddaughters: "I've heard stories of his life in Okanogan. He was not a nice man." (Granath collection)

"Deeds" in 1920. Growing up in St. Maries, Gregory not only acted like a pugnacious hellion, he looked like one. "It seemed to me like back in those days, even as a little kid, I was always in fights," he said. (Granath Collection)

Gregory (front row, fifth from left) was a member of the Finned "L" Club during his senior year at Lincoln High School in Tacoma. Life in the Hallenbeck home was as grim as Gregory's countenance. (Tacoma Public Library)

Gregory's senior portrait was altogether more flattering. Said his classmates of his swimming and wrestling prowess: "He can't be beat." (Tacoma Public Library)

Cadet Boyington's pinched expression made him appear older than his 23 years. He had reason to scowl, having recently learned of the Hallenbeck deception. Down-checks during flight training would soon cause greater concerns. (National Museum of Naval Aviation)

"Rats" with Janet and a neighborhood boy in Pensacola, early 1941. Gregory junior stands with the maid, whose 86-year-old mother posed for her first-ever photograph. Helene is at far right. Baby Gloria was probably napping. (Keith Boyington collection)

Boyington brandishes a revolver, perhaps the one he used occasionally to shoot out his barrack room light. Other pilots from the 1st Pursuit: (left to right) Croft, Burgard, Rossi, and Probst. Rosbert kneels in front. (Flying Tigers Association)

(left) Olga Greenlaw was never far from her Elizabeth Arden makeup case, even during a tire-changing stop. "I still can look fairly snappy when I make an effort," she wrote, "and I get along swimmingly with men I like." (Author's collection)

(right) Boyington during his brief combat tour as CO of VMF-122 at Guadalcanal in April 1943. He fought no enemy aircraft, but battled alcoholism and his own pilots instead. In late May, he broke his leg in a wrestling match. (USMC)

After acquiring command of VMF-214 in early September, Boyington talked tactics with several pilots at Turtle Bay. Left to right: Rinabarger, Boyington, Bourgeois, Begert, and Bailey. (National Archives)

Boyington's webbed parachute harness—with its heavy parachute, jungle pack, and inflatable raft—made for strenuous climbing. The Corsair's cockpit sill was eight feet off the ground. (Walton collection)

Boyington usually wore nondescript utility clothing, even while flying. On Turtle Bay's coral flight line, he reaches for a fastener on his Mae West while Moon Mullen looks on. (Walton collection)

Living in pyramidal tents was not unlike the logging camps where Boyington spent summers as a boy. In the fall of '43, he made a vain attempt to combat the slovenly conditions at Munda, New Georgia. (Walton collection)

Fighting was a way of life for Boyington. His baleful glare spelled trouble for wrestling opponents and enemy pilots alike. (USMC)

In a rare appearance in regulation uniform, complete with garrison cap, Boyington partied with his second-tour pilots at Turtle Bay, November 1943. Days later he was placed under house arrest by Col. Joe Smoak. (Walton collection)

Artists love to depict this F4U as Boyington's "personal" combat plane, but *Lucybelle* was doctored only briefly for publicity at Turtle Bay on November 26, 1943, hundreds of miles from the forward area. Note backwards victory flags. (Walton collection)

Wearing a derby passed around at parties, Boyington enthusiastically belts out a drinking song with the Black Sheep at Vella Lavella, Christmas Eve, 1943. He was on day two of a four-day binge. (Walton collection)

Suffering a severe hangover during his next fighter sweep, Boyington managed to down a Zeke on December 27 to bring his total to twenty-five victories. He wanly acknowledged the kill immediately after the mission. (National Archives)

Later that afternoon he posed with the first-tour veterans in one of the best-known squadron photographs of World War II. Six current aces held bats: (left to right) Magee, McClurg, Mullen, Boyington, Bolt, Fisher. (USMC)

Also on the same day, Boyington and "Wild Man" Magee (note bandana) did their part for public relations by staging an exchange of victory stickers for ball caps. (USMC)

Judging by these expressions, Boyington wasn't the only intoxicated Black Sheep on New Year's Eve. He made limeade with the medicinal brandy kept by derby-wearing Doc Reames. (Walton collection)

A day or two before being shot down, a puffy but uninhibited Boyington breakfasted in the makeshift mess tent at Torokina airstrip, Bougainville. (National Archives)

Ecstatic former POWs cheer the relief force approaching Omori prison in Tokyo Bay, August 29, 1945, two weeks after Japan capitulated. Flags of U.S., Great Britain, and Holland were made from sheets. (National archives)

Plump compared to other ex-POWs when he greeted Cmdr. Harold Stassen, former governor of Minnesota, on August 29, Boyington passed a flight physical within days of his release. (National Archives)

After landing at NAS Alameda on September 12, 1945, Boyington was hoisted to the shoulders of his jubilant Black Sheep: (left to right) Magee, Bragdon, Reames, Matheson. Sims is visible over Matheson's shoulder. (Walton collection)

Wearing his newly bestowed Medal of Honor, Boyington receives a firm handshake from President Harry Truman, October 5, 1945. The military's highest award for valor brought more trouble for Boyington than rewards. (National Archives)

In the fall of 1945, "Pappy" appeared at a football game with his lover, Mrs. Lucy Malcolmson, and his friend, Maj. Frank Walton. His relationship with both ended badly within months. (Walton collection)

After jilting Lucy Malcolmson, he married the former Frances Baker on January 8, 1946. They posed the next day in the Los Angeles home of Boyington's attorney. (Associated Press, courtesy of Bob Butler)

Although Pappy tipped the scales at 200 pounds, he was dwarfed by heavyweight boxers at Camp Pendleton in April 1951. Often "half blind from vodka" as a referee, he appeared to be well on his way this night. (National Archives)

Pappy and his third wife, actress Dolores "Dee" Tatum, posed at Keith Boyington's home in 1962 with their poodle, Clicquiot. They separated in 1970 and divorced three years later. (Keith Boyington collection)

The old and the new. During a business trip to Da Nang in 1965, Boyington enjoyed an overnight visit with a younger generation of Black Sheep, who flew attack jets with VMA-214 at Chu Lai, South Vietnam. (National Archives)

Robert Conrad, aka "Black Sheep Two," on the set at Indian Dunes with "Black Sheep One." No other fighter pilot in U.S. history has been the true-life main character of an action-adventure television series. (Courtesy of John Schafhausen)

Pappy and his fourth wife wait for the start of a Kodak hula show in Hawaii, November 1976. A recovering alcoholic, Josephine died of respiratory failure four years after Boyington's death. She was just 64. (Walton collection)

Pappy was only 63 when this was taken in Honolulu during the first Black Sheep reunion. "His deeply lined face," wrote Frank Walton, "showed every mile of the torturous road he'd traveled over the years." (Walton collection)

Just three days after the second attack, Boyington and two dozen others ferried replacement Wildcats up to the scene of the action. They landed at a strip known as Fighter Two and turned their planes over to VMF-221, which had scored the highest number of kills during the attack but also lost seven airplanes.* Others were severely damaged. As 1st Lt. Warner Chapman put it: "We were knocked out of the air regarding airplanes; we had only four still flying the next morning."

After delivering the Wildcats, Boyington and the other ferry pilots remained for a short tour of duty. He stayed briefly at the transient quarters ("the famous Hotel De Gink, a real rat hole"), before moving into a tent city near the Lunga River. Having experienced Burma, the oppressive humidity was nothing new to him, but the living conditions and sanitary facilities at Guadalcanal were primitive, and the food was not much better.

Boyington abruptly became commanding officer on April 19 when Elmer Brackett was reassigned for murky reasons—though one pilot said he "gave up the squadron." Overnight, Boyington became a commodity. Noting that he was a former Flying Tiger, combat correspondents sent the story of his AVG service to several newspapers, the pitch being that he was "back in harness" with his beloved Marine Corps, ready to resume the fight. They cast him as "a popular figure" with his pilots (who were only too glad to be rid of the tyrannical Brackett), explaining that as a Flying Tiger, Boyington had "shot down six enemy I-97s and destroyed more than thirty on the ground."

There, for the first time in print, were the six aerial victories that would become so important to Boyington's place in aviation history. The fact that he claimed six makes sense, even though it was a lie that he had shot them all down. In reality, he had received credit for two aerial victories from

---

* One pilot, 1st Lt. James Swett, shot down seven Vals and probably an eighth in a span of minutes before ditching his F4F. He later received a Medal of Honor.

the AVG, and the details of his service show that he did not down more.

His rationale for claiming six was the raid on Chiang Mai. Arguably, he should have earned 3.75 credits for his effort (based on the agreed-upon total of fifteen destroyed planes shared by the four shooters) and thus should have been paid for a grand total of 5.75 aircraft. For him, rounding the total up to the next whole number was no big deal, but there was one important problem. When considering individual victory credits, the U.S. naval air services have never recognized aircraft destroyed on the ground. Boyington's *aerial* record as a Flying Tiger was two victories (which should be considered valid regardless of actual Japanese losses), yet he inflated his record, no doubt rationalizing that he had been robbed by Jim Howard's review board. Lying came so easily to him that he once proclaimed, "I'm a psychopathic liar," though he meant to say *pathologic* regarding his compulsive behavior. Either way, as the new commanding officer of VMF-122, he gave his aerial record a head start.

For the next week, Boyington experienced only quiet routine at Guadalcanal. Nothing of note happened during his few flights, most of which involved defensive patrols around Guadalcanal and over the Russells. He participated in some strikes against two Japanese fields—Munda on New Georgia and Vila on the nearby island of Kolombangara—escorting Douglas SBD or Grumman TBF dive bombers, but he "never saw so much as the vapor trail of a single Japanese plane."

According to the memoirs of Hunter Reinburg, a captain in VMF-122 at the time, Boyington spent much of his free time drinking. Familiar with his legendary binges in the prewar days, Reinburg wrote: "Greg had not changed because I never saw him sober as CO of VMF-122 and I was continually flabbergasted how he could fly so well. As the squadron's operations officer, I was responsible for mission assignments. Greg liked my work and gave me a free hand, telling me to just let him know when he was on the schedule. Greg never missed a mission assigned to him thanks mostly to the fact that his plane captain literally 'poured' him in the Wildcat's cockpit."

As an alcoholic in an area where liquor was in short supply, Boyington applied any means necessary to acquire it. "He came up to me one night when it was just about time to go to bed," recalled pilot Herb Long. "I was the only one in the squadron that had any whiskey left—two or three bottles—and he told me that he'd just met a Seabee down at the beach who had a Japanese officer's jeweled sword. He told me the Seabee wanted three or four bottles of whiskey for it. You don't say no to your boss, so I gave him what I had. Well, I have never seen any sword, or any jewels, or anything else. Didn't see much of him either."

VMF-122's combat tour on Guadalcanal was probably the shortest on record, lasting just sixteen days. The flight echelon returned to the relative comfort of Turtle Bay, then received a real gift. As Boyington described it, "There had been some doubt as to whether our squadron would be sent on the usual 'week's rest and recreation,' as it was termed, for we had had only a very brief, no-action tour in the combat zone. However, we managed to luck out, and away we went."

By "usual," he referred to Sydney, Australia, where squadrons were sent for a week between combat tours to unwind. In a cultural atmosphere that closely resembled a cosmopolitan American city, the pilots could drink, dance, and find a young woman to help them pass the time. If London was the mecca for Yanks on liberty in England, Sydney served the same function during the Pacific war with one important difference. Londoners were stereotyped as resentful that the Yanks were "overpaid, oversexed, and over here," but the Australians were friendly, giving credit to Uncle Sam for saving them from the Japanese. Americans were welcomed with open arms, which in turn encouraged the visitors to open their wallets.

Normally a squadron had to complete a six-week combat tour to be eligible for a trip to Sydney, but as Boyington noted, VMF-122 lucked out. After passing a rudimentary health screening, the pilots climbed aboard a South Pacific Combat Air Transport Command (SCAT) plane on April 30 for the flight from Espíritu Santo to Tontouta, New Caledonia. The next leg spanned more than twelve hundred miles of ocean, this time in a transport dangerously overloaded with additional fuel tanks in the cabin. After a cold, nerve-wracking flight through the middle of the night, the Douglas R4D reached Mascot Airport outside Sydney at dawn on the chilly morning of May 2.

In his memoirs, Boyington described the standard routine that pilots usually followed upon arrival. After living in the tropics for months they were slovenly, even by civilian standards, and their best-kept uniforms were mildewed. No one felt or looked decent enough to go downtown, so their typical first stop was the Red Cross hostel at Kings Cross. There, they enjoyed hot showers while the hostel staff cleaned and pressed their uniforms. After getting slicked up, their next stop was the Royal Australian Hotel, either to register for rooms or just to ogle the girls.

Boyington disappeared almost immediately, recalled Herb Long. "I was right behind him when he registered. He had a winter flight suit on, and I think he traded it for whiskey. Anyway, as he was walking up to the registration desk, some cute little gal latched on to him, then another one came up and grabbed his other arm, and they walked up to the registration desk with him. He said, 'What's your name, honey?' That's the last I saw of him for several days."

The hotel lobby had a large mahogany bar where drinks were served for an hour in the afternoon. The marines were well prepared. When the bar opened at 4:30, they lined up at a section where a big-bosomed blonde named Freda took their orders. "When Freda poured a marine a drink, she poured a marine a *drink*," Hank Bourgeois reminisced. "You could go in there and order all your drinks and she'd fill up the glasses, and when the bell rang, everybody would grab four or five drinks and gulp them down."

The lobby itself was dubbed the "snake pit." With

Australia's young men off to fight elsewhere for the Crown, the sheer number of available women was astounding. They were supposed to be at least eighteen years old to gain entry to the lobby, but not all were of legal age. "This one girl looked a hell of a lot younger than eighteen, but we spent the night," recalled Bourgeois. "In the morning, she confessed that she'd borrowed her sister's identification card, and she was only fifteen."

Forewarned of the perils, the pilots settled into a pleasurable routine, downing drinks at happy hour, picking up dates, then heading to a nearby nightclub for dinner. They favored Prince's, the only club that served drinks after regular bar hours. During the day there was plenty of sightseeing. Most took taxis to the Royal Australian Air Force supply depot, where they drew fleece-lined gloves and boots. (They were ridiculously hot in the tropics but comfortable during long hours of high-altitude flying: it was damn cold at twenty thousand feet.) In the late afternoon, the marines headed back to the hotel lobby to start the routine all over again.

After a week of such living, they were more run-down than before. Fortunately, when they departed Sydney and flew back to Turtle Bay, they did not have to rush into another combat tour. VMF-122, scheduled to transition to Corsairs, was the fourth squadron currently in line for the new fighters, so Boyington and his pilots were sent back down to Tontouta for a week, both to ease congestion at Espíritu Santo and to ferry aircraft.

While on New Caledonia, Boyington ran across Norm Anderson, one of his friends from the weekend party house in Pensacola when they were cadets. Now a major, Anderson took him to the officers' club one night and introduced him to "Doc" Whitaker, an intercollegiate wrestling champion from the Big Ten conference. "They naturally began wrestling each other," recalled Anderson. "You could hear them out in the bulrushes, wrestling away and having a whooping time, almost so loudly that it was difficult to sleep." Commenting on the same wrestling match in his memoirs, Hunter Reinburg recalled that the grapplers tumbled down a slope. "At the bottom, the two declared the match a draw and returned to the bar for more drinking. Then, however, the two officers were very much 'out of uniform' because their clothes were considerably ripped, exposing many superficial coral cuts."

The rest period ended during the last week of May, when VMF-122 returned to Turtle Bay for familiarization with the F4U. The transition from the boxy, mild-mannered Grumman into the beastly Corsair was a daunting one. More than a few pilots were hesitant during their initial checkout, and for good reason. Everything about the plane seemed enormous, beginning with the size of its cockpit. There was no floor, only two metal channels for the pilot's heels, with a black chasm down below. The cowling seemed endless, stretching fourteen feet from the pilot to the propeller, behind which lurked the incredible power of the "Double Wasp" engine. Pilots were also wary of the F4U-1's reputation for unforgiving aerodynamic tendencies, which had caused more than a few fatal crashes during the early history of the fighter. The worst flaw was the Corsair's habit of stalling without warning if a pilot got too slow while trying to land.

No doubt some of Boyington's pilots sweated through their first flights, but he had the experience and the engineering background to handle the plane with kid gloves. Praising the Corsair as "a sweet-flying baby if I ever flew one," he strapped into a fighter with the performance and firepower to maximize his natural skills. Tony Eisele, then a first lieutenant, characterized Boyington as an outstanding, naturally aggressive pilot. "When I flew with him it was never a simple formation flight but a series of tail chases with loops, rolls, and dogfights," he later wrote. "I would land covered with sweat after a real workout."

By late May, it appeared that VMF-122 would be ready to participate in the next phase of the island-hopping campaign in the Solomons. The invasion of New Georgia, scheduled to commence in barely a month, would require an umbrella of Allied fighters to contend with the swarms of Japanese aircraft that were sure to come from Bougainville, home to at least five airfields. VMF-122 was prepared to serve a major role in what was sure to be an intense air battle, but for Boyington, the Fates stepped in again to alter the plan.

As he later told the story, he was summarily relieved of his command in late May "by a superior officer who did not approve of the ways I and my pilots had chosen to unwind." This was none other than Lt. Col. Joe Smoak, the MAG-11 operations officer, who had given Boyington such an unpleasant time in Pensacola. Since coming to the South Pacific, he had been involved only in nonflying jobs and was the acting commander of the air group (Sandy Sanderson had detached in early March).

Opinions about Smoak differed. A few officers at the higher ranks respected his viewpoint, but subordinates considered him a bully. Pilots who came to Turtle Bay to recover from fatigue and stress after a combat tour, wanting only to restore their energy, instead faced Smoak's frequent admonishments about keeping their tents clean and using mosquito netting. Irascible and unsociable, he used the Articles for Governing the Navy and the Marine Corps Manual to enforce discipline. Because he was Boyington's polar opposite, conflict between them was inevitable.

Immediately after Smoak stripped him of his command on May 29, a livid Boyington encountered three Corsair pilots coming back from the Turtle Bay skeet range. Captain Bruce Porter and his friends, members of another squadron, urged Boyington to visit Brig. Gen. "Nuts" Moore, now chief of staff of the 1st Marine Aircraft Wing. They decided to help by giving him a ride to the general's quarters on the other side of the island.

After driving through a downpour, they dropped Boyington off at the general's door, then continued to the officers' club. They were still there when Boyington appeared later, already feeling no pain after celebrating his reinstatement as VMF-122's commander with the general's private stock.

According to Porter, Boyington downed another drink with his new friends, then hurled his shot glass at the club's imported mirror and ran out to the jeep with a pilfered bottle. The foursome continued to drink as they drove through the mud back to Turtle Bay, where Boyington joined his own pilots at the little club built from plywood Dallas huts.

The rainy Saturday turned into one of those wild nights, the kind where fights seem to flare up spontaneously from too much booze. At least three occurred that night, remembered Herb Long. In the first, a pilot broke a bone in his hand when he punched another pilot on the chin; then came another fight, its details eventually obscured because of the main event. This took place when Boyington reached his saturation point, got in an aggressive stance, and hollered his usual challenge, "Who wants to wrestle?"

Maybe he had postured once too often, or had prodded a little too hard. Ed Shiflett, a normally soft-spoken lieutenant, got up and answered, "I'm tired of this. I'll take you on."

It was past midnight when big Ed, "Double E" to his friends, squared with Boyington while the rest of the pilots cleared a space in the center of the small club. Shiflett was no patsy. A former college wrestler, probably familiar with Boyington's moves, he simply had not been compelled to take on his drunk skipper before. This was Boyington's undoing. Shiflett turned inside Boyington, grabbed him with both hands, and threw him. Somehow Boyington went through the door and ended up in the mud; perhaps they both did. Onlookers heard a bone snap with a sound like a dry stick, an apt description of the long, narrow fibula on Boyington's lower left leg.

A corpsman was summoned from the aid station about a hundred yards away, but little could be done that night. Ice was applied to the swelling, and according to some accounts, Boyington hobbled back to the club for more drinks. In the morning he went to the MAG-11 field hospital for a more thorough evaluation. An X ray revealed a simple fracture just above the distal end of the bone, near the knob on the outside of his ankle. Boyington wouldn't be going anywhere for a while.

As part of the evaluation, the navy doctor had to determine how the injury had occurred. Self-inflicted wounds, for example, were given special consideration. Luckily for Boyington, the doc was understanding. Instead of writing that Boyington had been hurt in a drunken brawl, he described the event as "athletics." The doctor applied a cast to Boyington's broken leg, but that didn't slow him down. As Joe Foss heard it: "[A] couple days later when the doctor came into the O'Club, there was old Rats with the cast off . . . jumping around on one leg. The doc got so mad that he was ready to kill him. So he said, 'I'll put a cast on that will take a blacksmith to remove.'"

Sure enough, a second cast was applied on June 9. Boyington was transferred to Lion One, a bigger hospital near the bomber strip, with the doctor's recommendation that he "be sent to a more temperate climate for convalescence, inasmuch as he has been in tropical duty for five months."

Two weeks after breaking his leg, Boyington was put aboard the hospital ship USS *Rixey,* which took him far from the combat area to Auckland, New Zealand.

It stood to reason that Boyington would encounter bad luck just before his squadron went into action against the Japanese. Collectively, VMF-122 had scored all of five victories before he joined, but the invasion of New Georgia brought a dramatic shift in the unit's fortune, if not his own. As a prelude, "Double E" Shiflett started the scoring with a lone Zero near Guadalcanal on June 16, when the Japanese sent their last massed attack against the island. Two weeks later, at the start of the New Georgia landings, the squadron bore the brunt of the Japanese retaliation. Over the next eighteen days, VMF-122's pilots racked up forty-two victories and several probables. There were losses, of course. Hunter Reinburg was recovered after being shot down on June 30; two other pilots were not. A couple more went down during the next two weeks and were never found, but despite the losses, the squadron scored a ten-to-one advantage over the Japanese.

Sitting in a hospital with his leg in a cast, Boyington foresaw little hope for improvement in his personal future. He realized that he might not receive medical clearance to fly again, in which case he would never restore his reputation with the Marine Corps or settle his score with Claire Chennault. Greatly discouraged, he figured he had just screwed up his last opportunity to lead a squadron in combat.

13

Boyington's Bastards

While Boyington fretted over the bad luck that had plagued him for years, he simultaneously discovered that Auckland wasn't a terribly difficult place in which to endure a month's recovery. Better off than most patients on the physical therapy ward at Naval Mobile Hospital Number 4, he became adept at getting around on crutches, and learned to hobble down the road to the nearest watering hole. Getting back to the hospital drunk and on crutches proved a different story. Tony Eisele, sent down to MOB-4 to recover from malaria, supported Boyington during the hike back, "once with a broken cast on his leg after another friendly brawl." When he was required to be in the hospital, Boyington occupied his time with poker games; when he could get away, he dallied with a divorcée named Carrie, "a truly fine woman" who made his stay "worthwhile."

On Independence Day, appropriately enough, his cast came off and was replaced with a heavy bandage for support. After two more weeks of physical therapy he could put full weight on his ankle, so the hospital discharged him. He flew to New Caledonia, got his orders straightened out, then hooked up with SCAT for a ride to Turtle Bay.

The flight aboard the transport led to another stay in a hospital. Fast asleep when the R4D began a rapid descent to land at Espíritu Santo on July 25, Boyington awoke in pain, unable to equalize his right ear fast enough to offset the sudden pressure change. It was aching when he reported to MAG-11 upon arrival, where his day took another turn for the worse. Smoak was now in command of the air group.

Boyington was in too much pain to fuss. His sinusitis developed into a full-blown tropical cold, then his ear became infected, and he was admitted to the field hospital at Turtle Bay for three days of bed rest. By the time he was discharged on the last day of July, he had nothing to show for six months in the South Pacific except a sore ankle. He was also out three hundred dollars thanks to Smoak.

There could be no doubt that Smoak had been furious over Boyington's visit to "Nuts" Moore on the night of May 29; that sort of subterfuge was intolerable to his type. Conveniently, Boyington had punished himself by breaking his leg, but Smoak managed to add insult to injury. Ever mindful of the regulations, he suspended Boyington's flight status as soon as he was medically grounded, thereby cutting his pay by $150 per month.

Ironically, Boyington was given command of another squadron upon his return to duty, which must have come as a surprise, though it turned out to be a squadron in name only. Furthermore, his duties required nothing more than shuffling papers, which he dreaded. He was stuck on the ground until he could pass a flight physical. "I could not beg or steal my way into an active squadron or get flying of any kind," he wrote fifteen years later. "Sometimes I believed I was so hard up I would have even jumped at a chance to fly dive bombers."

His "new" squadron, VMF-112, had been overseas for nine months and was due to rotate back to the States as soon as the veteran pilots, currently enjoying R & R in Sydney, returned to Turtle Bay. During their absence, the roster had been padded with several replacement pilots from other squadrons, along with about twenty new arrivals from the States. Together, they formed the squadron's rear echelon, currently a holding unit for fighter pilots awaiting assignment to active units. Corsairs were available, which kept the new replacements busy as they logged their first hours in the new fighters, while the experienced pilots flew a regular schedule of proficiency training.

Several of the veterans—Stan Bailey and Hank Bourgeois among them—had seen significant action that summer. Boyington's former squadron, VMF-122, had been deactivated and returned to the States, but not before the replacement pilots who had come with him aboard *Lurline* had participated in the heavy fighting over New Georgia. That had been their second combat tour, meaning that as individuals they each had to complete one more six-week tour with another squadron. Thus, they were transferred into VMF-112 to await new assignments. Hearing of their recent combat experiences made Boyington all the more anxious to pass his flight physical and join an active squadron, but nothing was available.

He finally received a physical from navy lieutenant Jim Reames, a twenty-six-year-old flight surgeon who had spent much of the past eight months doctoring wounded aboard hospital planes. A good-natured Arkansas native, he had soloed at Pensacola as part of his training syllabus, and was eager to work with fighter pilots for a change. He got off on the right foot with Boyington by pronouncing him fit to fly on August 4, despite the fact that the ankle remained weak and swollen.

Now that Boyington could resume flying, Joe Smoak was forced to revoke his flight suspension. By halting Boyington's flight pay for two months, a spiteful gesture at best, Smoak had managed to save the government a few hundred dollars, but he generated a small mountain of paperwork that required the attention of clerks all the way to Washington.

If Smoak considered it a form of punishment to place Boyington in charge of VMF-112's rear echelon, knowing his duties would be limited to paperwork, the idea backfired. It was all a matter of timing. Smoak had no control over the fact that four of the eight squadrons equipped with Corsairs had finished or were about to finish their combat obligations. VMF-122 had already departed for the States, VMF-112 was about to follow, and two others would go home by

September. Conversely, only two new operational squadrons were scheduled to arrive during the same period. The coconut grove encampments at Turtle Bay were crowded with replacement pilots, but there was a distinct shortage of cohesive squadrons.

This created a dilemma for Adm. William "Bull" Halsey's island-hopping campaign in the Solomons. The Corsair had quickly established itself as the premier U.S. fighter in the South Pacific, and was steadily improving its kill ratio over the best in the IJN inventory—the fast, nimble Mitsubishi A6M Zero. It could be argued that Halsey's success depended on the big fighters, for without effective escorts, the navy and marine dive bombers and army level bombers could not batter Japanese strongholds. The same could be said for air cover over the invasion forces. The Corsair squadrons, capable of moving ahead with each leapfrogging advance, were well adapted to operating from hastily prepared fields. The navy still used obsolescent F4F Wildcats until the F6F Hellcat made its combat debut, and could not fill the gap when Corsair squadrons departed. The army's best fighter in the theater, the Lockheed P-38 Lightning, while a good high-altitude fighter, could not hold a candle to the Corsair as a dogfighter or a bomber escort.

The shortage of Corsair squadrons had come at an inopportune time for Halsey, who decided to conserve his assets by leapfrogging the island of Kolombangara, cutting off ten thousand Japanese troops based there, and grab instead the lightly defended island of Vella Lavella. Navy construction battalions, the venerable Seabees, bulldozed an airstrip adjacent to the beachhead, from which more aircraft could be launched against the big island of Bougainville.

Naturally, the Japanese strongly opposed Halsey's effort to capture the island near their last, biggest stronghold in the Solomons. The amphibious landings at Vella Lavella on August 15 precipitated another huge aerial slugfest that lasted for weeks. The beachhead, called Barakoma, was located just ninety miles from Kahili, the main Japanese airdrome on Bougainville. Defending against heavy Japanese attacks almost daily, Corsair losses were significant, though pilots were regularly rescued.

Fighter Command at Guadalcanal was fully aware of the need for additional Corsair squadrons. The problem was where to get them. Squadrons were being vigorously trained in the States, but only two were currently en route to the South Pacific, and it would be weeks before they were fully ready for combat. The logical solution, which had the advantage of being more immediate, was to create a squadron using readily available components. There were plenty of Corsairs—a service squadron was kept busy cleaning the protective Cosmoline off newly received fighters—and plenty of replacement pilots eager to fly them.

That last qualification applied particularly to Boyington, who had been clamoring for an active squadron. Though he had a reputation for trouble, he was a top-notch pilot with combat experience, and was overdue for a chance to prove himself. The timing was perfect. When VMF-112 detached for the States in mid-August, he and the other replacement pilots scuttled like so many hermit crabs to another squadron, VMF-124. Renowned as the squadron that had flown the first Corsairs in combat, its forward echelon was about to complete its last tour in the combat area. Once again, Boyington was temporarily in charge of the rear element with its hodgepodge of pilots at Turtle Bay, but this time the arrangement turned out differently. Shortly after his arrival at VMF-124, Boyington was given authority to train his group of pilots for combat.

Although he took credit for conceiving the plan and running it past his superiors, the idea most likely came from the top down rather than the bottom up. Someone higher up the chain of command, such as Brigadier General Moore, would have recommended Boyington as the right man to lead such an ad hoc squadron. Moore liked Boyington's offbeat style, was widely reputed to be a drinking general, and, as the assistant commanding general of the 1st MAW, had the authority to put the concept into practice. Not to be overlooked, Moore's immediate boss was Maj. Gen. Ralph Mitchell, who just a year earlier had recommended Boyington for reappointment to the Marine Corps. Now that he was only a few miles away on the other side of Espíritu Santo, he was well positioned to see his recommendation pay off.

Regardless of who originated the idea, the process happened informally, with no official documentation to tell how the plan became a reality. Results were the only thing that mattered, and as it turned out, the results were legendary.

The new rear echelon of VMF-124 was an amalgam of newcomers from the States and veterans from an alphabet soup of disbanded units. Boyington knew many of the latter, having sailed overseas, flown, and shared liberty with them. Theirs was the kind of camaraderie that is not soon forgotten. Of the eight pilots from VMF-122, his first squadron, three had matched or exceeded his own aerial record—considering his true score with the AVG. Stan Bailey had downed two G4M Bettys over Rendova, Hank Bourgeois claimed a bomber and a fighter, and lanky Robert Ewing had three kills. Four other lieutenants also had victories: Paul "Moon" Mullen downed one Zero and shared in the destruction of another, while John Begert, Sandy Sims, and Bill Case claimed one victory each. The eighth pilot originally from VMF-122, 2d Lt. Virgil Ray, was a former NAP with no victories to his credit. He had combat experience, though, having miraculously crash-landed his smoking, shot-up Corsair after a harrowing battle in July.

A ninth veteran had more victories than any of them—a total of four—but had arrived by a different route. During combat tours with VMO-251 and VMF-121, 1st Lt. Allan McCartney had flamed three Zeros and claimed a "smoker," later upgraded to a full credit. As for ending up with Boyington he said, "I just showed up one day with orders to join the unit. I think it was all verbal."

The rest of the group consisted of replacements who had shipped overseas during the summer, bringing a wide variety of experience levels. Second Lieutenant Bob McClurg had been at Turtle Bay the longest without a combat tour, mainly because he slid through the training command with very little fighter experience. Originally assigned to VMF-214 upon his arrival in June, he struggled with the Corsair on takeoffs and landings. In July, he cracked up a fighter in a ground loop, so a more experienced pilot took his place. McClurg was sent back to the pilot pool to practice.

At the opposite end of the scale, first lieutenants Chris Magee, William "Junior" Heier, and Don "D. J." Moore had trained with the Royal Canadian Air Force before they were recruited back into U.S. service. John Bolt, Ed Olander, and Rollie Rinabarger had gained hundreds of valuable flight hours as instructors in Florida, and Capt. George Ashmun had instructed in California. They were joined by nine more first lieutenants—Bob Alexander, Bob Bragdon, Tom Emrich, Don Fisher, Denmark Groover, Walter "Red" Harris, Ed Harper, Jim Hill, and Burney Tucker—plus 2d Lt. Bruce Matheson. The newcomers had arrived in the South Pacific with no Corsair experience, yet in just a few weeks they would go into combat.

Boyington did nothing particularly demonstrative to establish a leadership style on the ground. "We weren't real impressed with him when we met him," recalled Fisher, then twenty-one years old. "He was just in the pool with us."

Boyington was indeed unimpressive. He rarely bothered with a regulation uniform, preferring utility dungarees and a comfortable shirt with the sleeves rolled up; likewise he shunned collar devices and other displays of rank. Uniforms (or at least paying for them) had caused him nothing but trouble in the past. Now that Lucy Malcolmson was receiving most of his income, he owned a meager wardrobe of nondescript clothing.

It was in the cockpit that Boyington came alive. From the very beginning he showed the newcomers that he was aggressive and highly skilled, a pilot who would lead by example. Fisher learned quickly not to misjudge him. One of the largest pilots in the group, "Mo" (he could acquire mo' of this and mo' of that than anyone) had been flying since he was a teenager. He also loved to compete. "I'll tell you what, Major, I'll shoot you for a case of beer," he said to Boyington before their first gunnery hop together.

"You're covered, son," Boyington answered, probably licking his lips in anticipation.

In the air, Fisher radioed to ask what the routine would be. "We'll just do a little bit of everything," Boyington said through his throat mike. "You follow me."

Just as Tony Eisele had experienced in VMF-122, Fisher tried to hang on while Boyington threw his Corsair into a series of loops and corkscrews around the target sleeve. Fisher's bullets, tipped with blue paint, left a dozen or so holes; he felt good about his score. "But, hell," he said of Boyington's colored slugs, "that sleeve was red. I never saw so many holes in a sleeve in my whole life. He sold me right then and there."

Boyington and Bailey, who would be his executive officer, worked the squadron hard. They flew section and division tactics, strafing runs, high-altitude familiarization on oxygen, escort and intercept problems, even a coordinated defense against an "attacking" squadron of dive bombers. Individuals flew twice a day, sometimes more. During August alone the rookies logged thirty to forty hours in Corsairs to build flight time; veterans required somewhat less.

Boyington, with his disregard for protocol and ground duties, and Bailey, with his scrupulous approach to organization, made an effective team. Having instructed together in Pensacola, both knew how to gauge pilots, saw where each would fit according to strengths or weaknesses. The choices for division leaders were easy. "Boyington and Bailey took all the experienced pilots," recalled John Begert, "and said, 'All right, now you're going to be a division leader, and here are the people that will fly with you, and it's your responsibility to make sure they're combat trained.'"

As the month of August drew to a close, Boyington and his pilots maintained a steady pace of training. Because the original squadron would become inactive as soon as the combat element concluded its current tour, a new VMF control number would become necessary for administration.

The suggested remedy was to take another squadron's number when its combat echelon came to Turtle Bay for R & R, an idea that was approved somewhere up the chain of command. The next squadron scheduled to finish a combat tour was VMF-214, still in action up at Munda, New Georgia.

Known as the Swashbucklers (the name was unofficial), the pilots of VMF-214 had begun their second combat tour on July 21. By the time they reached Munda during the last half of August, their commanding officer had been killed and another pilot was missing. In the next two weeks the rest of the pilots were practically used up, with another pilot gone and several others grounded by disease. Those that could still fly were emotionally and physically exhausted. In addition to the horrible living conditions on New Georgia, Japanese bombers harassed Munda nightly; during the day, Japanese artillery lobbed shells from the nearby hills. The squadron claimed twenty victories during the tour, but morale was low, mostly due to the pilots' disrespect for their inept interim commander. They hung on until the end of the month, but were ready for a much-needed rest.

Everything came together during the first week of September. The tired Swashbucklers were relieved on schedule and reached Turtle Bay on September 3, followed by the forward echelon of VMF-124 two days later. Between them, some fifty additional pilots crowded into the already-bulging encampments. Boyington's group, belonging still to VMF-124, mingled with the veterans from the original squadron. Among them were Boyington's old cadet friend Bill Millington, now the commanding officer, and Ken Walsh, who scored twenty victories to become the first Corsair pilot awarded a Medal of Honor.

Settling into a separate camp, the Swashbucklers heard immediately about the pending use of their number by Boyington's group. "Choice scuttlebutt of breaking up the squadron," someone penned in the unit's war diary. "Actual fact, too, but heavy pressures will be brought to bear." The "pressure" fizzled, however, amounting to a visit with Joe Smoak at his MAG-11 headquarters, where the two senior pilots in VMF-214 lodged a protest. Smoak had no control over the situation.

Boyington's pilots continued training for a few days, but all flying stopped when VMF-124 was deactivated and left for the States on September 7. Consequently, the rumor the Swashbucklers had worried about came true. Majors Boyington and Bailey, along with two captains, twenty-two first lieutenants, and two second lieutenants, were administratively transferred to VMF-214. The squadron had no assigned aircraft, hence the flight training was put on hold.

Later that afternoon, a ground officer from the 1st MAW arrived to serve as the air combat intelligence officer. First Lieutenant Frank Walton, a former cop from the Los Angeles Police Department, had been picked for the job (as he told it) because he was big and rarely drank. In other words, he was supposed to handle Boyington when it became necessary. That was his explanation, written years later, though it was somewhat exaggerated.

Thankfully he did not show up at Turtle Bay and assert himself as being morally and physically superior to Boyington. Had he done that, he wouldn't have lasted long. He was big and powerful, and had been a champion swimmer in the Hollywood Athletic Club, but as a "ground pounder" he was in a different league. A reservist for all of one year, he had never worked with a squadron before.

Wisely, he applied his talents and brought several assets to the squadron, including his maturity. At thirty-four, he was a dozen years older than many of the pilots and had sagacious advice to give. He did not patronize them, but made a sincere effort to learn about their hometowns, high schools, colleges, where they had trained, and whether they were married (several were, or had fiancées).

Already a published author, Walton was actually looking far ahead, hoping to transform his daily notes into a magazine story if not a book.* With his cop's mind, he was a nat-

---

* Dutton published *The Sea Is My Workshop,* about Walton's experiences as a lifeguard, in 1936.

ural intelligence officer, and eagerly gathered information about targets and missions, then debriefed the results to compile an accurate account of each action. Much like Bailey, his character and personality served as an effective counterbalance to Boyington's demeanor. The three of them got along well together in the South Pacific.

With no fanfare and no paperwork, just a wave of the proverbial wand, Boyington's assorted pilots became the flight echelon of VMF-214 on September 7. Soon after, while drinking beer in the triple Dallas hut that served as an officers' club, Stan Bailey, John Begert, Hank Bourgeois, Bill Case, and a couple of other veterans discussed their current state of affairs. Talk got around to Boyington, who wasn't present, and his difficulties with Smoak. "There was a lot of heat brought down from the group to the squadron," Case later explained, "and we felt that."

They also talked about their own orphaned heritage after bouncing from squadron to squadron. Someone professed they were all a bunch of bastards. When the laughter subsided, another said alliteratively, "Boyington's Bastards." That was all they needed. Approval was unanimous, and they immediately got to work designing an insignia.

The next day, they submitted their design to Capt. John De Chant, public relations officer at MAG-11. He did not endorse it. "When we turned it in," recalled Case, "it was rejected because they didn't like the term *bastards,* and the personality of the leader should not be part of the official squadron name." The pilots didn't have to start over from scratch, however. Someone remembered that in heraldry, a left-angling black slash across a family crest signified bastard ancestry. So they drew up a shield with a bar sinister, then cast about for a name to go with it. The solution was anticlimactic, according to Case: "We had English letters on the original logo, and so 'Boyington's Bastards' became 'Black Sheep' . . . just saving the *B.* It was no more historic than that."

It began as a compromise, but the pilots' creation was irresistible in its subtlety. Not only did the name fit their collective history after being bounced from unit to unit, but Black Sheep was a poetic bull's-eye for describing their commanding officer's reputation in the Marine Corps.

To complete the design, they turned to thirty-nine-year-old "Pen" Johnson, a self-described "half-ass artist" who had gotten a waiver to serve as a combat correspondent with a raider battalion. Currently stuck at Espíritu Santo while "writing stories about Pfc.'s making corporal," Johnson drew a clever logo shaped like a shield, with the top of the traditional crest framed by a head-on Corsair. A lonely-looking sheep filled the space next to the bar sinister.

The pilots needed a flight surgeon to look after them. Jim Reames, the navy lieutenant who had given Boyington his physical the previous month, was added to the squadron on September 11. Boyington undoubtedly asked for him by name. "Diamond Jim" was likable, a hell of a card player, and generous with medicinal brandy.

Later that day, Boyington made an electrifying announcement. The Black Sheep had received verbal orders from Major General Mitchell to move into the combat zone—not just soon, but the next day. "We're going to Cactus and then on up to the Russell Islands," he told them, using the code word for Guadalcanal. "We'll fly twenty planes up. The rest of you will fly up on a SCAT plane."

Now that the roster had been pared to the standard complement of twenty-eight pilots, eight pilots in addition to Walton and Reames would have to ride the transport. Boyington chose the Corsair drivers based on experience— inversely. The rookies and Moon Mullen would get to fly Corsairs, thus logging the extra flight time afforded by the 550-mile flight to Guadalcanal, while Stan Bailey and the two-tour veterans, along with one unlucky newcomer, would ride the R4D.

The SCAT passengers left Turtle Bay by truck on the morning of September 12 and crossed Espíritu Santo to take off from the bomber strip. At 7:30, Boyington gunned a

Corsair off the hard coral at Turtle Bay, followed by nineteen others over the next few minutes. Four hours later they touched down at Guadalcanal's Henderson Field, a busy staging base in what was now considered the rear area of the Solomons. While waiting for a late afternoon departure to the Russells, most explored the famous island, described by Walton as "a complicated scene of destruction, rot, flies, and stench."

The transport was grounded overnight, so Boyington switched most of the pilots around for the second leg to keep it fair. They took off at 4:30 that afternoon for the half-hour flight to the Russells and landed at Banika, a fighter strip only seventy miles from Guadalcanal but an enormous leap forward in comfort. They moved into Dallas huts with electrical wiring—something lacking at the Turtle Bay camps—in coconut groves that were clean and attractive. When the transport arrived from Guadalcanal the next morning, the Black Sheep were considered a fully operational combat echelon in the forward zone, ready for the mission orders that could come at any time.

Considering their unusual creation, the Black Sheep were actually better prepared for combat than any marine fighter squadron that had come before them, and many that came after. Ten pilots including Boyington were combat veterans; nine had served together for two previous tours. Of the eighteen rookies, the majority had been together for months, forming their own cohesion, and most had logged hundreds of flight hours. None of the Stateside marine squadrons could boast that level of initial experience.

The first mission came the next day, September 14, as Boyington and two dozen Black Sheep shepherded a dozen B-24 Liberators of the 13th Air Force on a strike against Kahili. The biggest airdrome on Bougainville, it was a daunting site for a first mission. Numerous antiaircraft guns, some atop hills, protected the facility, and a seemingly endless supply of aircraft came down from Rabaul. Two fighter air groups of the 11th Air Fleet, the 201st and 204th

Kokutais (Ku), could be counted on to put up fierce resistance with their A6M3 "Hamps" and A6M5 "Zekes," variants of the famed Mitsubishi Zero. To the southeast of Kahili, the island of Ballale held another runway that served the fast-climbing fighters. It, too, bristled with deadly accurate antiaircraft guns.

During the mission briefing that morning, Boyington assigned divisions to cover the bombers at different levels and warned the pilots to keep their speed up by weaving to match the bombers' slower ground speed. The newcomers were also cautioned not to dash after enemy planes. "If we attack," he told them, "it means we've been lured away from our job."

Arriving at the flight line, he waddled around a Corsair to preflight it before climbing in. He was weighted down by a webbed parachute harness, headgear, a Mae West, and a pistol; dangling awkwardly below his rump, a bulky triple-pack held an inflatable raft, a jungle survival kit, and a parachute. The effect was like walking around with a fifty-pound child hanging from his belt.

Soon the air was filled with smoke from cartridge starters and the throb of two dozen radial engines being warmed. Boyington waited until the cylinder-head temperature stabilized, then signaled for the chocks to be pulled from the Corsair's wheels. Coral dust flew as he throttled up to get the heavy fighter out of its revetment. On the hard-packed taxiway, he snaked his plane back and forth to see what was in front, the pilots behind him staggering their positions alternately to the left and right, giving themselves room to weave without clipping each other's wingtips. Slender noses angled high, the parade of variegated blue fighters rumbled along the taxiway through a coconut grove. Reaching the departure end of the white coral strip, Boyington revved his engine until it bellowed, ran his instrument checks, then throttled back to wait for a green light from the Aldis lamp in the control tower. It flashed at 8:35.

Shoving the throttle forward, Boyington initiated the first combat flight of his unconventional squadron. Lifting from the coral, he raised the landing gear, milked up the flaps, then climbed in a long, lazy turn, allowing the rest of his flock to quickly form on his wing. The Corsairs sorted themselves into divisions as he led them toward the island of Choiseul at nineteen thousand feet.

Arriving early at the rendezvous point, the Black Sheep orbited until they sighted the bombers en route from the southeast, then took their assigned stations while curving and swooping above the drab-looking Liberators. The slender-winged bombers did not fly a tight formation, making the escort job more challenging, but the fighters stuck with them during the flight up the "Slot" toward Bougainville.

From a long way off, a huge column of black smoke was visible, a signpost left by a previous strike. The Liberators climbed to twenty-two thousand feet, skirted Kahili to the north, then made a sweeping left turn that brought them over the target on a reverse heading. Half a dozen dust trails appeared on the runway: enemy fighters taking off.

Now the air was smeared in several places with angry black clouds of antiaircraft bursts, heavy stuff, all of it behind them. The bombers' sliding doors went up, the bombs tumbled out, the doors rolled down. The bomber pilots horsed on more power, every man for himself, and before long the Liberators were scattered along a five-mile stretch. Appalled at the lack of discipline, the marines were no more impressed to see a few bombs hit one corner of Kahili's dispersal area; the rest of the bombs killed fish.

The Black Sheep returned to base without a challenge from enemy fighters, but Boyington couldn't complain about the results. "Whenever you were out in the combat zone and saw enemy planes—you didn't have to necessarily engage them but you could see them in the air—that was supposed to be quite a shock to the nervous system," he later explained. "I could see those planes anytime, whether they were there or not there, [because] anytime you reported seeing them in the air, you got free brandy when you got back from the mission."

The next day he took most of the squadron on another

mission, an escort for five photoreconnaissance B-24s, but it was an exercise in futility. The Liberators wandered all over the sky, leading the formation up the northern coast of Bougainville (they were supposed to photograph the northern end of Choiseul), before doubling back on the wrong heading. Boyington withdrew his fighters and steered them toward Banika. Mechanical problems forced six pilots to land early, and one Corsair was wrecked when the brakes failed. Several of the squadron's Corsairs, older F4U-1s (known as the "birdcage" because of the latticework canopy), suffered more maintenance headaches than did the newer F4U-1A models.

Boyington might have expected the air to be full of Zeros, but after two missions, he had spotted only a few dust trails—free brandy or not. The second mission had been dismal, with a plane wrecked, and several pilots were briefly lost among the unfamiliar islands before they found their way back to the Russells. Thus, in the span of two days, he grew more than a little worried: "I was doing some tall hoping, for if this conglomeration that I called a squadron didn't see some action shortly, my combat-pilot days were over. I knew it. Age and rank were both against me now. Lady Luck just had to smile upon me, that's all."

Fortunately for Boyington, the smile was not long in coming.

14

Touchstone of Victory

Just after lunch on Thursday, September 16, Boyington and twenty-three of his Black Sheep manned Corsairs for another mission, a dive-bombing strike involving Douglas SBD Dauntlesses and Grumman TBF Avengers against the heavily defended island of Ballale. The multiservice escort would include New Zealand P-40 Kittyhawks and some of the first navy F6F Hellcats to reach the Solomons.

Boyington's four-plane division was a combination of newcomers and veterans. He put Mo Fisher on his wing, reasoning the youngster who had been cocky enough to challenge him at gunnery would make a good wingman. He would soon find out how right he was. Virgil Ray, the most junior officer in the squadron, led the second section because of his previous combat experience in VMF-122. His wingman was Red Harris, a twenty-three-year-old from Nebraska whose wife, Maurine, taught school in San Diego.

Boyington began his takeoff roll at 1:00 P.M., with the rest airborne in just seven minutes. The Black Sheep formed up and proceeded to New Georgia, where they met the dive bombers, then climbed to twenty thousand feet to provide roving high cover. More than a hundred aircraft—one of the largest Allied strike groups yet assembled in the South Pacific—turned westward toward the enemy island off the coast of Bougainville. The Black Sheep were slightly ahead of the bombers, with Boyington's division in right echelon,

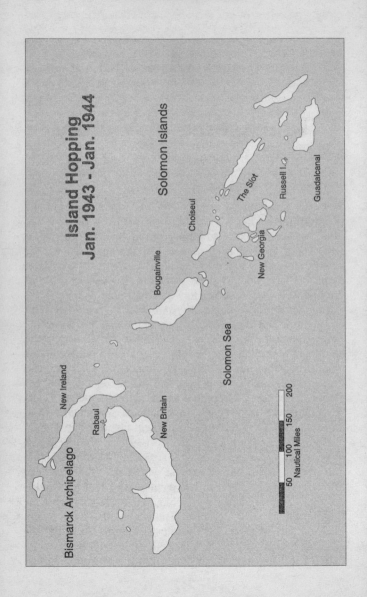

Island Hopping
Jan. 1943 - Jan. 1944

Bismarck Archipelago

New Ireland

Rabaul

New Britain

Bougainville

Solomon Sea

Choiseul

Solomon Islands

The Slot

New Georgia

Russell I.

Guadalcanal

50 100 150 200
Nautical Miles

as they passed south of the Shortland Islands, then pivoted to the right to attack Ballale out of the west. The sky was layered with fleecy clouds, preventing the fighter pilots from having a clear view of the target down below.

Boyington was evidently looking in the wrong direction when an estimated thirty to forty Zeros swarmed from a cloud bank. Hearing a "tally-ho" on the radio, he broke hard to the left, a move so sudden it caught Fisher napping, leaving a huge gap between their Corsairs. Virgil Ray lost Boyington completely. From that moment on, he and Red Harris fended for themselves.

Inexplicably, Boyington was not even ready to fight. Winging toward a heavily defended enemy island, shepherding not only his own squadron but a large number of friendly bombers as well, he had neglected to turn on his gun switches and gunsight, and had not charged the guns. Either he was lulled by "the monotony of flying herd on the bombers," as he later described the first phase of the journey, or he was hungover after a night of heavy drinking. Perhaps it was both. Years later he admitted to an incredible lapse for a combat veteran: "I don't know what I was thinking at that particular moment. Or what I was supposed to be doing."

Lady Luck was smiling now, even beaming, as Boyington narrowly avoided being shot down by a Zero he never saw coming. The Japanese pilot was commencing his firing run when Boyington made that sudden break to the left. Whether the radio call or a sixth sense prompted him to move, the erratic maneuver spoiled the enemy pilot's deflection shot. Skidding past Boyington, the Japanese failed to see Fisher, now recovering from his own surprise. The Zero swooped into the big gap between the two Corsairs, crossing Fisher's nose from the left as it overran Boyington. When the Zero pilot stopped his skid, he then swung back to the left, still unaware of Fisher, as he lined up for another shot at Boyington.

Directly behind the Zero, Fisher triggered a burst and the Zero tightened its turn until it rolled all the way onto its back. "I just flew right up his tail and got rid of him," Fisher

said matter-of-factly. His second burst went directly into the
cockpit. "Once you got in that close, they really filled up
your gunsight. And when those six fifties were firing and
they hit something, man, they just shredded it."

Unaware of the drama behind him, Boyington was
stunned to see an A6M3 pull alongside. The pilot, apparently
as befuddled as Boyington, waggled his wings as a signal for
Boyington to join up, then pulled ahead, "showing the huge
red roundel on his fuselage as he went by." At this point,
Boyington discovered his guns were not switched on or
charged. He spent what "seemed like an eternity" arming his
Corsair, then nudged in a small amount of rudder to bring
the Hamp into the illuminated reticle reflected on his windscreen. He triggered a long burst into the cockpit, which
flared: the pilot's oxygen exploded. The Japanese fighter
rolled over and began a long, terminal plunge straight down.

The cacophony of guns and tracers and flames yanked
Boyington back to reality as if he had been hit "with a wet
towel." He twisted around in his seat just in time to see
Fisher's coup de grace on the Zeke that had tried to assassinate him, then lost sight of his wingman again.

Boyington next joined with two Corsairs, took the lead,
and steered them toward Kahili. Moments later he realized
they were gone, and found himself flying into a narrowing
wedge of airspace with nothing but Zeros in front of him and
on both sides. He zoomed up into the protection of a cloud
layer. Emerging in clear air, he continued a spiraling climb
to twenty-four thousand feet, then spotted the friendly
bombers two miles below him as they raced from Ballale
with Zeros snapping at their heels.

Pushing over, his five-ton fighter plunging like an express
elevator, he started to pull out of the dive above ten thousand
feet to bring himself onto the tail of an A6M3. He opened
fire at three hundred yards, the optimum boresighting distance for the Corsair's six guns, but his speed differential
was so great that in seconds he had closed to fifty feet. At
that moment the enemy fighter burst apart.

Any number of pilots have expressed their amazement at

how instantaneously the unarmored Zeros could disintegrate. Besides lacking pilot armor, their fuel tanks were prone to explode if a single incendiary punched through. The Japanese pilots knew they were riding veritable Molotov cocktails, indeed demanded that their planes be kept as lightweight as possible in favor of maneuverability, and some of them were willing to forego the extra weight of a parachute. This was their warrior code of Bushido, which emphasized that they fight offensively at all times. It was frequently their undoing.

When the Hamp erupted, Boyington had no time to react. "It exploded so close, right in front of my face, that I didn't know which way to turn to miss the pieces," he wrote. He had neither the space nor the time to avoid them, and flew right through the expanding whorl of aluminum and pilot and vaporizing fuel. He was fortunate to miss the engine and its still-spinning propeller, but collected numerous dents on his cowling and leading edges of wings and tail surfaces.

Pulling back up—airspeed and altitude were his most precious assets—Boyington approached the formation of friendly bombers. He saw two Hellcats perched on the right at nineteen thousand feet, then tracers flashed as a Hamp dived at them and missed. It plunged past the retreating formation, then zoomed upward, the pilot intending to perform an Immelman at the top and resume the attack. One step ahead of him, Boyington dived down to get under the Hamp and cut him off with a deflection shot. The Hamp's airspeed decayed near the top of the loop, providing Boyington with a slow, vertical target. He got slugs into the Hamp and held the trigger in, pulling back on his stick to follow the Hamp's rise. At the apex, still on its back, the Japanese fighter blossomed orange and yellow. Momentum carried it through the loop until it reached the vertical heading down, leaving a spectacular arc of flaming fuel and black smoke.

Boyington again climbed, heading southeast toward home base. At about eighteen thousand feet, he sighted Zeros coming the opposite way, well below him, returning to their own field after harassing the bombers. Having learned from his recent experience with the exploding Hamp not to close too rapidly, he throttled back, singled out the rearward Zero, and glided down from two miles above. This one evidently saw him coming, but initiated only "a gentle turn to the left." It was too easy. Boyington sensed a setup, and sure enough, another Zero was off to his right, ready to pounce.

Ignoring the bait, Boyington suddenly reefed his heavy fighter around toward the second Zero, another A6M3. He opened up at three hundred yards in a head-on attack, could see chunks of debris flying off the enemy fighter's cowling (even the incendiary rounds struck with enough impact to knock cylinders off an engine), then dived under the Hamp as it flashed by. He performed a chandelle, pulling into a hard, climbing left turn, then rolled out on the reciprocal heading. Now behind the Japanese fighter, he could see it trailing smoke while descending in a flat, shallow glide toward Ballale. It appeared done for, so he climbed, watching as the Hamp continued to lose altitude until it finally smacked into the water.

Boyington could not find the Zero that had baited him, so he shaped a course toward the relatively safe haven of New Georgia and resumed climbing. Passing through ten thousand feet, he saw another pair of Zeros returning to Ballale. And they saw him. The pair immediately turned into him, so he parried by heading straight at them, then upped the ante by firing head-on at the leader. He was a maniac when it came to the game of chicken—he had rattled Cokey Hoffman in exactly this manner—and the Japanese pilot had no more stomach for it than the old NAP. The Zero yanked up and to the right, whereupon Boyington blew right past it and fired at the wingman. The second Zero allegedly belched smoke, but Boyington did not press this attack, wanting to conserve his dwindling fuel and ammunition. It was still a long way to the nearest friendly field.

Turning southeast, he remained level at ten thousand feet, and was approaching Vella Lavella when he saw a single Corsair low on the water. Two Zeros barreled in from the opposite direction and jumped it. They did not see Boyington, who opened fire "at extremely long range to drive them off." Predictably, one zoomed up, and Boyington was again ready. He followed, firing steadily as the Zero did a slow vertical roll until it gushed flames and fell off to one side.

Now Boyington was in trouble himself, having slowed too much while firing as he climbed. His Corsair clawed for altitude, airspeed bleeding away rapidly. The heavy fighter got over on its back and lost the race with gravity, stalling at only ten thousand feet. For an agonizing moment it hung like a breeching whale, then began to fall inverted in a disorienting flat spin. Boyington needed all of his skill and past experience to wrestle the fighter back under control before hitting the water. When he finally was able to look around again, he could see no other planes, friendly or otherwise.

Turning straight toward New Georgia, he adjusted the fuel-air mixture to squeeze every mile out of his remaining gas. When he finally set his streaked, dented Corsair down at Munda, according to the postmission report, he had ten gallons of fuel and thirty rounds of ammunition. After an hour and a half on the ground for servicing, he took off again and flew to the Russells.

It was nearly six o'clock when Boyington landed at Banika, where a jubilant crowd of Black Sheep, having landed almost two hours before, welcomed him back. They knew he could not be flying on his original fuel supply and had presumed him missing; Bob Ewing still was. Glad as they were to see him, they were equally exuberant about their own remarkable performance that afternoon. Frank Walton, still debriefing participants, faced a long night of writing.

The squadron's first engagement had evolved into an enormous free-for-all covering hundreds of square miles. Don Fisher added a second flamer to the Zeke he shot off Boyington's tail; Bob McClurg and Bob Alexander each scored single victories; Chris Magee, Ed Olander, and Bruce Matheson recorded Zeros as probably destroyed. Among the veterans, John Begert shot down two Zekes, Allan McCartney claimed two probables, and a probable apiece went to Stan Bailey and Virgil Ray. Counting Boyington's five victories—the "smoker" he supposedly hit was never recorded—the Black Sheep were officially credited with destroying eleven Zeros and probably destroying eight more.

That night, a raucous party was held under the coconut trees in the VMF-214 encampment. Boyington remembered, albeit vaguely, that Ashmun, Mullen, Matheson, and Fisher entertained the squadron with their harmonious voices. There was good reason for Boyington's addled memory. "Not even the possibility of a hairy hangover bothered me the slightest," he wrote. "So I took aboard a load of issue brandy, which our flight surgeon . . . had been so kind to supply."

Although Walton had never piloted a plane and had been in the service for only a year, he had the power to award or deny aerial victory credits. During his debriefings after an engagement, he decided whether claims sounded reasonable. If so, the accounts were recorded in his government-issue notebook, then retyped monthly as the official squadron war diary. He was good at asking the right questions, but rarely was he able to get independent confirmation of a claim. After Boyington's first combat engagement in the Solomons that afternoon, he was officially recognized for five victories, though he had fought alone for practically the whole engagement. The Japanese did lose enough planes to cover his claims—barely.

Decades after the fight, author-historian Henry Sakaida extensively researched the casualty lists and other documents of the 11th Air Fleet fighter groups. They showed that on the afternoon of September 16, the Black Sheep were jumped by twenty-six Zeros of the 204th Kokutai led by Lt.(jg) Tetsuji Ueno, joined by several Zeros of the 201st Ku. The total number of Japanese fighters matched the marines' estimate of thirty to forty Zeros, validating the accuracy of that portion of their records.

The day had been a costly one for the Japanese, with five pilots from the 204th killed, including Ueno, and one pilot from the 201st. A Zero pilot was seen bailing out of his fighter just as it broke up, raising the possibility that if he survived, the plane was destroyed with no corresponding entry on the casualty list.

Muddying up the equation is the fact that the two Hellcat squadrons claimed five Zekes and a probable over Ballale, bringing total claims on the American side to sixteen victories and nine probables. This obviously makes Boyington's victories difficult to reconcile, as does the fact that he fought alone. If he did get five, only two of all the other claims were valid, including several made by Hellcat pilots. Nevertheless, his claims cannot be arbitrarily denied. As the commanding officer of the squadron, he claimed to have downed five, and Frank Walton wrote them up. As a result, Boyington became only the third marine to shoot down five or more planes in a single flight, and more uniquely, was the first to do it in a Corsair. He had put himself in good company: all of his predecessors were awarded the Medal of Honor.*

Boyington launched most of the squadron for another photoreconnaissance mission at 7:30 the next morning, after which they were to land at Munda and remain there for extended duty in the forward area. The escort went awry—the Black Sheep never rendezvoused with the photo planes—so they flew on to New Georgia after a half-hour search.

Boyington stayed out of the cockpit for the rest of the day, and at some point reported to Brig. Gen. Francis Mulcahy, commander of Allied aircraft in the New Georgia group. The old general, who had once chastised Boyington for landing

---

* Joe Foss shot down 5 Zeros during two flights on October 25, 1942, in defense of Guadalcanal. James Swett downed 7 Vals and got a probable in a single flight (using 18 seconds' worth of firing time) on April 7, 1943, also at Guadalcanal; Jefferson DeBlanc shot down 3 Zeros and 2 Rufe floatplanes on January 31, 1943, near Kolombangara. Swett ditched and DeBlanc bailed out, a testimony to the difficulty of the single-flight achievement.

his fuel-starved F4B-4 at the Quantico rifle range, now greeted him as the Pacific war's newest hero. Mulcahy had a private stock of scotch, according to Boyington, whose fortunes were changing for the better.

Word that he had bagged five Zeros in his first combat spread quickly. The wire services picked up the story, which was published in U.S. newspapers within a week, generating additional references to his six apparent victories as a Flying Tiger. Now that his AVG record was indelibly linked to his composite score, there was no going back.

But while his feat was making headlines in the States, there was not much to rejoice about at Munda. The environment Boyington and the Black Sheep endured was a great equalizer. The airfield straddled a narrow finger of land jutting into the Solomon Sea at the western tip of New Georgia, where the Japanese had been well dug-in. Heavy bombardment had been necessary to dislodge them, followed by vicious fighting that had ended just a few weeks earlier. The earth was scorched and raw, with unburied bodies and parts of bodies giving off a sickening stench. The climate itself was hellish.

At night, sporadic Japanese air raids kept the marines awake. Exhausted after two nights without sleep, Boyington asked for permission to take a Corsair aloft after dark and hunt for the raiders, known collectively as Washing Machine Charlie. The Corsair was no night fighter, but there were no other types available. Ground-controlled radar could provide a vector to incoming targets, which Boyington believed made the attempt worthwhile.

Accordingly, he was off the schedule on September 19, having flown two tiring patrols the day before. He took off at 1:00 A.M. on the twentieth, set the fuel mixture for maximum loitering, then waited for the radar controller to provide contacts. Occasionally he dropped down to fifteen thousand feet to conserve his oxygen supply, but each time he did, the bogies that had stayed on the fringe of the radar net would come closer. When he climbed back up, they withdrew. "Charlie chose to be cagey," he wrote.

Within minutes of his 5:00 A.M. landing, a Mitsubishi G4M roared over and bombed the field. Reporting that he had seen a signal light on Japanese-held Kolombangara, Boyington surmised that an observer was informing the bombers of his presence, hence the raid as soon as he landed. He had not been able to prevent the dawn attack, but as Walton later pointed out, "A good many thousand men blessed [him] for giving them the first uninterrupted night's sleep they'd had in a long time."

A personnel problem cropped up unexpectedly soon after the combat tour began. Boyington's second section leader, Virgil Ray, had lost his nerve after the encounter over Ballale on the sixteenth. Emotionally scarred by an earlier combat experience in VMF-122, he was now serving his third and final tour, having come over on *Lurline* with Boyington. He claimed a probable over Ballale, but flew only one more mission—the aborted attempt to escort photo planes—before going quietly to Boyington. "I don't feel comfortable anymore with this," Ray said, according to one of the other pilots.

Boyington had seen enough during his career to know what types of leadership were effective and what types weren't. From his experience with the Sandells and the Bracketts of the world, he realized it would serve no purpose to embarrass or berate Virgil Ray. "Okay," was all he said, "we won't force you." After taking Ray off the flight schedule, Boyington gave him an opportunity to work it out for himself. He might have sensed that the shy, unsmiling ex-NAP would never fly another combat assignment, but he did not send him away in shame.

For himself, Boyington itched for more aerial action, especially after other pilots added to the squadron's score. The most dramatic effort was by made Chris Magee, who dumped two Vals and claimed another as a probable on September 18, when the Japanese attacked the landing fleet at Vella Lavella. He was written up for a Navy Cross. Subsequently, Boyington added Magee's division (led by John

Begert) to his own for a strafing mission on September 21. Magee did figure prominently, but for unexpected reasons.

The assignment that morning was to interdict surface vessels reported in a cove off Choiseul, north of New Georgia. Having replaced Virgil Ray with Moon Mullen, Boyington took off at 8:30 and led the Black Sheep toward the designated cove, where they found the vessels and began to work them over. Their primary target, reported as a small cargo vessel, turned out to be a seventy-foot Chinese junk. Boyington initiated a series of strafing runs, and by his second or third pass was actually following Magee by several seconds. Suddenly, an airburst just above the target startled him. "They're firing at us!" he yelled on the radio. Magee, barely able to contain himself, called back "Forget it, that was a grenade." Having found an unused weapon at Munda, he decided to bring it along, then chucked it at the vessel as he flew overhead.

Several hours after the first mission, Boyington took his division aloft again, this time to provide high cover for a strafing attack on Kahili. It was an adrenaline-filled adventure for the four shooters, but uneventful for Boyington and his patrolling Corsairs. The next day found him grounded for a fungus infection in his left ear canal. Doc Reames scraped out the accessible region and washed it with boric acid, then packed the ear with a mixture of acid and sulfa powder. Medically grounded for the next couple days, Boyington had to endure this painful remedy daily for more than a week.

A growing trend of mechanical ills among the Corsairs got even worse on the morning of September 23, when Boyington led five divisions aloft for a strike escort. Their mission was to protect two dozen SBDs and TBFs as they tried to wipe out a heavy AA position at Jakohima, a few miles west of Kahili, while B-24s escorted by army P-38 Lightnings would strike at Kahili airdrome simultaneously.

The effort began badly for the Black Sheep, five of whom either never made it off the ground or turned back after takeoff. Boyington led the remainder toward Bougainville after they rendezvoused with the dive bombers, but they had not yet reached the target when the B-24s came hustling toward them from the opposite direction, having hit Kahili earlier than they were supposed to. Thirty to forty Zeros were in pursuit, while the P-38s were nowhere in sight, justifying the marines' disdainful nickname for them: "high-altitude fox-holes."

Boyington's division had been rearranged because of the various aborts, such that Bill Case was now on his wing, with Moon Mullen and Denny Groover in the second section. Boyington climbed to twenty-four thousand feet and began circling down to attack the swarm of Zeros, but for some reason never made contact with the enemy. His complete lack of engagement is difficult to explain. Other Black Sheep claimed four Zeros, and his own second section came under heavy attack. Mullen was wounded superficially when a bullet struck the birdcage framework of his canopy, sending fragments into his left shoulder; other Zeros pumped cannon shells and machine-gun bullets into Groover's Corsair. One 20mm shell detonated in the cockpit, breaking his right arm and slicing him in several places with shrapnel. Despite his wounds and the fact that his Corsair was crippled by five cannon hits and fifty machine-gun slugs, Groover nursed the plane back to Munda. He was subsequently evacuated to Guadalcanal for a month before he rejoined the Black Sheep.

Two hours after the mission ended, Boyington was back in the air again, this time with an ad hoc division consisting of Stan Bailey, a patched-up Mullen, and Case. The foursome flew at low altitude to the Treasury Islands, south of Bougainville, to scout locations where PT boats might be able to retrieve downed aviators. After finding some promising beaches, they disguised the purpose of their flight (lest enemy coast watchers had observed them) by strafing Faisi, a Japanese seaplane base in the nearby Shortland Islands. Wary of possible airborne fighters and antiaircraft fire, they increased speed to four hundred miles per hour and made a single pass, exploding the boiler of a steam launch under way in one of the channels, then hammering a bivouac area and a gun position. They were half a mile past Faisi before the AA gunners got off a few useless rounds.

After that accomplishment, Boyington was frustrated by days of insignificant missions. Even worse, his division was stuck with a mundane escort for a Lockheed Ventura on September 26, when three other divisions of Black Sheep got into a fight with Zeros. Rollie Rinabarger was wounded and had to be evacuated. Ten days had elapsed since Boyington's big score on the sixteenth, but he had not encountered a single enemy plane. His pilots, in the meantime, had downed eight and added three probables.

Boyington had an opportunity to improve his score on the twenty-seventh, but the mission was fouled up from the beginning. Bourgeois and Begert took their divisions on the dawn patrol that morning and landed shortly after 8:00 A.M., then were called a few hours later to join Boyington's division for a B-24 strike on Kahili. They were given only fifteen minutes' notice and nothing was organized; some of the planes had not even been serviced. Immediately after taking off at 11:05, Bourgeois had an instrument failure and returned to Munda, bringing Junior Heier as an escort, which left only six Corsairs to protect twenty-seven bombers. Boyington's division, airborne late due to the delay in servicing the aircraft, was directed to proceed straight to Kahili rather than join with the Liberators.

Despite his delayed departure, Boyington was able to race to Kahili ahead of the formation. High overhead, he saw "a twin-tailed ship heading north across the field emitting intermittent twin streamers of black smoke." Thinking it was "a signal for the Jap fighters to take off," he lowered his division (Fisher, Case, and Sims) to ten thousand feet, hoping to knock off any fighters that climbed up from Kahili. A couple of aircraft were visible on the field, but they appeared to be bamboo mock-ups, so Boyington climbed again. Spotting two airborne groups of Zeros approaching from the southeast, he circled to get above them.

When he had the advantage, Boyington nosed over to attack, somehow losing Fisher again. Unaware that he was alone, he picked out a Zero, slid into firing position, and squeezed the trigger. Nothing happened. Incredibly, he had forgotten to arm his guns again. To have flubbed it once, on his first combat engagement since leaving the Flying Tigers, could be chalked up to human error; to repeat the blunder was bordering on ineptitude, especially for a squadron leader. Thankfully there had been no planes aloft when he had taken his division down to ten thousand feet—his guns had not been armed then either.

Seeing that Boyington was alone, Bill Case caught up by nosing straight down while the skipper spiraled around on the tail of the Zero he was chasing. Case opened fire whenever the Zero crossed his nose, then released the trigger as Boyington's Corsair drifted in range. They did this through a couple of turns, spiraling downward, until Boyington pulled up. "I pulled up and joined him," recalled Case, "and he led us back to the rest of the formation area, to do the job we were supposed to be doing. When we got back on the ground he said, 'Who was that on my wing?' I told him who it was and he said, 'Well, you got that Zero.'" Boyington explained to Case that his master gun switch was not on; he never fired a shot at the enemy plane.

Case's recollection that Boyington pulled up and led them back to the formation contradicts Walton's war diary input, which described Boyington in another engagement with a Zero after he "cleared his guns." (Walton kindly allowed that they had jammed.) Boyington supposedly followed the Zero down until it struck the water, after which he "almost crashed into the water himself." If so, he broke one of his own cardinal rules about preserving altitude. More importantly, he took himself away from the formation and his own fighters, which were under attack.

Whichever way it went, Boyington made no further attempt to get back into the fight, and was conspicuously absent from a heavy battle in progress around the B-24s. Case and Red Harris, meanwhile, went to the aid of the bombers.

The worst of it was that both were subsequently hit: Case was forced down at Vella Lavella with several holes in his plane, and Harris was shot down, never to be seen again.

In Boyington's defense, aerial battles such as this were spread across hundreds of square miles, making it impossible for a squadron leader to be responsible for all his pilots once a fight began. It was every man for himself. Even so, on this particular day Boyington's participation was ineffective. After starting to lead his division back toward the bomber formation, he disappeared, leaving Case and Harris to fend for themselves in the middle of a fight.

There is no need to look further than alcoholism to explain his effort that day. Based on his past tendencies and the fact that the mission was added to the schedule with little advance warning, he was either experiencing a "hairy hangover" or was actively drinking when the strike was ordered. Why else would an otherwise superb pilot fail to remember basic cockpit procedures such as arming guns, or nearly fly himself into the ocean? The Black Sheep collectively acknowledged that he sometimes flew drunk, backed up by Hunter Reinburg's earlier statements regarding his performance in VMF-122.

Judging by Japanese records, which appear highly accurate in this case, Boyington's claim of downing a Zero on September 27 was an attempt to save face. The two air groups involved scrambled their Zeros against an estimated count of twenty-seven bombers—exactly the number of Liberators involved—but no losses were recorded by either kokutai.

Detractors have long claimed that Japanese losses were deliberately underreported. Such a notion, however, goes against an essential element of the Bushido code—that death in combat was not only a duty to be served for the emperor, but a privilege. Individuals who made the sacrifice were fully identified by name and rank in Japanese casualty records so that their families could maintain shrines in their honor. To deny a certain number of those losses would have required denying the existence of the individuals and their entire families.

Boyington managed to shrug off his mistakes, putting his pilots at ease with his self-deprecating manner. As good as he was, he made the same errors they did. Nobody realized the extent to which he was under the influence. His bodacious drinking and occasional brawling were attributed to his charismatic personality, which made him seem all the more charming. He was outgoing, with a quick homespun wit, and was admired because of his legacy as a former Flying Tiger. In the airplane, his aggression rubbed off on the pilots, resulting in a sensational start for the Black Sheep—twenty-three victories and eleven probables in a span of eleven days. The record grabbed far more attention than Boyington's character flaws, which everyone considered minor.

Such aggression could also be dangerous in the wrong hands. Bob Alexander, a handsome fitness buff with perfect white teeth, was described as having "an attitude that he was going to win that war." With one victory already to his credit, he was flying as Stan Bailey's tail-end Charlie when four PT boats were sighted near Kolombangara just after dawn on September 30. American boats were not supposed to be in this region after sunrise, but Bailey recognized them as friendlies and rocked his wings, simultaneously broadcasting a warning to his wingmen not to open fire. Failing to heed the radio call or visual signals—including some from the boats—Alexander triggered a burst that smothered the stern of PT-126. A sailor in the engine room was killed instantly, an ensign on his first week of duty was mortally wounded, and a young gunner's mate was blown overboard. Reflexively, gunners on the 126 boat returned fire, hitting Alexander's Corsair. It curved toward the island and slammed into the jungle just inland from the shoreline.

The four deaths were not only needless but also ironic: hours later the Black Sheep learned they were to get a well-earned break from the miserable conditions at Munda. Exhausted, poorly fed, diseased, and dirty, they were ordered to pull back to the Russells that same afternoon. Eight pilots flew worn out Corsairs to Banika (from whence they would be ferried to the rear for refurbishment), while the rest rode aboard a SCAT transport. The opportunity to work out of Banika was a welcome respite in the middle of the combat tour, and for the next three days the Black Sheep took turns standing scramble alerts. Otherwise they were free to swim, relax, and enjoy the immeasurably better food.

The temporary break ended for Boyington on October 4, when he led two divisions to escort SBDs to Malabeta Hill, another strong AA position near Kahili. Participation was limited because the squadron had but eight planes—the same ones that had been flown down from Munda, supposedly with too many hours to be combat worthy. Now they were to be used again, from a base that added 260 miles to the round trip.

Not surprisingly, Mo Fisher and "Long Tom" Emrich suffered engine trouble soon after taking off at 11:15. Boyington and the remaining Corsairs chugged up to meet the dive bombers at ten thousand feet over Rendova, but the rendezvous time passed with no sign of the formation. After waiting an extra fifteen minutes, Boyington heard a radio call from the bombers indicating that they were going home, so he led his small force northwest to look for them.

The strike that day had been planned as another of those coordinated events, with army Liberators scheduled to hit Kahili at the same time that the dive bombers struck the AA position. Reaching Bougainville, Boyington saw dust trails as Japanese fighters streaked off the ground to meet the attacking bombers. Unfettered with escort obligations, he took his Corsairs down to meet the Zeros as they climbed in a right-hand spiral. Descending toward the tail-end Charlie in the first division, Boyington nearly overran it due to the Zeke's phenomenal rate of climb. He opened fire from high astern at three hundred yards, then chopped his throttle while kicking right rudder to slew his Corsair around in a skid. Settling back behind the Zeke, he pulled the trigger again and his slugs "chopped the Jap's tail to pieces." His momentum pulled him around to the next Zeke in line, so he triggered another burst from above and slightly left of its tail. Before he could even determine whether his aim was true, the Zeke's pilot parachuted from the plane. Boyington quickly lined up on yet another Zeke, which flamed at the right wing root and headed down.

He had downed three Zekes in a single 360-degree turn in less than a minute. Several of his own pilots were in the immediate vicinity, making it easy for Walton to get supporting statements. No other marines submitted claims that day and Boyington was credited with all three, but the Japanese records show the loss of just one pilot: Petty Officer Miyanishi of the 204th Ku.

Never one to shy away from publicity, Frank Walton invited Pulitzer Prize–winning war correspondent George Weller, on assignment for the *Chicago Daily News,* to interview some of the Black Sheep. Three were from Chicago, Walton pointed out to Weller, who subsequently filed half a dozen nationally syndicated articles about the squadron. The first story was a dramatic, blow-by-blow account of Boyington's big dogfight over Ballale in mid-September; another quoted his reaction to the home front's belief that the Allies owned aerial superiority in the Solomons. "My outfit has been in dozens of air battles over the islands from Guadalcanal to Buka," Boyington was quoted as saying. "Every time the Japs fight us, they outnumber us. And they fight us every time we strike."

Weller's accounts gave Boyington terrific national exposure. Soon other correspondents were writing about his string of nine victories in just three engagements. One article, published on the eve of the World Series, portrayed him as "an ardent baseball fan" who was "willing to offer a Zero for the ball cap of a World Series winner." The Black Sheep as a whole were supposedly eager "to put up as collateral for their offer the thirteen enemy planes with which they have been officially credited in the past two weeks." It was all for publicity, but the squadron's ante was on the table.

Oddly enough, Boyington did not fly for an entire week, an unusually long hiatus for a squadron commander during a combat tour. At the same time, he shunned the collateral duties and responsibilities usually carried out by a commanding officer. "Bailey ran the squadron as far as administration was concerned," said one pilot; "Boyington was a horror as a CO," echoed another. The Black Sheep considered it his modus operandi, and didn't seem to mind that he let others handle matters on the ground.

The breather ended on October 10, when Boyington and sixteen of the Black Sheep returned to Munda via SCAT, with the remainder following in new or reconditioned Corsairs. Later that morning, five divisions were in the air for strikes on Bougainville, but once again Boyington wasn't among them. He reported instead to the Commander, Allied Air Forces, Northern Solomons (ComAirNorSols)—now in the hands of his old drinking general, "Nuts" Moore—making it highly probable they spent part of the day sampling the general's scotch.

Boyington finally participated in a strike the next day, escorting B-24s to Kahili with two divisions of Corsairs. Contrary to his earlier assertion that the Japanese always outnumbered them, only a handful of Zeros challenged the rear of the Liberator formation after the bomb run. If Boyington saw them, he never deviated from his course. Bill Case, however, swung around and triggered a short burst at the lead Zero while it was still half a mile away. Incredibly, his "lucky, wild-assed shot" hit the Zero and it went down, confirmed by P-38 pilots.

Two days later, the squadron suffered another setback. Virgil Ray, who had not flown since being pulled from the flight roster in September, took off for Guadalcanal on the morning of October 13 to collect the mail. He was expected back at Munda at 4:30, but hours later was declared missing "in a heavy storm." It was a miserable yet somehow consistent end for the former enlisted pilot, who had been treated as an outcast in VMF-122 and was practically invisible among the Black Sheep. His request to be removed from combat flying had not helped. Whatever happened that day, he just flew away and never came back.

Boyington's next mission, two days after Ray's disappearance, was designed with a new twist. The plan called for two Black Sheep divisions to escort B-24s to Kangu Hill, a supply dump near Kahili, while Boyington's division held deliberately at Munda. After taking off late, his division would perform a fighter sweep, free to engage any Zeros that had chased the bombers from the target. In practice it turned out differently.

The bombers zigzagged en route to the target on October 15, putting them twenty minutes behind schedule. Boyington had reached Kahili ahead of them and saw Zeros racing skyward, an ideal setup for his free-roving division. Accompanied by Burney Tucker of Tennessee and the effective team of Case and Emrich, Boyington waited until the Liberators dumped their bombs, then dived into an estimated ten to fifteen Zekes. The Japanese fighters were at four thousand feet, vulnerable in their climb, when the Black Sheep hit them from above. Boyington shot down one Zeke and claimed two or three others probably destroyed, Case and Emrich each downed two, and Tucker was credited with one. In minutes, the division earned credit for six planes destroyed and at least two probables; the 11th Air Fleet indeed lost a total of seven Zeros that day.

What mattered most was the result of Boyington's freelancing. The Japanese fighters were caught at a tremendous disadvantage, allowing the Black Sheep to swat them down without receiving arrows in return. This was Boyington at his best—taking advantage of a situation that presented itself, using his initiative to go on the offensive after the original plan became invalid. Knowing that the squadron's action reports were read carefully up the chain of command, he had Walton add to the narrative: "It is recommended that such a fighter sweep be sent up early on every strike to engage the enemy fighters. An additional sweep should go out to protect the [bombers] on the return trip."

The idea was enthusiastically received, but the main event for the following day had already been planned. Three divisions of Black Sheep (led by Begert, Bailey, and Bourgeois) escorted an SBD strike against AA positions at Kara Airfield, south of Kahili, while Boyington and Ed Olander took their divisions up to protect a formation of Liberators returning from a simultaneous strike on Kahili.

In the vicinity of Bougainville, Boyington's mission began to unravel. Visual navigation was prevented by a solid layer of clouds below the formation, while "dead reckoning" was hampered by huge thunderheads that forced pilots to zigzag haphazardly. "The weather was terrible," confirmed John Bolt, leading Olander's second section. "We got up to the target area and it was socked in solid. The clouds were way the hell up there, towering over the bombers' altitude. The bombers went into some clouds and we lost them; we didn't know where the hell we were."

To find a reference, Boyington led his eight Corsairs carefully down through a hole in the clouds, leveling off at just five hundred feet above the ground. Realizing that they were halfway up the west coast of Bougainville, he turned southeast to lead them back toward Munda. Soon they could see Kahili to their left, through the rain. "Stick in close," Boyington broadcast as they crossed the beach and flew over the water between Kahili and Ballale.

Down below, barges and craft of every description plied the channel, obviously taking advantage of the lousy weather. Boyington spotted five good-sized cargo vessels but was intent on getting away from Indian Country. "Nobody shoot," he radioed, nervous as a cat sneaking through a dog pound. Years later, he gave a condescending rationale for ignoring the vulnerable targets: "It was a temptation to stop and shoot at them, but I knew that if I ever took a shot at these I would have my clowns all spread out, and then they would never get back home."

After clearing Bougainville, he did not lead his Corsairs straight home. "He did a rather poor job of navigating back," Bolt said years later, with reason to feel uncharitable. Instead of leading them southeast toward Munda, Boyington felt his way from island to island, first taking them east until they reached Choiseul, then south to Vella Lavella, adding half again as much mileage as the direct route. The extra distance cost Tom Emrich too much fuel, and he was forced to ditch his Corsair near Vella Lavella. Four of the Black Sheep circled overhead until a rescue boat picked him up, after which they landed for fuel while Boyington and two others continued to Munda.

Bolt, one of the four to refuel at Vella Lavella, decided to return to Bougainville and strafe the vessels he had seen. He tried to entice the others to go with him but none would, so he took off alone, found Bougainville, dropped beneath the clouds, and roared up Tonolei Harbor. He poured slugs into barges, a junk with no sails, a small steamer. At the end of the harbor he chandelled and raced back out, drawing fire from only one AA gun.

An angry Boyington was waiting at Munda. "When Jack Bolt finally returned to our field and made his report," he later wrote, "it was up to me to bawl him out." Although he was a maverick himself, Boyington would not or could not tolerate the same from his subordinates. "I was always breaking established rules," he boasted, but there was a double standard.

Two days later, no less an icon than Bull Halsey sent a telegram congratulating Bolt on his "one-man war." Forced to acknowledge the achievement, Boyington painted himself as paternally forgiving by claiming that he recommended Bolt for a Navy Cross. It never happened. "I never got anything for that Tonolei Harbor strike," said Bolt. "Where Boyington said he gave me the Navy Cross for it, he in fact zeroed it by burying it in a DFC which related three Zero kills. Boyington never cottoned to me much after that."

In their combat reports, the Japanese word for planes that disintegrated was *jibaku,* meaning "self-exploded," implying that the pilots deliberately blew themselves up for the emperor. Plenty of IJN pilots performed the ultimate honor dur-

ing the next two days as the air war over Bougainville
reached its crescendo.

Boyington's recommendation for a preemptive fighter
sweep had gotten the attention of Nuts Moore, who called
him into a conference to discuss plans for a dedicated fighter
mission. Moore later wrote, "It was my feeling that Boyington and his squadron could invite Tojo to fight and could
whip him. It is general knowledge that pilots prefer to fight
over their own airdrome or near home (every cock fights best
on his own dunghill). The possibility of success of circling
Kahili and inviting a fight was discussed with Boyington.
Major Boyington was so anxious, enthusiastic, and sure of
victory that I ordered the mission."

The sweep was laid on for October 17. Boyington briefed
fifteen Black Sheep along with eight Fighting Falcons from
VMF-221 on his idea of how to get the Zeros to come up.
"We'll send a couple of your divisions to fly over Kahili," he
said to the Falcons, "and about fifteen minutes later we'll arrive and knock the hell out of the guys who took off to cream
you all."

Jack Pittman, a former flying sergeant, complained, "Hell,
that's making bait out of us!"

Boyington quipped, "That's the kind of odds I like!"

The Corsairs were airborne by 8:30, save for one Fighting
Falcon that could not get started and two Black Sheep who
were forced to abort after taking off. The remaining Corsairs
headed straight for Kahili, with the Fighting Falcons parked
in front at six thousand feet, just as Boyington intended. The
plan worked to perfection.

In bright sunshine, with only a few scattered clouds dotting the island panorama, the marines arrived over Kahili
and watched as Zeros took off in twos and threes. The
Japanese fighters formed into larger groups and climbed out
in different directions; more launched from Kara or Ballale
until there were fifty-six Zeros aloft. With remarkable accuracy, the marines counted fifty-five enemy fighters in the sky.

Descending in lazy S-turns, Boyington led eight Corsairs
down to ten thousand feet and hit eighteen to twenty Zekes

in their climb. The numerical disadvantage was offset by his hit-and-run tactic, making the most of the Corsair's superior weight and firepower. The ensuing fight, lasting more than half an hour and covering a huge expanse of water, was "a sight to behold."

Boyington hounded down and splashed three Zekes; Magee, Tucker, and Heier claimed two apiece; three other Black Sheep got singles or probables. Only two Zekes were nailed in frontal attacks; the rest were shot from behind, their pilots unable to escape the fast, heavy, dominant Corsairs. The Black Sheep hogged the take, with but one Fighting Falcon laying claim to two Zekes and a probable. Combined, the squadrons claimed fourteen kills and three probables. The 201st Ku lost one pilot, while the 204th and 253d lost three apiece: seven pilots killed. At least two pilots were seen to parachute, indicating that more Zeros might have been destroyed than the casualty lists revealed. Even if the claims and actual losses did not match, it was a morning of mayhem for the Japanese.

The cost to the marines was minimal: three Corsairs shot up (one damaged beyond repair), and two Purple Hearts for the Black Sheep. Bruce Matheson and Ed Harper, wounded by 7.7mm fragments, landed at Munda in a heavy storm, the latter bellying in with his Corsair's hydraulic system shot out. Both men were anesthetized with Le Jon brandy and patched up by Doc Reames.

The day after the triumphant fighter sweep, Boyington again led Corsairs toward Bougainville, this time as medium cover for an SBD strike on the notorious antiaircraft gun positions at Ballale. In a perfectly coordinated attack, TBFs simultaneously dive-bombed the runway, followed by B-24s that released their bomb loads from high overhead. Everything came together like clockwork. Dauntlesses plastered the AA sites, the Avengers' bombs crisscrossed the strip, then the ordnance from the heavies walked right down the runway centerline. Because the island was so small, the effect was like blasting an anchored carrier. Two clusters of Zeros were sighted, but Boyington held his Corsairs close to the SBDs and the Japanese never challenged, probably because an overwhelming number of P-38s, P-39s, and New Zealand P-40s also maneuvered nearby.

That afternoon, Boyington led his second mission of the day to Bougainville—a repeat of the previous day's fighter sweep. Two divisions of Fighting Falcons were involved, one led by Maj. Nate Post, commanding officer of VMF-221, the other by Jimmy Swett, who had received a Medal of Honor after downing seven Vals during a single flight.

At ten minutes to four the Corsairs reached Kara Airfield and began circling at eighteen thousand feet. From their perch, the marines could see some sixty planes parked over at Kahili, but none took off. Puffs of black smoke began to dot the air, coming uncomfortably close. Boyington moved the formation over to Kahili and circled it twice, drawing more AA fire, but still the Zeros would not budge. Their losses the previous day had evidently taken the fight out of them.

Keying his throat microphone, Boyington taunted the Japanese, knowing that someone who spoke English was monitoring the American frequencies. A few days before, a clipped voice had come on the channel, asking, "Major Boyington, what is your position?" His answer: "Right over your damn airport, you yellow bellies, come up and fight!" He repeated the challenge again on the afternoon of the eighteenth, shouting, "Come on up and fight, you yellow bastards!"

Fifty years later, Jim Hill remained almost in awe of the results. "[Boyington] baited the Japanese Zeros to come up and we could see them taking off, and lo and behold they just kept climbing up around their field, instead of going out, getting some altitude, and coming back. [He] said, 'Well, they're going to make it easy for us, let's go get 'em. Pick out your target.' We just kept peeling off and down onto these Zeros."

The Corsairs hit the Japanese as they climbed through six thousand feet with results almost identical to the day before. "Off the end of the Kahili strip, which stopped right on the edge of the ocean," Boyington later wrote, "I saw eight splashes, with oil gradually spreading in larger circular patterns on top of the water."

The Black Sheep drove the Zeros downward, picking them off one at a time. Boyington claimed one, as did Olander, Case, and Emrich; Hill got his first and only kill of the war, while Magee scored a hat trick. "I saw him flame three on first bursts," noted Boyington. The Fighting Falcons also contributed, including two for Nate Post, three for Jack Pittman, and one for Jimmy Swett.

Not surprisingly, the total claim of fourteen Zeros destroyed exceeded the 11th Air Fleet's actual losses by a wide margin. The 201st Ku suffered the worst, losing four pilots, while the 204th lost two. Still, the Japanese had expended some fifteen Zeros during two days of fighting over Bougainville, and admitted that thirteen pilots were killed. In exchange for this, Lt. Milton Schneider of VMF-221 was shot down. Boyington saw his plane go in.

The Black Sheep were charmed. They claimed twenty Zeros between the two sweeps at the cost of one crashlanded Corsair and some minor wounds. From any perspective, it was an extraordinary accomplishment. Boyington had upped his personal record by eight in the past two weeks, bringing his total score to fourteen as a marine.

The news got even better. The boisterous pilots had barely finished debriefing when Frank Walton announced that VMF-215 was going to relieve them. That night, most of the Black Sheep moved out of their sloppy tents and into a newly erected Quonset hut. "We drowned out the lizards and the tree toads," wrote Walton, "as we sat, naked, on our canvas cots, babbling about the day's action, singing, and talking about Sydney." Doc Reames was persuaded to break open his footlocker of Le Jon brandy. In no time, a raucous party got under way.

A rude awakening came far too early. John Begert, having finished a "rat-holed" bottle of scotch by himself to celebrate his survival of three combat tours, was shaken to semiconsciousness by a shape bending over him in the darkness. "They want planes to strafe Kahili and it's your division's turn," grumbled Boyington. It was 4:00 A.M., and Begert was still drunk. So was Boyington, who watched as Begert wrestled with his mosquito netting and struggled to get up from his cot. "You're in no condition," he said. "I'll take it, I'll take the flight." If anything he was even drunker than Begert, but flying in that condition was nothing new to him.

The unexpected wake-up had developed after someone at the command level decided Kahili needed a dawn strafing. The Black Sheep were not officially off duty yet, and their replacements had never seen Bougainville in broad daylight, let alone in the darkness. Meanwhile, the party in the Quonset hut had lasted until two o'clock. Boyington had slept for only a couple of hours before he was roused by a runner from operations. Reames groaned that the pilots needed rest. "Never mind, Doc," Boyington said sourly. "They want Kahili strafed, we'll strafe it."

He asked for volunteers. George Ashmun, Chris Magee, and Bob McClurg agreed to go along. They put together a simple assignment—the first two would hit Kara while Boyington and McClurg strafed Kahili. There wasn't enough room for all of them to strafe one target in the tropical night.

Wearing his sweat-stained flying clothes, Boyington crawled into a truck for a ride to the flight line. He was shuffling around a Corsair to preflight it when a flashlight shone on his feet—still clad in slippers. "Hell, Greg," said Reames, "you don't have any shoes on."

"I don't need shoes to fly an airplane," growled Boyington, but the doctor took off his own and held them out. "You'll certainly need them if you go down."

Boyington laced them on.

It was still pitch-black and raining lightly as the Corsairs were fired up and warmed, then moved toward the strip. An hour earlier Boyington had been passed out; now he was in a high-performance fighter, preparing to take off in detestable weather and strafe a dangerous enemy base that he had to locate in the dark. No one else would have been crazy enough to try.

He took off at 4:50, hit the scud layer at two thousand feet, then bounced through the goo on instruments until he broke out on top. Ashmun, Magee, and McClurg, dazzled by moonlight and countless stars, formed on his wing before they entered a turbulent cloud bank. Ashmun got separated from them, so Boyington turned on his running lights for the benefit of the two remaining. Over Choiseul he inexplicably doused his lights and dropped from view into the clouds, whereupon Magee and McClurg decided to stick together and hit Kara by themselves.

Breaking through the weather alone, Boyington flew to Kahili, barely able to see it against the dark landmass of Bougainville. He made a pass but could detect nothing worth shooting at in the blackness, so he came around for another run, this time headed inland. He sprayed three bombers parked at the far end, drawing sporadic AA fire as he streaked over the runway, then curved to the right and flew low over Tonolei Harbor. Spotting the silhouette of a warship, he poured a long stream of slugs into it, then turned east toward Choiseul, where he strafed a barge at the mouth of a river before finally heading home.

Instead of landing back at Munda, however, he stopped at Vella Lavella to see his friend Nate Post, primarily to inform him that he had seen Milt Schneider, currently listed as missing, crash into the water the previous afternoon. After Boyington arrived, Post contrived to keep him there. "We needed an airplane," explained Warner Chapman, a division leader in VMF-221. "Our aircraft availability was down to nothing, and Post simply said, 'Boys, Boyington is here. I'll keep him busy, you fly his plane.' So we flew his aircraft at least two flights that day." Boyington had no objection, for Post shared a gift he had received earlier—a case of Schenley's, known in the islands as "Black Death."

During the day, Chapman managed to stop by the tent while Post entertained his guest. Content to listen as the others sipped Black Death and talked, Chapman observed that Boyington was disgruntled. As he continued to drink, the Black Sheep skipper complained first about his family troubles, then about the media, then his lack of recognition for victories, and finally about his own pilots. He described them, remembered Chapman, as "a group of irresponsible, harum-scarum people who were not as disciplined as they ought to be."

Among the episodes Boyington bitched about was John Bolt's impromptu strafing attack of three days before, which he resentfully labeled "a cock-and-bull tale." He was obviously having a difficult time swallowing the accolades Bolt had earned from Bull Halsey, and thus resorted to characterizing him as a liar.

Here was Boyington at his worst: intolerant and hypocritical. Viewed objectively, however, a couple of his points could be considered valid. There had been unfortunate or unusual acts exhibited by some of his pilots, including Bob Alexander's blunder that had killed three sailors and caused his own demise, followed by Virgil Ray's decision to quit flying combat missions and subsequent disappearance. And there was "Wild Man" Magee, the original beatnik, who wore a bandanna like a gypsy, studied metaphysics, and tossed a grenade from his airplane.

It was also true that Boyington had not received any sort of recognition for his own accomplishments. A Distinguished Flying Cross was routinely awarded for downing three planes; based on that criterion, he should have received four already. As for the lesser Air Medal, he was due a pocketful.

He flew back to Munda late that afternoon (Doc Reames got his shoes back), concluding a day as unorthodox as any he'd experienced in his flying career. The next morning he led sixteen Black Sheep back to Vella Lavella, where they turned their Corsairs over to VMF-221 before boarding an R4D for a ride to the Russells.

Their combat tour now officially over, the Black Sheep lounged for the next few days and enjoyed simple pleasures: cold beer, swimming, a game of poker or cribbage.

Contrary to his assertion that the press had dropped him, Boyington was back in the headlines. With his score now recognized at twenty victories, including six as a Flying Tiger, he was the high-scoring U.S. pilot currently in the combat zone. Suddenly he was being mentioned as the next possible candidate to challenge the record shared by Joe Foss and Eddie Rickenbacker.

In the funny pages one October Sunday, Frank Tinsley featured him in his full-color comic strip, *Fighting Marines*. The text described how the ace had knocked down "his twentieth Nip during a sweep over Kahili," accompanied by a dramatic rendering of swooping Corsairs and flaming Zeros. Boyington was also noted prominently in an excerpt from Olga Greenlaw's new book that was published in the August issue of *Cosmopolitan* (then a family-oriented magazine). He began to receive coverage in several other major magazines, as well. Writing for *Collier's,* Jack De Chant described Boyington's leadership as "a spark, a touchstone of victory—there was magic in his name."

Thus, despite his gripes, Boyington had gained nationwide acclaim with his sizzling record. As he drew tantalizingly close to the all-American tally of twenty-six victories, the only question was whether he could sustain the pace.

15

Gramps

Sunday papers weren't the only place military cartoons appeared in 1943. A new character named Grandpaw Pettibone was introduced that year in *Naval Air News,* the Bureau of Aeronautics's weekly newsletter. A cantankerous old-timer with a bony physique, long white beard, corncob pipe, and Wellington boots, Pettibone gave voice to caustic commentary about real aviation mishaps in the newsletter's safety column. Blurting his trademark "Jumpin' Jehoshaphat," he railed against careless accidents and bonehead mistakes. "Gramps," as he was called, became so popular that he endured as the sage of naval aviation safety for fifty years.

At least two thirds of the Black Sheep had enjoyed the column featuring "Gramps" back in flight school; when they met Greg Boyington in the summer of 1943 they naturally made comparisons. He had been in the Marine Corps when they were just starting puberty, and although he wasn't the oldest in the squadron—Walton had him beat by four years—his bedraggled appearance made him look like he was. "Hell, I don't see how anybody that old can get up in the morning," Don Fisher once joked. "After all, he's thirty or thirty-one, with a couple of kids."

Eventually, someone called him "Grandpappy," which was soon shortened to "Gramps" in keeping with the Pettibone character. Bob Bragdon, for one, began using the nickname after the first tour, and it caught on. Boyington had already made it clear that he didn't like to be saluted or called "sir," and he ran a loose enough ship that there was no harm in dropping all conventions of protocol around him.

For the ever-theatrical Moon Mullen, however, there was a problem. In adapting the Yale "Whiffenpoof" drinking song for the squadron's use, he realized that neither "Gramps" nor "Grandpappy" fit the syllabic count. Another variant worked best:

> To the one-armed joint at Munda,
> To the foxholes where we dwell,
> To the predawn takeoffs which we love so well.
> Sing the Black Sheep all assembled
> With their canteen cups on high,
> And the magic of their drinking casts a spell.
> Yes, the magic of their singing
> Of the songs we love so well,
> "Mrs. Murphy," "One Ball Riley," and the rest,
> We will serenade our "Pappy"
> While life and breath shall last,
> Then we'll pass and be forgotten
> Like the rest.
>
> We are poor little lambs who have lost our way.
> Baa, baa, baa.
> We are little Black Sheep who have gone astray.
> Baa, baa, baa.
> Gentlemen Black Sheep off on a spree,
> Damned from here to Kahili,
> God have mercy on such as we.
> Baa, baa, baa.

Taking the kidding in stride, Boyington demonstrated that he was no old-timer. The squadron was still at Banika in late October, enjoying drinks in one of the triple-Dallas huts, when he and a pilot from another squadron began to debate whether boxers or wrestlers made the better pound-for-pound fighters. Their argument heated up, and the inevitable contest began.

At first the boxer held the upper hand. He slugged Boyington in the face several times, drawing blood, while deftly staying outside the wrestler's bullish attempts to grapple. Boyington's face was soon a mess as he absorbed punishment, but he kept crowding the boxer until an opening appeared. With a rush he grabbed the boxer and threw him to the floor, then continued to throttle the helpless man, slamming his head against the plywood floor even after Walton said, "Okay, Greg, you've proved your point. Let him go." Several more Black Sheep convinced Boyington to release his victim, whose face was by then turning purple.

The combatants sat down, wiping blood, rasping for breath. Cold beer helped. The boxer wasn't ready to concede.

"That was a lucky hold you got."

"No, it will always end the same way. The wrestler will always win."

They started again. The boxer cautiously kept his guard up, connecting several times, but Boyington had an iron chin and the fight ended the same as before. He could have killed the other man. The damage to his face didn't bother Boyington, who considered it a small price to pay for proving his point—that he was still tough enough to whip just about anyone.

After an oh-dark-thirty breakfast on October 25, Boyington and the Black Sheep boarded a transport and departed the forward area. While they winged their way to a well-earned rest, Col. Ray Hopper, commander of the Russells' air group, sent a remarkable piece of correspondence to Guadalcanal. His two-page letter, addressed to Maj. Gen. Nathan Twining, USA, Commander, Allied Air Forces, Northern Solomons (ComAirNorSols), was entirely about Boyington.

Somehow, Hopper discovered that Boyington had received no official recognition for his numerous accomplishments. Nothing whatsoever had been done about his five-victory combat back in September, though the first three marines to achieve the feat had received a Medal of Honor. Hopper took it upon himself to jump-start the process, hurdling all lesser awards by submitting a recommendation for the same award—a Medal of Honor. Citing "outstanding heroism and courage above and beyond the call of duty," his correspondence to Twining presented a compelling account of several combat engagements, while richly praising Boyington's "matchless vigor," "dauntless inspiration," and "indomitable spirit." The main thrust of his testimonial was that Boyington and his entire squadron always faced numerically superior enemy forces, yet, because of his aggression, aerial leadership, and superior tactics, had succeeded in knocking down a lopsided number of Zeros.

While Twining considered the recommendation, Boyington and the Black Sheep settled into a recently vacated camp at Turtle Bay. Hardly had they retrieved their belongings from the storage compound when Colonel Smoak came by to complain about the mess in the Dallas huts. John Begert, referring to him as "an idiot colonel," later explained: "He actually made us go out and police the area, pick up cigarette butts and stuff like that. One night I remember he was hot on mosquito nets, so he came around and poked his head in every one of those [huts]. He's lucky he didn't get shot."

Petty though his rules were, Smoak could not be disobeyed. Boyington made everyone use their netting and straighten up the camp, then he and the Black Sheep devoted themselves to doing as little as possible. Time blurred as they played cards, got in line for chow, watched the nightly outdoor movie, sipped whatever drinks they could procure, talked with great anticipation of Sydney, and enjoyed songfests led by the Choral Society.

Nine languid days passed at Turtle Bay, during which Boyington's only notable accomplishment was to pass a medical checkup before the Black Sheep departed for Sydney on November 3. They flew to Tontouta, then milled around while waiting to take off for the long leg to Mascot

Airport just after midnight. As they drew nearer to Australia and sang loudly in the dark cabin, their skipper's vigor grew proportionately. "Boyington was bragging," said Hank Bourgeois, "that he was going to screw five times a day for the seven days we were there."

Sydney hadn't changed much. It was still a hedonistic playground that boggled the senses, where the real fun began when buxom Freda lined up drinks at happy hour in the skirt-filled lobby of the Royal Australian. Subtle things were different, however, now that Yanks on R & R had been throwing around their money and celebrating to excess for months. Restaurants and nightclubs still put up a cheerful front, but they were all too happy to take advantage of drunk Americans by double- and triple-billing if they could get away with it. The marines could have cared less. "We figured on spending a month's pay each; some of the boys spent as much as a year's salary," Walton later wrote.

When Boyington showed up at the airport for the return trip on November 12, it was the first time most of the Black Sheep had seen him since their arrival. Prior to boarding, they were held up by the R4D's loadmaster, who wouldn't let them bring a case of Australian lager: too heavy, he told them. Boyington didn't ponder the dilemma. "Drink the beer, boys," he ordered, and the contents disappeared. The only weight the loadmaster saved was that of the glass and the packaging.

During the flight, Boyington claimed that he'd accomplished his goal. "I kind of think it was with Freda," concluded Bourgeois. "She was always trying to get an American to marry her. She had to be around thirty, maybe older; big breasts, a little on the heavy side, but she always had a smile."

Boyington encountered plenty of changes and more than a little trouble during the next two weeks at Turtle Bay. After losing five pilots who had completed their obligations, the roster was upped by twenty-one members in order to meet a mandated increase to forty pilots. Among the newcomers

were several veterans from other outfits, including the new
executive officer, Maj. Pierre Carnagey, a handsome blond
athlete with two probables to his credit. The Nebraska native
was also someone else's victory, having been shot down
once over the Vella Gulf.

Next in seniority was Maj. Henry Miller, closely aligned
with the original VMF-214. A diligent, influential member
of the old Swashbucklers, he had strongly opposed their dis-
mantling when Boyington's echelon took over the squadron
number back in September. He was meticulous to a fault
(the Black Sheep nicknamed him "Notebook Henry"), creating some awkward moments between him and Frank
Walton in the reorganized squadron.

Another veteran, newly promoted Capt. Fred Avey, had
shot down a Zero during a tour with the Hellhawks of VMF-
213 and received a half-credit for a Betty. He was a week
older than Boyington, making him one of the oldest active
pilots in any fighter squadron.

In contrast, J. Cameron Dustin was just twenty-two, and
already a captain. He and Capt. Gelon Doswell, a year older,
were two-tour veterans of VMF-123 but had no confirmed
victories. Neither did the last two veterans, first lieutenants
James Brubaker and Bruce Ffoulkes, both former Hellhawks.

Except for Capt. Marion March, an instructor for the past
two years, the rest were greenhorns recently arrived from the
States. Harry Bartl, Glenn Bowers, John Brown, Rufus
Chatham, Ned Corman, Bill Crocker, Bill Hobbs, Herbert
Holden, Al Johnson, Harry Johnson, Perry Lane, Fred
Losch, and Al Marker were part of an alphabetically aligned
draft of replacements from ARS-2 in San Diego. The only
one of the bunch with previous Corsair time was Losch; the
rest had been tutored by Henry Miller, who served as an instructor with the MAG-11 headquarters squadron after the
Swashbucklers were disbanded.

Boyington faced several challenges. The newcomers outnumbered his original Black Sheep, yet in the span of two
weeks he had to integrate them with the squadron while si-

multaneously training them in tactics *and* in the F4U. As Corman explained, "You're out there as a new boy, and you're learning how to get in and out of the airplane. Literally. Since I'd had one hour, I was practically an experienced pilot in the plane; the other guys had nothing."

The flying schedule was a blur. Familiarization flights in the F4U, intercept problems, gunnery, and division tactics had to be crammed into the short training period. There were plenty of Zero killers among the veterans, and they made effective teachers. "We knew that we were in an outfit that had seen some action," said Corman, "and it was reassuring to know that these were combat-experienced pilots. They weren't just giving us something out of books—it was something they had learned."

The rookies and veterans jelled quickly. As a solution to a nearby garbage dump's problem with wild hogs, John Bolt organized a hunt one night. The next day, the squadron had a huge barbecue with six whole roasted pigs, plenty of beer, and a songfest. The combination was magic. "We weren't new boys for very long," remembered Glenn Bowers. "We got right into it with them."

A rarity that night was Boyington's appearance in a neat khaki uniform, complete with proper collar devices and a garrison cap. In an effort to deny Smoak the slightest reason to find fault, he tried his best to look sharp. Despite his efforts, he could do nothing about the fact that Smoak simply didn't like him. Whatever lay at the root of Smoak's resentment—no doubt jealousy reared its ugly head—he became vindictive. The result was a clash of egos that made Boyington's quarrel with Claire Chennault seem comparatively mild.

Smoak sent for Boyington on Friday, November 19, and informed him without preamble that Vella Lavella needed an operations officer. Boyington was stunned. He would lose his squadron and be transferred, a clean sweep of things. He returned solemnly to the Black Sheep camp, told Walton of his meeting with Smoak, then concluded, "Looks like he finally caught up with me."

Walton challenged, "You're not going to stand for that, are you?" He urged Boyington to see General Moore, unaware that he had made the trip under virtually identical circumstances six months earlier. If Boyington had any misgivings about repeating his visit, he ignored them or reconciled them later, for he set off across the island in a jeep that afternoon.

Too late Smoak realized that Boyington had nothing to lose by trying to circumvent him. It had worked before. Realizing his tactical error, he stopped by the Black Sheep camp at four that afternoon and found a group of concerned pilots gathered in the hut Walton shared with Boyington. "When he comes in," Smoak told Walton, "I want to see him." He checked again an hour later, then once more at six o'clock. Finally, an angry General Moore reached him by telephone, dispelling any doubts about where Boyington might have gone.

Moore did the talking—or shouting—during the brief exchange. Walton later reconstructed it: "What's this about taking Boyington out of his squadron? . . . What? . . . Well, I don't care how senior he is; he's the best combat pilot we've got, and he's to be left in command of his squadron where he belongs, understand?"

Boyington celebrated for hours. It was past midnight when he finally returned to the camp, but Don Fisher fetched him a beer while he told his jubilant Black Sheep how he got back into the squadron. Moore had tongue-lashed Smoak over the phone, he told them, then turned on his own chief of staff: "There's too goddamned much of this business of transferring squadron commanders around without my hearing about it." Moore was "banging the desk and swearing," so Boyington thanked him and beat a hasty retreat out of his quarters.

Smoak had lost the battle, but Boyington still had to face the music in the morning. He returned from the meeting carrying a report of his own arrest. Smoak had dredged up an obscure general order, written ten months earlier, which stated: "All officers of this group will not make trips to the [1st MAW or higher] offices for personal or departmental benefits without specific permission of the group commander."

Violation of such an order would normally have resulted in a verbal reminder, perhaps even a mild reprimand, but Smoak stretched his authority to the extreme and placed Boyington under arrest for "disobedience of orders." To ensure that Boyington remained within the confines of the airfield, Smoak even posted a guard outside his hut.

Boyington cooled his heels for a few days before filing his official response. He wrote: "I violated Group General Order Number One (1), dated 17 January, 1943," then quoted its two short paragraphs. Ever a slave to paperwork, Smoak immediately forwarded Boyington's statement and the original report of arrest up the chain of command, thinking it would cause fatal damage to Boyington's career. Instead, Smoak was essentially slain by his own sword. In quoting the silly order for all to read, Boyington revealed Smoak's arrogance and pettiness. The CO of MAG-11, unable to fathom that there was a war on, continually wasted everyone's time with unnecessary administrative matters.

Nuts Moore had a little paperwork of his own for Smoak's eyes. A commendation dated November 15 from Fighter Command on Guadalcanal praised Boyington's performance during the past combat tour. His conduct, it read, was "marked by a brilliant combat record, readiness to undertake the most hazardous types of missions, and a superior type of flight leadership." The commanding general considered Boyington "one of the five outstanding fighter pilots that have operated in this theater since the beginning of operations." Moore added an endorsement, then made Smoak sign off that he had read the commendation.

In the meantime, Boyington flew with his refurbished squadron, ate his meals, and lounged in his hut. From time to time, someone rapped on the back of his hut and surreptitiously passed a cola bottle through the window. The original contents had been replaced with something stronger, of course. Bowers, who helped in such efforts, simply acknowledged, "He needed some booze."

• • •

Six days after his arrest, Boyington posed for publicity photographs at the flight line. A Corsair was doctored with temporary graphics, including twenty small Japanese flags pasted to the fuselage and small white lettering identifying the pilot as "Gregory Boyington, Maj. USMC." A personalized name was applied to the engine cowl with the same water-based paint. In the only known surviving photograph, the name—partially obscured by a bystander's arm—appears to be *Lucybelle*. It makes sense, as Boyington maintained a torrid letter-writing affair with Lucy Malcolmson, whom Frank Walton referred to as "Lucy Belle" in a 1993 interview. Years later, however, Boyington claimed the name was *Lulubelle* when the photograph became public. By that time, he had about fifteen thousand reasons to want to forget Lucy Malcolmson, each one worth a dollar.

On the afternoon of the photo opportunity, Boyington received verbal orders from Major General Mitchell to commence the next combat tour. Within twelve hours he was aboard an R4D bound for Vella Lavella, hundreds of miles from the rear area. Thus, he never flew the colorfully decorated Corsair on a combat mission, yet countless artists have subsequently depicted *Lulubelle* as Boyington's personal combat plane, even over far-off Rabaul.*

With the blessing of Mitchell's verbal orders, Boyington got the last laugh on Joe Smoak. He and the Black Sheep moved out of their encampment at 2:00 A.M. on November 27, then took off from the bomber strip a few hours later in a transport. When Smoak walked down to his headquarters from his separate and pretentious set of huts a few hours

---

* The markings are popular on die-cast and plastic models too. One sharp-eyed modeler wrote to Boyington and asked why a few of the tiny victory flag decals were reproduced in the wrong direction. Boyington's response confirmed that they were true to the original: "The flags were only pasted on for PR shots—and removed immediately afterwards. Some clown pasting the flags on accidentally stuck a few on backwards—simple as that."

later, he discovered they had left. Worse, he had to sign an official letter for delivery to Boyington, stating, "You are hereby released from arrest this date and restored to duty, as your services cannot be spared."

Not many days later, serving up the last bit of justice, Nuts Moore relieved Smoak of his command and sent him to Vella Lavella as the operations officer. Later still, Smoak was sent to a staff job at Bougainville, even closer to the fighting.

Boyington knew he was flying on borrowed time as he settled into his new home. Vella Lavella was new in the sense that it had been taken from a tiny Japanese garrison just three months earlier; otherwise it was hot and humid, the same as all the rest. Fortunately, it was cleaner than most, having been spared the devastation of heavy bombing or a prolonged ground battle. The airstrip had been constructed right along the protected shoreline, and the Black Sheep lived in a nearby tent encampment among the coconut palms. Tent life was not unpleasant when the ocean breezes blew.

The increasing tempo of the island-hopping campaign lent a transient feel to Vella Lavella. Almost four weeks earlier, the assault on Bougainville had gotten under way with amphibious landings at Empress Augusta Bay, midway up the western side of the island. The 3d Marine Division and 2d Raider Regiment established a semicircular perimeter large enough to begin construction of a fighter strip at Cape Torokina; later two more fields were built farther inland. The Japanese tried to repulse the landings with hundreds of planes based at four airfields surrounding Rabaul (a fifth was started, but never completed), but by late November the air war had stagnated.

The timing was poor for Boyington and his squadron when they commenced operations on November 28. Although he participated regularly in combat air patrol (CAP) over the beachhead and the convoys that resupplied the perimeter, he failed to sight a single Japanese plane during the last days of November and the first two weeks of December.

With little else to interest him, Boyington led a small excursion to Kolombangara in the hope of locating Bob Alexander's crash site. Seven Black Sheep—including Burney Tucker, the only man remaining who had seen Alexander's plane go in—boarded a PT boat on Sunday, December 5, for the forty-five-mile run across the Vella Gulf in a driving rain. Tucker guided them around the southern shoreline to a small promontory, then pointed: damaged treetops still showed the swath cut by Alexander's Corsair.

The Japanese garrison had supposedly been evacuated, but the Black Sheep armed themselves before boarding a rubber boat. After landing on a narrow shelf of hard coral, they chopped and struggled through a tangled mass of jungle, looking overhead at the scarred trees to guide themselves. They reached the grim terminus of their search, as described by Tucker: "The plane had cut a path through the palms fifty feet wide and a hundred feet long. It was demolished but not burned. We found Alexander's body with it. We brought rocks and coral up from the beach and made a protective mound. We scratched Bob's name on the propeller blade and used it for a headstone. Then we stood at attention in the rain and saluted our last respects."

Alexander's body had been reduced to bones, most lying near the seat that had been torn from the cockpit on impact. There was simply no way for the marines to assimilate the pitiful remains with the pilot they had known—the handsome, all-American boy. Boyington wanted to say a eulogy, but admitted later the "words would not come."

It sounds contrived in today's cynical world, but the silent salute was reported unanimously. So was the simple farewell Boyington finally did utter: "So long, Bob."

The day after the excursion, Boyington flew a routine strike escort to Kieta Harbor on Bougainville, another uneventful mission without any sort of opposition. He did not fly at all for the next four days, resigned to the fact that his score would remain stuck at twenty until Corsairs could reach Rabaul. That would not happen until the strip at Torokina was ready, so he began to regularly check its progress. The first opportunity came on December 8, when Captain Dustin's division landed at Torokina for fuel. Ed Olander reported to Boyington that the field was still under construction, the landing surface too soft, "a quagmire."

Two days later, Boyington decided to see for himself. He took off alone in midmorning and reached Torokina fifty minutes later, where he found the runway surface already much improved. After returning to Vella Lavella in the afternoon, he led his division on the dawn patrol over Bougainville the next morning, extending their time on station to almost four hours before landing at Torokina for gas. The strip was in even better shape, showing improvement with each passing day.

Convinced that Torokina was ready for regular operations, Boyington flew to Munda on December 12 to meet with Nuts Moore about hitting Rabaul. They had lunch, talked of fighter sweeps, and probably shared a snort or two before Boyington returned to Vella Lavella. That they drank together is not a gratuitous assumption, for they had good reason to celebrate. The day after the Black Sheep left Espíritu Santo, Moore had strongly endorsed Boyington's Medal of Honor recommendation, calling him "the most audacious and successful fighter commander it has ever been my pleasure to know." At Munda, he must have cautioned Boyington not to mention the recommendation, which still had to be endorsed at half a dozen command levels and could be stonewalled at any time.

Boyington kept the news of the recommendation under wraps with the exception of a letter to Grace that month:

Well, Mom, you wrote a long time ago and asked why I didn't do something so that you could buy a new outfit and go to Washington like Bob Galer's mother did. You are going to do this little thing when I get back, because they have recommended me for the Congressional Medal of Honor out here.

I never dreamed that some day I was going to get the highest honor they give. But you said you wanted one for a trip to Washington, D.C., so I had to go out and knock down a mess of Japs to give my mom her wish. . . . Thank God I had the opportunity.

Boyington evidently felt a burst of energy after his meeting with Moore. As though to justify his assertion that Torokina was operational, he took two divisions there the following morning, remained overnight, then spent all the next day flying three complete missions—two patrols and a surface search—before landing back at Barakoma at the conclusion of the last patrol. After almost seven hours in the air, he rested all day on December 15, but was galvanized when a special notice appeared in the operations order for the sixteenth: "All squadron commanders report to Com-AirSols, Munda, 1430 for conference."

Arriving at Munda on schedule, Boyington joined eight squadron commanders for a discussion with Major General Mitchell (now ComAirSols) and Nuts Moore regarding a fighter sweep to Rabaul. The details were hammered out in an hour and a half. Boyington would lead the sweep, designed for the sole purpose of enticing Zeros to come up. Rabaul had been bombed repeatedly by Army B-24s and B-25s, but this would be the first raid by land-based, single-engine Allied aircraft.

The honor of being placed in charge of the epic event was great, but so were the responsibilities. The effort would be huge—eighty aircraft stacked in three layers—which would hopefully look like a bombing formation to Japanese radar controllers. Each service had campaigned for a share of the action, resulting in an unwieldy conglomeration of thirty-two Corsairs, two dozen Hellcats, and an equal number of Kittyhawks. From their different fields on Vella Lavella and New Georgia, the fighters would take off early the next morning, land at Torokina to top off tanks, then await the signal to launch.

There was much to coordinate. Boyington returned to Vella Lavella early that afternoon with the exciting news, then selected the pilots who would accompany him. Sandy Sims's division (including John Brown, Junior Heier, and Bruce Ffoulkes) got the nod, while Boyington would fly with Bob McClurg on his wing, followed by Chris Magee and D. J. Moore in the second section.

By early evening, Frank Walton had gathered the necessary material to brief the Vella Lavella contingent, including tall, lean Maj. Marion Carl, the first ace in the Marine Corps and now in command of VMF-223. Walton gave out altitude assignments, posted the latest photographs of New Britain and Rabaul, highlighted the Japanese airfields, then got down to explaining emergency plans.

Two Dumbos (PBY Catalina flying boats) would be standing by at Torokina; pilots in distress were to radio "Dane Base" to alert them. If a pilot came down on New Britain, his probability of being rescued was very poor, but if he could reach New Ireland, the odds were better. First, however, he would have to evade the many Japanese on the island and reach a village near the Weilan River, then try to locate a supposedly friendly native named Boski. A water landing offered the best overall probability of survival, though success depended largely on whether Dane Base received an accurate report of the downed pilot's location. If he wasn't picked up within the first twenty-four hours, the variables of weather and currents conspired against him, and the opportunities for rescue began to diminish exponentially.

None of the pilots had any illusions about the dangers of hitting Rabaul. They would have to cross the largest expanse of open ocean they had yet encountered, strike the most daunting enemy base in the South Pacific, then complete a long, nerve-wracking trip home. Because they were piloting single-engine planes, any relatively minor mechanical problem could rapidly become serious trouble—real or imagined. A pilot whose plane didn't hold together was virtually guaranteed of spending considerable time in his inflatable rubber boat, leading Moon Mullen, one of the premiere songsters in the area, to write a tune called "In a Rowboat at Rabaul." The lyrics poked fun at a downed aviator's puny hopes, and became popular among South Pacific fliers.

When Walton finished his portion of the brief, Boyington said a few words, then asked if there were any questions. Correspondent Dan Bailey, sitting in, saw Boyington laugh at one of the young pilots who asked what strategy he planned to use against Zeros. The lieutenant was visibly embarrassed. "Seeing this," Bailey wrote, "the major apologized and said: 'There's no such thing as strategy in fighting up there. Gambler's guts would be better to describe what a fighter pilot needs. Good aerial fighting is a gamble. And you've got . . . to be willing to take the consequences if you lose. It's just like street fighting. If you hit the other guy first, and hit him hard, you'll probably strike the last blow. That he'll hit you back harder than you hit him is the chance you have to take.'"

Awake before 4:00 A.M. the next morning, Boyington ate breakfast, conducted his preflight in the dark, then took off at 5:15 to lead the Vella Lavella fighters up to Bougainville. True to his reputation for frequently taking the oldest-looking plane on the line, he flew an F4U-1, an old birdcage version that had been in the Solomons for months.

At Torokina, a fleet of gas trucks moved from plane to plane, topping off tanks. The field was packed with fighters, all of which began turning up in time for the scheduled departure. Boyington released his brakes promptly at 9:00, but it proved time consuming to get all the fighters off the single strip. The "Kiwis," minus two P-40s that aborted with mechanical difficulties, reached their assigned altitude well before their American counterparts, who had to climb significantly higher. Wing commander Trevor Freeman promptly raced toward Rabaul with his Kittyhawks rather than waiting as directed, leaving the Americans far behind.

Boyington gathered his Corsairs and Hellcats at twenty thousand feet, then guided them northwest along the

Bougainville shoreline. He was forced to go around a weather system before resuming a direct heading for Rabaul, putting the American fighters even farther behind. By the time they reached the coast of New Britain, the New Zealanders had already engaged a dozen Zeros from the 204th Kokutai, subsequently joined by elements of the 201st and 253d.

While the melee swirled at the lower levels, Boyington crossed Cape Gazelle and proceeded toward Simpson Harbor, where the town of Rabaul was tucked inside a protective ring of volcanic mountains. At the north shore of the harbor, Lakunai Airdrome reportedly housed some sixty-five fighters. Sure enough, from twenty-eight thousand feet above, the marines could clearly see thirty to forty aircraft lined up along the reddish-brown earth of the airstrip. None took off. A few bursts of heavy AA dotted the sky, as if the Japanese were content to take potshots. Frustrated, Boyington reverted to the challenge that had worked over Kahili, shouting over the radio, "Come on up and fight!"

On the ground at Rabaul headquarters, a Nisei named Chikaki Honda was listening to the chatter on the American frequency. A year older than Boyington, he had been born and raised in Hawaii and developed a passion for baseball at McKinley High School, where he used the American name of Edward. He pursued the sport after his parents sent him to their homeland for a religious education, playing for Keio University, then working briefly as a sportswriter for Domei News, and eventually becoming an assistant coach for the Nagoya Dragons. When America entered the war, he forfeited his U.S. citizenship, joined the IJN as an interpreter, and reached Rabaul in the summer of 1943. He had been away from the States for twelve years by the time Boyington's voice boomed over the radio, but had not forgotten his ballpark vernacular: "Come on down, sucker," he invited.

Boyington did just that. Dropping to ten thousand feet, he sprayed about nine hundred rounds in the direction of the field. If any Zeros subsequently took off, none came up to challenge the Black Sheep skipper, who continued to circle the area for thirty-five minutes without making contact. For him, the sky remained empty.

McClurg, meanwhile, left Boyington's flank after spotting a lone Zero far below. It turned out to be a Rufe, the floatplane version, which he claimed as a victory, though he was admonished by Boyington for leaving the division to go after it. Moore likewise left the formation (he waggled his wings first, but no one saw him) and engaged Zeros, claiming two.

After winging back to Torokina for a fuel stop, Boyington reached Vella Lavella that afternoon in a foul mood. He threw down his helmet as he walked into the operations tent, complaining, "They wouldn't come up. Just a few strays." As more reports filtered in, it became all too evident that the first sweep of Rabaul had been unsuccessful. Wing Commander Freeman had been shot down, another New Zealander was captured after colliding with a Zero, and D. J. Moore was overdue. (He was safe but injured, having crash-landed on Sterling Island in the Treasuries.) Aside from the two Black Sheep, none of the other Corsair pilots registered claims, and only one Hellcat pilot received credit for a victory among navy units. The Kiwis claimed five planes, bringing the Allied total to nine, but the Japanese lost just two fighters and one pilot for the whole day.

Walton's report was used as a medium to lobby for smaller efforts. "Far too many fighter planes were sent on the sweep," he wrote, urging that all aircraft should be of the same type, "thus eliminating the necessity for continually checking other planes in the sky." No repeat missions were currently planned, however, and Boyington found himself off the schedule for the next three days. His next appearance on the operations board was December 21, when he was scheduled to lead three divisions of Black Sheep to escort a planned B-24 strike on Rabaul, but after he reached Torokina the mission was scrubbed. The rainy season had arrived, bringing violent fronts that sprouted among the islands with little warning.

With deceiving speed, half of Boyington's combat tour had slipped by. Two months had passed since his successful sweeps over Kahili, during which he'd not so much as laid the pipper of his gunsight on an enemy plane. Another two days dragged by because of foul weather, a seemingly interminable wait while the days remaining in the combat tour rapidly dwindled. He didn't realize the lull would end soon, and dramatically; nor could he know that when the proverbial sword fell, its blade would cut both ways.

16

In a Rowboat at Rabaul

Boyington's outlook changed dramatically two days before Christmas. A large B-24 strike on Rabaul was planned for December 23, after which several Black Sheep would participate in a mop-up fighter sweep. Despite the success Boyington had demonstrated in October with his preemptive sweeps over Kahili, the mission planners seemed determined to schedule the fighter sweeps to arrive after the bombers had already cleared the target—in this case a full hour and fifteen minutes later. On the other hand, some of what Boyington had recommended after his first Rabaul sweep did sink in: this event was planned with just four dozen fighters, including twenty-eight P-38s from the 44th Fighter Squadron on Guadalcanal, eight F4Us from VMF-214 led by Boyington, and a dozen more Corsairs from VMF-223, with Marion Carl in tactical command.

The event began at Vella Lavella when Pierre Carnagey took off with two divisions of Black Sheep for the bomber escort, followed by Boyington forty minutes later with two divisions of his own for the fighter sweep. They reached Torokina shortly after nine o'clock, where they were joined two hours later by Henry Miller and John Bolt, who attached themselves as latecomers. The enlarged group was airborne again at 12:30, having delayed until the prescribed time to allow for the Liberators to accomplish their mission.

Perhaps the Black Sheep flew to Rabaul that day with a

sense of overconfidence, based on the squadron's reputation for lopsided victories over Kahili during the recent tour and the quietude of the past few weeks. If so, it was a costly letdown, for a storm of aerial combat unlike anything the Black Sheep had ever seen broke over Rabaul that day. In a dramatic reversal of their effort six days earlier, the Japanese scrambled an overwhelming force when the bombers approached Rabaul. The 201st Ku launched thirty Zeros, the 204th sent thirty-eight, and the 253d added another thirty-one. The Zeros hounded the bombers and overwhelmed the escorting fighters, downing Pierre Carnagey and Jimmy Brubaker along with a Hellcat pilot from VF-33.

Fortunes for the fighter sweep were far better, but not without cost. As had happened over Kahili earlier, the bomber formation was behind schedule and the fighter sweep was early. Carl's forty-eight fighters reached Rabaul just fifteen minutes after the bombers had plastered the town and harbor. Many Zeros were returning to Rabaul in small groups, making easy targets. Leading his designated "low flight" of eight Black Sheep, Boyington spotted a gaggle of planes off to his right. "This is it, fellows," he called on the radio, and the Corsairs scattered after individual targets.

Boyington turned toward the general melee off to his right, then spotted a lone Zero well below him heading toward Rabaul. He dropped behind the mottled green fighter in a throttled-back glide. As he later put it: "Never before had I been so deliberate and cold about what I was doing." He set up the shot from dead astern, letting the range close to just fifty feet, knowing the pilot was "a doomed man" before he flamed the Zeke with a single burst. A parachute billowed as the pilot drifted toward the channel; and he splashed beside the ring of water that lingered after his Zero hit the surface.

Boyington had been able to make such a nonchalant attack—as easy a gunnery pass as he ever made—because of the Japanese pilot's failure to "check six." Likewise, Boyington made himself vulnerable by flying straight and level behind the Mitsubishi, but he always seemed to get away with it because he measured the odds, then played by his own rules. The Black Sheep marveled at his amazing intuition, his ability to know when to hit and when to be cautious. As Fred Losch later said, "He was smart, he was aggressive, and he was an excellent pilot. You can be a great pilot, and fly fighter planes, but that doesn't make you a great fighter pilot."

In the cockpit Boyington was as good as they got, possessing just the right combination of talent and apparent invincibility—a quality that was perhaps his greatest asset, intangible though it was. Somehow he *knew* that he wouldn't fall from the grain elevator beams over the tracks at St. Maries, just like he knew there wasn't an unseen enemy pilot trying to assassinate him over Rabaul. At least not this day.

After flaming the careless Zeke, Boyington pushed the throttle forward and began to climb. Reaching eleven thousand feet, he saw two more A6Ms slightly below and to his right, heading for Rabaul. One streamed smoke; the other weaved protectively. Boyington curved around to get behind them, then came in from dead astern again. The Zekes saw him coming, and the cripple dived away while the wingman rolled out to one side. With the advantage of speed and altitude, Boyington simply continued his run on the damaged Zeke and triggered his guns at one hundred feet. The little fighter ignited, and again the pilot jumped clear. Apparently the survival instinct was stronger in some Zero pilots than their desire to "self-explode" for the emperor.

By this time, the victim's partner had maneuvered around to start a run on Boyington. He responded by nosing over, building airspeed to gain separation, then pulled up hard to reengage. But the Japanese pilot had already turned away and was circling the parachutist, who drifted above St. George's Channel. The second pilot's gesture was gallant but wasted. Low and slow, he made an easy target. "I closed in on him from the sun side and nailed him about a hundred feet over the water," Boyington later wrote. "His Zero made a half roll and plunked out of sight into the sea. No doubt his swimming comrade saw me coming but could only watch."

Working his way back up to eighteen thousand feet, Boyington steered toward Rabaul and circled the harbor for twenty minutes. It was a terribly long time to be flying alone above Indian Country, with just his pair of eyes to keep a swiveling lookout for the surrounding enemy. When he spotted them, he was slightly outnumbered. A cluster of nine Zeros in a classic V passed by almost a mile and a half below.

In what was becoming a repetitive maneuver, Boyington pulled back the throttle and dropped behind the formation with the sun at his back, allowing him to steadily approach the rearmost Zero. At three hundred feet and closing rapidly, he held the trigger in. The Zero erupted and nosed out of the way just as Boyington barreled down through the formation, scattering the others. Quickly regrouping, they chased him for ten minutes—actually gaining, he thought—until he built enough airspeed to pull away heading toward the west, away from home.

The shooting was not quite finished. After pulling around to the proper heading, Boyington cleared the eastern coast of New Britain and was skirting the edge of New Ireland when he spotted a submarine just offshore. He dived at the sub "and managed to get in two or three bursts before it submerged," according to Frank Walton's entry in the war diary.

Stretching his fuel to reach the Barakoma strip at 4:30, eight hours after departing for Bougainville that morning, Boyington was met by a cluster of pilots and correspondents. His four victories were a huge leap toward the existing Foss-Rickenbacker record, justifying the excitement beside his revetment on the flight line. "The minute his plane landed and he announced his victories," wrote Dan Bailey, "the pilots picked him up and carted him around on their shoulders, yelling, 'Just three more, old man, and you'll do it!'" Boyington tried to downplay it, telling the Black Sheep they were "expecting a hell of a lot."

Another correspondent, Sgt. James Hardin Jr., steered

Boyington into a Marine Corps radio truck parked near the revetment, where a portable transcribing machine recorded his description of the four victories. He was modest, speaking in his homespun style with a slight Western twang. "I caught this one on fire," he said of the first victim, and made the downing of the fourth sound equally humble. "I came down unknown to the Zekes and picked off the tail-end man, and then ran like a son-of-a-gun."

His account also went into Walton's action report, making the four victories official. Plenty of others logged claims, bringing the total to nineteen Zeros destroyed, two probably destroyed, and six others damaged.

It had been a devastating day among the Zero pilots, with seven killed in action, and at least two were seen to bail out. Therefore, seven and possibly more Zeros were shot down, making it numerically feasible that Boyington downed all four of his alleged victims, although accepting them at face value negates many of the other claims. The Black Sheep alone were credited with eleven Zeros destroyed.

Conversely, it was the squadron's worst single day thus far regarding losses. In addition to Pierre Carnagey and Jimmy Brubaker, Bruce Ffoulkes was missing. After the fight started, he had remained with his section leader for a while, but later ignored Junior Heier's radio warning not to climb into a gaggle of Zeros. None of the three were ever found.

Sobering though the losses were, Boyington was in a celebrating mood. "He was a noisy, cheerful, and talkative Boyington," observed Sergeant Bailey. "Anything the press wanted to know he answered." He chatted about a broad range of topics, even his divorce. Of his children, he talked most about Bobby, then eight years old, who knew more about planes than Boyington did. Fueled by Le Jon brandy, he also talked about himself, enjoying the attention as his emotions climbed. Finally he declared, "I'm working with the best bunch of guys in the South Pacific. I'm flying. I'm fighting. I'm killing Japs. I'm the happiest man in the world."

This was probably the night that Marion Carl paid a visit

with his executive officer, Maj. Bob Keller, who later described Boyington as "exuberant." During the ensuing party, Boyington heckled Carl about the Cactus Air Force on Guadalcanal, teasing him that Wildcat pilots couldn't dive-bomb like the Flying Tigers. "K.O." Toomey, another of VMF-223's pilots, was also present that night, being such a regular around the Black Sheep that they almost considered him one of theirs. (No freeloader, he contributed his repertory of songs "with a fine Irish brogue in a hoarse whiskey tenor," and always wore a derby to the songfests.) As the party continued, the normally reserved Carl had his fill of Boyington's ribbing. "I'll show you how it was done on Guadalcanal," he shouted. Putting the derby on his head, he climbed on a table and dived off headfirst. "Fortunately," wrote Keller years later, "his trajectory was interrupted by two well-wishers. No one was hurt. These two multiple aces actually got along exceedingly well together, and a strong mutual respect existed between them."

Boyington's high spirits continued the next night, Christmas Eve, as an even bigger party got under way in the tent. Doc Reames and Frank Walton made "eggnog" from powdered milk, powdered eggs, sugar, nutmeg, and five quarts of booze. Most of the Black Sheep crowded in, taking turns wearing Toomey's black derby while they dipped their canteen cups into the high-octane concoction, belted out their favorite songs, and shared stories of Sydney. Then the atmosphere took a somber turn. Perched on a footlocker, "Meathead" Bragdon voiced a concern that most of the pilots were feeling: "Listen, Gramps, we all want to see you break the record, but we don't want you to go up there and get killed doing it."

"Don't worry about me," said Boyington, still feeling invincible. "They can't kill me. If you guys ever see me going down with thirty Zeros on my tail, don't give me up. Hell, I'll meet you in a San Diego bar six months after the war, and we'll all have a drink for old times' sake."

Moon Mullen raised a toast to the skipper's resolve and the Black Sheep launched into another round of songs, but

Boyington's mood began to change that night. First his high spirits reached a plateau, then, later still, hit a brick wall. He went on a binge that lasted another two days, and when the inevitable crash came on the morning of the twenty-seventh, he was physiologically drained. Later he admitted to being "anything but happy."

There is no way to determine exactly what depressed him, but the possibilities are endless. Stress and fatigue affected all of them, but were proportionately worse for Boyington because of his alcohol intake. Then there was the empty bunk, the one the likable Carnagey had so recently occupied. ("It's sure lonesome here without old Pierre," Boyington told his other tent mates). If he had indeed exaggerated some of his victory claims, the likelihood that guilt crept into Boyington's conscience would be all the greater.

His demons can only be supposed, but his behavior was suggestive of a manic-depressive; one of his own relatives, a health-care professional, has described him as bipolar. Over a stretch of three days and four nights, he binged instead of flying, though he had less than two weeks remaining as a squadron commander. While he drank, the Black Sheep flew successful Rabaul missions and scored victories.

Some of them occurred on Christmas Day, the holiday Boyington had come to despise since childhood. During an escort mission over Rabaul, Ned Corman flamed the tail-end Zeke from a formation of five—his first and only victory of the war. "I was just elated," he said years later. "I thought it was the best Christmas present I'd ever had. And then Boyington debriefed me, and he just chewed my ass from one end to the other. One, for leaving the formation, and two, for not getting all five."

Fred Avey also scored a victory that day, and Boyington later tried to pick a fight with him. So skinny that his chest was practically concave, Avey was not the type of opponent Boyington normally looked for. "I weighed about 110 pounds then, and I was soaped up for a shower when Boyington came staggering in and wanted to wrestle me," he later told Walton. It was one of Avey's worst scares on the ground, for he was standing on a slippery section of pierced steel planking, and knew he would be seriously cut if Boyington threw him down. He used every ounce of persuasion to get the skipper to leave.

Toward the end of his Christmas binge, Boyington's demeanor was much different than it had been after his successful fighter sweep. Associated Press correspondent Fred Hampson learned this during a short interview.

> I asked him on the night of December 26 if he was really as interested in the record as everybody seemed to think.
>
> "Sure I am," he snapped. "Who the hell wouldn't be? I'd like to break it good and proper. If I could just get on the ball again I might even run it up to thirty or thirty-five. Lord knows the hunting's good enough when the weather lets you in there, but I'm not right. I'm not right at all."

The binge ended on December 27. It might have lasted longer, but Boyington was awakened before dawn to get ready for a mission. He was the tactical commander for a dedicated fighter sweep over Rabaul, scheduled to take off at 6:20, and he was still hungover. As he later described the morning: "I was staggering about the tent, searching for my fatigues without much success. Knowing this would never do, I wobbled out of the tent to a rain barrel that was kept constantly full of the waters shedded [sic] by the tent top, and there I submerged my head and shoulders into the cool water. I repeated the dunking several times, blowing bubbles from my mouth and nose until I was able to steady myself down a bit. This little aid had become standard procedure with me by then, for the pressure was really on me, I felt."

He was still feeling "really rough" when he rode down to the flight line with the other pilots, some of whom claimed later that he habitually put little bits of tobacco under his eyelids to keep his bloodshot eyes open. Accustomed to manning one of the older planes, he took a drab-looking F4U-1A that had been around for several months. Appearances were deceiving. The Corsair was mechanically refurbished, having just been ferried to Vella Lavella on Christmas Eve after an overhaul. Much like its pilot, it was rough looking on the outside, but ready to perform strongly all day.

Boyington got the sweep under way from Torokina at 10:00, leading forty Corsairs and twenty Hellcats toward Rabaul in a stack that stretched all the way to thirty thousand feet. The Japanese were waiting above St. George's Channel with upwards of forty Zeros, which orbited in a huge, canted Lufbery Circle. Despite his hangover, Boyington did "a masterful tactical job" of dealing with the unusual Japanese concept, maintaining his force's altitude advantage to bottle up the Zeros. Over the next fifteen minutes, peeling off for overhead runs, Corsairs and Hellcats hacked an estimated ten to twelve Zeros out of the sky—this according to Japanese records.

The Black Sheep combined for five victories, including two for Don Fisher and one for Moon Mullen, who joined McClurg and Bolt as the newest aces. Boyington scored once, making a classic overhead attack on a Zeke at fourteen thousand feet. It torched after he hit it from a hundred yards.

When the sweep was over, he landed back at Torokina and remained on the ground for nearly two hours before finally lifting off for Vella Lavella at 3:15 P.M. Touching down an hour later, he pulled his helmet off, letting the breeze fan him as he taxied number 883 through the dappled shadows of palm trees. Approaching the flight line, he could see a crowd of pilots, reporters, and photographers waiting by his revetment. They were anxious to hear about the sweep, hoping he had tied or beaten the Foss-Rickenbacker record.

Frank Walton was loving all the publicity. Having put himself in a position to conduct a live interview from Sergeant Hardin's radio truck when Boyington returned from the record-breaking flight, he was standing by with pages of carefully prepared script. After being introduced by Hardin, he would say: "Thank you, Sergeant Hardin, and how do you do, America. Our pilots—and they're your pilots, too, of course—have gone all the way to Rabaul today on the kind of mission they've been looking for. . . ." His handwritten script went on like that, filled with hyperbole. In addition to figurative descriptions of Boyington ("a real fighting man"), the pages included prompts and appropriate blank spaces for the yet-unknown number of planes he would shoot down. "And here he is now—keep your fingers crossed, ladies and gentlemen, while I bring him to the microphone. He did it, ladies and gentlemen, _____ more Zeros for a total of _____. Meet America's new Number One Ace—Major Gregory Boyington."

But Walton was denied this day. Boyington swung 883 around in the revetment and shut down the growling Pratt & Whitney. In the sudden silence, he leaned his right elbow on the cockpit sill and held up his index finger—one victory. A photographer jumped onto the wing and snapped his picture, the flash revealing the weariness in Boyington's eyes, even through his Ray-Bans. Walton salvaged the afternoon by climbing onto the wing to shake Boyington's hand, a gesture staged purely for the photographers. Boyington did not smile.

Correspondents lingered for interviews. To Fred Hampson he explained: "The hunting was fine, but I wasn't right again. God, but I'm doing some dumb things up there!" Another reporter quoted Boyington as saying, "Damn it, I couldn't hit the broad side of a barn with bass viola today. I guess the tension was too great."

Someone had hit his Corsair, though. A neat hole from a Japanese 7.7mm round was discovered in the right wing. It was a minor hit, but it seemed to crack Boyington's façade of invincibility. One of the Black Sheep later said, "It shouldn't have been anything to rattle anybody, but this one damn round through his wingtip shook Boyington up."

Another public relations event that afternoon served as a welcome distraction. To everyone's surprise, a World Series team had answered Boyington's offer to trade Zeros for ball caps. The St. Louis Cardinals lost the series in five games, but took game two from the New York Yankees and subsequently shipped a thick stack of caps and several Louisville Sluggers to the Black Sheep. Several photographs were taken that afternoon, including one with the six current aces holding baseball bats beneath the nose of a Corsair while the other Black Sheep stood atop the sturdy wings. Boyington grinned widely in what would become one of the most oft-published squadron photographs of World War II, enjoying the moment with his equally happy Black Sheep.

The smiling soon stopped, however. By the middle of the following morning, a popular veteran and two more of the new Black Sheep were gone.

The ill-fated Black Sheep were supposed to have been idle on December 28, as were all of the marine squadrons at Vella Lavella. When the operations order was posted the previous afternoon, only one event was listed, a flight of F6Fs to cover a task force. Late in the afternoon, word spread that Maj. Rivers Morrell, commanding officer of VMF-216 up at Torokina, was taking a fighter sweep to Rabaul in the morning.

Quickly, Boyington rounded up three divisions and left for Bougainville just before 6:00 P.M. The twelve Black Sheep grabbed some chow at Torokina, found tents for the night, then arose before dawn to join Morrell's mission.

On paper, the size and composition of the sweep was to Boyington's liking with forty-six Corsairs assigned, but the hastily conceived plan had flaws. In the first place, two of the squadrons had little experience. A few divisions from Morrell's squadron had participated in two previous fighter sweeps, but their only victories had come just the day before, when several pilots claimed a total of eight Zeros. They lost three of their own in the process—hardly an auspicious beginning. VMF-321 was even greener, having just arrived in the combat zone four days before the mission. Morrell had never led a strike before, and the force he commanded was cobbled together with odd numbers of planes: twelve from the Black Sheep, nineteen from Morrell's squadron, nine from VMF-223, and just six from VMF-321.

In the predawn blackness on December 28, Boyington taxied a slightly newer Corsair over the Marston matting for a 6:00 A.M. takeoff. The plane he had flown up from Vella Lavella, 883, had carried him four times the previous day and was overdue for maintenance, so he borrowed 915 from one of the Black Sheep on standby.

The departure went smoothly, but within an hour two Black Sheep turned back due to mechanical trouble. The rest proceeded uneventfully toward Rabaul until reaching St. George's Channel, whereupon Morrell turned the formation in a huge arc that took the Corsairs north of Rabaul. Gradually he brought them around to the southwest, then finally turned them east, toward the channel again. The formation was descending the whole time, according to the VMF-214 war diary, while "making such a wide sweep that enemy planes taking off from Lakunai Airdrome had plenty of time to climb to altitude before the formation had completed its first circle."

Unseen by the Corsair pilots, a large group of Zeros had climbed above them to the east, gaining the upper hand. Hiding in the glare of their beloved rising sun, they waited for the right moment, then pounced with a tenacity and coordination never before experienced over Rabaul.

Popular Texan D. J. Moore, lagging at the rear of Boyington's division, was overwhelmed by aggressive IJN pilots newly arrived from the carrier anchored in Simpson Harbor. Over in Capt. J. C. Dustin's division, he and his tail-end Charlie, Harry Bartl, climbed blindly into the sun and were likewise shot down, while veterans Bruce Matheson and Ed Olander split away and dove for their lives.

The various Zero units claimed twenty-one Corsairs destroyed and eight others damaged, though the three Black Sheep were the only victims. The exaggerated claim reveals that large numbers of Zeros had ganged up on them, with each pilot's account subsequently recorded as a victory. Due to a standing order, the *kokutais,* rather than individual pilots, received the victory credits.

The six remaining Black Sheep were forced to fight defensively. Boyington sighted a fighter four thousand feet below and nosed over, approaching from his usual position directly aft, but when he opened fire the enemy plane zoomed with "a terrific rate of climb." He identified it as a Tojo, the Allies' nickname for the Nakajima Ki-44 flown by the JAAF, but that type was never based at Rabaul. In all likelihood, he shot at a Hamp, which had square wingtips not unlike the Nakajima's. Credited with a probable, which did nothing for his overall score, Boyington uncharacteristically failed to reenter the melee after that single pass.

Four of the Black Sheep managed to account for Zeros, including Olander and Matheson, who shot their way out of trouble. Meanwhile, the other three Corsair squadrons made outrageous claims for twenty-two additional Zeros destroyed, seven probables, and ten damaged. In reality the fight had been a draw, with three Japanese pilots lost and two additional fighters damaged. As a measure of the poor validation surrounding claims, two pilots from VMF-216 were credited with victories even though they could not state definitively whether they shot at in-line Tonys or radial-engine Zekes.

A few of the surviving Black Sheep made it back to Vella Lavella, but the rest, including Boyington, stopped at Torokina. After landing at 9:30 A.M., he decided to remain at Bougainville and avoid the press waiting at Vella Lavella. He had nothing to show for the mission, and three of his pilots were missing. In the past five days, six Black Sheep had disappeared, the heaviest blow of all being the loss of D. J. Moore.

Boyington slept on a cot at Bougainville for the second night in a row, lucky if he carried a "bingo bag" with a toothbrush and razor. The living conditions were primitive enough that he didn't feel self-conscious about shedding his sticky clothing and tramping about in his boots and underwear. It was all he wore while standing in line for at least one meal served in a tent without tables. He helped himself from pots set precariously on a sagging cot; coffee was dipped from a garbage can.

Miserable weather moved in, keeping him at Torokina until the afternoon of December 29. By the time he reached Vella Lavella, the operations order for the next day had already been posted. He was not on it. Instead, Marion Carl was scheduled to lead the next fighter sweep. In his official oral history, Carl recalled the dialogue that occurred when Boyington came to him with a request:

> "How about trading flights tomorrow? Let me take your hop tomorrow."
>
> "What's the problem, Rats?"
>
> "Well, I'm due to rotate, and I don't think they'll let me come back up again. I've got [twenty-five] airplanes and I'd like to get the record."
>
> "Okay, I'll trade you," Carl agreed. "I'm going to be up here for a while. I'll just slip mine one day and it won't make that much difference."

It was all for naught. Boyington took off just before seven o'clock on the morning of December 30 with two divisions of Black Sheep, but after they reached Torokina the fighter sweep was canceled due to poor weather. Two other divisions participated in a bomber escort to Rabaul, where the weather created havoc for the mission.

A dejected Boyington brought his flight back to Vella Lavella, having wasted the trade. He was nearly at wit's end. "I was helpless," he later wrote. "And even during this strain I came to realize that a record meant absolutely nothing; it would be broken again and again, in spite of anything I did. I was worried only about what others might think of me."

He was not scheduled to fly on New Year's Eve, which turned out to be no loss—those that did attempt a mission aborted again—but idleness did nothing to improve his mood. "He went off by himself and stared at the rain," wrote Walton. "He was jittery."

At evening chow, Fred Hampson sat across from Boyington at a wooden table and pressed him with more questions. "Are you going to get another chance at the record?" After a noncommittal response from Boyington, he tried harder: "Well, if you do, are you going to break it? Are you going to be satisfied with just one or two, or are you going after more?"

"Goddamn it," shouted Boyington, crashing his fist to the table and flipping his plate of food onto Hampson, "why don't you guys leave me alone? I don't know if I'm going to break it or not. Just leave me alone till I do or go down trying." He retreated to his tent and Walton followed, but not before telling the food-smeared correspondent, "You guys never learn."

While the rain beat down, Boyington got another party started. Reames and Walton, concerned about his condition, tried to get him to ease up, but Boyington had his own ideas. According to Reames, he grabbed a hammer and went to the footlocker where the medicinal brandy was stored, shouting, "Here's a ball, and here's a peen!" Timing his swing with the word *peen,* he knocked off the lock with a single blow.

Boyington poured the booze into a Thermos jug, then stirred in juice from fresh limes that grew on the island. "They certainly made a wonderful punch," he later wrote, "when mixed with crushed ice, medical alcohol, and issue brandy."

With Boyington's limeade and the help of the Choral Society, the Black Sheep rang in 1944. At midnight, several of the pilots went outside and fired flares into the sky with Very pistols until Henry Miller ran out and put a stop to it. Ship captains out in the anchorage believed an air raid was in progress.

Boyington was off the schedule New Year's Day, so Walton and Reames urged him to go hiking with a photographer and one of the younger pilots. Boyington wore himself out in the jungle that afternoon, then lay down on his cot to have a nap before dinner. He slept almost twelve hours.

At 7:00 A.M. on January 2, he took off for Torokina with

Fred Losch, Tom Emrich, and Denny Groover to attempt another fighter sweep. True to past form, he left Vella Lavella in an old birdcage Corsair, but by the time he reached Bougainville he doubted the plane's ability to carry him the whole way to Rabaul and back, especially as he would be in tactical command of the sweep. He contacted Barakoma to request a new plane, and within fifteen minutes Bill Crocker took off in 883, the F4U that had performed strongly for Boyington on December 27, delivering it to Torokina with time to spare.

Forty minutes later, leading twenty Hellcats and twenty-eight Corsairs from six squadrons, Boyington took off for his fifth fighter sweep over Rabaul. But his bad luck continued, as his decision to switch planes turned out to be the wrong one. A few minutes past noon, just as he neared Rabaul, the usually reliable Pratt & Whitney engine began throwing oil. An opaque film soon covered his windscreen, blocking his forward view.

Down on the ground, the worn-out 201st Kokutai was preparing to retire to Truk Atoll in the Carolines later that day, but when the approaching fighters were picked up by radar, the group managed to put nineteen Zeros in the air. These were joined by thirty-one Zeros from the 204th Ku and an equal number from the 253d, eighty fighters in all. The sky was swarming with them—and Boyington couldn't see to shoot.

Exasperated, he chopped the throttle, slowed to just above stall speed, then slid back his canopy. Losch, Emrich, and Groover, retarding their throttles to stay with him, stared slack jawed as he unsnapped his parachute harness, rose from the seat, and tried to wipe away the oil. Standing four miles above the earth, using a handkerchief in a hundred-mile-an-hour slipstream, his attempt was nothing more than an act of defiance.

In disgust, Boyington turned back for Vella Lavella at reduced speed, bringing Emrich along to navigate and provide cover. As before, the revetment at Barakoma was crowded with writers and photographers and the radio truck when he landed, and as before, he had to explain that he'd had "a little tough luck up there." The original record stood. Compounding his frustration, Losch and Groover returned to report action, Losch having downed a Zeke and damaged another, while Groover got a probable and damaged one as well.

When the schedule was posted that afternoon, nothing was shown for the Vella Lavella squadrons on January 3. Boyington did not want a day off. With the monsoon weather causing so many aborts, he was down to just one or two more attempts to beat the record. He had no favors left to bargain with, but he campaigned for one more attempt anyway. Somehow, he succeeded. He would lead a fighter sweep early in the morning—takeoff was at dawn—meaning that he would have to fly back up to Torokina that afternoon to be ready.

Knowing that several of his pilots had not yet had a crack at Rabaul, Boyington selected three who were eager for a turn. George Ashmun, popular and experienced, had led his own division for the entire tour, but had never been on the "gravy train." In fact, after two tours with the Black Sheep, he had not so much as damaged an enemy plane in the air. J. J. Hill, also on his second tour, had not done much shooting, either, since downing a Zeke in mid-October. Al Johnson, one of the replacement pilots, had likewise missed opportunities during the tour.

The four pilots were in the air by 5:30 that afternoon, Boyington in 915 again in place of the leaking 883, while Ashmun manned the same birdcage Corsair that Boyington had cast aside the previous day. Upon reaching Torokina, he escaped the ever-present correspondents by seeking out John Condon, now on the staff of ComAirNorSols. Condon had the perfect hideaway: "We had a little camp just off Piva Trail, which was some distance away from Torokina—not that far, perhaps a few minutes. It was comfortable and we were well set; we'd been there since the first of November. He came over and had dinner, then shot the breeze. He did not stay up and carouse around. He went to sleep."

Refreshed, Boyington was up before dawn for one more sweep of Rabaul. His division was joined by Ed Olander's (Rufus Chatham, Bruce Matheson, and Perry Lane), plus eight Corsairs from VMF-223, twelve from VMF-211, and sixteen Hellcats from VF-30. They took off at 6:30 and subsequently rendezvoused without incident, but en route to Rabaul mechanical ills began to whittle away at the formation. Olander turned back with oxygen-system trouble and landed at Vella Lavella; Lane returned to Torokina with a hydraulic problem; Hill's radio went out and his guns wouldn't fire, so he also reversed course. Seeing that Hill was on the wrong heading (his compass had also failed), Al Johnson wheeled around and gave chase, then led a grateful Hill to Vella Lavella.

The remaining four Black Sheep rearranged themselves into a single division, Matheson and "Mack" Chatham forming the second section, as Boyington led the formation over New Britain. At approximately 8:00 he initiated a wide, right-hand sweep over the heart of the enemy stronghold, which appeared dark and murky, the effect of a solid overcast above and thick haze down below.

The Corsairs and Hellcats had been detected long before. Already climbing to intercept them were seventy Zeros from the two remaining air groups at Rabaul: thirty-three from the 204th Ku, the balance from the 253d. Boyington's formation had completed 180 degrees of turn when the first contact was made at 8:15. He saw a formation of six Zekes at fifteen thousand feet, pushed over, and approached the trailing Zeke with his trademark stern run.

Here at last was the opportunity he had been waiting for, trying too hard for, but he was neither patient nor deliberate. Like a hunter with buck fever he opened fire at twelve hundred feet, almost a quarter of a mile behind the Zeke. Normally the tracers would alert the Japanese pilot, who would instantly split-S and be gone, but this Zeke held its course. Boyington closed the distance rapidly, and at three hundred feet his converging rounds occupied the same space as the A6M. The lightly built Zeke shuddered under the impact of the slugs, some of which had ignited as they exited the Corsair's gun barrels at more than twenty-eight hundred feet per second. An instant before the Zeke's high-octane fuel torched off, the pilot jumped free. Several pilots from VMF-223, along with Matheson and Chatham, saw the Zeke's demise. Boyington had more than enough eyewitnesses for his twenty-sixth victory. The record was tied.

Ashmun remained in close formation, but Matheson went after a different Zeke and Chatham was forced to withdraw after suffering an electrical gun failure identical to Hill's. While dealing with their individual concerns, neither Matheson nor Chatham saw the first two Corsairs descend farther into the murky haze over Rabaul.

Boyington was thinking only of more victories. Spotting a gaggle of Zeros below him, he continued down another three thousand feet. Somehow—he could never watch every piece of the sky at once—he failed to notice a much larger group of Zeros until they swooped down, roofing him in. The trap was sprung.

Remarkably, considering his oft-repeated edicts about using the weight of the Corsair, Boyington did not dive away when the Zeros pounced. Perhaps there were simply too many. Overwhelmed by twenty or more Zeros, he and Ashmun began weaving defensively. The maneuver constantly changed the enemy pilots' firing solutions while he and Ashmun cleared each other's tail, but it also slowed the Corsairs.

The Zeros swarmed at them from above and both sides, and even from below. Ashmun had completed just a few turns before his plane went into a shallow, smoking glide as the Japanese boresighted him in a shooting frenzy, sensing the kill. The Corsair drifted downward with Ashmun already dead or incapacitated, never altering course. Smoke changed to bright flames, the glide became steeper, and finally his Corsair smashed into the surface of St. George's Channel.

Turning on Boyington, now alone, the pack of Zeros showered his Corsair with a similar fusillade. His fighting days ended the instant a 20mm shell entered the belly of his

Corsair and exploded down in that big, dark void below the steel foot channels. Jagged pieces of shrapnel burst upward into the cockpit, some striking the back of his lower left leg and ankle, causing two or three wounds. A large, misshapen piece entered the inside of his left thigh and punched out a few inches above, spraying blood as it tore large entry and exit holes. A U-shaped sliver embedded itself into the meat of his thigh next to the first big hole. Another chunk passed between his legs but sliced his forearm, which was exposed because his hand was gripping the control stick. The last wounds, perhaps caused by shards of fragmented armor plate, were in the left side of his head: almost like birdshot, tiny pieces of steel peppered the back of his lower jaw, the flesh of his ear, and the scalp behind his ear, having punched through the earphone in his cloth helmet.

Bleeding from a half-dozen wounds, Boyington tried to escape by diving, but was forced to level off above the surface of St. George's Channel. What happened next, as described in the earliest contemporary account (a supplemental report to the air combat action form), was nothing short of miraculous:

> He had only gone half a mile when his main gas tank went up in flames, filling the cockpit with smoke and fire.
>
> Unable to see, Boyington took his safety belt with one hand, his rip cord with the other & pulled both & kicked forward on the stick with his foot at the same time. He was thrown clear by the negative G's—either going through the canopy or pulling it off as he went out.
>
> He was 100–200 feet off the water at the time.
>
> He felt one tug on his shoulders as the chute caught & then crashed into the water on his left side with sufficient force to crush his canteen & smash his wrist watch.

That account, submitted to headquarters in September 1945, was virtually identical to Boyington's 1958 memoirs. The cockpit fire, he wrote, was "the same as opening the door of a furnace and sticking one's head into the thing."

Oddly, neither account mentioned burns, nor were any reported during his subsequent medical examinations. The huge main tank was located immediately in front of the cockpit, and other pilots encountering such fires received grievous burns—if they lived at all.

The real story of how Boyington came down, although speculative, was written almost as an afterthought in Walton's original January 3 war diary. When the returning pilots were debriefed, they stated that "someone was heard to call Dane Base reporting that he was going to have to make a water landing." Their statement was duly recorded, yet little attention was paid to the distress call.

By process of elimination, however, the call was almost certainly made by Boyington, based on several facts. First, no missions to Rabaul were scheduled that day until Boyington campaigned to have the fighter sweep added. Secondly, among the Corsair and Hellcat squadrons employed on the sweep, only two planes failed to return—those of Boyington and Ashmun. If Ashmun was shot down in flames, as Boyington later reported, the only remaining candidate for the emergency call to Dane Base would be Boyington.

More evidence was provided in a letter he wrote to researcher Henry Sakaida in 1983. "I ended up in the water almost abreast of Cape St. George, New Ireland," he stated, "about five miles from shore. I knew we had a coast watcher at this point, and had high hopes of having him rescue me."

His wording and the Dane Base radio call strongly indicate that he deliberately ditched, a crucial element being the site: Cape St. George was some fifty miles from Rapopo Field on New Britain, where he and Ashmun encountered the Zekes, and was also the last landfall before reaching open ocean. Wounded, bleeding profusely, with his plane in bad shape, Boyington had the presence of mind to pick the one location that maximized his chances for a Dumbo pickup or a coast watcher's assistance. Being low on the water when he radioed, Dane Base would not have picked up his call, but the airborne fighters heard it.

Of the struggle that followed after he came down, he wrote an equally implausible account that included a strafing attack by four Zeros until they exhausted their ammunition, followed by two hours of treading water without his bullet-torn Mae West—though he somehow retained his harness with its heavy survival pack and unopened raft. He stripped off his clothing in the water, he claimed, then eventually toggled the CO_2 cartridge on the raft and struggled aboard, still holding on to the survival pack with its first-aid kit. Dubious as the whole thing sounds, no one can say with absolute certainty that he lied. The remarkable fact is that he survived at all.

Whatever happened, he was brought down by enemy gunfire at approximately 8:45 on the morning of January 3, 1944, the most extraordinary day of his life. He had experienced flashes of raw, jagged emotion during the combat engagement: elation at flaming a Zero, anguish at seeing Ashmun die, the shock of explosions, blood, and pain. Then came elation again, the euphoria of survival, followed by uncertainty after he climbed aboard his raft. Naked, unprotected from the tropical sun, he drifted in a tiny rubber boat with his wounds immersed in salt water. The nearest dependable help, a PBY Catalina, was more than two hundred miles away; a coast watcher was supposedly on New Ireland, but Boyington could see only the dark outline of jungle on the horizon. He wasn't drifting any closer.

There was not much to do much except sit there and ride the current, the swells running about seven feet apart with a mesmerizing rhythm comparable to a train's wheels, "pounding out some tune, over and over, and never stopping." He wrote later that Moon Mullen's song "In a Rowboat at Rabaul" got stuck in his head. No small irony, that.

17

Mr. Prisoner

By midday, word that Boyington had failed to return spread across Vella Lavella "like the chill wind." Witnesses reported his twenty-sixth victory, but no one had seen him or Ashmun since. When they failed to appear after several more hours, it was all too obvious they were down somewhere. Walton nervously checked with various airstrips where the missing men might have landed, but no one had a positive answer. That afternoon, Henry Miller and Moon Mullen took their divisions up to Torokina in order to launch a search, but the weather on arrival was terrible. They would have to delay their attempt until morning.

Boyington's revetment at Barakoma became eerily quiet. An air of disbelief prevailed, as if his disappearance in the act of tying the record was almost too coincidental. "In the movies it would be labeled pure corn," wrote Fred Hampson. "Things like that don't happen." He and George Weller and other correspondents sent out newswires about Boyington's record-tying achievement without mention of his disappearance. Evidently, the public-relations people decided it was best to withhold the news for the time being, in case Boyington showed up.

Due to normal delays for censorship and transmission, the first stories published on January 6 proclaimed, "Boyington Blasts 26th Jap Plane." Several cities in Washington hailed him as a local hero, and the Hallenbecks, awakened during the night, were interviewed in time for the evening editions. Grace said matter-of-factly that she was "not surprised" to hear of Boyington's feat. "We knew he'd do it, but we are tickled to death to hear it."

One account, forwarded via Guadalcanal, contained the first known public appearance of "Pappy" as Boyington's nickname. Although the pilots didn't use it, Fred Hampson was probably the first to coin the name in print, having heard it in the Black Sheep song. The story's author wasn't cited, but the writing was vintage Hampson: "This Methuselah among the marine fliers has logged about 2,500 hours in the air. Stocky and square-jawed, he looks not unlike a bulldog; in the air he fights like one."

In Okanogan and Seattle and many other places, Boyington's record was widely celebrated that day, but the cheering ended abruptly the next morning. Grace had received the bad news the night of the sixth, mere hours after hearing the glad tidings of her son's latest score, in a telegram from the Navy Department that had been inexplicably delayed. The new commandant, Maj. Gen. Archibald Vandegrift, stated merely that Boyington was missing in action. He added that further delays should be expected in receiving more details.

Hardly had the teletype machines cooled from the previous day's story when they chattered with the latest news. The Hallenbecks, grim but composed, answered the reporters' questions again. Ellsworth said, "We are praying for Greg's safety and we have every faith that he will turn up okay." Grace also remained upbeat, at least in public: "I am confident that he is all right and he will show up somehow, somewhere."

Reporters had to look no farther than Boyington's children for touching angles to the story. The studio portrait taken in Okanogan was printed two columns wide, showing the ace and his two oldest kids looking appropriately somber. In Seattle, Gloria posed sweetly with her dog in the Wickstrom home. She was described as "too young to understand, but she knew something was wrong." At bedtime that night, she was quoted as praying, "Please God, bring Daddy back."

Bill Hallenbeck took leave from army training at Camp Riverside, California, and went to Okanogan to be with Grace, while Greg junior and Janet were sent to stay with neighbors. Ellsworth said he would break the news to them gently, assuring them that their father was safe.

Boyington was indeed alive and out of immediate danger, though there was nothing inherently safe about captivity in the hands of the Japanese. His daily existence was far from comfortable, his future in no way certain.

Some eight hours after splashing down in St. George's Channel, he saw a submarine nearby. His hope that it was an American boat quickly faded when he saw a white flag with its red "meatball" lashed to the conning tower. Hauled aboard, he was interrogated by an English-speaking pharmacist's mate while sitting naked on the deck. Tea, cookies, and cigarettes were offered during the surface run to Simpson Harbor, which took more than two hours by his estimate. Uncomfortable as it sounds, he later described it as the best treatment he received as a captive. According to Japanese records, submarine I-181 arrived at Simpson Harbor on January 3, confirming that segment of Boyington's amazing day. The capture of an airman cannot be verified from the sub's log, however, because I-181 was sunk just thirteen days later.

Boyington was blindfolded and put in a small boat with an armed escort, then delivered to a wharf. From there, he was poked and shoved with rifle butts along the coral streets, his progress slowed by "a shattered ankle." (This turned out to be another of his exaggerations, but the pain of hobbling barefoot on the coral, "like walking on broken glass to feet that are not used to it," must have been excruciating.)

He was finally ordered to halt. Standing naked in the street, unable to see his surroundings, he heard music and female laughter. Other prisoners confirmed there was a "house of joy" nearby, where prostitutes—many forced or under conscription—entertained enlisted men during the day; at night their services were reserved for officers.

Having arrived at an IJN headquarters building, Boyington underwent a rough interrogation. He claimed that when the standard line of questioning came to his serial number, he couldn't answer correctly because he had not been issued a new one (he had, but evidently didn't memorize it). The guards slugged him, stubbed out cigarettes on his neck and shoulders, and tightened the ropes binding his wrists "like tourniquets." He contradicted himself in his memoirs, however, writing that he threw up his hands in disgust when a "snaky-eyed individual" tried to get him to identify radio calls. He couldn't have done that if his wrists were bound.

During his first night of captivity, Boyington was interrogated by Chikaki Honda, the baseball-playing Nisei who had challenged him on the radio back in December. Honda, the principal interpreter, was a clever interrogator, adept at using his familiarity with American culture to draw out answers. A year older than Boyington, he looked young enough that the prisoners referred to him as a "kid." John Arbuckle, a PBY pilot shot down near Rabaul, described him as "about six feet tall with only slightly Oriental features and a good athletic build. He had a good voice and bragged of singing for popular bands in Honolulu before going to Tokyo for college education sometime around 1936–37."

Honda knew how to soft-sell prisoners into divulging information. His ploy was to enter the interrogation room after a beating had been administered, then offer tea and cigarettes. He was the nice guy, a classic element of psychological warfare. Prisoners were often talkative, susceptible to gentle persuasion, after enduring a beating.

Boyington did not learn his interrogator's real name during several sessions with Honda, who insisted on being called *tsuyaku*. Unaware that this was the word for interpreter, Boyington thought it was his name. "I came to like Suyako in a very short time," he wrote, evidently forgetting that Honda was the enemy, no matter how friendly or sincere he seemed. Boyington even gave him his Model A-11 government-issue Bulova wristwatch.*

Between interrogations, he was confined to a planked cell in the jail run by the Imperial Japanese Navy's 81st Guards unit. Throughout the day, he sat at attention on the wooden floor of his cell, shared with an aviator named Crocker who had been shot down over Ballale. They were forbidden to converse, though they could get away with it when the guards weren't watching. Interrogations, brief meals, and the occasional trip to empty the *benjo* bucket were their only distractions. A diet of moldy rice and soup, containing little or no protein, was barely enough for subsistence.

The cells were devoid of furniture except the bucket, and their only bedding consisted of "a couple of gunnysacks." Having arrived with no clothes, Boyington was probably provided with a *fundoshi,* the traditional loincloth. It was essentially a T-shaped garment; the horizontal piece tied around the waist, and from it a wider strip of cloth hung behind the buttocks. This was pulled between the legs and looped over the string in front, leaving an overhanging flap. The prisoners wore little else, nor would they have wanted to. Rabaul was just three hundred miles from the equator, and the heat inside the cells was smothering.

After several days in this bug-infested cell, Boyington's wounds began to fester, giving off an even fouler odor than did his unwashed body. Relief, when it finally came, was minimal. A quasi doctor who had been trained in the islands was permitted to treat Boyington's wounds, but his capability consisted of little more than applying hot saltwater compresses.

---

* After the war the watch was confiscated from Honda, who claimed Boyington gave it to him. Responding to a U.S. Army request for verification, Boyington wrote: "I never did know the name of the interpreter at Rabaul. It is true that I gave an interpreter my watch. This fellow if he is the same one deserves any consideration you can give him. He performed many acts of kindness for us prisoners."

Malaria came next. Between waves of bone-rattling chills and delirium from high fever, Boyington still had to sit at attention on the hard wooden floor. If he started to slump or close his eyes, he was beaten. The only distraction came from the daily interrogations, accompanied by what Arbuckle defined as "the usual slapping, harsh discipline, and occasional beatings."

Though such treatment seemed particularly cruel, it was not reserved exclusively for prisoners. Recruits and even trained personnel in the Japanese navy, especially among the lower ranks, were routinely beaten with bats or sticks. It was as much a part of their military culture as marching or eating. The disciplinary system went hand-in-hand with the Bushido warrior philosophy, under which prisoners were considered as having dishonored themselves by being captured, rather than dying in combat. The idea of surrender was abhorrent to the Japanese, who consequently did not feel compelled to honor the Geneva Convention. Thus, Boyington and those with him at Rabaul were captives, not prisoners of war. The threat of liquidation always hung over their heads.

During one interrogation, Boyington was allegedly informed that all of the prisoners would be shot if he did not provide the name of his base's commanding officer. According to his memoirs, he complied by pointing out Joe Smoak's "compound" on Bougainville in an aerial photograph and telling the Japanese how to skip-bomb it. It was either pure fantasy or treason. Nevertheless he wrote, "I smiled to myself, thinking: 'I would love to see that no-good son of a bitch's face if it is at all possible for them to get through.' I never did find out whether they had been able to drop this bomb near [Smoak], and I'm afraid to ask."

Ironically, Rabaul was on the receiving end of aerial attacks that came day and night with nerve-wracking regularity, the Allied high command having determined that a ground assault was unnecessary. The fortress could be strangled from the air. Conditions became dire as the bombing intensified throughout January and into February, affecting prisoners most of all. Eighteen military "captives" in the nearby Kempeitai prison died of malnutrition or related diseases, but the most horrendous statistic is that more than three times that number were executed. In the final count, only eight emaciated men out of 126 known military captives were alive at war's end.

Boyington's chance of survival would have been minuscule if not for "Chicky" Honda, who was determined to get out of that hellhole himself. In what amounted to a ruse, he requested permission to escort Boyington and a handful of other captives to Tokyo before Rabaul was completely cut off. Boyington was probably considered a high-profile case, but the others had little military knowledge. Honda merely used the prisoners to get out of Rabaul. Six of them, including Boyington, Arbuckle, and Flt. Lt. Brian Stacy of the Royal Australian Air Force, were heavily bound and loaded aboard a GM4 Betty on February 15. Almost immediately after taking off, the bomber landed again due to an incoming air attack. The captives "were herded into the woods" until the next day, when the flight was attempted again.

This time, the Betty flew eight hundred miles north to Truk Atoll in the Carolines, the largest IJN fleet facility outside the Japanese home islands. Protected by a near-perfect ring of reefs and barrier islands, the enormous anchorage was considered a true bastion, hence its nickname among the Allies as the Gibraltar of the Pacific.

Years later, Boyington wrote that he eternally regretted not having tried to commandeer the plane during the long flight. The crew, consisting of a pilot, copilot, and rear gunner, was protected by a single armed guard; Chicky Honda was the only other Japanese. Boyington was disappointed, he wrote, at "not having had five of my own Black Sheep with me there as captives . . . instead of the boys I did have." Further disparaging his fellow captives, he wrote that one of them guessed he was plotting a takeover, and urged him not to try. "None of my Black Sheep would have talked like that," he continued, "and everything would have been so damned easy if only I had had five of them there with me."

But this was merely another fantasy. The prisoners were too trussed up to do anything except daydream, according to Arbuckle, who reported that they were blindfolded, handcuffed, bound with rope by the arms and feet, and gagged. Hence, they could not have conversed in the first place.

Nor did Boyington need to add dramatics to the flight. Beginning that very day, nine U.S. carriers of Task Force 58 launched two days of massive air strikes against Truk. The first attacks were planned to neutralize Japanese air strength, thereby establishing aerial superiority; somehow, the Betty managed to sneak in undetected from the south and slip through the screen of Hellcat fighters. Even more amazing, the bomber made its landing approach just as a fresh wave of strikes commenced. None of the passengers disputed Boyington's recollection that the Betty made an emergency landing, or that after it stopped, they were tossed out of the bomber and took shelter in a concrete slit trench, huddling there for the remainder of the day.

After nightfall, they were taken by boat to a nearby island, where they were deposited in a stockade. One small disparity: Boyington claimed all six prisoners were jammed into a single cell, whereas Arbuckle testified later that he, Boyington, and Maj. Don Boyle, another Corsair pilot, shared one. Either way, the conditions were extremely uncomfortable. One of Boyington's most vivid memories was of terrible thirst. Three cups of water were provided each day—not nearly enough to replace what they lost from perspiration in the poorly ventilated huts. After sixteen days (Honda explained that it had taken that long to effect repairs to the shattered airfield and bring in more planes), the trip to Tokyo resumed. The prisoners were flown northeast to Saipan and spent the night in a chicken coop, evidently the only place where they could be kept under guard, then proceeded by twin-engine transport to Iwo Jima. In the span of two days, Boyington went from the sweltering equatorial heat of Truk to a barren rock that jutted from the vast Pacific, where the winds blew cold in early March. He huddled with the other captives in a flimsy lean-to.

The next day, March 7, the prisoners were flown to an airport outside Yokohama on the main island of Honshu. The local populace gaped in fascination as Honda escorted them out of the city and into the surrounding hills, which Boyington found as beautiful as the mountains near his boyhood home. The last part of the trip was on foot, down a dirt road that led into a remote valley a dozen miles from Yokohama. They passed through the gate of a wooden stockade, for all the world like a Wild West fort except that the walls stood only six feet high. Two long, narrow buildings formed the east and west perimeter, connected by stockade walls to enclose a rectangular compound. The dirty captives were herded into an isolated barrack, where they would remain secluded from the main body of prisoners until they could be given a proper orientation. Before he was put inside, Boyington got a brief glimpse at the knot of men in the central yard. One of them was Jim Condit, his poker-playing buddy from the *Yorktown* cruise before the war.

The camp staff—enlisted men in naval uniforms—quickly processed the new prisoners and issued "a minimum of cotton clothing." Honda left them, saying, "Well, boys, this is it at last. This is going to be your new home." Boyington never saw him again. Furthermore, he soon learned that his "new home" was Ofuna, a secret camp run by the Imperial Japanese Navy. Contrary to the image Honda projected, Ofuna was not a nice place at all, nor were the people who ran it.

Boyington would have been incredulous at the amount of media coverage still being given to him in the United States, two months after his disappearance. Other pilots made headlines, of course, and the victory record was eventually eclipsed as he predicted, but no other pilot matched him as a media sensation during World War II.

There were so many fascinating angles for the press to explore: Boyington the maverick, the hell-raising, two-fisted drinker, the deadly accurate fighter pilot, the beloved commander of the aptly named Black Sheep. Grace received "hundreds and hundreds" of letters, her most treasured coming from the families of almost twenty Black Sheep, including several from the wives and parents of missing members.

Frank Walton maintained a regular correspondence with Ed Sullivan, then a radio personality and columnist for *The New York Times,* who published a number of stories about Boyington and the Black Sheep in his "Little Old New York" column. Then came major articles in *Time, Liberty, Collier's,* and even a new, breathless tribute by Olga Greenlaw in *Cosmopolitan.* Aviation magazines ran plenty of articles, including one by Walton with the quirky title "Black Sheep . . . Run!" Boyington's disappearance had merely heightened his fame.

While the media speculated about his disappearance, Boyington's name also received a quieter form of attention. Aside from Grace, only a few people at upper command levels knew about the Medal of Honor recommendation. A huge boost had come from Bull Halsey, who endorsed it on Christmas Day, deeming it "an honor and a pleasure to recommend approval for the recognition of the outstanding exploits and heroic achievements of this officer."

By the time the growing stack of endorsements reached Adm. Chester Nimitz, Boyington was declared missing. Nimitz recommended the award be given "in absentia" and forwarded the paperwork to Adm. Ernest King, who concurred, but despite the high-profile signatures, the navy's Board of Decorations and Medals began to meddle. Information was needed, the members said, regarding Boyington's second combat tour.

Herein lay a notable difference between Boyington's recommendation and virtually every other MOH awarded: his was based mostly on a period of service, whereas the medal was intended for "a specific act or acts of gallantry above and beyond the call of duty." When the information requested by the board arrived, it showed that Boyington had achieved some amazing results with the Rabaul fighter sweeps during his second tour, and the board pushed the award through quickly. On March 15, President Roosevelt signed the citation, officially awarding a Congressional Medal of Honor.

Grace was notified in a letter from headquarters on April 10, accompanied by a copy of the citation. She was reassured that the medal was not being conferred posthumously, because her son was officially carried on the records as missing in action. The original citation and the award would be held in Washington "in case he should be available for personal presentation at some time in the future."

Some people at headquarters were not so publicly optimistic. A few days after the award was announced, Edna Loftus Smith, a Marine Corps historian with a commission in the Women's Reserve, wrote to illustrator Frank Tinsley: "Since Major Boyington has just been posthumously awarded the Congressional Medal of Honor, and in view of his never having been previously decorated . . . would you consider a second strip on him?"

Tinsley created a new *Fighting Marines* strip, depicting the Medal of Honor and its loop of pale blue ribbon along with a dramatic rendering of Boyington's last dogfight. He made no reference to a posthumous award, yet for the next fifty years the general public believed that Boyington's medal was awarded only because of his disappearance— helped by the fact that Boyington later perpetuated the story. His absence was a matter of coincidental timing, of course, as the process had been initiated more than two months before he was shot down, but his apparent loss on January 3 probably influenced decisions to endorse the award at higher levels.

Also by coincidence, the navy's highest award followed the Medal of Honor. Joe Smoak's replacement as the commander of MAG-11, Col. William Manley, had an entirely different opinion of Boyington than his predecessor. Unaware of the MOH when he recommended an award in late January, he praised Boyington's legacy of "inspirational leadership, selfless devotion to duty, extraordinary heroism, indomitable fighting spirit, gallant intrepidity, and remarkable flying skill." Manley did not name a specific award, so

Admiral Nimitz endorsed it as a Navy Cross on March 22. The Board of Decorations and Medals turned it down, concluding that the dates that formed the basis of the Navy Cross had already been used for the Medal of Honor.

When General Vandegrift learned of the board's decision, he sent a lengthy correspondence to James Forrestal, the new secretary of the navy, practically shouting for a reconsideration. He revealed that the original MOH recommendation had been endorsed by a long list of heavy hitters based on Boyington's *first* combat tour. It was only because the board requested details of the second tour, he argued, that the dates were added to the citation. Forrestal agreed. His "For the President" signature was placed on a Navy Cross citation in June.

Boyington had become somewhat acclimated to life at Ofuna during the past several weeks. Not that familiarity made him any more comfortable, but at least he knew what was expected. His first discovery had been that Ofuna was nothing more than an intimidation camp, run by the IJN solely to extract information. As he succinctly put it, "The purpose of this place was to make your life as miserable as possible in the hopes of getting military secrets from you. Hell, I had about as many secrets as my mother!"

But that didn't stop the Japanese from trying. In what was essentially a protracted version of the routine he had experienced at Rabaul, the staff at Ofuna performed a coordinated good guy–bad guy ritual with Boyington. The environment was slightly cleaner and thankfully lacked the oppressive tropical heat, but the Ofuna staff had refined the art of abuse.

The camp population fluctuated constantly between roughly sixty and ninety prisoners, with one man per cell in two long barracks. New prisoners were usually held for a period of solitary confinement in "Ikku," a long barrack with cells along both sides of a central corridor, located on the camp's western perimeter. The exterior of the frame building was sheathed with pine, as were interior walls, ceilings, and floors. Thus, the cells did not look unattractive—knotty pine being visually warmer than concrete or stone—but the tiny rooms were absolutely bare except for a straw sleeping mat. Small windows of frosted glass high on the outside wall helped to brighten the cells during the day, but at night the unlit, unheated rooms were bone-chillingly cold.

The prisoners had little in the way of clothing. At the beginning of their confinement most were issued well-worn tennis shoes, though many with feet too big for Oriental footwear had to settle for rags. Glenn McConnell, a tall B-24 pilot who arrived at Ofuna a month after Boyington, listed a meager inventory: "Green cotton two-piece Jap work fatigue uniform, two cotton blankets, no pillow. No toiletries except cardboard box of Jap combination metal polish and dental powder. Since I had a toothbrush, they must have provided it."

There were no *benjo* buckets. Instead, Boyington had to ask permission in Japanese to use the separate latrine, which consisted of several narrow stalls with the traditional slit in the floor rather than a Western-style toilet. During his period of solitary confinement, he was escorted under blindfold by a guard. Frequently, permission was denied until he learned how to speak rudimentary Japanese and conduct himself properly in the presence of camp personnel. He picked up the words while being shouted at, slapped, punched. More importantly, he learned that he had to bow whenever a guard came near, while saying good morning or good evening at the appropriate time of day, likewise in Japanese.

Curiously, the politeness, though forced, worked both ways. The word *san,* an honorific, was applied equally to the prisoners. Whenever Boyington bowed and said, *"Ohio, Heitai-san,"* to a guard in the morning, he would usually hear, *"Ohio, Horio-san,"* in response—literally, "Good morning, Mr. Guard," and "Good morning, Mr. Prisoner." To amuse themselves and their fellow captives, prisoners habitually smiled while offering the appropriate greeting, then uttered in the same pleasant tone of voice the foulest sorts of curses in English. The guards smiled politely and bowed back.

Those moments of personal satisfaction were fleeting,

Boyington discovered. The routine at Ofuna was constant harassment. The guards were not as small as he might have envisioned, and they were tough—capable of inflicting considerable pain with a slap, let alone with a closed fist. One of the biggest brutes was the senior enlisted man, Chief Pharmacist's Mate Kitamura, nearly six feet tall and well muscled. He or one of the other guards would appear at Boyington's cell without warning, sometimes to rough him up, at others to pull him out and haul him to an interrogation room.

Enter the "Quiz Kids," three English-speaking interrogators for the IJN general staff who came out to Ofuna from the Yokosuka Naval Base. The most senior of these, Captain Sanematsu, was in overall command of Ofuna from late 1942 until the end of the war, though he did not live there. He and the other two took turns grilling Boyington and the new arrivals (along with the regular prisoners at less frequent intervals), much as Chicky Honda had done at Rabaul. They were crafty at loosening a prisoner's tongue with feigned kindness after the guards had done their part.

According to Boyington, his first interrogation was conducted by the junior member of the trio, an interpreter the prisoners called "Handsome Harry." This was "James" Sasaki, born Kunichi Sasaki in 1898. Raised in Japan, he completed his secondary education before sailing in 1915 to California, where his parents resided in Oakland. Although he was several years older than his American classmates, he went through grammar school and high school again, then received a two-year junior certificate from the University of California at Berkeley. He finished his degree at the University of Southern California, majoring in political science, then worked for ten years as secretary of the Japanese Association of Gardenia Valley, a jurisdiction of about twelve hundred families. From approximately 1934 until the war began, he worked in the Office of the Japanese Naval Attaché in the embassy at Washington. At that point, he was sent back to Japan as part of an exchange of prisoners.

By the time Ofuna opened in 1942 Sasaki was a lieutenant

(senior grade), but he appeared at the prison dressed as well as any gangster in the movies, wearing snazzy suits and saddle Oxfords. Hence, "Handsome Harry." After twenty-six years in the States, his English was without inflection, and he spoke it more properly than most prisoners.

Boyington started out with his usual spiel. From the time of his capture, he had given Chicky Honda and other interrogators his real name, but tried to convince them he was an underling. He presented himself as an operations officer, merely along for a ride the day he was shot down, because of his inexperience, he had no Japanese planes to his credit. Sasaki stopped him cold. "I know you are lying like hell, Boyington," he said, "but stick to it, as it sounds like a good story."

With that one bit of advice, Sasaki convinced Boyington that he was sympathetic to the American cause. He had actually given up nothing. Generous with cigarettes and tea, Sasaki made Boyington feel as though he were visiting with an old friend. Later, Boyington wrote that the two of them had "many a delightful conversation during those brief intervals when we were certain we were alone." He believed Sasaki's story that the Japanese had coerced him to work for the government, and believed that Sasaki truly liked him. Later, Boyington conceded that he was "a man who just wanted to be *wanted,* and for some reason or another had felt that he never had been since childhood."

The interrogators were skilled at making prisoners feel they were on their side, giving tiny concessions that seemed sincere. For a gregarious personality like Boyington, talking and smoking was far preferable to sitting alone in a barren cell. He enjoyed chatting with Sasaki, and he certainly knew more than his mother about the war and the U.S. military. Even if nothing he revealed was singularly harmful to his fellow servicemen, he aided the Japanese intelligence-gathering machine simply because of his garrulous nature.

Boyington's fellow prisoners were also eager to talk with him. Though he had been a captive since January, he could provide updated news about the war to those who had become prisoners before him. Jim Condit, shot down and captured six months before Boyington arrived, was finally able to converse briefly with him when Boyington earned yard privileges.

The established prisoners, allowed to talk and mingle in the central yard during daylight hours, got their exercise by walking around the perimeter of the bare yard. Those in solitary were permitted outside for only brief periods in an area near Ikku Barrack. For some reason, the Japanese never figured out that the two slowly circling groups of prisoners passed near enough to each other to grab snippets of conversation. Condit described his abbreviated first talk with Boyington.

> I timed it so that I'd be abeam from him in the middle. I said, "Hi, Greg," and he said, "Hi, Junior."
>
> The next time around: "How long's the war going to last?" That's what we always asked the new prisoners. He gave some ungodly length of time.
>
> The next time around I said, "I'll bet you a case of whiskey it'll be over in forty-five."
>
> The next time around he said, "Okay."

Eventually Boyington and his group were moved into "Sanku," the barrack for established prisoners. Aside from getting to mingle more freely in the yard, however, there was little to look forward to. Each meal was exactly the same as the one before: "a cup of rice and some soybean-paste soup, three times a day, day after day."

Later it was discovered that the Japanese had cut the prisoners' rations by a fourth, and because of additional theft, the prisoners actually received no more than three hundred calories per day—a starvation diet. Weight loss was rapid. Boyington testified in a postwar affidavit that he dropped from 170 pounds to an estimated 110, consistent with John Arbuckle's assertion that prisoners lost "about 50 or 60 pounds." Vitamin-deficiency diseases such as beriberi (a

Singhalese word meaning "I cannot") were practically un-
avoidable. The men grew weaker as their legs swelled and
joints became painful, making walking difficult. Recalled
Condit, "You could stick your finger in your leg, and it
looked like you were sticking it in dough."

The starvation, boredom, and regular physical abuse were
all deliberately calculated by the Japanese to affect morale.
Prisoners' names were never reported to the outside world,
an issue the Japanese interrogators frequently pointed out.
"They told us that we were not official prisoners of war,"
said Arbuckle, "that we were merely captives; that they had
not notified our government or Geneva and at any time they
saw fit they could liquidate us. They held that over us."

Escape was hardly worth considering. The prisoners were
too weak to go far, looked too different from the indigenous
population to blend in, and Japan was an island. The camp
builders realized there was no need to make it escape proof.
The flimsy stockade was just six feet high and had the horizontal braces on the inside, making it easy to climb. Glenn
McConnell could look over the top and watch farmers tend
their rice crops. "I thought about going over the fence a
number of times," he admitted, "but I thought, then what? If
I go over the fence, I'm gonna get caught; when I get caught,
I'm gonna get the living bejeezus beat out of me; if I don't
get the living bejeezus beat out of me, I'm going to get
killed. Activity one will be followed by activity two and I'm
going to be killed, just for insulting the emperor."

Yet, even at their lowest ebb, the prisoners showed re-
silience and defiance, if only by making up nicknames for
the guards. The on-site camp commander, Warrant Officer
Iida, was "the Mummy," and Seaman Guard Asoma's silver
teeth earned him "Metal Mouth"; Pharmacist's Mate Kitamura was known as "Konga-cho," meaning doctor, but behind his back he was "the Quack"; they called Seaman
Guard Yamazaki "Swivel Neck," and Hata, the civilian cook,
became "Curly" because of his long hair. "We used the
names right in their presence," said Condit, "but one day one
of them started beating the hell out of somebody when he

found out what his name meant. That's the way it went: win some and lose some."

The smallest acts of defiance were sometimes the most meaningful. "We had this little presentation deal where we all lined up and bowed to the emperor every morning, like reveille," pointed out McConnell. "It was a wonderful time to pass gas, on purpose. I don't understand how the Japs never could figure that out."

In the spring of 1944, the Japanese did figure out plenty about Boyington, thanks to intercepted radio bulletins. He was brought before Captain Sanematsu, who opened his briefcase and pulled out a transcript. "He handed me a piece of paper," Boyington later told a reporter, "on which I could see a few words like *Medal of Honor* and *shot down twenty-six planes* and *tied Rickenbacker's record,* and then I thought, *Uh-oh.* But all he did was tell me that the broadcast and my story didn't jibe, and that lying was bad. He said that the Japanese people didn't like lying."

The next piece of news the Japanese intercepted was about his mother. In March, at about the same time that Frank Knox endorsed Boyington's MOH recommendation, he designated Grace Hallenbeck as the sponsor of a soon-to-be-launched escort carrier under construction in a Tacoma shipyard. Although not front-page news (except in the state of Washington), it was a terrific honor for Grace. The proud moment occurred at flood tide on the night of June 10, when she christened USS *Sunset* to the accompaniment of more press coverage. Each piece referred to her missing son and the Medal of Honor.

The news had an unexpected effect on the Japanese. Heretofore, wounded prisoners were generally denied medical treatment, resulting in numerous deaths for lack of the simplest attention. Likewise, those who fell seriously ill were ignored and food was withheld, which merely hastened their demise. With Boyington it was different. "Greg had some shrapnel in his thigh, and it started bothering the heck out of him," said Condit. "By that time, the Japs had found out who he was, and that the president was ready to give him the Medal of Honor. That caused a little stir around camp in a few different ways. In any case, this was one of the few times that the Japs called a doctor out to camp, to look at Boyington's leg. The doctor told the pharmacist's mate to cut Boyington's leg open and get the shrapnel out."

Boyington confirmed the episode soon after the war, writing in a magazine article that his infected leg was "puffed out like a small barrel." After Kitamura took a surgical knife and cut away the flesh around the piece of shrapnel, it popped out. "Then we started squeezing," continued Boyington, "and my leg was just like a big tube of toothpaste. Neither of us said very much, but I stared at the stream of pus and decided it was too late."

On a different occasion, McConnell was with Boyington when both were treated in Kitamura's pharmacy, located in one of the cells at the north end of Ikku Barrack. Kitamura cursorily swabbed a hole in McConnell's foot with salve, then turned to Boyington, whose entry and exit wounds in the upper part of his thigh were open and festering. "Konga-cho would take these medical scissors, the kind that have the forty-five-degree angle at the tip, clamp them onto a piece of gauze, dip the gauze into a jar of petroleum jelly, and stick the gauze into this big hole," remembered McConnell. "Greg would go 'Ughh,' and pass out sitting straight up. Konga-cho would push this thing in a little bit and get it down to the end, release the scissors, come back in the second or third hole down and grab the bottom of the gauze, and pull it through."

Despite the deference the Japanese showed for the Medal of Honor, it did not prevent Boyington from being singled out for a beating. When he overstepped the camp rules, he was treated just like any other prisoner. As Condit explained: "He was addicted to smoking. The Japs gave us one cigarette in the morning after breakfast, and another one after dinner. And nobody was supposed to smoke other than that. Old Boyington wanted to smoke when he wasn't supposed to, and got caught."

The incident took place on July 4, a year to the day after the cast was removed from his leg. When Boyington was caught, the other prisoners were assembled in the central yard for the public punishment. Seaman Guard Yamazaki, "Swivel Neck," drew a circle in the dirt and ordered Boyington to stand within it, feet apart, hands in the air. Wielding what Condit described as "a small fence post," Yamazaki slugged Boyington's buttocks until he tired, then a guard known as "Crummy" took over. When they were done, Boyington was still standing, but his rump had swelled such that he could glance over his shoulder and see it "sticking out there about a foot."

Fifty-five years later, Condit was still amazed that Boyington stayed on his feet, but acknowledged with a bit of resignation that stubbornness cut both ways: "Boyington never batted an eye. The punishment didn't stop him from smoking, though."

A month or so later, all the prisoners were called out into the yard again and made to file past "the Quack" and "Swivel Neck," who struck each prisoner in turn with bats. The mass beating occurred "because one of the prisoners had been caught smoking when he was not supposed to be," according to prisoner Carl Cannon. He did not name the culprit.

There were other vicious beatings, the most brutal in August, when two prisoners were punished in front of the others for deciphering a map from a Japanese-language newspaper they had found in the latrine. Petty Officer Kitamura used a prisoner's crutch to beat the offenders, both of whom were weak from beriberi, then struck them with his fists and savagely kicked them. They were delirious for days, but eventually recovered. In exchange, they had learned about D-Day and the progress of the war in France—encouragement the Japanese couldn't beat out of them.

Collectively, the prisoners received beatings that were later discovered to have coincided with Allied victories in the Pacific. "We knew when the Japs had gone through a terrible mess, like the Marianas Turkey Shoot," contended

McConnell. "We knew within a day or two, because, Jesus, all of a sudden everybody got mad and started slamming us around, banging people. We went through that a number of times. Every time our troops would invade another island, we'd get another round of punishment."

As the routine dragged on, the starving prisoners talked mostly about food, dreamed about it in their sleep, then tried to ignore the gnawing hunger that remained after each meager cup of rice. The perpetual menu was maddening, altered only by the occasional mixing of the contents from the two big pots—one of rice, the other of watery soup—that the prisoners called "all-dumpo."

Then came Boyington's "lucky break."

In a foul mood after the public beating he had received on July 4, he asked camp commander Iida for an audience with Captain Sanematsu. "The Mummy" denied his request, but Boyington brushed past him defiantly and "went right in anyway." His action was so audacious that he got away with it. "The captain was quite surprised," he said later, "and he asked me to sit down and have a cigarette while I cooled off. I talked with him and told him that I wanted a job in the kitchen. I did not get it right away, but about two or three months afterwards I was put to work there."

Sure enough, Boyington began his job as a cook's helper in September. Meals for the guards and prisoners were prepared in a large, open kitchen with knotty pine walls and high windows like the other buildings, though it had a cement floor. Along the back wall sat a huge wood-burning stove used to prepare the guards' meals. Beside it, an even larger brick oven held two enormous kettles where the prisoners' rice and soup were stirred.

Boyington's duty was among the most desirable in the entire camp. He arose before dawn to get the fires going in both ovens, then worked sixteen hours a day hauling wood and water and bags of rice, but he could remain in the warm kitchen all day, especially in winter. Best of all, he had access to food and cooking ingredients, such as a tub of lard. When no one was looking, he would "scoop out a big handful of this stinking lard" and swallow it down. To a starving man, even a fistful of greasy fat "tasted like honey."

The kitchen also had a relatively friendly atmosphere. In addition to assisting "Curly," Boyington worked with a grandmother named Oba. He correctly referred to her as "Oba-san," but did not fully understand the honorific, and misinterpreted her name as Obason in his memoirs. Described by Boyington as a "little old civilian lady," Oba harbored no apparent grievances against prisoners, or at least none against him, and kept a lookout while he helped himself to the lard barrel or stole morsels of food. Between meals, they sat together near the oven to drink tea and smoke—Oba using a small pipe, Boyington finishing the butts of cigarettes thrown on the ground by the guards. He sanitized them by smoking through a holder fashioned from bamboo.

His acquisition of the kitchen job was well timed, for the winter of 1944–45 was "cold, bitterly so," he wrote. Bill Leibold, a survivor of the submarine *Tang* that had been sunk by her own errant torpedo, said of the Ikku Barrack: "The cracks through the walls were large enough for snow to sift in on the decks of the cells and it was very hard for us to keep warm." Even the mainstream prisoners were forced to crowd together for warmth, lining up in the sun three or four rows deep against the side of a barrack. "After fifteen minutes," said McConnell, "the guys in the front row would go to the back row with their backs up against the barracks—that was the warmest place—and everybody else would shift a row." The men would rotate constantly and await their turn at a few minutes of relative warmth. "We had no gloves," added McConnell, "no galoshes, no scarves, coats, or sweaters."

By comparison, Boyington was comfortable. He remained by the stoves during the day, stealing food when he could, and not only regained everything he had lost, but actually started to exceed his optimum weight. Almost every night he bathed in a hot tub after the guards had finished, whereas the general prison population got to bathe perhaps once a month. Having learned to tolerate very hot water, he would walk to his cell, wrap up in his blankets, and "sleep warm all night long."

At Christmas, a couple of Red Cross parcels were distributed to each prisoner, but no one could explain their origin. Ofuna was a secret camp and the Swiss had not sent a representative to visit. As it was, items from the boxes delivered to Ofuna were missing, particularly chocolate and cigarettes, which were "flaunted by the guards," according to Leibold. Aside from the parcels and the guards' permission to sing carols, the holiday received little attention at Ofuna. The New Year's celebration was another matter, creating an unexpected dilemma for Boyington.

According to a detailed story he related years later, the trouble began when Kitamura asked him to stay up late and keep the fire going in the cast iron stove. He gave Boyington a box of cigarettes in return, then brought in a wooden case filled with bottles that Boyington recognized as sake. "I knew that I was supposed to keep these warm at a certain temperature," Boyington said, "and I could have my tea and smoke a package of cigarettes to my heart's content."

Kitamura had no concept of what he was doing when he placed powerful rice wine under the nose of an alcoholic, but Boyington had no intention of stealing it. He figured he'd be shot or bludgeoned to death if he were caught, and getting caught would be easy. Nightly blackouts had been in effect since the first B-29 raids started in November; recently the bombers had struck as close as Yokohama and Yokosuka, just twelve miles away. Because of the blackout curtains at the windows and doorway, he would have no warning before a guard came into the kitchen. Furthermore, he was proud of the fact he'd gone an entire year without drinking, and was convinced that his abstinence helped his infected wounds heal faster after Kitamura had treated them. It was good simply to be in the warm kitchen.

I was just as happy as I had ever been in my life up to that date, sitting there all by myself, thinking about when the war would be over and smoking cigarettes and drinking tea. I was perfectly content until the guard came in for the first refill. The little guard, a nice fellow—'College Boy'—we used to call him, had never been anything but nice to us, and immediately I resented this little squirt. Why? Because he had half a jag on and was feeling very happy, and I could smell his breath.

I thought of telling him what a bunch of no-goods they were; I could get away with it . . . and I knew it. I said, "How come you don't give us all we want to drink every day, Haiti-san?"

He said, "Well, I will get beaten if I get caught giving you any sake."

I kept on, and he said, "Hurry up and get your cup."

We were issued tin utensils: a cup, a little larger rice bowl, a little larger container, then a soup bowl. These I had in a corner of the kitchen, in the dark. I went over there and I didn't even touch that cup; that was out of the question. I did think momentarily about that rice bowl, then I thought: *To hell with it, I will never get another chance.* So I took the soup bowl back. The poor little guy's eyes popped right out of his head.

I said, "Well, let your conscience be your guide, just put what you want in there."

He filled this a little over half full, and he cautioned me to keep this in the dark and get it down as fast as I could, and if I got caught, not to tell them where I got it.

My arm was on his shoulder and I said, "We are friends; you can count on me to the ends of this earth." And I got that thing down. Not because *he* wanted me to get it down in a hurry, [but] because *I* wanted to get it down in a hurry. It took just a couple of gulps to get it down.

Well, I was waiting for that warm glow, and lighted up a fresh cigarette and sat down. Then I started down on these guys and said, "What the heck are these squares doing? There isn't even any kick in this junk."

That glow didn't come—at least I thought it didn't.

During the evening I lost track of time, but several other guards came out [to the kitchen], and some of them were nasty ones. But they weren't nasty to me anymore. When I would hear their footsteps, I would run over and I would have that blackout curtain open so that they could walk in. My arms were around some of the real rough ones, too, and I got sake out of everybody that came in there.

What a bum.

Eventually, Boyington staggered out of the kitchen. Leibold heard him enter the barrack where the *Tang* men were still being held separately from the other prisoners, a classic case of a man stumbling drunk into the wrong building. Boyington finally found his own cell and slept late the next morning. He got away with that, too, as the guards were in no better condition.

Thousands of miles to the east, Grace Hallenbeck had her own cause to celebrate. A plain, typewritten card had arrived in the mail, containing a hidden message that her son was alive. Before this, only a pitifully small collection of personal effects, inventoried by John Bolt and Bob Bragdon, had arrived in Okanogan. The items included a Longines wristwatch, sixteen dollars, his shellback certificate from the *Boschfontein* voyage, a few money-order receipts. His overseas trunk was delivered two months later packed with assorted clothing and all the other worldly fodder he had accumulated since she last saw him. Her son was lost, yet his things kept showing up at her doorstep.

Then in early August, she was galvanized by a letter from General Vandegrift: Boyington's name had been found among documents at Saipan. A correspondent for *Leatherneck* magazine saw it in a flight log and reported the information to headquarters, but the story was effectively squelched to spare possible repercussions for prisoners. The Marine Corps, unable to verify the details, cautioned Grace to keep everything confidential.

Now, exactly a year after her son disappeared, she received a postcard addressed to Gregory Boyington, Esq., from Flt. Lt. Brian Stacy, RAAF, Zentsuzi War Prison Camp, Nippon. Stacy's message was addressed to Boyington, but it was really a signal to Grace. Before his transfer from Ofuna to a regular POW camp the previous October, Stacy had managed to memorize a nickname Boyington had given him, along with Grace's address. The card finally reached her in early January 1945. As she read through the usual holiday greetings, her heart must have stopped at the line "'Deeds' is alive and OK." That single word was all she needed. No more than a handful of people in the whole world knew about "Deeds"; she hadn't heard it herself in almost twenty years.

Headquarters agreed that the information was "very interesting," but reminded her not to divulge any of the information. She must have been bursting to tell her family and friends, but she obeyed, knowing Gregory was safe even if the Marine Corps seemed skeptical.

The late winter and early spring of 1945 were relatively anticlimactic. As the frequency and intensity of the B-29 raids increased, more of the bright aluminum bombers were brought down. Surviving crew members received some of the most brutal treatment meted out in the camps, which actually made life a little easier for the veteran prisoners. In February, Boyington and the others were thrilled to see dark-blue carrier planes overhead, knowing it meant the Japanese had been kicked out of the Philippines.

Afterward, his kitchen thieving "became even more brazen," and by spring he weighed 190 pounds. The other prisoners could not help but notice. "The Japs treated Boyington better than they treated the rest of us," stated McConnell, without rancor. "They respected someone who was skilled enough, in their estimate, to shoot down twenty-six or twenty-eight Japanese planes. They didn't care much for the rest of us, though we received deference for being combat veterans, but they really had affection for Boyington. He had a great personality."

Leibold had a similar assessment. "I do not think Greg Boyington was ever 'cozy' with the Japs; he was considerate of his fellow prisoners and stood his ground with the Japs. While at Ofuna, he was commended by an IJN admiral for his combat accomplishments (as were the *Tang* survivors in a later ceremony). I think he was probably assigned to the kitchen because the Japs respected him to a degree."

Although Boyington was downright plump, the Ofuna staff became concerned about the rest of the prisoners, who were in such poor health they could not be sent to regular camps. They were too weak to work. In an apparent effort to reduce the head count, thereby increasing the ration for the remaining prisoners, Boyington and eighteen of the healthiest men were transferred to Omori, a regular army POW camp near Yokohama.

Walking out of the Ofuna stockade on April 6, Boyington glanced behind him. "I wasn't conscious of the quiet wooded scenery in the same way," he later wrote, "for I saw no beauty in looking back."

The ragged prisoners were escorted to a rail station, rode a streetcar to Yokohama, then hiked to the Omori district on the western shore of Tokyo Bay and tramped across a long wooden causeway to a tiny man-made island. A POW camp housing several hundred prisoners occupied the northern half of the dredged-up landmass, where Boyington and the other newcomers were separated from the general camp population. Still considered "special prisoners," they found themselves crowded into a section of Barrack Number One, which had its own fence around it. They were kept under constant watch by a guard within the room, his rifle always at hand with its bayonet attached.

If anything, the living conditions at Omori were worse than those at Ofuna. The barrack was infested with fleas, lice, and cockroaches; there was no plumbing, and the prisoners shared a single bucket of water for cleaning their utensils, washing, and brushing their teeth. They were issued several blankets each, but had to share space on two wooden sleeping platforms, raised knee-high above the dirt floor with a center aisle between them. The food, slightly more substantial than they had received at Ofuna but less than Boyington was accustomed to, was delivered to the barrack three times a day. The diet was almost identical: a cup and a half of pasty milo-maize, made from rice, beans, and corn, sometimes augmented by soup.

Beginning with morning roll call at 5:00 and lasting until 9:00 P.M., the prisoners were continually harassed by the guard on duty. Throughout the daylight hours they were forced to stand; anyone trying to sit or lie down was clubbed back to his feet with a rifle butt. To use the latrine, situated between the barrack and the stockade wall, prisoners had to request a "*benjo* ticket." Sometimes the guards would make them plead and argue for fifteen minutes.

A week after Boyington arrived, a huge B-29 raid on Tokyo lit up the night sky across the bay from the man-made island. It was a colorful sight, but too far away to be considered threatening. Two nights later, however, the communities nearby were targeted, including Yokohama, Kawasaki, and Omori. The ground shook, shrapnel rattled on the roofs, and the blast of antiaircraft guns was heard at the south end of the island. Miraculously, no bombs fell on the camp, though it was only eight hundred feet across the channel from the mainland—close enough that the prisoners could feel the heat of raging fires. At first light, they saw that Omori had been transformed into ruin. Only the exterior walls of a few concrete buildings stood; everything else within view had burned down to heaps of rubble.

The special prisoners remained in their barrack for the entire month of April while Boyington lobbied to get them on a work detail, where they could "get out in the sunshine and get some exercise," remembered Leibold. Finally, around the first of May, they were marched across the causeway into Omori to clear debris and grow vegetable gardens. The guards kept them isolated from the main prisoners, and in spite of the fact that they were now doing physical work, their food ration was not increased. They discovered later that it was significantly smaller than what the regular POWs received.

Boyington labored hard during the next few months, with little change in the routine. The gardens were fertilized with human excrement, as was common in Japan, requiring him to spend a good part of his day searching for recessed-style toilets among the ruins. As he later described the task: "The buildings were completely gone, but the toiletlike affair [was] just kind of a cement bowl under the ground, and we dipped this human crap out of these old toilets." Working in teams of two, the "honey dippers" lowered a bucket fastened on a pole into the cesspool, then ladled the contents into a larger bucket. When it was full, they strung it on a twelve-foot bamboo pole, hoisted it to their shoulders, and trudged back to the garden.

The army guards were generally more tolerant than the thugs at Ofuna had been, but did beat prisoners on occasion. "Horseface," cursed with buck teeth and thick lips, was in charge of the special prisoners during work details. At a site one day, he beat Lawrence Savadkin of the *Tang* nearly unconscious with a pair of pliers that belonged to a civilian; he had mistaken them for camp property. At the opposite end of the spectrum, a private named Kano, fairly fluent in English, performed "acts of kindness too numerable to mention," according to Boyington. The special prisoners were denied medical attention, but Kano occasionally smuggled Lloyd Goad, an American doctor imprisoned with the regular POWs, into the barrack at night.

One such effort was made when Pvt. Arthur Gill, suffering from dysentery and malnutrition, began to fade during the summer. Unable to digest food, he stopped eating. Leibold testified that Boyington and Kano repeatedly tried to get medical attention for the sick aircrewman, but were refused at every turn. At noon on July 5 (the date varies slightly between accounts), Gill lapsed into a coma. Finally the guards brought in Dr. Fugii of the Japanese army, who administered a shot of blood plasma. The effort was far too puny, so at 8:30 that night Kano smuggled Dr. Goad into the barrack; he administered glucose, but Gill died within the next thirty minutes. Boyington felt he had let Gill down, and wrote of "a sorrow that came from my own inadequacy to keep one poor little fellow alive," as though he might have kept him from dying by force of will.

In mid-July, a detail of special prisoners started a new job approximately six miles from the camp, where a cave was being enlarged. Boyington was among the group, as was Cmdr. Richard O'Kane, the *Tang*'s skipper, who had become the senior special prisoner when he was transferred from Ofuna in June. A future recipient of the Medal of Honor, he figured the caves were to be used for stockpiling supplies or as bomb shelters, as an Allied invasion seemed imminent.

The prisoners worked in the cave for twelve hours a day, wrote Boyington, "just like muckers in a mine." He failed to mention whether the hours accounted for the twelve-mile round trip on foot, which required incredible stamina considering that nearly all of them had swollen legs and painful joints from beriberi, were weakened by hunger, and wore inadequate footwear. When they reached the cave, their workday was just beginning. From the entrance, they walked fifty feet into the mountain to an intersecting cross tunnel about three hundred feet long. Their job was to dig three new tunnels from this passage, farther into the mountain. After two weeks, only ten of the original thirty men were still able to make the round trip, let alone dig. Somehow, they managed to excavate three chambers, each measuring approximately six feet wide, six feet high, and twenty feet deep, by mid-August.

One day while Boyington worked in the cave, a Japanese noncom attempted to tell him about an amazing weapon that had laid waste to a city. Boyington had difficulty understanding the story: "I couldn't fathom at first that it was only one bomb he was talking about. I thought it was just some more Japanese propaganda. But he said no, that his family had lived in the city of Nagasaki, and that only one bomb had been dropped on the city. He said that people were still dying there, and that he had not been allowed even within the city limits to look for his lost family."

Assuming Boyington's geography was correct, he'd learned about the *second* atomic bomb, which had been detonated over Nagasaki on August 9. That he knew nothing of the first bomb, dropped on Hiroshima three days earlier, was not surprising. He and the other special prisoners were completely cut off from outside news.

Less than a week later, the prisoners overheard a momentous broadcast on the cave's public address system. Throughout the morning of August 15, a radio announcer urged all of Japan to listen to an important speech from the emperor at noon. Work stopped in the cave as the guards and civilians clustered around the receiver. Electrical power was low, making the broadcast difficult to hear as the prisoners stood at a respectful distance. They could understand little of Emperor Hirohito's solemn speech (actually being played from a record cut the night before), but they could interpret enough from the bowed heads of their captors to know the end had come. Japan had capitulated.

The impact of the speech brought jumbled emotions to Boyington and the other shaggy prisoners in the cave, who were completely uncertain about how the Japanese would react. But the guards were quiet. The entire populace of Japan was in a state of shock. The prisoners just put down their tools and returned to Omori, their safe arrival a welcome sign to those at the camp that the Japanese intended no form of mass retribution.

For Boyington, waiting with hundreds of prisoners to see what would happen next, more than a period of confinement was coming to an end. His life would be forever defined by his participation in the greatest war of the century: five months with the Flying Tigers, four more as the leader of the Black Sheep, nineteen as a captive.

Although that part of his story was over, his greatest battles were yet to come.

18

Chicken, Peas, and Bourbon

The days immediately following the surrender of Japan were among the strangest in Boyington's life. From an unwashed, half-naked prisoner, he rose to become a ticker-tape hero in a matter of weeks. Even then, his was a different sort of rags-to-riches story, because he never had more than a few dollars to his name.

The Japanese did not immediately abandon Omori after Emperor Hirohito's recorded speech, leading to a bizarre incident two nights after the pronouncement. Some of the guards got drunk on sake and began to threaten the former special prisoners, focusing their alcoholic rage on the B-29 men, but Boyington, the *Tang* crew, and several others were also holed up in the same barrack. Nervous moments ensued while the guards, screaming threats and waving their swords in the air, staggered around the yard outside the barrack. Occasionally one would become bold enough to launch a sort of banzai attack on the door, but the prisoners had barricaded themselves inside. When the Japanese finally wore out, the good-hearted Private Kano and a duty officer herded them back to their own quarters.

Afterward, the senior Allied officers at Omori called a conference and decided to let the remaining Japanese guards keep their weapons in case of "possible incursions," but designated a team of twenty American and British men to take over the weapons if necessary. Boyington was chosen to lead the group. Years later, Robert Martindale claimed in his prison memoir *The 13th Mission* that he informed the ace of this very assignment. Boyington allegedly snubbed him, saying, "I won't do it. That's Mickey Mouse stuff." Martindale made it sound as though Boyington had disobeyed an order, but his scenario was improbable, even in a prison setting. Officially, Martindale was three ranks junior to Boyington, who would not have stood for being told what to do by an army lieutenant, and a B-24 copilot at that. Asked later to clarify his role, Martindale rephrased it, saying Comdr. Arthur Maher, the senior American officer, sent him to relay the assignment. If so, that was Maher's mistake. Furthermore, the surviving *Tang* crewmen refute Martindale's claim that he took the duty, contending that Boyington did serve as the camp's provost marshal.

The bickering stopped when U.S. carrier planes began to fly over the camp, first dropping notes, then returning to deliver larger packages. The ex-prisoners painted P.W. in large white letters on the rooftops, resorting to foot powder and tooth powder when they ran out of paint. Other messages began to appear like so many billboards: 500 MEN, OMORI WE THANK YOU, and, after several aerial deliveries crashed through roofs: DROP OUTSIDE— THANK YOU.

One navy pilot, Lt. Jim Hoisington of the carrier *Hancock,* snapped a picture from his Corsair with a Kodak. The developed print revealed a message painted on a narrow roofline, just inside the eastern stockade wall, calling attention to the prison's best-known occupant. PAPPY BOYINGTON was painted neatly on one roof, and HERE! was added exuberantly to the next. Nobody outside the prison realized the lettering had been applied to the *benjo* roofs.

As various photographs were brought back to the fleet, the rooftop messages were analyzed and the information transmitted to staff planners, who in turn organized relief drops. B-29s started hauling the big stuff on August 27, releasing bomb bay loads of supplies in fifty-five-gallon drums from low level. The parachutes worked only part of the time. Buildings were damaged and a few injuries were sustained, but fortunately no one at Omori was killed. There were minor complications, however, as men ignored the army's warnings about overindulgence. The drops included coffee and candy bars, including a whole case of Mounds that landed in the "honey pit" beside the *benjos* ("we pulled it out, washed it off, and got out those candy bars for sure," remembered B-24 pilot Tom Cartwright). Compulsive as ever, Boyington got wired on caffeine and stayed awake all night, entertaining his fellow ex-prisoners. "He had a crowd around him," said Cartwright, "which he loved."

On the morning of August 29, the former prisoners recognized the distinctive outline of U.S. warships steaming into Tokyo Bay. The airdrops had given the weakened men hope; now euphoria swept the camp. They crowded onto rooftops, climbed the stockade, then lined the seawall. Several from different nationalities began fashioning flags from scrounged materials.

Bull Halsey was out there, having completed one major campaign after another (some better than others) since meeting Boyington at Munda twenty-two months earlier. He now sent Commodore Roger Simpson to lead a Prisoner of War Liberation Force deep into Tokyo Bay aboard the cruiser *San Juan,* accompanied by destroyers, minesweepers, empty troop transports, and a hospital ship. Halsey also sent his chief of staff for administration, Comdr. Harold Stassen, who had resigned from his third term as governor of Minnesota to serve in the naval reserves. "Roger and Harold," the admiral radioed, "those are our boys, go and get them."

As soon as a flotilla of Higgins boats could be lowered, the relief force headed straight for Omori under a bright sun. More than six hundred exultant men—Omori had absorbed dozens of ex-prisoners from surrounding camps—followed the boats' progress around the north end of the island to the protected channel, where a small dock jutted out.

Navy photographers aboard the craft captured heartrending scenes. Crowded three and four rows deep on the seawall, men cheered wildly, waving their makeshift versions of

Old Glory and the Union Jack and the flag of Holland. The ex-prisoners looked a little strange from a distance, like children's renditions of stick figures. Some wore shorts several sizes too big; others were nearly naked, dirty loincloths their only modesty. Two of the stick figures jumped off the seawall and swam out to the boats, unable to wait any longer. They were picked up, half drowned, before the boats nudged against the flimsy dock. Simpson, Stassen, and their crews went ashore, swarmed by men whose jubilation was the only thing holding them upright.

The landing party moved into the camp and Simpson gave a short speech, then his group toured the island while the photographers recorded pictures of starved men. "The B-29 people were just like skeletons," said Cartwright. The camp had been fastidiously maintained under Japanese control, but after two weeks of relief drops the ground was littered, as were the barracks. The visual effect was all the more damning.

Stassen shook hands with a shirtless Boyington, who was among the first to leave the island. The evacuation proceeded as fast as the Higgins boats could race back and forth to the hospital ship *Benevolence,* where Boyington climbed the gangway. Many others, such as B-29 navigator Lt. "Hap" Halloran, had to be hoisted aboard in cargo nets.

After a shower with delousing solution and a medical exam, Boyington donned navy dungarees and a work shirt, then sat down to eat in the ship's wardroom. A reporter from *Time* watched him consume eight eggs, two servings of ham, and two helpings of mashed potatoes. Across the table, unable to eat, a half-starved B-29 pilot could only shake his head and watch.

Details of Boyington's recovery from Omori were flashed to the communications ship *Ancon* in Tokyo Bay, then transmitted Stateside. It was still August 29 on the other side of the dateline when the nation awoke to the news, and a more complete story was printed under banner headlines the next day. Boyington granted a lengthy interview from a different hospital ship, USS *Reeves,* telling an amazing tale of his bailout, during which he flipped his burning Corsair on its back and "dropped a hundred feet to the water, stunned." Elements of his story would change as time passed, but nobody was going to refute him, as his account was among the first to be published regarding the treatment of prisoners.

Within a few days of being moved to *Reeves,* Boyington was transported to Kisarazu Naval Airfield outside Tokyo, where he boarded a four-engine Douglas R5D transport bound for Guam. Unassisted, he climbed the steep boarding ladder with an armload of new clothing and several souvenirs, including a Japanese rifle. After two nights on Guam, he flew to Kwajalein and thence to NAS Barbers Point, Hawaii, where he set foot on U.S. soil for the first time in thirty-two months. A crowd met the planeload of ex-prisoners, but the cameras and reporters were there for him. Nuts Moore, now wearing two stars, gave Boyington the kind of warm embrace a man might give a prodigal son.

The next several days were transitional. Boyington rested at Ewa, a marine air station eighteen miles west of Pearl Harbor, while the Marine Corps decided how to handle his return. The public relations people were fully aware of his status as an elite hero, especially his appeal as an ace fighter pilot. He had gone down fighting, earned a Medal of Honor, and emerged phoenixlike from a secret prison after being tortured. This was a PR dream come true.

Boyington discovered how famous he had become while reading through a collection of articles covering the past two years, including "a lot of stories that were quite flattering indeed." Even so, he did not realize the extent to which the Marine Corps was planning the next phase of his life.

The first step was to have him accept his regular commission. A mere five weeks after he was shot down, the Committee on Naval Affairs had met at the House of Representatives to consider bill S. 1427, an act to authorize his appointment to the regular Marine Corps. A letter from James Forrestal to Speaker of the House Sam Rayburn was read into the *Congressional Record* on February 16, 1944. Perhaps the most crucial information presented was the statement: "He is credited with having shot down at least six Japanese planes during his service with the Flying Tigers." The record had become virtually irrevocable.

An examination was required before the promotion could become official, so Boyington underwent the works, including a flight physical on September 6. In order to document his wounds, he was X-rayed from head to toe, revealing two small shrapnel fragments in his scalp along with "a few minute metallic particles" in the skin of his lower jaw. His arm and leg wounds had completely healed with no traces of fragments, though the scars were visible. He told the examining physicians that his left ankle had been fractured when he was shot down, but X rays taken from three different perspectives revealed only the old break in his fibula; otherwise his ankle was normal.

As for his general condition, he had mild beriberi in his legs and his skin was jaundiced from the diet at Omori, but the medicos were amazed at his health. "Considering his time of confinement and treatment as a prisoner of Japan," wrote the senior flight surgeon, "I am of the opinion that his physical condition is excellent." A mere eight days after being released, Boyington passed his flight physical, the most restrictive medical qualification in the armed forces.

Later the same day, standing before a huge Marine Corps flag, he accepted his appointment as a first lieutenant and raised his right hand to be sworn into the regular service. Immediately afterward he was promoted to lieutenant colonel, with Nuts Moore having the honor of pinning the set of silver oak leaves onto Boyington's collar. Moore then invited him to stay at Ewa for a few extra days, offering his own quarters while he was away on a trip. Boyington was not about to argue with his beloved superior. He intended to use the time to work on his image, later writing, "I decided that I would smarten myself up a bit, so I might be in accord with the public's conception."

His resolve did not last long. Norm Anderson and Bill Millington, both future generals, were outdoors one day when Boyington spotted them. Millington recalled:

We were playing tennis outside the general's quarters, when all of a sudden this guy came out of the house. He said, "I saw you guys through the window. Goddamn, it's good to see you again!"

I said, "Jesus, Greg, I'm glad you made it—you're looking pretty good. They've got you all nice and trim. I'll bet they didn't feed you much over there."

He said, "Hell, no. But I want you guys to know something. During my confinement with those damn nuts, I saw life in an entirely different fashion. I'm a different man now, and, by God, I'm going to prove it too."

I said, "More power to you, Greg. That's great."

Well, that night he went out and totaled a jeep—he'd gotten skunked. He couldn't resist it. One taste of alcohol in some damn bar, and he was off on a binge again.

On the night of September 11, Boyington boarded a Douglas R5D for an overnight flight to NAS Alameda, outside Oakland, to begin the next part of the plan put together by the Marine Corps. The idea was simple: a cross-country public information tour. Remarkably, the complete itinerary had been prepared by September 7, the day after Boyington was green-lighted for promotion. From California, he was to depart on a two-month tour of the biggest cities in the land—Seattle, Chicago, Washington, New York, Philadelphia, Detroit, and Los Angeles—with numerous side trips to intermediate cities. The planners knew ahead of time that the White House was presenting several Medals of Honor on October 5, "Nimitz Day" in Washington. Boyington would be first in line.

It would have been unthinkable to send Boyington on such a junket alone, so the Marine Corps arranged for a full-time escort, looking to the one officer who had adroitly kept him in the public eye, Maj. Frank Walton. He was well placed, currently serving as the information officer at Miramar, headquarters for marine aviation on the West Coast. The public relations machine worked so well that by the afternoon of the seventh, Walton was on his way to San

Francisco under orders to arrange a gala reunion of Black
Sheep at the St. Francis Hotel. Afterward, he would accompany Boyington on the proposed tour.

Given carte blanche to do whatever was necessary, Walton
arranged suites at the St. Francis, sent TAD orders to the former Black Sheep on the West Coast, organized a reception
dinner, and notified the media, including *Life* magazine.
Chance Vought agreed to host the reception, preparing to reap
the benefit later when Boyington and Walton toured the
Corsair facility in Connecticut as part of their itinerary. The
Seattle *Post-Intelligencer* also stepped in with an offer to fly
Boyington's mother and kids down to San Francisco on
September 12, presumably in exchange for exclusive cover-
age.

With no detail overlooked, Walton and a sizable crowd
gathered at Alameda well before dawn on the twelfth.
Boyington's flight from Hawaii was scheduled to land at
4:30, not an atypical hour for the Black Sheep. Stan Bailey
was among them, having taken a short break from his job as
CO of the reconstituted VMF-214, as were Jim Reames and
former adjutant Art Little, who somehow worked his way
into the reunion even though he hardly knew Boyington.
Fourteen pilots had been brought in, along with navy chaplain Melanchton Paetznick, who had befriended Boyington
at Turtle Bay, then performed a memorial service for him
and George Ashmun after they disappeared.

The Black Sheep were joined by reporters, photographers,
a dapper radio announcer from KFRC, and a throng of air
station personnel. The excited crowd moved outside as the
Douglas transport touched down and taxied up to the terminal. A boarding platform was pushed up to the cargo doors
high on the fuselage, then Walton clambered up and disappeared into the darkened cabin.

A few minutes later, wearing a leather flight jacket,
Boyington emerged onto the platform. Grinning, he waved
as camera bulbs flashed and the crowd cheered. If it wasn't
quite like Charles Lindbergh's welcome outside Paris, the
reception was just as heartfelt and spontaneous. "This is the

most wonderful thing that has happened to me," he shouted, starting down the ladder. The Black Sheep surged forward, lifted him to their shoulders, and carried him into the terminal with boyish whoops. Caught up in the moment, he thrust his fist into the air, shouting, "This is great, boys!"

The reporters didn't let him get farther than the lounge. Despite the fact that he had just completed an all-nighter from Hawaii, Boyington was obliged to explain the adventure of the past twenty months. He didn't even take off his flight jacket, just sat in an armchair and sipped from a cup of coffee someone set on the table in front of him. A small lamp illuminated his face as the crowd leaned in theatrically, reporters hunching over notepads. Boyington began his story.

Normally, according to the old adage, he who gets home first writes the history; everything that follows is revision. As the last member of his group to come home, Boyington alone knew the final chapter. He had used the layover at Ewa to make a few changes.

During his so-called rest there, he had become cynical after reading the accumulated articles about himself. "It was truly fantastic, the legend of bravery and idealism that had been concocted during those twenty months since I had been seen going down in a ball of flames," he wrote. "And, on top of it all, the majority of all this had been released from Marine Corps Public Relations. There was no question in their minds that my watery grave would hold me, and that I would never return to disgrace them or haunt them."

He was credited at the time with twenty-six victories, preserving the tie with Joe Foss, who had failed to add to his score during another tour of duty late in the Rabaul campaign. Army and navy fighter pilots had since bested the score by a considerable margin (P-38 pilot Richard Bong was tops with forty), but the Marine Corps record remained deadlocked. Or so everyone assumed.

Boyington evidently felt there was nothing to lose by amending the story. During this first interview in California, he claimed *three* Zeros during his last dogfight over Rabaul, and said that the late George Ashmun had also flamed one. The additional victories occurred, he said, while he and George scissored defensively. Each shot one Zero off the other's tail, then Boyington got one more while trying to force the swarm away from George.

He also gave a dramatic rendition of miraculously escaping his flaming Corsair, after which he was strafed in the water by four Zeros until they exhausted their ammunition. He described his various wounds in detail: "My scalp was hanging down in my eyes, my left ear was almost torn off, and my throat was cut. I had a hole in my upper left leg and both arms had been hit by shrapnel. My left ankle yes, it was the bad one—had been broken." He later embellished the injury, describing the ankle as "shattered" with a compound fracture. The doctors at Ewa must have scratched their heads at that one.

Boyington had no reason to worry that his victory claims would be challenged—there were no eyewitnesses to refute him. In this case, however, dead men do tell tales. Among the Japanese, only Petty Officer First Class Hideshi Tanimoto and Superior Seaman Yoshige Kitade, both of the 204th Kokutai, were lost that day, and a pilot from the 253d was wounded. By claiming two additional victories plus Ashmun's single, Boyington elevated the day's total claims to nine Zeros. Obviously, with only two actually shot down, his claim fell well short, even with the unfair presumption that everyone else wrongfully claimed theirs.

Nor are the Japanese records necessary as an argument that Boyington invented the additional victories. During the interviews he gave aboard *Benevolence* and *Reeves,* he described his bailout, capture, and subsequent prison treatment in detail, but never mentioned additional aerial combat, let alone more victories. He didn't know then that the Marine Corps record was still tied. By returning practically from the dead, he saw an opportunity to become the high-scoring marine fighter ace, and simply took it.

Considering his lifelong need to be accepted, there was nothing sinister about his decision. When he was young, he deliberately scratched and bloodied himself to draw attention, to be seen as the hero. Nothing had changed.

Across the bay that afternoon, Boyington's second reunion of the day was as gratifying as the airfield reception. Accompanied by a reporter and a photographer from the *Post-Intelligencer,* Grace arrived at the St. Francis with Greg junior and Janet. Wearing a fur coat despite the fact that it was summer, Grace wrapped her son in a loving embrace and kissed him very fully on the mouth, hamming for the photographer. "Bobby" and Janet, in their Sunday best, beamed as their father got down on his haunches to visit with them. He produced a couple of presents—a Japanese bugle for Bobby, a locket and bracelet for Janet (who was missing two front teeth). His time with them lasted only a few minutes before he was swept up in the crowd of people wanting to shake his hand, but the children didn't seem to mind. "We just wanted to see Greg," Grace explained. "Now we're ready to go back home and wait for him."

That evening, the squadron reunion at the St. Francis drew a large crowd, including representatives from *Life.* A three-page photo layout appeared in the October 1 issue, one of them showing Boyington at the bar with four of his aces, supposedly the first time the magazine had pictured a drinking event. After dinner, the pilots surprised Boyington with a gold watch, inscribed, *To Gramps, from his Black Sheep.* Genuinely touched, he went around to each table to chat with his friends and let them admire the gift. *Life* explained: "It was not a boisterous party. The men talked over their family affairs, including births of children, later told stories of narrow escapes, some funny, some serious."

Lucy Malcolmson was conspicuously absent from San Francisco, having moved back to Manhattan in the summer of 1943, but would meet Boyington when the upcoming tour reached the East Coast. In the meantime, her absence didn't seem to trouble him, for he wasted little time making a play for an attractive blonde he spied at the Top of the Mark, a popular nightclub at the Mark Hopkins Hotel. She was Ann-

Marie Elwell, wife of his boyhood pal Reed, who was currently serving aboard a destroyer. Boyington had met with Reed just before going overseas and evidently saw Ann-Marie's photograph—an easy one to remember. She looked like movie star Carole Lombard, and had been offered a stand-in role not long before the actress was killed in a plane crash. After seeing her at the Mark with her coworkers from the Presidio Army Base, Boyington called the following night and invited her to the St. Francis for dinner, drinks, dancing, "then whatever" at his suite. He would send a limousine. "Reed wasn't home at the time," she recalled, "so of course I declined. But an hour later Greg called and said, 'If the Saint Francis isn't good enough, we'll go to the Top of the Mark.' Well, that really finished it. Women and liquor were his top priorities."

Boyington had one other priority: he was broke. Bad as his financial situation had been before the war, it was now in complete disarray. With the exception of his allotments, his pay had been held since his disappearance, and his new role as a public figure allowed no time to straighten matters out. For the time being he would have to live on the seven-dollar-per-diem allowance he was paid. Fortunately, wherever he went during the coming tour, his accommodations in some of the most luxurious hotel suites around the county would be free. He wouldn't have to plunk down so much as a nickel for a cup of coffee, let alone pay for drinks.

Worried mostly about the latter, Frank Walton laid his opinion on the line while sitting with Boyington in the St. Francis's steam room just before the tour started. "Greg, you're a worldwide hero. You can be anything you want to be. You could be a senator. You could be governor of this state if you want to be. Whatever you want to be. But you've got to lay off the booze."

"I learned my lesson about that," Boyington responded. "You won't have any problem with that."

Although both men realized Boyington was famous, they were still unprepared for the wild reception at their first stop,

Boeing Field, on September 17. A military band and a thousand cheering spectators gave a hint of the welcome Seattle had planned for its hometown hero. Met by Mayor William Devin, the two marines were led to a waiting motorcade, which moved slowly downtown while the band continued playing from a flatbed trailer. Boyington sat on the folded top of a huge Lincoln convertible, waving in disbelief as "a veritable snowstorm" of shredded paper fluttered from office-building windows.

The media had done a thorough job of promoting him as a Seattle native, even commenting on his employment at the Olympic Garage. He was dumbstruck as the motorcade reached the same square where he had parked cars just three years earlier, jammed with a crowd conservatively estimated at more than five thousand people. Suspended in the air above what was now called Victory Square, giant banners proclaiming WELCOME HOME PAPPY hung on cables. Near the bandstand, governor Mon Wallgren waited to greet Washington's most famous war hero. After an army band played the national anthem, the speechifying began. When it was Boyington's turn he stepped to the microphone, wholly unrehearsed, never having expected this while waiting to be rescued from Omori.

"You've shown that you're glad to see me," he said, "but I want to tell you that I'm ten times as glad to see you." The crowd roared its approval. "I can't tell you how grateful I am," he continued. "This wonderful welcome simply overwhelms me. It's too good to be true." He had Seattle eating from the palm of his hand.

After three days of luncheons and dinners, with a side trip to Oregon and a visit with five-year-old Gloria at the Wickstrom home, he and Walton were met by a delegation from Okanogan. They crossed the Cascades and drove into the Columbia River Basin on September 20, arriving in Brewster ahead of schedule. School had let out early, but the children missed seeing Boyington's car as it cruised through town on the road to the Hallenbeck ranch. Two miles past town, Boyington got his first glimpse of the small ranch where his mother and two oldest children now lived: a peaceful place, with a small white house under an old apple tree, a view of the Columbia River, a barn, and orchards in back.

Ellsworth greeted him with an embrace, asked, "How are you feeling?" then answered his own question. "You're looking pretty good. A little fat, maybe."

Boyington took the barb with a grin. "I'm feeling fine."

A car drove up—the neighbor with a phone message that all the schoolchildren were waiting on Main Street. "We can't leave those kids standing there," said Boyington, whose own son and daughter were among them. Reaching town, he was surrounded by two hundred children, several carrying WELCOME HOME placards.

Later, Janet showed him the chicks that had hatched in the barn, and she rode her bike around the yard. Boyington hiked with her to the hazel-colored hills of prairie grass overlooking the Columbia, where they stood together just below a windswept ridge, she holding his big hand with her little one as they gazed across the river valley, hauntingly alone in a vast landscape of prairie and rugged mountains.

Bobby demonstrated that he could drive the ranch car, then showed his father the Kraut helmet and rifle Bill Hallenbeck had sent from Germany. Boyington took his son hunting for a day, but too soon it was time to go up the valley to Okanogan, where a huge homecoming for all of the county's veterans was planned. Boyington was the guest of honor.

The celebration was incomparable. The afternoon weather was gorgeous that first Sunday of fall as a crowd of fifteen thousand gathered to watch the big parade. Boyington sat in an open car again with Frank Walton and the official party, surrounded by the kind of colorful, locally flavored convoy that only a genuinely patriotic small town could produce. When the parade reached the city park, Boyington and his whole family took seats in the giant gazebo. The program included a special presentation by the president of the local wildlife council. "We believe the best way for veterans to forget war," he said, handing Boyington a new sport rifle, "is to go out into the wide open spaces with a gun. . . ."

When the microphone was turned over to Boyington, he proved he was no one-speech wonder. "With days like years in a Jap prison camp," he began, "my fondest dream was of driving up the highway into the Okanogan country. Now my dream has come true." He was just as good at winning crowds as he was at shooting down Zeros.

The rest of the tour was a dizzying schedule of one public appearance after another, several times a day—the "chicken, peas, and bourbon" circuit. Boyington was the draw. His sole purpose was to encourage the public to purchase Series E treasury bonds, mostly called War Bonds out of habit, though Victory Bonds had come into vogue.

After being fêted for two days in Chicago, he and Walton arrived in Washington, D.C., on Tuesday, October 2. Two days later they went to the commandant's office in the Navy Annex on Columbia Pike for a special ceremony. General Vandegrift pinned a Navy Cross on Boyington, who was immediately disillusioned with the navy's highest award for valor—or at least with the politics surrounding it. He categorized it as a "booby prize," a description that in his case was probably valid.

Vandegrift had argued for the award after the review board initially turned it down, and Frank Knox ultimately overruled the board, but the citation was weak for such a valued medal. It referred to just one specific event, when Boyington scored his last official victory before being shot down. Navy Crosses simply weren't issued under those circumstances. Boyington was convinced that the award was political, issued in response to radio and newspaper commentary that he had received no recognition before he disappeared. Jaded ever after, he was often heard to grumble: "Nothing is too good for you when you are dead."

At headquarters that morning, Boyington took care of a matter that was more important to him than the Navy Cross. The additional victories he claimed during his last flight were as yet unofficial, and would have to be accounted for in the squadron war diary in order to be recognized. Walton accompanied him to the intelligence department, pulled the war diary, and found his original typed entry for January 3, 1944. Feeding a blank action report form into a typewriter, Walton typed the entries necessary for a supplement: a narrative of the final dogfight, with two extra victories for Boyington and one for Ashmun, plus an account of Boyington's bailout, injuries, and subsequent capture. When Walton was done, Boyington signed the form as the approving authority. The original with the new supplement went back into the diary, and Walton kept a carbon copy for his own records.

That was all it took. With a stroke of his own pen, Boyington was credited with twenty-eight victories, making him the high scoring ace in the Marine Corps.

Early on Friday morning, another beautiful fall day, Boyington stood in formation with thirteen other sailors and marines on the South Lawn of the White House, waiting for President Truman to appear. Dozens of the most influential politicians and flag officers in the United States sat nearby, a remarkable peanut gallery with more "scrambled eggs" and stars than Boyington had ever seen in one place. One general, never identified, approached Boyington from behind. "There are those who never counted on your showing up again," he whispered.

Without turning his head, Boyington shot back, "Yeah, they say a lot of nice things about you when you're dead that they wouldn't say when you're alive. But I sure screwed 'em, didn't I, Dad?"

Everyone snapped to attention when the navy band launched into "Ruffles and Flourishes," then Harry Truman strode onto the lawn. The ceremony began with Boyington's award. He stepped forward in his crisp greens as a naval officer spoke into a public address system.

"The President of the United States takes pleasure in presenting the Medal of Honor to Major Gregory Boyington, U.S. Marine Corps, for service as set forth in the following citation:

'For extraordinary heroism above and beyond the call of duty as Commanding Officer of Marine Fighting Squadron TWO FOURTEEN in action against enemy Japanese forces in the Central Solomons Area from September 12, 1943, to January 3, 1944. Consistently outnumbered throughout successive hazardous flights over heavily defended hostile territory, Major Boyington struck at the enemy with daring and courageous persistence, leading his squadron into combat with devastating results to Japanese shipping, shore installations, and aerial forces. Resolute in his efforts to inflict crippling damage on the enemy, Major Boyington led a formation of twenty-four fighters over Kahili on October 17 and, persistently circling the airdrome where sixty hostile aircraft were grounded, boldly challenged the Japanese to send up planes. Under his brilliant command, our fighters shot down twenty enemy craft in the ensuing action without the loss of a single ship. A superb airman and determined fighter against overwhelming odds, Major Boyington personally destroyed twenty of the numerous Japanese planes shot down by his squadron and by his resourceful leadership developed the combat readiness in his command which was a distinctive factor in Allied aerial achievements in this vitally strategic area.'"

Boyington hoped to hear the pet phrase Truman was said to utter when draping the blue ribbon around a recipient's neck ("I would rather have this honor than be president of the United States"), but the president simply shook his hand and said, "Congratulations, Major."

The Nimitz Day ceremony came next, with a huge parade and speeches. Frank Walton joined Boyington on the dais, with its huge mocked-up battleship as a backdrop. Afterward, at a round of parties and receptions, Boyington celebrated the crowning moment of his military career.

Despite his busy schedule, Boyington made some time to

settle an old bet. Jim Condit, raised in the city, was recovering at home from his three-year imprisonment when Boyington called. "Hey, Jim," he said, "I got a present for you." He brought over a case of whiskey, making good on Condit's bet that the war would end in '45. When Boyington arrived, Condit recognized immediately that his former prison mate was in rough shape. Boyington admitted that he was losing control: "This is killing me," he told Condit, "I just can't go anyplace without somebody giving me a double shot of whiskey."

But the Victory Bond tour was not yet half over, and the second segment proved even more demanding than the first. Boyington and Walton flew to New York on October 7, where they stayed in *Look* magazine's suite at the Waldorf Astoria for the next nineteen days. Almost daily they made excursions into Pennsylvania, New Jersey, or Connecticut; between trips, there were plenty of public relations events in Manhattan, including radio programs, promotional photographs ("Pappy" drinks Borden's milk), even a studio interview for one of the city's first television stations.

Because of the frantic schedule, Walton had an increasingly difficult time monitoring Boyington's well-being. "At each one of these places they would have a little reception," he recalled. "They were all shaking his hand and bringing drinks to him. I'd caution him, 'God damn it, Greg, watch that booze.' Finally it got that he was sneaking them. Then it got to where he was getting drunk and having difficulty making his speeches."

As soon as he reached New York, Boyington resumed his affair with Lucy Malcolmson, who was still married to Stewart Malcolmson. They spent time together between Boyington's public appearances, and she hosted a party for him at her house in Greenwich Village. Walton, who had to fend for himself while they shared the weekend of October 13, grew increasingly concerned that the affair would lead to bad publicity if the media learned Boyington was sleeping with another man's wife. Walton made his disapproval clear to Boyington, and likewise "took no pains to conceal it from Lucy."

Ignoring Walton, Boyington professed his love for Lucy and backed it up with a letter to Stewart Malcolmson. He wrote that Lucy was going to move to Nevada to qualify for a divorce in absentia, after which he would marry her. Next, Boyington gave her a photograph of himself with the inscription: *Dearest Lucy—I shall always love and adore you. There is not enough space on this earth to separate us, my darling. All my love—Greg.* Finally, he arranged for his pay record to be transmitted to the Brooklyn Navy Yard. A small insurance allotment and the $420 deposited each month in Lucy's account were still in effect, but his back pay had grown to more than four thousand dollars.* Almost immediately after collecting it from the local paymaster, he purchased a Lincoln Zephyr for Lucy to drive to Reno. Without too much difficulty, she convinced him to put the title of the car in her name. "She didn't want to drive it if it was in my name," he later explained, "for fear she might get in a jam on the road."

Finally refocusing his attention on the tour, Boyington flew with Walton to Detroit on October 26. Two days later they moved on to Seattle, their hub while they ranged out to events throughout the Pacific Northwest, after which they drove to Portland, Oregon. By the time they checked into the Hotel Benson on the afternoon of November 3, they had been wining and dining and traveling for fifty-two days. Walton sent their last serviceable uniforms to the valet for a quick cleaning while they rested in their suite.

Still wearing their skivvies, they learned that a "dinner" had been laid on when a small welcoming committee joined them in the sitting room. Walton was too exhausted to make small talk and retreated to the adjoining bedroom for a nap,

---

* In his memoirs, Boyington claimed that the Treasury Department placed liens on his property for failure to pay taxes on income held while he was a prisoner. Not only did he collect his back pay (which was taxable at the time), but in 1952 he became eligible for a tax refund for those years.

but was soon disturbed. "God Almighty, I woke up and heard this commotion next door," he later recalled. "I looked in and there were about ten people in there. Boyington was down on the floor with my bathrobe on, rolling around drunk as a skunk. So I picked up the phone and called him and said, 'You get those people out of here or I'm going to come in and throw them out.' He turned around to them and I could hear him say, 'That's my partner, and he said if you don't get out of here he's going to throw you out. And he will.'"

Walton helped Boyington get dressed for the dinner, which turned out to be a Victory Bond event attended by hundreds of the city's most influential citizens. "I got him down there at about seven o'clock," continued Walton. "He sat up there at the dais with the town's elite—the mayor and all—and I was sitting down looking up at him, just dying, with him blinking like a goddamn owl. I was sick to my stomach, almost."

Eventually Boyington was called to speak. Staggering to the microphone, he said, "I know what you want me to talk about: you want me to talk about how I shot 'em down. I was flat on my back at forty thousand feet—that's what you want, isn't it? That's what you want! I'm here to sell War Bonds. Buy War Bonds. Why? I don't know, just buy 'em."

This time, no one clapped.

19

The Low Road

From his pinnacle as America's top marine ace, with a seemingly boundless view of potential opportunities, Boyington spun into an abyss of alcoholism, debt, and public notoriety in a matter of months.

After flying down to Los Angeles with Frank Walton on November 5, he announced his plans to remain in the Marine Corps pending the outcome of a flight physical. In reality the choice was not his to make. By virtue of accepting the regular commission in Hawaii, he had locked himself into a Marine Corps career. Regular officers, unlike reservists, were not eligible for discharge.

That the victory tour concluded in Los Angeles was no coincidence. While in New York, Boyington had received a call from headquarters placed by Brigadier General McKittrick, his former commanding officer at Quantico. McKittrick had ascertained more about Boyington's true medical condition—a slightly enlarged liver, a history of beriberi and malaria, a case of jaundice, and still-healing wounds—and wanted to put a stop to the tour. At Boyington's request, he authorized the rest of the scheduled events, but sent orders for Boyington to report to the Long Beach Naval Hospital when he reached Los Angeles. It wasn't a bad deal. For pay purposes, Boyington was attached to the casual company at the Terminal Island Marine Barracks, and reported for duty as an outpatient while he underwent a thorough evaluation.

Walton's home was in Los Angeles, so while the two tired marines recuperated from their arduous tour, they got together to discuss the idea of writing a book. Walton even proposed that Boyington stay in the spare bedroom of his house in Panorama Terrace. "I'll take you down to the Hollywood Athletic Club," he offered. "We can go on a diet, lose some weight, and work out there every day." After Boyington accepted, Walton arranged for a police secretary to come over after her regular duty hours. "We'd sit there and I'd get him to start talking about his experiences—where he started, where he was born, and all that stuff," Walton recalled years later. "She was getting pages and pages of text, and he did pretty good for a while."

In the meantime, Lucy Malcolmson held up her end of the bargain and provided regular updates on her progress across the country. Her effort to drive west seemed to indicate that she was not out to bilk Boyington: if it had been her intention to cut and run, she already possessed most of his wealth. Furthermore, she had committed herself to the relationship by selling her Greenwich Village house before leaving New York. She forwarded her itinerary, to which Boyington responded by sending saccharine messages to each night's stopping place. She reached Jamestown, New York on November 8 to find: *I love you. Hurry up and get out here. Miss you terribly. All my love.* Next came Gary, Indiana *(Doing fine baby darling. Keep it up)*, followed by Omaha, Nebraska *(Practically nuts now. You and time are closer)*. When she reached Reno, Boyington planned to fly out in late November and return two days later.

Maybe it was fate—but more likely it was planned—that Carol Walton would introduce Boyington to a coworker a week before he was to meet Lucy. Over a duck dinner at the Chinese Theater in Hollywood, Boyington fell in love with Frances Baker, a divorced X-ray technician. The thirty-two-year-old blonde bombshell was equally smitten with him.

Described as "a Hollywood actress" like countless others in the city, she had begun a degree in medicine at the University of Southern California before dabbling in the movie business. She had divorced Russell Baker, a restaurateur and insurance man, in 1942.

All but forgetting Lucy, Boyington immediately proposed marriage to "Franny." Lucy's six-week residency in Reno would last through the first week of January, which he evidently believed would give him time to resolve the situation. In the meantime he and Frances drew local media attention during their weekends together. They were invited aboard *Blue Moon,* a yacht owned by a Consolidated Vultee Aircraft executive, and later cruised as guests aboard *Sirocco,* a yacht formerly owned by Errol Flynn. When not cruising the coast, they drank and danced at Rosarito Beach, Mexico. Despite all the fun, Lucy maintained a powerful grip on Boyington, who would lose a frightening amount of money if he stood her up. Considering his history with finances and women, there didn't seem to be a positive outcome in sight.

He was too busy to visit the athletic club with Walton, and although he received a clean bill of health during his flight physical in mid-December, he tipped the scales at 190 pounds. The doctor described him as "slightly obese." Afterward, Boyington was ordered to Miramar for duty—coincidentally at the same time that Walton went off leave and returned to his former intelligence position—so the two of them decided to share an apartment.

Suddenly, everything seemed to unravel for the marine ace-of-aces. He was simply too well known to solve his dilemma quietly, particularly now that the war was over and the nation was eager for frivolous news. His weekends with Frances had been publicized in southern California, and now the stories of his entanglement with Lucy began to appear across the country in Sunday tabloids, even in *Time* and *Newsweek.*

The tailspin began on New Year's Eve, when Frances evidently decided to push Boyington into breaking off his relationship with Lucy by driving him to Reno. In his pocket, he carried a three-carat engagement ring purchased for $2,900 "because it looked like a bargain." (He had borrowed the funds from a Reno bank, evidently during his visit in November.) According to a litany of he-said-she-said statements, Boyington did attempt to end his relationship with Lucy after Frances dropped him off, but he was rebuffed. Worse, Lucy used her considerable financial leverage to get the engagement ring. Later, Boyington claimed he was "hypnotized" into giving it to her, but his explanation only made him seem daffy. More likely he was outfoxed: Lucy was willful, clever, and held almost all of his money.

Whatever romance might have existed between them quickly evaporated while they argued over the allotment. As Boyington later told the *Los Angeles Times:* "[A]fter two days of heated battle about money matters I told her, 'As far as I'm concerned it's good-bye.'" He left Reno in a daze, having resolved little aside from verbally dumping Lucy. She still had his money, and now she had his rock on her finger.

The main wave of publicity came just a few days later, when Lucy held a press conference in Reno. The Sunday gossip columns reported on January 6 that Boyington, "the toughest air combat leader to come out of the Pacific war," would marry "the girl who inspired all his deeds" as soon as Lucy's divorce hearing was completed two days hence. The announcement came as a shock to Boyington, who was reportedly "aghast" when approached by the press back at Miramar on Monday. "I don't know why Mrs. Malcolmson disclosed that she planned to marry me," he said. "We made no such plans. At one time she wanted to marry me, but I told her I did not want to marry her." To another reporter he allegedly blurted, "We're just good friends," a brush-off that stunned Lucy. "In spite of all I've heard on the radio and seen in the papers," she said, "I just don't believe Greg would do what he appears to have done."

The press gleefully reported every new twist in the hero's love affair, sending Boyington into hiding, so Walton fielded phone calls for a couple of days. Frances got more directly involved also, as Walton explained.

> Franny phoned, and she was getting panicky, reading the stories in the paper about this gal Lucy Belle in Reno, who was having press conferences, saying she was going to get married to Boyington.
>
> In the meantime Greg was sitting there one night and said, "Gee, Frank, I don't want to marry anybody."
>
> I said, "Greg, you don't have to marry anybody. You're not hooked until you say those words, and if you don't want to marry anybody, just don't answer the phone."
>
> "Well, that's what I think I'd better do."

But rather than wait for Boyington to reach a decision, Frances took matters into her own hands. She drove down to San Diego, picked him up and took him back to Los Angeles, then flew with him to Reno. Carol Walton was also aboard the plane, and served as matron of honor when Boyington and Frances exchanged vows before a justice of the peace on January 8.

Scheduled to appear that very day in district court for her divorce from Stewart Malcolmson, Lucy was a no-show. "My client is on the verge of complete collapse," her attorney told reporters. Attempting to divert attention from her absence, he trotted out several telegrams Boyington had sent Lucy during her cross-country trek. Couched in sweetness, the love notes were widely published by the press.

Meanwhile the newlyweds returned to Los Angeles and held a press conference of their own at the home of Boyington's attorney, Arthur Miller. When Boyington wasn't mixing double bourbons for reporters, he happily smooched with Frances. In order to satisfy all the requests for pictures, he was compelled to carry her across the threshold three times. Then he answered questions.

His short romance with his new bride? "It was love at first sight."

His relationship with Lucy? "It was strictly a long-distance romance by mail, and you know how mail romances can build up."

Lucy's relationship with his children? "She had been their guardian for four years and she simply assumed we would get married."

The engagement ring? "I was so involved with Lucy there wasn't much else I could do. I can handle Japs okay, but can't do much with women."

Front-page headlines announced the nuptials and Lucy's jilting. Subsequently, intimate details of Boyington's life were rehashed in the tabloids, spotlighting his earlier divorce from Helene, the situation with his allotment, and his convoluted romances with Lucy and Frances.

By coincidence, Boyington received orders to a new duty station on the same day that his wedding was announced. He was authorized ninety days of "rehabilitation leave" en route to Marine Corps School, Quantico, and announced immediately that he would use the time to conduct a lecture tour with his new bride. Verbal approval had already been obtained, with the understanding that he would not be an official representative of the Marine Corps. In the wake of the embarrassing publicity surrounding his marriage, headquarters urged him to cancel most of the events, but Boyington was not about to comply. He needed the money.

Unfortunately, the lecture tour had neither the backing nor the billing of the Victory Bond effort. The venues were smaller, as were most of the cities where the lectures were scheduled. Beginning with the first stop, Cleveland, it was evident that his recent "marital confusion" had harmed his credibility. Press coverage of his wartime adventures was secondary as reporters devoted more space to his marriage, calling it "the subject of a lot of light reading." In Buffalo, his "tangled marital adventures" received similar attention. Over a span of more than sixty days, the Boyingtons traveled to nine cities ranging in size from Chicago to Harvey, Illinois, but too much time elapsed between speeches for the newlyweds to realize any profit. Instead of unpacking at

Quantico, they returned to Los Angeles in the third week of March. Things went from bad to worse in a hurry.

Out of money, the Boyingtons moved into the Waltons' spare bedroom temporarily, making for a crowded house. Walton had since gotten out of the Marine Corps Reserves and returned to his former job with the LAPD, having advanced his career by passing promotion exams for lieutenant during the war. Using his public relations experience, he arranged a press conference at his office on March 22, hoping to publicize the book he and Boyington had worked on. The coauthors—Walton in his police blues and Boyington in his greens—posed with their eighty-thousand-word manuscript, which traced the development of the Flying Tigers, then the story of the Black Sheep squadron ("composed of inexperienced pilots nobody else wanted"), and finally how the Black Sheep carried on in Boyington's absence, while he "underwent twenty months of Jap prison brutality." The project soon collapsed, however, and with it their friendship.

The culprit was no mystery. Walton's work schedule was based on twenty-four-hour watches. On days when he had the duty, he arose at four in the morning in order to take over the watch at six, then remained on duty until he was relieved the following morning. The Boyingtons kept no such hours and were often disruptive late at night. They talked about losing weight, so Carol tried to accommodate them. "My wife fixed us salads and lean meat meals, that sort of stuff, and no drinking," recalled Walton. "Every night they raided our refrigerator and ate up everything in our refrigerator. This went on for maybe a week or two, and I was getting more and more pissed off about it."

One night in April, the Boyingtons came home late, roaring drunk. Somehow Walton slept through the first part, but eventually Boyington slumped to the floor and threw up, swearing loudly at no one in particular. Carol Walton could take no more. "My wife came in and shook me awake," remembered Frank, "and said, 'The son of a bitch has got to go!'"

When he saw the mess in the kitchen, Frank had to agree. "Greg," he demanded, "I want you out of here tomorrow. When I get home from work tomorrow, I don't want you here." By the time he returned, Pappy and Frances were gone.

Within days of the episode at the Walton home, Boyington returned to San Diego and checked into the naval hospital. Curiously, he was not hospitalized for alcohol treatment, but for arthritis. He complained of painful knees, ankles, fingers, and wrists, symptoms that supposedly began in 1943 and had become worse. His left knee and ankle, he said, were "painful enough to be almost disabling."

Nothing in Boyington's medical record suggests he was admitted to dry out—presuming a sanctioned treatment program even existed in the naval system at the time—but his hospitalization for arthritis appears to have been a partial smokescreen. During his second day, April 16, a thorough series of lab tests and evaluations revealed nothing more than stiffness in fingers and "slight joint pain . . . present at times and not noticeable at others." He complained of low back pain lasting three months, which happened to coincide with his carrying Frances over the threshold three times. Boyington was diagnosed with polyarthritis, indicating symptoms in many extremities, and the press was duly notified. The navy's official spin was that the "illness he contracted during twenty months of imprisonment never fully left him."

In the meantime, his orders to Quantico were postponed and he was put on a program of physical therapy for ten days. Then he was given a series of intravenous typhoid vaccine injections to deliberately induce fever. By mid-May he reportedly felt better, and his diagnosis was changed from polyarthritis to arthralgia, a minor distinction indicating that the pain in his joints was caused by groups of nerves, not arthritic inflammation. He was released from the hospital to go "inland" to the desert for two weeks, "to observe effects of the drier climate."

Rather than heading to the desert, however, he spent the time attempting to recover the money that Lucy had received by allotment. She still lived in Reno, stranded there after Stewart Malcolmson cut off her monthly allowance, but had proved resourceful by hocking the engagement ring for a grubstake in a rooming house that catered to recently divorced women. Business was reportedly good enough that she had begun negotiating with the owners to purchase the property. Boyington disrupted her plan by charging in a criminal complaint that she had stolen more than nine thousand dollars of his pay. A municipal judge issued a warrant for her arrest, so she came to San Diego with her Reno attorney, Joseph Haller, to surrender. Bail was originally set at $25,000—an enormous sum at the time—but an outraged Haller argued it down to $10,000. Immediately after Lucy was booked into the county jail, Haller posted her bail and they returned to Reno, whereupon they called in the press.

Once again Boyington found himself headlined in such stories as HE LOVED HER IN DECEMBER BUT NOT IN MAY. Tabloids provided the eager public with every detail, among them Boyington's financial woes (he claimed to be $6,000 in debt). Lucy was charged with seven counts of grand theft, including her withdrawal of $4,500 from the allotment funds nearly a year after Boyington was imprisoned. She had cleaned out the account with a withdrawal of more than $1,100 six days after he married Frances.

The hearing was postponed for several weeks, apparently while Boyington underwent more treatments, but finally the opposing sides met in court on August 20. The case never went to trial. Haller offered as evidence a number of letters establishing Boyington's relationship with Lucy, including a note he had written during the war: "Honey, will you still love me if I never get to be America's leading ace?" Lucy likewise documented Boyington's authorization for the allotments, saying she had used the money for its intended purpose. "He knows darn well what happened to his money. Not only can I account for it, but for a lot of my own I spent settling Pappy's accounts and taking care of his kids, his mother, and all his bills. Nobody knows that better than Pappy."

The hearing was in its second day when the judge decided he'd heard enough. He called a halt to the testimony, declaring there wasn't "probable cause to hold the defendant guilty of this charge or any of the charges." Lucy's eyes filled with tears of relief; Boyington walked out of the courtroom in stony silence.

In the span of a year, he had gone from lionized hero to tabloid fodder. The Marine Corps, all too happy to benefit from his earlier fame, now viewed the publicity surrounding his personal affairs as a discredit to the service.

Boyington was photographed at the San Diego courthouse using a cane, but his reliance on it was questionable. He returned to the hospital for another evaluation, after which the physician noted that Boyington's condition was "not aggravated by malnourishment, malaria, or dysentery while in a Japanese prison camp." No one seemed to notice the contradiction of the navy's earlier press release, or that just seven months previously, Boyington had passed a strenuous flight physical. Now, at the age of thirty-three, he received yet another diagnosis for his physical complaints—this one the most curious of all—an "acquired deformity" of the left ankle. Apparently ignoring the X-ray evidence, a medical board accepted Boyington's statement that he had sustained "a compound fracture of his left ankle by shell fragments," and that somehow, after his capture, "it had healed without treatment." The board reached a secondary finding of rheumatoid arthritis in the ankles, knees, hands, wrists, and back, and ultimately determined that he was "permanently unfit for service."

If there was a degree of arthritis, Boyington later made a remarkable recovery. Almost certainly, the medical maneuvering was meant to retire him. For several reasons—his renewed drinking, the negative publicity surrounding his marital and legal troubles, and probably that old general opinion that *he was no damn good and never would be*—his health was systematically documented to render him unfit for service. Boyington declined to submit a rebuttal, an indication that the process was mutually agreed upon.

The next step was a naval retirement board. While waiting for one to convene, Boyington left active duty on August 21 with orders to proceed home, there to await the further orders of the board. In the meantime, he was authorized to wear civilian clothing and to "engage in any occupation not contrary to law." Heavily in debt, with no home or means of employment, Boyington was uncertain of what to do or where to go for the first time since college. As a graduate he had been fortunate to land an immediate job with Boeing, but the situation at the end of World War II was vastly different, with a glut of highly qualified young men in the job market. He knew one thing after working for Boeing: drafting was not for him. If anything, he was even less capable of a desk job after flying fighters for more than a decade—not to mention drinking for just as long.

While waiting for something else to come along, he took Frances to visit his family, an awkward situation due to the fact that they were once again in a new place. The Hallenbecks had left the pleasant ranch in Brewster and moved to Grants Pass, Oregon. Bobby and Janet were still with them. In no position to take responsibility for the two children, Boyington was henceforth never more than an absentee parent. Nor did Gloria reenter the family. She was adopted instead by the Wickstroms, who continued the decent start on life they had given her in Seattle.

She was the fortunate one. Bobby and Janet were raised in a dysfunctional setting by alcoholic grandparents. Bill Hallenbeck's daughters—Tiffany, Ramona, Patricia, and Holly—were around during their cousins' high school years, witnessing to varying degrees their unhappy life with Grace and Ellsworth. "Because of alcoholism and other things, they kept themselves isolated from other people," said Ramona, referring to Grace and Ellsworth. "They didn't have a community of friends, and they moved so much." The "other things" essentially meant Ellsworth's pedophiliac behavior. Her own father had been victimized, Ramona stated, and Ellsworth hadn't stopped there: "I'm positive it happened to [his] grandchildren, because it happened to all of us. I can't imagine what it would have been like for Bobby and Janet to grow up in that household. It had to be horrible."

Indeed, Gregory junior was pleasantly accommodating when it came to authorizing next-of-kin access to his father's records for this book, but he would not talk about his life or family relationships. "It's all a big secret," he declared, and let it go at that. Ramona acknowledged, "Back then it was the family secret. That type of behavior is still hard to bring up today or get treatment for."

Somehow, Boyington remained unaware of his stepfather's sickness. Bobby was not yet twelve, and Janet was three years younger, when he left them with the Hallenbecks.

Upon their return to Los Angeles, the Boyingtons moved into a modest ranch-style house on Verdugo Avenue in Burbank. Their income dropped significantly not many months later when a letter from the Marine Corps arrived, informing Boyington that he had been placed on the retired list effective August 1, 1947. He was advanced one rank because of the Medal of Honor, but his retirement pay, formulated from a percentage of his active duty pay, was reduced to approximately $250 per month; the Medal of Honor was worth just ten extra dollars.

Thus ended his storied career in the Marine Corps. For more than ten years, the organization had allowed him, in one form or another, to pursue the two things he truly enjoyed—flying and fighting. Not surprisingly, his return to civilian life was extremely difficult. "Shortly after the war," he wrote, "the glamour was gone and there was nothing in my life but turbulence for nearly ten years." His words, written in 1957, were an understatement, for his life lasted another three decades, and the turbulence did not end with the publication of his memoirs. The truly tumultuous period began with his entry into the job market. "I set the business world on fire," he said with sarcasm, "six jobs that lasted about four months, the longest of any of them."

After discovering that the only people interested in him were those who hoped his fame or notoriety might move their products, he became a salesman. Like many starting out in the industry, he called his friends and acquaintances first. "Over the years, I would hear from him occasionally," remembered Frank Walton. "He'd want to sell something. He sold me insurance one time, some stock in an insurance company. And he was selling jewelry, and was a salesman for a beer company."

At the onset of each new job, Boyington worked frantically, remaining relatively sober, but the pace and his sobriety would soon end. "I knew a big, fat drunk was coming up," he later commented. "They forgave you if you were bringing the company some business, so when I figured the handwriting was on the wall, I'd go in and resign. I couldn't resign like a normal human being, I had to go in and put on a show."

While struggling to become a civilian again, Boyington improved his financial situation by means of an unusual job, one he described as "a money-making hobby." It also provided some excitement and was certainly well suited to his boisterous personality. In 1949, he entered the zany world of professional wrestling as a referee.

Back in the days of cathode ray tubes and flickering gray images on television, pro wrestling bore little resemblance to the current parade of ultrahyped, outlandishly costumed characters. Nearly all of the wrestlers wore the same style of outfit, consisting of high-topped shoes and a pair of form-fitting trunks. To differentiate heroes from villains, the good guys had sculptured bodies and handsome "baby faces," while their opponents were fat men, often with beards.

For Boyington, the paycheck was secondary; he was in it for the carnival atmosphere, the action in the ring. Ironically, he claimed to despise the "milquetoast creatures" in the live audiences, probably using them as his excuse to get "half blind from vodka" before the start of the first match. Television brought in viewers from across the West as he worked arenas in southern California. Occasionally he traveled, such as the time "Hap" Halloran, his fellow prisoner from Omori, saw him at the Indianapolis Arena. Boyington officiated the main card featuring Lou Thesz—a legend whose career spanned five decades—and some forgotten "heel." He continued to referee for several years until the arenas began to close. "They'd chase you from San Diego to Bakersfield for jobs and there wasn't much money in it," he said in mid-1955, "so I quit." The amazing thing was that five years earlier, he had been rated seventy percent disabled by the Veterans Administration, which authorized him to receive increased tax-free compensation. All that time, he spent several hours each week running around the ring as a referee. In May 1950 he weighed a cherubic two hundred pounds, yet his ankle held up fine and no further mention of arthritis was ever made.

While Boyington hobnobbed with wrestlers and the underworld of promoters, Medal of Honor recipient Joe Foss was establishing a strong career in politics. He was national vice chairman of the American Legion Aeronautics Committee in 1949 when the two aces met during a reception at the Biltmore Hotel. The memorable event was attended by an impressive list of VIPs. "Half the U.S. Senate was there," Foss recalled, "and a lot of state senators, governors, congressmen, and so forth." Despite all the dignitaries, Boyington could not resist getting drunk. Then he challenged Foss.

> I was just walking around, visiting with people in that mass of humanity there, when all of a sudden he appeared in front of me and said, "Let's wrassle!"
> I said, "I'm glad you got that crap out of your system."
> And he answered, "I've always wanted to kick hell out of you."
> I said, "Don't ever try it, or I'll kill you."

With that, he sprung at me. He hit me in the chest with his shoulder and drove me into the wall; I hit so dang hard that I thought I'd fractured my skull. He had his hands clasped behind me, with his knuckles between my shoulder blades, and kept bashing me against the wall. I got my heels against the wall, kicked out, and just plowed U.S. senators and people out of the area.

We hit a big stuffed chair, and with the two of us on it, that thing came apart. Down he went and hit his head on the floor, so he let go of me. I checked to see if my neck was broken, wiggling it around, and here he came again. I hauled off and hit him a good one along side of the head. That sort of stunned him and he bent over. Then I gave him another one that just about laid him in the daisies, and flipped him upside down. I got on top of him and yelled at Duke Corning, my business partner, who used to officiate at wrestling and boxing matches: "Count this jerk out!"

Carried to a bedroom to sleep it off, Boyington knocked on Foss's door the next morning and said, "Boy, I guess we had some fun last night!" But Foss, whose only decent suit had been torn, was in no mood for wisecracks. "He'd pull dumb stunts after he'd had a few drinks," he concluded. "He went nuts—just came unhinged—and thought it was a joke the next day."

Boyington attended the reception because of Len Peterson, a millionaire and "a hotshot with the Legion" who had recently hired him as a sales executive with the East Side division of the Los Angeles Brewing Company. Peterson "sort of adopted old Greg and was trying to help him," according to Foss. This explains why Boyington managed to keep the job for six years, for he took advantage of Peterson's tolerance almost immediately. "Three days after I started," he later agreed, "I found out it was a job where I didn't have to report in every morning. Now, that's very convenient for a guy. Sometimes I had a little trouble getting the old eyeballs back to where they looked halfway decent, and

I was putting lotion on my face to look halfway respectable. Not having to report in, a couple of times it was ten days before they heard from me."

After his binges, Boyington would "sober up and work like a dog," so Peterson kept him on. Boyington acknowledged that it would have been far better if Peterson had fired him. As it turned out, he earned a decent salary and had access to a large expense account, but still had to send Frances to a local bank on occasion to borrow money. "I didn't know how many checks I'd written," he later explained. "The expense account wasn't enough."

Given so much leeway, it was a miracle that Boyington didn't hurt himself or kill someone as his drinking reached ever-higher levels of tolerance. "Even if I was laying on the floor," he said, "as long as I could see you and talk to you, I was not drunk. But when I was blacked out and couldn't remember, then I would admit to being drunk."

He was picked up on numerous occasions by the Los Angeles County Sheriff's Department or the LAPD, and at least one drunk driving arrest was widely publicized. He was also involved in several traffic accidents, yet he never lost his license because drunk driving laws were practically nonexistent. Civil penalties were another matter. By 1955, judgments totaling approximately eleven thousand dollars had accumulated, causing him to perpetually struggle with debt.

Under such conditions, Frances stayed with him far longer than might have been expected. "[He] became simply impossible," she later told *Life* magazine. "No one could have stayed with him in that condition. I got him an apartment of his own. Once I went there and found he'd been bingeing and there was fried egg all over the rug. There didn't seem to be anything to do except wait for him to want to be helped. But I cleaned up the rug."

Eventually, Boyington agreed to enter a weekly program with a psychiatrist, but lost interest when he discovered how the system worked. At a speaking engagement a few years later, he brought the house down with his explanation:

[The doctor] brought in, free of charge, psychiatrists from the University of Southern California and UCLA. I filed blocks, I did pictures, I did everything. I liked the reactions on their faces—they were dead giveaways, these guys.

Well, after about six months something happened. One night my wife received a telephone call from a bartender in Hollywood. He said, "You'd better come down and get Pappy before the police get him. He's asleep in the middle of the barroom floor."

So Franny came down and got me in the car. About the time we were going over the Cahuenga Pass into the valley, I started coming to a little bit. I noticed she didn't turn at the turnoff which went our way; she went straight ahead. I said, "Hey, you aren't going home."

She said, "No. You've forgotten, this is your night with the psychiatrist."

I said, "I can't go there, I'm drunk."

"Oh, yes, you are."

So she drove me down there, and this was consultant night; some young doc was there from the university. I noticed right off the bat that he was frightened with my appearance. This pleased me, so I grabbed him by the coat. I leered in his face, laughed, and I picked him up and set him on the table and said, "Let me do it to you tonight, Doc."

Claiming he was sorry to have ended the program in such a fashion, Boyington tried "a high-class sanitarium," where he received occasional doses of carbon dioxide combined with oxygen to help him through the detoxification process. Then he was given a portable "gas treatment" device to use at home. "I thought this was a good idea, and the doctor did too," he said. "It was just the same as a blackout drunk. But there's only one thing wrong with this—you come out and you feel good. A drunk doesn't like that. When he comes out of a blackout, he wants to have his clothes a mess and find puke all over himself, and he wants to have his money and his watch gone. You can't do it with this gas in your own home, so I didn't want any part of that."

Psychiatry had failed, and an expensive treatment program failed. Boyington had to reach the bottom of the abyss on his own. "I got sick and tired of drinking," he conceded. "I even got sick and tired of being sick and tired." His blackouts had become so severe that he would find himself back at home, having been dropped off by the police or a friendly cabdriver, his pockets stuffed with tracts from Alcoholics Anonymous and other groups. He had absolutely no memory of where he had been. "I finally got to the point that I knew my periodic blackouts were going to merge into one," he said. "Some people are afraid of death; I was afraid of a permanent blackout."

His last drink, he claimed, came on his forty-third birthday, December 4, 1955. He resigned from the brewery, called Alcoholics Anonymous, and attended his first meeting in Beverly Hills. Seeing people he had imbibed with in the past, he was impressed by their blunt honesty. "The big thing was, rather than hiding all this stuff, there they were laughing and joking about it. And some of these things were pretty doggone grim."

He did well for several months, then skipped meetings for four weeks when he found a new job, thinking he had his problem under control. Deciding to have some vodka one night, he discovered what "a slip" was all about. The chemical reaction hit him harder than ever, and the next night he was back at AA. "I knew where I belonged," he stated, "and I went back, and I wasn't the least bit ashamed. I liked these people. Some of them were crazier than others, but that's not for me to judge."

Alcoholism, according to AA literature, is an incurable, progressive, fatal disease. If untreated, alcoholics will drink themselves to death, die from associated diseases, or die from accident, suicide, or homicide. For Boyington to halt his skid took nothing less than his most tenacious fight. In one way he was fortunate to be so stubborn. He called upon the trait that had helped him face the Kenneth Fishers who wanted to beat him up, and the Joe Smoaks who wanted to shove him down. None of those struggles compared to alcoholism, which had been developing within him for twenty years. It took him that long to realize it was the one thing he would never beat. Once he came to grips with the realities of the disease, he learned to live with it. Afterward, he maintained long periods of sobriety, interrupted by regular slips, but he would always be an alcoholic (or, as he called himself, "a drunk").

As AA members are fond of pointing out, a pickle cannot turn itself back into a cucumber.

20

Tinseltown

At the end of his first sober year, Boyington was featured in a syndicated newspaper story on the lives of Medal of Honor winners. Pictured in his Burbank home, he looked remarkably changed from his chubby appearance in 1950. The years on the low road had aged him, making him look more like a man in his late fifties than one of forty-four.

He had become like Claire Chennault. His skin hung loosely on his face and neck, mostly because the collagen in his skin was breaking down after decades of absorbing chemicals from cigarette smoke. He had also lost weight. When he quit drinking, he cut off his main source of calories—alcohol. Frances once remarked that Boyington "craved sugar something terrible," the result of a chronically low blood sugar level. Paradoxically, whenever Boyington consumed sweets his blood sugar spiked, then plummeted lower than before, causing behavioral symptoms and mood swings.

Living with him under such conditions was a challenge. "The first year he wasn't drinking it didn't seem worth it to me," Frances later told a writer for *Life*. "When we first got married I loved him so much I thought if he only stopped drinking everything would be all right. But without liquor he was worse than ever; he was mean and cruel and threw things."

His situation was not uncommon. In the MOH article,

which focused on his battle with alcohol and inability to hold a job, Boyington was depicted as the classic example of a struggling war hero. He was bitter about his postwar handling by the Marine Corps ("They used me for publicity"), and even spoke out against the Medal of Honor itself: "I'm not [as] sensitive about that medal as before, but I still wish I had never gotten it."

The article ended with optimism for Boyington's future. In the spring of 1956, twelve years after he had last piloted a plane, he enrolled in a civilian flight training school. The flying was not challenging, but he had to learn new regulations imposed by the Civil Aeronautics Administration, and the communication procedures were more complicated than those of his military days. When he got his license, he began a weekend job ferrying executives and passengers in a light plane owned by the Flying Tiger cargo line.*

In the meantime, Gregory junior (called Bobby only by his immediate family now) had made his way into aviation. As the son of a Medal of Honor recipient, he was eligible for appointment to a service academy, so he took the entrance exams for the brand-new Air Force Academy in the summer of 1955. Having enlisted in the Marine Corps after high school, he was older than most of his classmates when he became a member of the first freshman class that fall, but was also savvier than they were.

Janet likewise followed her father's footsteps, though in a much different fashion. At eighteen she married a middleweight prizefighter eight years her senior, then moved into a North Hollywood apartment with him. As if that wasn't enough of a parallel, her husband, Rocco "Rocky" Slater, resembled her father physically. A former neighbor described Slater as "short, very stocky; his face looked like he'd had a few fights."

---

* Bob Prescott, who once had left Boyington stranded during a dogfight over Rangoon, founded the company. From its humble start just prior to the war's end, the Flying Tiger Line became the top global air cargo carrier by 1980; later it was absorbed by Federal Express.

Boyington was making changes of his own. In 1957 he landed a new job with Coast Pro-Seal, a company that manufactured pressurization sealants for the aviation industry. Soon thereafter, he and Frances moved into a home on North Maple Avenue, where he also found time to rewrite the manuscript he and Walton had started in 1945. Walton obligingly sent all the old notes after Boyington requested them, but it was a solo authorship now. Boyington merely mentioned Walton in the text a few times, significantly increasing the manuscript with new material about his triumph over alcohol, with philosophical observations interjected throughout. He also used his typewriter as a hammer to bash the hidebound military, not bothering to disguise his contempt for Claire Chennault, Harvey Greenlaw, and the Chiangs. Curiously, he used phony names for Joe Smoak ("Colonel Lard") and other Marine Corps antagonists, apparently out of concern for government reprisals.

His writing style reflected his knack for extemporaneous storytelling. When he reached a tangential subject that interested him, he went with it, then eventually wandered back to the main topic. He wrote with enough profanity to give his story the proper veneer for a tough marine, and the showman in him created more than a little John Wayne adventurism, but he was wholly unconcerned with factual accuracy. Events were out of chronological order, had the wrong date, or had actually been experienced by other people; some stories were heavily embellished, others were simply fabricated.

Few people if any would have recognized the inaccuracies, and the manuscript was well received. Back in 1946, Boyington had met Max Miller, a reporter for the *San Diego Sun* and best-selling author of *I Cover the Waterfront,* who at the time was working on *Blackburn's Squadron,* a manuscript about a navy Corsair squadron in the Solomon Islands. Boyington credited Miller with helping him get the memoir started (evidently forgetting the role Frank Walton had played), and perhaps called on him for an endorsement to get the manuscript in front of an agent.

The first interested publisher wanted to make changes, "soft-pedaling the rough parts," as Boyington put it, so he took it to G. P. Putnam's Sons. There, he allegedly told the editors: "Just point out the misspelling and grammatical errors, and I'll fix them." Judging from the published version, they agreed to his stipulation. The book's sentence structure was awkward, platitudes and distracting observations were left intact, and surnames were regularly misspelled. On the other hand, marketing elements such as the title, *Baa Baa Black Sheep,* were well conceived. The concluding sentence, Boyington's now-famous ridicule of heroism, was equally inspired. Borrowing directly from F. Scott Fitzgerald, he wrote, "Just name a hero, and I'll prove he's a bum." Its impact was tremendous.

Baa Baa Black Sheep was released in mid-July 1958 at $4.50 per hardcover copy and became an overnight success. *Time, Life, Saturday Review, The Wall Street Journal,* and many major newspapers applauded Boyington's courage. Because of his apparent candor and humility, literary faults were forgiven, and the book flew off the shelves. Ed Sullivan invited the Boyingtons to attend the first show of the 1958 season, which they did on Sunday, September 14. Seated in the audience, they watched the usual fare of acts—puppets, pie-plate twirling, a comedy routine by Mickey Rooney— then Sullivan briefly welcomed visiting personalities. First he introduced Jerome Robbins and Stewart Granger, who rose from their seats to acknowledge the audience, then Sullivan talked a little longer about Boyington. He mentioned his book by name and praised Boyington as one of the Marine Corps's "greatest all-time heroes." Given such an influential boost, *Black Sheep* enjoyed sales of sixty-five thousand copies in six months; by the end of its first year there had been fourteen printings, with more than a hundred thousand copies sold.

Boyington hired Harry Sokolov of Famous Artists in Beverly Hills to handle the bidding over dramatic rights. Producer Fred Kohlmar won out for Columbia Pictures with an option that would pay Boyington $250,000. One of

Hollywood's biggest stars, Robert Mitchum, was cast in the leading role to play Boyington. *Black Sheep* reached number one on the *Los Angeles Times* nonfiction best-seller list, and by May 1959 was still entrenched at number three on the *New York Times* list. It was declared the top-selling autobiography of the publishing season.

For the first time in his life, Boyington was financially flush. The fee Columbia paid to secure the movie option was not disclosed, nor were the terms of his deal with Putnam, but conservatively, he made more than $30,000 by the end of the year.

When *Life* came to Burbank to shoot a big layout, the Boyingtons did a lot of smiling. Greg junior even grinned broadly during a brief reunion at the Air Force Academy, much to his father's relief. "I've got my son back," he declared. The feel-good story focused mainly on his recovery, and Frances talked openly about the challenges of that first year of sobriety. "But the second year was better," she said, "and this last has been best of all. Now his periods of exhilaration and depression are spaced further and further apart and we both think we're out from under. Heaven only knows about tomorrow, but today is wonderful!"

The "wonderful," the sobriety, even the marriage, were all too good to last. The collapse began when Boyington departed on a thirty-city tour. During a restaurant interview in Manhattan, he revealed that the book's success hadn't cured his resentments at all. Asked about his military awards, he snapped, "They only gave me the Medal of Honor when they thought I was dead. That medal is a whole story all by itself. I keep it out in the garage along with the other stuff we don't want in the house."

As time passed, his contempt for the medal grew even stronger, or at least his feelings were manifested as contempt. Perhaps he was burdened with guilt, knowing that some of his wartime claims and parts of his autobiography were less than truthful. As an editorial in *Time* described Medal of Honor winners: "The hero . . . aware of his own weakness, must always fight the fear that he does not deserve all of the accolades."

Boyington continued to go on book-signing trips through the spring of 1959, and as the money poured in from book sales, he spent it. Among the big-ticket items he acquired were a Lancia sports car and a twin-engine Cessna 310C airplane, the latter purchased for seventy-five thousand dollars, currently equivalent to a quarter of a million. Most of the airplane's cost was financed with a loan.

Spin-offs from the book were impressive. Executive producers Burt Ross and Frank Danzig approached Boyington about hosting a new television show called *Danger Zone*. He signed a contract to appear on the program, described as "a weekly documentary series exploring the sources of danger and man's reaction to it," with the first syndicated broadcast scheduled for early 1960. In his role as host he interviewed several personalities, including the captain of a tanker hit by kamikazes, a race-car driver who crashed at Le Mans, a Malibu lifeguard attacked by a shark, and R. T. Smith of the Flying Tigers. Three guests would appear per episode, their stories accompanied by "authentic film footage."

Boyington also received an undisclosed fee from Putnam when Dell Publishing acquired the paperback rights to *Black Sheep,* subsequently released at fifty cents per copy in 1959. The cover featured the same true-grit portrait of Boyington in his aviator's cloth helmet, but with a new blurb. He was now known as "the 'bad boy' hero of the Marine Corps."

While maintaining a frantic pace of appearances around the country, Boyington still worked for Coast Pro-Seal and consulted for the Columbia Pictures movie. Somehow, he also found enough time to begin writing another book. With such a schedule, he rarely came home. On those rare occasions when he was at home, said Frances, he threw tantrums.

In early 1959, while searching for aircraft to use in the feature film, Boyington visited Carson Shade's air service near Riverside. He intended to inspect some vintage bombers that were being converted for use as aerial firefighters, but what caught his eye was Shade's thirty-three-year-old wife, Dolores. With her smoldering green eyes and slender figure, she was another dark-haired beauty cast in the Helene-Olga-Lucy mold. Acquaintances remembered her as having Latin features, and she claimed to have been schooled in Mexico and Argentina. An alleged star of European films, she came to Hollywood for "guest television spots" in 1950, but her career went nowhere. For seven of the past nine years she had been with Shade, her second husband.

She might have seen in Boyington her ticket back to Hollywood. It didn't matter that he was older by thirteen years and was now a grandfather (Janet had given birth to a daughter the previous spring); his charisma was undiminished. He was a best-selling author, drove a flashy sports car, and worked on movie and television projects. Using her Hollywood name of "Dee Tatum," she was seen around town with him that summer.

They were together a couple of times when Boyington visited Janet, who had separated from Rocky Slater just six months after her daughter was born. Boyington tried to cheer his daughter up, and even brought his dog, Lord Alvin, along on one of his visits to her Willowcrest Avenue apartment. "The reason I remember that," said Paula Forbish, a downstairs neighbor, "is because it was a bassett hound and it peed on Jan's couch."

For the people in the apartment, if not for Alvin, the mishap was an omen of what lay ahead.

In early July 1959, after thirteen and a half years of marriage, Pappy and Frances were separated. A month later, Boyington had the unique experience of filing for divorce one day, then sitting in court again when his daughter filed for divorce just a few days later. Janet charged that Rocky Slater had threatened to harm her and take away their daughter, Candice, now seventeen months old. "He said the only way she was leaving was on a slab, feet first," recalled Forbish, who accompanied her friend to the hearing on

August 26. Dee Tatum and Boyington were also there for moral support.

When it came to his own divorce, there was no mention of his relationship with Dee, who was already undergoing a divorce from Carson Shade. Instead, Frances blamed the marriage's collapse on the fact that Boyington was away too much. Gossip columnists managed to drag some of the proceedings into the open, but there was far less frenzy than when Boyington was mixed up with Frances and Lucy after the war.

Working relatively quickly with their respective attorneys, the couple reached a property settlement that would haunt Boyington for years to come. In lieu of alimony, Frances got the house and all its furnishings, half of all rights and proceeds from *Black Sheep* (and its related contracts), and half of any monies or other considerations from *Danger Zone*. Boyington kept the Lancia and the airplane (with its $48,000 loan), his personal property and clothing, plus whatever money was currently deposited in his name. When the case was heard in Los Angeles County Superior Court on October 13, the findings and agreements were settled quickly. The most notable aspect of the case was that Boyington had a future celebrity as company in the courtroom. The bailiff, deputy sheriff R. J. Burrell, would later serve as Judge Wapner's stoic helper "Rusty" on *People's Court*.

Exactly two weeks after Boyington's divorce, he and Dee Tatum were married in Denver. Neither had obtained final decrees, so for legality they got quickie divorces in absentia in Montgomery, Alabama, which allowed them to get hitched in Colorado. They did not let the fact that it was their third marriage each prevent them from having a church wedding, and Dee even wore white. The Air Force Academy's chaplain performed the ceremony at a Methodist Church, with Greg junior as best man.

Almost from the beginning, their marriage was characterized by an anxious need to demonstrate its legality. In February 1960, when Boyington's divorce from Frances became final, he and Dee went to Las Vegas and underwent a second marriage, this time with a justice of the peace. Then they celebrated the occasion of Dee's final decree from Carson Shade in December by getting married yet again, with Rusty Burrell as best man at the L.A. County Courthouse.

They returned to Colorado for another wedding when Gregory junior got married on the day of his graduation from the Air Force Academy. PAPPY JR. MAKES IT went the headlines. The son shared more than a nickname with his father—his marriage produced a son and two daughters before it ended in divorce, and he also rose to the rank of colonel in his chosen branch of service. The biggest difference between them was that alcoholism did not take over Gregory junior's life, sparing him from that particular misery.

Despite the numerous wedding distractions, Boyington finished his novel in 1960. *Tonya* was purchased by Bobbs-Merrill, a subsidiary of a New York publishing house, but the little-known company was unable to give the book's October release much of a promotion. The publishers evidently hoped Boyington's name and the alluring dust jacket would be enough to entice buyers, with adult males being the obvious targets.

Tonya was the sixties version of a sex novel. The cover featured a shapely, green-eyed brunette in a red cocktail dress and high heels, glancing back over her shoulder to make suggestive eye contact with the Potential Buyer. In case her come-hither gaze didn't get him to buy the book, the first page began with a postcoital setting on a hot Burma night. Ex-marine Rusty Bush lay abed with the main character, Tonya Brownfield, the nymphomaniac wife of the ineffectual, watery-eyed executive officer of the Flying Sharks, a volunteer group of P-40 pilots stationed at Paygoo, Burma, just before Pearl Harbor.

Tonya was little more than the AVG segment of *Baa Baa Black Sheep* with a minimum of fictional veneer. Not only was the main character a barely disguised Olga Greenlaw, but the names of other principal characters were concealed even less. Jack Newkirk was Kirk Jackson; Dick Rossi was Ross Dickey; Curtis Smith was Courtland Lee Smith; Robert Sandell was Robert Sanderson. Of course Boyington included himself—as Rusty Bush, a debt-ridden former marine—while Claire Chennault's character was represented by Francis Stud (or simply Colonel Stud), who in turn was manipulated by the cunning and inherently evil Empress, clearly Madame Chiang Kai-shek.

The only fictional twist to the story was laughable—Tonya was cast as a spy. Just like his real counterpart, the Kirk Jackson character dies in a ball of flames during a strafing mission, whereupon a Japanese major discovers a photograph in the dead pilot's wallet, miraculously unburned. The officer recognizes the beautiful woman in the photograph as one who sold him information in Saigon—Tonya!

There were no rave reviews this time. The *Los Angeles Times* called it a "peep show of the Burmese battlefront," and a "wacky and very believable adult version of *Terry and the Pirates*." Boyington himself said, as he handed a copy to a reviewer: "It's lousy writing, but you'll find it interesting reading." Based on his own endorsement, he was probably not surprised that the book fizzled instead of sizzled. It was reprinted a few times, and probably sold even better after its risqué dust jacket was replaced with a plain red one, warning, "Not Recommended for Children."

The Flying Tigers were especially unreceptive. *Baa Baa Black Sheep* had disparaged Claire Chennault enough, they thought; *Tonya* merely picked up where the autobiography left off. Since Chennault's death of lung cancer in July 1958, Boyington had vilified him at book signings, speaking engagements, or anywhere he had an audience. Later, when the Flying Tigers Association was formed among surviving AVG pilots and ground crew, they refused to let him join. Their bylaws required members to have an honorable discharge, they said. Boyington simply used their argument as his license to speak out, and for the rest of his life, he was ostracized from the group. More than a few Flying Tigers protested his claim of six victories, and some even discussed his record with the Marine Corps's aviation historian, Robert Sherrod, but nothing came of it.

Boyington's multiple weddings to Dee Tatum and the publication of *Tonya* in 1960 were among the few highlights he enjoyed during the next decade. Prior to that time, he could always find something positive to remember from each decade of his life: the flight with Clyde Pangborn in the teens, the fun of growing up in St. Maries in the early twenties, piloting fighter planes in the thirties, his military triumphs of the forties, his best-seller in the fifties. But the sixties were unkind.

The movie version of *Baa Baa Black Sheep* faltered first, killed off before it went into production, and Boyington's payoff from the option never materialized. Then *Danger Zone* languished after the first several episodes, fading into the oblivion where so many television properties disappear. In a major change of direction, Boyington tried politics next. Evidently, he had grown accustomed to talking to the public during the *Black Sheep* book tour, and decided he could make the leap. He was described by one newspaper writer as having "strong convictions about world affairs, U.S. foreign policy, and the nation's financial structure," but he would soon learn that beliefs had little to do with getting into the game.

Registering as a Democratic candidate for the new Thirtieth Congressional District surrounding Los Angeles, Boyington encountered a small snag. The rules prohibited use of quotation marks or parentheses around a nickname—only legalized names were allowed—so he could not enter the 1962 election as a candidate named "Pappy" Boyington. The solution was simple: he changed his name. The court approved his petition to make Pappy his legal middle name in December 1961, after which he all but dropped the use of his given name. For the rest of his life, he referred to himself as Pappy far more often than Greg.

The nickname probably gave him better public recognition, but it did not help win elections. Former Black Sheep

Fred Losch had just started his own building supply company in Altadena, near Los Angeles, when he encountered Boyington on the campaign trail while driving through a remote part of the valley.

Under a couple of palm trees was an old car. On top of it was a big sign that said VOTE FOR PAPPY BOYINGTON, and he was sitting behind a card table. He probably didn't have five hundred dollars for his whole campaign. I mean, literally.

You say, "Why the hell was he running?" It wasn't for money, because, cripes, back then they were only making five grand a year. In talking to him, he said, "Somebody's got to do something." He was a patriot. He loved his country. He came in third.

Although the salary was low, Boyington might have been in the race because of the money after all. He was no longer employed by Coast Pro-Seal and relied entirely on his government pension. A successful campaign required far greater funds than he could raise, and even before the election took place he and Dee scaled back, moving into an apartment on Colfax Avenue in North Hollywood.

Just three years earlier he had seemed wealthy, with the promise of more riches from subsidiary rights and Hollywood options. One by one the deals had fallen through, his money evaporated, and his campaign for state representative ended dismally. He started to drink again, and before long, back in debt, he went over the edge for his second plunge into the abyss.

Less than a year after the failed campaign, the Boyingtons attempted to bolster their self-image by going on an ego trip to Spokane, where Keith Boyington was a budding architect. They also made several side trips to St. Maries and other towns, presenting themselves wherever they went as a successful Hollywood couple: the best-selling author with television interests, and his beautiful actress wife. They were thus portrayed by reporters from Spokane and Coeur d'Alene, who spread the story that the couple was considering a move to the area. They were looking at property, they said, where they could build a ranch for their prize quarter horses.

A news article in the Spokane paper stated that Dee was "the most photographed model in America," and was featured on the cover of more than five hundred magazines in a single month. The *Spokesman-Review* printed the news that Dee had starred in "a great many films," spoke six languages, had personally drawn the blueprints for converting a B-24 into a firefighting plane, and owned several horses—one of them a champion with hundreds of ribbons. Boyington was equally fantastic, with a prize quarter horse of his own, and he was currently putting together a new television series "on antisubversive activity cases based on material from the National Police Association."

The Boyingtons probably stopped to see Bill Hallenbeck in Oregon at some point during their trip. As one of his daughters later recalled, "[Greg] used to drop in every so often, and it was fun when he did. There was a lot of drinking and stories. I don't know whether you could say he was manic-depressive or bipolar, but he was always 'up.' There were other times when he would go away and binge-drink. My dad did the same thing."

During one of these visits, Boyington discovered the awful truth about Ellsworth's pedophilia, somehow learning that the sickness went back years and involved two of his own children. The combination of that agonizing news and the reality of his currently unhappy life caused him to turn his back on much of his family. He became bitter and cruel, creating even more alienation within his family.

Gregory junior and Janet suffered the most, according to letters Dee wrote in 1964, the year Boyington hit bottom, virtually ending what little relationship he still had with his children. He went so far as to claim that Gregory junior was not his son. But even that denial paled in comparison to his devastating relationship with Janet.

She had rejected much of her own past, and never talked

about Gloria. Her friend Paula Forbish was stunned to learn in 1999 that Janet had a younger sister. "The only one she ever talked about was her brother," Forbish said. "Over all the years I knew her, she never mentioned a sister, and even after we left the apartment, we kept in contact."

Attractive and bold, Janet turned her back on traditional conventions and lived with a man in the San Bernardino Mountains. She had given birth to two more children by 1964, but also struggled with drug and alcohol abuse, conduct Boyington could not tolerate. Self-righteously, he sought intervention from the courts. When Janet attempted to show she was married, he obtained a copy of her license and declared that it had been falsified, thus helping Rocky Slater, now in his mid-thirties and living with his mother, to gain custody of Candice. But Slater was no gem as a parent, so Boyington and Dee adopted Candice prior to 1965, listing her as a dependent grandchild for several years thereafter.

After her own father went against her in court, Janet withdrew from him completely. "She always told me she wouldn't have a damn thing to do with him ever again," said Forbish, recalling that Janet stuck to her word when Boyington was hospitalized two years later, gravely ill. He eventually recovered, but the relationship never did. Several years later, Forbish and her husband visited Janet in Oxnard, California. She was still living with the same man, now with four children, and made a disturbing comment to Forbish: "She said there was a balcony upstairs. That's what she was going to fly off of. I said, 'Jan!' And she said, 'Yeah, I've followed in my dad's footsteps.'"

Janet kept her word on that, too, dying around 1971 of an apparent suicide involving alcohol or drugs. Efforts to learn more details through state offices and social security records yielded nothing. Apparently no death certificate was issued under the surnames Boyington, Slater, or Welsh—the name of the man she had allegedly married. Similarly, the youngest child from that relationship, a daughter, tried for years without success to discover what had happened. Still, the vagueness of the details is consistent with the family history of erroneous and misleading documents. Even if the details were known, they would provide only dry statistics as to how, when, and where Janet died—not why.

The most plausible conclusion was voiced by her cousin Ramona, who succinctly described Janet's sad life: "I know she was a tormented soul."

Boyington's third marriage lasted a surprisingly long time, considering that he had plunged back into alcoholism, suffered bitter disappointments, and was unemployed for the first three years after marrying Dee. He finally started a new job in the fall of 1963, but was fired within three months for drinking.

At the beginning of 1964, he was hired by an avionics firm located in Glendale. Electronic Specialty Company provided a good salary, an expense account, a Chevrolet Impala, and sent him on regular business trips to Dallas and other major cities. Dee was suspicious. After receiving phone calls from one of the "girls" Boyington had met in Texas, she hired a man to "observe his activities." One day, opening Boyington's mail, she discovered his wedding ring tucked inside a letter addressed to him from Dallas.

Logic suggests she made the discovery on March 20, the day she "clawed, belted, and committed mayhem" on her husband. Boyington fought back and, in a later statement to the press, admitted that he "pushed her and she fell." Dee complained of a back injury, described as an "agonizing" compression fracture of her spine, complicated by a chipped bone. A news article pictured her lying in a hospital bed in her living room more than a week after the altercation. Boyington had not returned, not even for his clothing.

He went to court to get their marriage annulled, claiming Dee had obtained an invalid divorce from her first husband, Richard Tatum (who supposedly divorced her in Mexico City). In an attachment, he claimed that she had concealed his Medal of Honor and Navy Cross and refused to return them. Lastly, he charged that the man Dee had hired to shadow him was not a licensed investigator.

In the midst of all the negative publicity, he left a beachside bar and turned into the wrong lane of a freeway, whereupon he collided with an oncoming car, injuring two passengers. The domestic situation became even more embarrassing when Dee, from her sickbed, phoned a Western Union telegram to President Johnson at the White House, appealing directly to him for a duplicate Medal of Honor. The White House referred the matter to the Marine Corps, which in turn responded tersely that only the recipient could request a duplicate award.

Suddenly, Boyington dropped the divorce suit. Dee had found his missing Navy Cross at the apartment, she claimed, and the Medal of Honor eventually showed up as well. Perhaps he was convinced by her plea to the White House that the medal's disappearance was not her fault, and the couple managed to coexist for several more years.

Electronic Specialty was likewise forgiving. After the circus atmosphere quieted in late 1965, Boyington was sent on a business trip to South Vietnam. At Da Nang, where a marine photoreconnaissance squadron used some of the company's avionics equipment, he learned that his old squadron was in-country at a small base just fifty miles away. The marines obligingly provided air transportation for a short visit.

Built by Seabees next to a beach—in this case on the South China Sea—Chu Lai was remarkably similar to the jungle strips Boyington had flown from more than twenty years earlier. It had even been surfaced with the familiar Marston matting, and just like the old days, the marines lived in World War II–vintage tents and ate basically the same kind of chow.

There were equally amazing differences. The squadron had been redesignated as an attack squadron, VMA-214, and flew the Douglas A-4C Skyhawk. The diminutive jets, carrying a huge external ordnance load, blasted from the three-thousand-foot runway using small ejectable rockets that literally threw them into the air on a plume of smoke and flame.

Captain John Rooke, one of the Black Sheep pilots, recalled that Boyington's plans changed after he arrived at Chu Lai. "He was just supposed to spend the afternoon and then go back, but as it turned out, we started a little party. We had an outdoor barbecue with whatever rations we had, and it turned into an all-night affair." That, too, was like turning back the clock, as Boyington sat around and drank beer with marine pilots in a tropical wartime setting, doing his best to answer questions from the new generation of jet jockeys. Rooke thought he seemed modest about his accomplishments, but as the evening wore on Boyington became remorseful, talking about family troubles. The hero image quickly tarnished.

The trip to Vietnam turned out to be the last good thing to happen to Boyington for a long time. In a photograph taken at Chu Lai, he appeared in good health, with a full, robust torso, but appearances were deceptive. He suffered from emphysema, causing him to work so hard to draw each breath that he used more muscles than just his diaphragm. The muscles in the upper torso and neck, even those between ribs, became enlarged due to his efforts to pull more air into the lungs. Thus, he looked strong, but the inside of his chest was another matter. Thirty years of smoking had caused irreparable damage to his lungs, and he was also diagnosed with chronic bronchitis.

After he had been constantly sick for two years, a chest X ray in 1967 showed a suspicious spot. He went to see an old friend in Montebello, East Los Angeles, where Jim Reames had opened a successful general surgical practice after retiring from the navy. Boyington elected surgery in nearby Beverly Community Hospital, undergoing two major operations in June. Reames assisted in one, a resection of the diseased lung; newspapers reported that Boyington had "abdominal surgery" during the same period.

Once again his name was widely published. This time, the

newspapers reported that Boyington was not only gravely ill, but destitute, owing eight thousand dollars in hospital bills. Public response was immediate. From all over the country came gifts of money. The White House received letters from concerned citizens wanting to know how this could have happened. The queries were forwarded to the Pentagon, where an officer responded to each one, answering that Boyington was eligible for hospitalization through the Veterans Administration but had elected a civilian medical facility.

Boyington never did quit smoking, despite the fact that the pathology on his lung was reportedly cancerous. Even so, he responded well to surgery, with no further cancer scares for many years. After his lengthy illness he was no longer employed, so he relied once again on his disability pension, augmented by Social Security and the Medal of Honor stipend, which had increased to one hundred dollars a month. His books had gone out of print and the royalties were all but dried up, leaving him with a total income of about twelve thousand dollars per year. Instead of beating the pavement to look for a conventional job, he did the unexpected. He began to paint.

Perhaps the bout of illness helped Boyington rediscover the artistic talents of his youth, for he had not drawn seriously for more than thirty years and had not painted since his lessons in Tacoma. Concurrently, Doc Reames might have urged him to leave the smog of Los Angeles. Soon after Boyington was released from the hospital, he moved his wife and adopted granddaughter to Rancho Mirage, near Palm Springs. Later still they moved to the neighboring city of Cathedral City.

The location provided plenty of inspiration for painting, as he did not have to travel far in any direction to reach the remoteness of the California desert. He started before dawn, just like the long-ago missions in the Solomon Islands, armed now with only a sketch pad and a Thermos of tea. After reaching his chosen vantage point, he waited for the sun to come up, then absorbed nature's show. Occasionally he sketched basic outlines, but did no painting at the site.

Instead, his mind was the canvas. "Do you know," he once asked a reporter, "that the sun's hues in the desert change thirty times in twenty minutes?"

Before the sun had climbed high, Boyington packed his tools and returned home to paint. Working with oils, his style impressionistic, he finished about six landscapes a year. One critic was said to have characterized him as "a very competent craftsman," and Boyington seemed genuinely pleased with his own achievements. That was indeed a rarity in his life.

He may have found solace in painting, but by the end of the decade his relationship with Dee was in a fatal tailspin. There would be no saving the marriage this time, particularly after he sued for divorce and moved out. Encountering a hostile judge in Palm Springs, he decided to put some distance between himself and the desert community, and called Bruce Porter, the marine pilot who had once helped him at Espíritu Santo. After the war he had enjoyed a visit at Porter's home in Los Angeles and kept in touch, and now he reached out again to his friend, who currently lived in Fresno.

Porter was caught slightly off guard when Boyington asked straightaway about the local courts. "I'm getting a divorce, and these guys are crucifying me down here in Palm Springs," he explained. "They hate my guts. I want to get out of this area and come up there."

Porter was willing to help. With hardly a word to anyone, Boyington moved up to Fresno in 1970, leaving Dee and Candice on their own while the rest of his relatives scratched their heads, wondering where he had gone. He rented an apartment, and was gradually introduced to Porter's circle of friends in the Sunnyside neighborhood. Among them were Carl Christiansen, owner of a local supermarket and staunch member of AA, Jack Gibbons, an ex-marine whose family owned land in the foothills of the Sierras, and Josephine Moseman, a divorced friend of Porter's wife.

When Gibbons invited Boyington to move onto a parcel

of land near Auberry, he accepted, buying a small travel trailer that he parked in a picturesque meadow at Alder Springs. At one point Boyington announced that he was going to build a house on the parcel, telling everyone that he was friends with Governor Ronald Reagan and could get a favorable GI loan, but he was merely boasting again. He lived in the trailer for at least two years while going through a protracted divorce from Dee—the closest he came to completely dropping out. During this period of isolation his estranged daughter died, and he remained inaccessible until the spring of 1972. By then, his health had declined again, and he was in far worse shape than anyone realized. Ironically, his illness allowed his family, aided by a local reporter, to track him to the Fresno VA hospital.

The Associated Press picked up the latest story of his condition, and soon a tale of pathos circulated from coast to coast. "The type of life I lived, the old machine was bound to wear out," he was quoted as saying. "I've been quite ill the last five years. I just want to pass on without a fuss. I've had a pretty full life and nothing lasts forever. Any way the wind blows, I won't kick."

Boyington was approaching sixty. Considering the alcohol he had consumed and the damage cigarette smoke had caused to his lungs, the wind should have blown him dead with little effort. Yet the old bulldog refused to roll over. In time, he not only got back on his feet, but regained a surprising level of spryness.

Much of the credit for his recovery goes to Jo Moseman, then forty-five, divorced from a wealthy highway contractor. "She had a beautiful home—probably the biggest home in Sunnyside," remembered Christiansen. "She was very social and played golf. Fact is, I didn't much care to play with her, because she beat me all the time." Jo was also a recovering alcoholic and attended AA religiously, thus helping Boyington get back into a regular schedule of meetings as well as take up golf. They began to see a lot of each other. "She was a damn good little golfer," echoed Porter. "He had played before, but she got him playing regularly and it was a good thing to keep him occupied."

Jo possessed boundless willpower when it came to abstinence. During Boyington's weak moments, she refused to have anything to do with him. Through sheer stubbornness, she helped him regain control over his drinking. Gradually settling down because of her perseverance, he enjoyed a quiet period of painting and golf while he put his life back together. He slipped from time to time, but he wasn't an oaf. "A lot of people underestimated him," Porter said. "Boyington was brilliant, talked on any subject, and spoke eloquently. In other words, he was a charmer."

Jo Moseman thought so and, on August 4, 1975, married Boyington in a quiet ceremony at her home overlooking the country club's fourteenth fairway. There was still one more matter Boyington had to settle with Dee, however. After their divorce in 1973, she had gone to Mexico and married a Hungarian immigrant, then failed to notify the California courts. She continued to collect support payments from Boyington until he won a termination in 1976.

His fourth marriage brought an end to the most difficult period of his life. He had wallowed for fifteen years in alcoholism, debt, and family turmoil—a combination that would have swamped most men for good—but in Jo he found an unselfish partner with the stubborn strength to help him discover a meaningful life. He probably would have been content to live out the rest of his days on the golf course and in front of an easel, perhaps flying a private plane once in a while, but the amazing turnaround in his life was not quite complete.

Thanks to a dog-eared copy of his memoirs, he was about to become famous again, even more so than ever.

21

The Entertainer

Two hundred miles from Fresno, a forty-five-year-old executive read his "pretty beat-up" hardcover copy of *Baa Baa Black Sheep* for the second time. He had served aboard the carrier *Coral Sea* in his younger days and remained interested in aviation, but in his current business he didn't read strictly for pleasure.

Frank Price, former sailor, was the head of Universal Television. He read widely, always looking for new material, but the timing wasn't right when he first picked up *Black Sheep*. When he read it again in 1975, everything clicked. "Pappy Boyington and the whole thing with the Black Sheep, that really hit home for me," he later said. "I liked it a lot, and I'd say at that particular time, the military certainly wasn't big on television. So I thought it could be fresh and different, and it was dealing with the last good war. I thought it was a terrific idea for a series, something that Steve Cannell would be very good at, so I bought it first. You don't want to start selling people on something you don't own, so we acquired the rights to it."

Price's next step was to create a two-hour movie to shop to the networks. Time was short before the next pilot season began in the summer of 1976, so he gave Stephen Cannell, a writer-producer on a hot streak with *Baretta* and *The Rockford Files,* just two weeks to write the script.

Cannell read *Black Sheep,* then tried to call Boyington.

He left several messages with Jo, but they weren't returned. Boyington sometimes headed up to Auberry for a binge, and might have been experiencing one of his slips. "There was a running joke: 'Boyington's up with the Indians, drunk in some bar,'" recalled Bruce Porter. "They loved the guy; they were always throwing their arms about him and drinking with him. He was always having some escapade up there."

Lacking the time "to sit around and wait for Greg," Cannell wrote the script on his own. Freely admitting he took "some pretty good liberties," he used real names for some characters, including Pappy Boyington, Claire Chennault, and Admiral Nimitz, and also kept Boyington's nickname for the aptly named antagonist, Colonel Lard. He was nearly finished with the script when Boyington finally phoned. "Oh, that's great! I love that," he said when Cannell presented the outline.

Flying Misfits was likewise approved by the studio. As word spread that a new aviation-themed project was on the fast track at Universal, agents began to call. David Shapira was one of the first. "I've got Pappy Boyington," he told Cannell. "You've got to put this guy on—he's the perfect Pappy Boyington."

When Shapira identified his client as forty-year-old Robert Conrad, however, Cannell had reservations. "He had a reputation of being a real tough guy. I thought: *He's just about the perfect guy to do it, but, man, I don't need to get a new dentist.* But David wouldn't quit. He kept saying, 'You've gotta meet this guy.' I had this meeting, and thought: *God, everything about this man is Pappy.* So I hired him."

Meeting with Boyington and Conrad in early 1976, Cannell was struck by the natural similarities between the two men: size, build, even mannerisms, were remarkably alike. Afterward, the actor and the old marine walked to Universal's hotel to get better acquainted. "We had a few cocktails," remembered Conrad. "I had read his book; we chatted about the book and then just generally had a bull session."

Jo joined her husband in the hotel dining room, but because she did not watch television she was unfamiliar with Conrad. "He was drinking wine and smoking cigarettes, and I asked him why he wasn't eating," she later told a reporter. "He told me he was celebrating because he had gotten the part of playing Pappy Boyington." So I told him, "You're assuming the role fast."

Cannell had a script and a star; now he needed a squadron. Rather than casting twenty-eight pilots to portray the Black Sheep, he hired several youthful-looking regulars, including John Larroquette and James Whitmore Jr., then filled in the rest with extras.

Universal acquired the most historically accurate aircraft possible by renting six vintage Corsairs and a P-40, among other types. They were expensive. Each fighter cost the studio $400 for the first two hours of each workday, then $350 per hour thereafter. Pilots received $350 per day just for walking on the set. The reward for the studio was viewer support. Too often, war movies settled for readily available T-6 "Texan" trainers to represent planes of different nationalities, merely by changing the markings. Universal's decision to use classic Corsairs was a real coup, although a few purists still complained about differences between the rented Corsairs and the ones Boyington had flown during the war.*

To simplify the aerial choreography while filming from his modified B-25 camera plane, second unit director James Gavin gave each pilot a call sign. Former navy pilot John Schafhausen, owner of an F4U-7 originally built for the French navy, became "Black Sheep One" by virtue of his Corsair experience. He and the other pilots, reduced to five after the first day because one old Corsair developed engine trouble, flew from Van Nuys Airport over Santa Barbara Sound, where they entered mock battles with Japanese "Zeros"—five of the venerable T-6s painted light gray, with Rising Sun insignia.

* All of the Corsairs were later models than Boyington had flown, and were painted in the late-war dark sea-blue instead of the variegated blue-to-white scheme of 1943 and early 1944.

By mid-June, Conrad and the cast had completed filming at several locations around southern California. Hired as a consultant, Boyington watched his story come to life in the studio and at Universal's back lot, followed by a three-day stint at Camp Pendleton, another day and night at a beach (for a luau scene with a bevy of nurses), and five days at Indian Dunes near Valencia, where a remote airstrip served as a South Pacific setting. After the studio's crew re-created a tropical island base along the perimeter of the twenty-eight-hundred-foot strip, the second unit brought in the Corsairs for ground segments of the movie.

Camera dollies, support crews, and lighting equipment did not distract Boyington from watching the familiar gull-winged fighters take center stage. "When those Corsairs taxied one by one out onto the field and they started giving it the old gun to take off," he later said, ". . . a little shiver went up my spine."

Despite the fact that illnesses had prematurely aged his face and robbed him of his once-beefy build, he was still an icon to the cast. "He was a rough, tough guy," remembered Conrad, a private pilot. Boyington provided input on his character and also claimed he had a hand in authenticating the dialogue and various wardrobes used by the cast, but the hairstyles, "off-duty" clothing, and tight flight suits worn by the Black Sheep clearly reflected the fashion influences of the 1970s, not the '40s. He was also unconcerned that the script had been written for entertainment. "His feeling about the show was that if the producers wanted to embellish it, if they wanted to 'Hollywood' it, that was fine with him," acknowledged Conrad. "Poignant moments between the commanding officer and his pilots were important to him, how his character related and played that part. Esprit de corps was very important to him. Anything that was fictionalized didn't bother Boyington."

Hoping the Department of Defense would endorse the movie, Universal sent a copy of the script to the Marine Corps Historical Center in Washington, D.C., but the center was unable to "correlate the script with any known set of facts." Nevertheless, Universal purchased almost twenty-one thousand feet of archival film from the organization. Color gun-camera footage of actual aerial combat was then spliced with Jim Gavin's aerial sequences to portray dog-fights as realistically as possible.

By a narrow margin, "Flying Misfits" was completed in time for the pilot season, ahead of which NBC ordered a series of twenty-two episodes, to be called *Baa Baa Black Sheep*. Boyington discovered at this juncture that he had signed away the rights to the name in his original contract with Universal. In what turned out to have been an extremely "soft" deal by industry standards, he signed a contract to serve as a technical advisor for a reported five thousand dollars, whereas extras were paid "scale" of up to a hundred dollars a day, often to just to stand around. His role was off camera, but he could have negotiated for ten times as much. He blamed his agent, saying that he mistook the contract for an interoffice memorandum. "I was lied to and cheated by Hollywood," he complained, but seemed to implicate himself by adding a hollow defense: "I wasn't just a naïve fool."

Meanwhile, the network's order created a dilemma for Stephen Cannell, who was "absolutely stymied" about how to write the show after NBC bought it. "How the hell are we going to do twenty-two episodes of guys just going up and flying against nameless Japanese pilots?" he wondered aloud. "I don't want to do a racist show and reignite hatred of the Japanese. I'm doing a series in the South Pacific, and everybody's going to be watching this on a Sony TV. This is an impossible show to do."

He brought in writer-producer Philip De Guere, who helped him style the show much like the book. The recurring theme would be Pappy's war against the Marine Corps, particularly Colonel Lard. They also personified the enemy. "Instead of treating the Japanese as the bandy-legged yellow devils that the propaganda films of World War II did," said Cannell, "we would treat our Japanese opponent as a noble enemy—almost like a knight in the sky. As many episodes as we did like that, I never got anything but favorable mail from Japanese Americans."

Filming of the hourly series began almost immediately on a schedule of an episode every six days. Because of the long hours and the distance to Indian Dunes from Hollywood, Conrad stayed in his thirty-five-foot Vogue motor home several nights a week. He let Boyington use it during the day. "He hung out there," recalled the actor, "and had a few cocktails." One day, according to Conrad, Boyington's access to alcohol resulted in a verbal exchange while they walked together on the runway.

> Greg was in a challenging mood, hungover. He looked at me and said, "You know, Conrad, I would have loved to have had you in my squadron."
>
> I answered, "Colonel, I would love to have flown with you."
>
> "Not to fly with me—so I could kick your ass. You're an arrogant little bastard."
>
> I stopped and looked at him and said, "Sir, you mean *try* and kick my ass."
>
> He said, "You want to go now?"
>
> "No, Colonel. I don't want to go now. You win." And I started to walk.
>
> He called after me, "Hey, Conrad, it would've been fun a few years ago, wouldn't it?"
>
> "No, Greg, I love you. I don't think so."
>
> That's the word-for-word encounter; that's the Greg Boyington that I thought was hilarious.

NBC's announcement of the movie and the forthcoming series led to another sort of trouble for Boyington. In July, during an interview with a staff writer from the *Los Angeles Herald Examiner,* he substituted the Hollywood version of events for his real exploits during World War II. He had indeed stolen a plane from the Flying Tigers, he said, and ransomed it to Chennault for three thousand dollars; his Black Sheep were all awaiting court-martials when he found them, but after they performed particularly well one day, he threw the disciplinary files away. "That took care of that," he said. "I saved the government untold money with that move." In an *Air Classics* magazine interview, he sounded equally disdainful: "I had to go and pick out these guys who were sittin' in the pilot's pools and waiting court-martials, getting ready to be shipped back home, people who had been kicked out of squadrons."

His words came back to haunt him. More than a year earlier, Frank Walton had begun to organize a Black Sheep reunion—the first since the war—inviting all the former members to meet in Hawaii, where he and Bruce Matheson had retired with their wives. In March 1976, responding that he was uncertain of his schedule, Boyington described the new movie project to Walton. It was "loaded with humor," he wrote, "somewhat similar to *M*A*S*H*."

Thus alerted, Walton saw the *Herald Examiner* piece and clipped it out, having underlined the exaggerated and derogatory comments about the pilots. He found Boyington's dismissive remarks unconscionable. More than a few of those pilots had died in battle. He, not Boyington, had been their Boswell, had looked after them, had done the things Boyington never cared to do as their commander.

Later, when Boyington indicated that he and Jo could attend the reunion, he made sure to let Walton know that Universal would be finished with the filming by then, and that the two-hour movie would air on Tuesday, September 21. Walton watched it—he couldn't help but watch it—and came away disgusted with the repetitive brawling and the persistent theme that the Black Sheep were all disciplinary cases. More than a little resentment must also have dwelled beneath his frustration. Boyington's book, begun with Walton's help, had done well without him; now this.

Most of the other Black Sheep had less reactive impressions. For them, it was a thrill to have been one of the pilots portrayed, to be part of the first American aviation unit singled out for its own network television show. The majority of them watched each new episode, perhaps ignoring the fistfights and the nurses, but enjoying the aerial action with the vintage Corsairs.

However, all of them objected—some vehemently—to the show's introduction. Every episode began with a soundtrack of a male chorus singing "We are poor little lambs" from the squadron song, while the screen displayed what purported to be a history lesson: "In World War II, Marine Corps Major Greg 'Pappy' Boyington commanded a squadron of fighter pilots. They were a collection of misfits and screwballs who became the terrors of the South Pacific. They were known as the Black Sheep." Next came a segment resembling old newsreel, setting up the plot as though it had been historically documented.

Walton put together a booklet about the squadron, writing short biographies of the original members (including those lost in combat) and duplicating several photographs. Copies of "The Black Sheep Story" were printed for each of the surviving members, sixteen of whom arrived in November to join Walton and Matheson, a good representation considering that most of the men were still actively employed. One dynamic was vastly different from thirty-three years earlier: most of the Black Sheep were accompanied by their spouses for the weeklong tour of the islands. They were guests at several venues including a standing-room-only Kodak hula show, where some of the Black Sheep were called out as "students" for lessons. Boyington, tending to dress like a carnival barker, was far from the tallest in the hula line but overwhelmed everyone with his plaid bell-bottoms.

The Black Sheep and their wives roundly declared the reunion a success, but the days had not passed without friction. Many had voiced their objections to the television series. "We asked Boyington, 'Why the hell did you do this? Why did you put that crap in that TV show?'" Walton recalled. "He said, 'Well, I needed the money.'"

Walton became more determined than ever to correct the character damage caused by the show, as publicly as possible. He got several newspapers to report that the pilots weren't behind the series, then succeeded in selling a three-page article to *TV Guide*. The television series was "as phony as a three-dollar bill," he charged, explaining why the real Black Sheep weren't what Hollywood portrayed them to be.

Cannell and Boyington submitted separate rebuttals, printed in a subsequent issue. "Walton expects you to buy his writing as 100 percent fact," wrote Boyington. "Another important item is that he is not a pilot and hasn't the slightest knowledge of how a combat pilot thinks."

Riding the momentum of his first article's success, Walton forwarded "Pappy Boyington, Tragic Hero" to *Reader's Digest*. It was rejected, but instead of giving up he vowed to interview every one of the surviving Black Sheep and write an entire book about their collective experiences. Ten years passed, but he eventually accomplished his goal.

At the end of the first season, NBC announced that *Black Sheep* would not be renewed. If it seemed to Boyington that Walton had prevailed, the *TV Guide* article actually had little to do with the decision. The programming chief who originally bought the series had been fired just before it aired, and his replacement put *Black Sheep* into the time slot opposite ABC's *Happy Days* and *Laverne & Shirley*—the top two shows of 1976.

Conrad campaigned to renew the show, arguing that it had received higher ratings in some regions than the executives realized, particularly in the South; Universal also received piles of fan mail. NBC agreed to shoot five more episodes as a standby. After several of the network's new shows failed, the series got a second start in December 1977 as *Black Sheep Squadron*.

Other changes were afoot. Seeing what three lovely sleuths had done for ratings in *Charlie's Angels,* Frank Price urged that more female presence be added to *Black Sheep*. Hence, "Pappy's Lambs" were introduced as four nubile nurses. To the real Black Sheep, the show had become a travesty, but the ratings indeed climbed to a survival level.

Between shooting seasons, Boyington went with Conrad

on several publicity junkets, including parades and golf tournaments. They sang the "Marine Corps Hymn" together on *The Mike Douglas Show* and appeared in the 1978 Bing Crosby pro-am golf tournament at Pebble Beach. Boyington was reacquainted with Hap Halloran, whom he had last seen at a pro wrestling match in Indiana. Now a top executive for a major freight line, Halloran had managed a company where Conrad worked prior to becoming an actor. The three men established a mutual friendship that Boyington considered among the most genuine of his senior years.

He and Conrad connected especially well, to the point that Boyington didn't have to use words to communicate. They were sitting in the back of a jeep during a parade, recalled Conrad, when the procession bogged down in a Baltimore street.

> The colonel gave me a gesture—three fingers held sideways—which led me to believe he wanted a drink. I said, "Hey, Greg, what can I do here? We're in the middle of a damn parade, for God's sake!" He pointed over to a tavern. I thought, *Well, whatever,* and hopped off the jeep. I walked in there, and a bunch of people were watching the parade from the bar, sitting on barstools. I said, "Can I get three shots of bourbon?" The bartender said, "You can't take that out there—it's a parade!" I said, "Hell, I know what it is. This is for Greg Boyington."
>
> "Pappy?!"
>
> "Yeah!"
>
> "We'll put it in a cup."
>
> So he poured bourbon into this waxed cup that advertised Coca-Cola, and I took it out and handed it to the colonel. He was waving with his left hand and drinking with his right.

The two of them often cosigned autographs—Boyington as "Black Sheep One," Conrad as "Black Sheep Two"—and appeared together on the series when Boyington played a visiting general at the end of the second season. "He loved putting that suit on and playing a general in the series," said Conrad. "He loved that. Boy, I'll tell you, you couldn't have gotten enough photo-ops."

After thirty-seven episodes, *Black Sheep* ended its prime-time run in the spring of 1978. Considering Cannell's struggle to come up with the first scripts, it was remarkable that so many others had followed. Conrad earned respect for his tenacity while fighting to save the show, but forces beyond his control were responsible for the demise of the series. The biggest culprit was violence during the so-called "family hour." Viewers had complained after discovering that real Japanese pilots were inside those burning planes in the archival footage.

For Boyington, the end of the show was not the disaster it might have been. Thanks to the power of television, his name was a household word. As Conrad put it, "Greg was back." This time, he was back to stay.

His final career began even before the show ended. Having reacquired the publishing rights to *Baa Baa Black Sheep,* he and Jo arranged to have a new hardcover edition printed under the name Wilson Press, using Jo's maiden name, and began to travel the air-show circuit together. The popularity of the television series had boosted interest in vintage warplanes, drawing ever-larger crowds to fly-ins and static displays nationwide. Taking a personal interest in flying again, Boyington began building his own kit plane, an RV-3 single-seat sport flyer, and joined the Experimental Aircraft Association. Soon he became a fixture at the annual EAA convention in Oshkosh, Wisconsin, where he often spent more than a week among hundreds of thousands of visitors. Dressed in a fancy flight suit—sometimes blue, sometimes gold, with patriotic epaulets on the shoulders and his name and pilot wings embroidered on the front—he attended a regular schedule of major air shows across the country.

In 1977, seeking more marketability, he went into a recording studio and cut an unrehearsed two-record set containing some ninety minutes of storytelling. It was a low budget, unedited production, an atypical medium for a memoir, but it gave listeners the opportunity to savor his western accent and gravelly voice. Most of his stories rang with the kind of authenticity that only an eyewitness could provide. When he talked of exploring the Milwaukee Mill in St. Maries, where the chief sawyer was "a big Polack named Mike Kudzorio," the volume and tone of his voice dropped, betraying his longing for those simpler days. At air shows, he autographed the album cover for *Pappy Boyington, World War II Ace: A Personal Reflection on His Life,* along with copies of *Black Sheep* and *Tonya,* art prints, memorabilia, even Flying Tiger items—cash, checks, and credit cards accepted.

When he wasn't sitting in an air-show booth, he was earning a speaker's fee at conventions, symposiums, or corporate functions. He spoke candidly, coloring his speech with mild profanity and using favorite techniques to work the audience. He warmed the crowd by subtly watching for someone near the front, invariably a woman, looking back at him with a puzzled expression. He'd stop what he was saying, make eye contact, and say: "What are you looking so funny for, lady? I'm Robert Conrad with wrinkles!"

He thought of himself as an entertainer. "Say you're at a convention of medical people," he once told a reporter. "Hell, they don't want to listen to some boob with a bunch of charts talking about upper sinus tubes. They want to be entertained." As a result of being in constant demand, he and Jo traveled across the country "like it was going out of style." To his half-brother Keith he wrote: "I can't complain, because it is making us a darn good living."

Life was not entirely rosy, however, as Boyington's celebrity status and the renewed fame of the Black Sheep brought a host of profit seekers and impostors to the surface. Surprisingly, the most tenacious among them was not an American impersonator but a former enemy pilot from the 253d Kokutai at Rabaul.

No sooner had the television series premiered in 1976 than pleasant-faced Masajiro Kawato contacted Boyington, saying he had looked over his personal records, compared them to details in Boyington's book, and determined that he was the pilot who had downed the great Pappy. (The fifty-one-year-old Kawato also boasted that he had set a trans-Pacific nonstop record in a modified single-engine Piper Comanche, claiming to have flown five thousand miles from Tokyo to California in early September. Author and researcher Henry Sakaida subsequently found numerous flaws in Kawato's statements; no aeronautic agencies in the U.S. or abroad recognized the flight.)

Boyington, intrigued by Kawato's statements about Rabaul, met him at the local NBC affiliate in Los Angeles. They got along well, so Boyington arranged for "Mike" to visit the set of the series. A few months later, as the featured guests at a huge luncheon celebrating Brotherhood Week in Los Angeles, they publicly embraced. Boyington told the assembled press that he agreed with Kawato's statements: the circumstances of the aerial combat on January 3, 1944, "were completely the same."

Privately, Boyington urged Kawato to get a translator to assist with a memoir he had written in Japan years earlier. "I said I would write a real selling foreword for his book," Boyington wrote later. "He could make a climax in his book of Pappy Boyington's last duel over Rabaul, and take full advantage of all this tremendous TV-series publicity. I firmly believe Mike could have a best-seller—and a motion picture in the side benefits." Boyington even suggested some rousing titles, such as *Duel in the Sun* or *Last Dogfight over Rabaul*.

Obviously, accuracy was secondary as long as Kawato's account made a good story—the way Boyington approached his own historical record. Publicity would be just as beneficial for him as it would be for Kawato. He invited the Japanese pilot to cosign the combat art prints he sold at air shows, most of which depicted him flying Number Eighty-six, the so-called *Lulubelle*. Kawato agreed and drove up to

Fresno, but their partnership disintegrated even before he got inside Boyington's house. His girlfriend, a Japanese national, jumped out of the car and told Boyington emphatically, "Mike gets half!" Offended by such a brash display, Boyington stated later that he could "smell the lawyers coming." He wrote a check to Kawato, took him to the bank and gave him the money, then told him he never wanted to see him again. Kawato's book *Flight into Conquest,* published by a vanity press in 1978, was a confusing memoir filled with cheesy schoolboy expressions: "The tank on my right burst into flames. Yipes!" Only two pages were devoted to his alleged shoot-down of Boyington, but they provided ample evidence that Kawato's claim was fabricated. He remarked that the distinctive appearance of Boyington's plane was vivid in his memory, and the accompanying artwork showed the familiar Number Eighty-six Corsair. Boyington had never flown the plane in combat. Misled by the copious amounts of artwork he had seen, Kawato was caught in a lie that was mostly Boyington's doing.

Later, Henry Sakaida unearthed Kawato's original memoirs, published in a 1956 Japanese magazine. The text never referred to combat with Corsairs. Furthermore, none of the Rabaul air groups recognized individual victory claims due to an imperial order issued on June 1, 1943. Air groups, not individuals, were credited with victories, meaning that every member of the 253d Kokutai participated equally whether he was airborne or not. Kawato, who had been an enlisted pilot, boasted after the war of being an ace with eighteen kills, but Sakaida found evidence of only one victory and a quarter-share of another. Finally, the Zero Fighter Pilots Association in Tokyo got involved, issuing a statement that Kawato's claims were "ridiculous and disgusting." His patently false statements, clearly intended to capitalize on Boyington's popularity, caused the organization genuine embarrassment.

Kawato continued to shadow Boyington until he eventually outlasted him. Although he never gained much popularity or sold many books, he did have a sense of humor. An abridged edition of his book was reprinted under the title *Bye, Bye Black Sheep*.

As phonies go, Kawato has plenty of company in the form of individuals who falsely claim to be former Black Sheep. At least he was a real Japanese navy pilot, deserving of some respect for that accomplishment, but American counterparts—those legions of wanna-be Black Sheep that surfaced after the television show made the squadron famous—deserve only to be exposed as the frauds they are. The sheer volume of them amused Boyington. "It would seem that nearly everyone I run into has a good friend who was a member of the Black Sheep," he once wrote. "Perhaps we are one of the largest organizations in the world and don't know it."

Ironically, he was a major contributor to the problem. At an air show in Chino, California, he met a volunteer at the Planes of Fame Museum who had passed himself off as a Black Sheep pilot since the end of World War II. But instead of revealing that he was a phony, Boyington befriended him, autographing a copy of his book *From Your Old Skipper,* perpetuating the lie. He wasn't forgetful; he still needed that feeling of acceptance he got from the man's fawning attention. (A few years later, when the names of the real Black Sheep were published in Frank Walton's book, the same individual confessed privately to Walton that he had been an enlisted man. He had lied to everyone after the war. Still unwilling to give up the charade, he tried to cajole Walton into autographing a copy of his new book, *To One of the Black Sheep*. Rightfully, Walton ignored him.)

In another strange case, Boyington conferred an honorary membership upon an expatriate living in Japan for helping him investigate Kawato's claims. He mailed a certificate of appreciation referring to the individual as "the youngest and last member" of the Black Sheep, not realizing that the recipient, who called himself a former marine captain, had flunked out of flight school. The individual had never been a marine, and was only twelve years old when the Black Sheep were in combat.

One man in Montana, highly respected in his town, convinced the local citizens that he was the pilot wearing shorts in the famous squadron picture taken at Vella Lavella (John Bolt was the only one in shorts). In another case, an enlisted ordnance man from the VMF-214 ground echelon deceived his family and friends for years by claiming he was a pilot in the flight echelon. Only when his widow requested his service record was the bitter truth revealed.

There seems to be a Black Sheep impostor in almost every city across the land. The irrefutable fact is that only forty-eight other pilots and two ground officers served with Boyington in the combat echelon of VMF-214 during World War II. More noteworthy, a third of them were casualties, with eleven dead. Sadly, each time Boyington made some barfly an honorary member, he showed contempt for those who had legitimately served with him—especially those who died. Similarly, the countless individuals who have falsely claimed to be Black Sheep are guilty of scorning the real members. Those who served with Boyington are named in the Appendix. No one else can claim membership—period.

Due to his schedule of air shows and speaking engagements, Boyington worked hard and enjoyed long periods of sobriety, but when he slipped, he fell hard. Stephen Cannell recalled an incident that occurred a few years after the series ended: "Boyington got arrested for drunk driving up on the highway in Fresno. Here he was, nearly seventy years old, and it took four cops to arrest him. They had to mace him to get him. He was a tough guy. Jo called me—he was in jail—and said, 'I don't know what to do. We have to get him out.' Greg was a really nice person, but there was a maniac in there."

Jo was usually more decisive. Bruce Porter told of a patrolling police officer who discovered Boyington in a seedy section of Fresno, "down by the railroad tracks; a horrible place." Somehow Boyington hadn't been rolled yet and still had his wallet. Finding his address, the officer gave him a ride home, then knocked on the front door.

"I've got your husband here," he told Jo when she answered.

"Take him back and throw him in jail," she said, and slammed the door.

Boyington struggled with other compulsions. He still smoked heavily, could drink half a dozen cups of coffee at a sitting, and, even when he hadn't bombed his system with caffeine, was restless, staying up at night to watch old movies on television.

During calmer periods he drove to the desert, sometimes into Nevada, to capture sunrises and sunsets in his mind's eye. "It seems rather incongruous," he once said, "but I think of myself as a genuinely delicate, artistic person." By the mid-seventies he had completed some sixty paintings, if his claimed output was accurate, and he evidently had no trouble selling them.

One that Jo had wanted for herself was a source of conflict. "He did the most gorgeous painting and gave it to some attorney down in Palm Springs," remembered Porter. "I guess the guy had done some favors or something, but Jo was madder than hell at Greg because she wanted to keep that painting. But he was a marvelous artist."

Jo, as unselfish in supporting his career as she was demanding of his sobriety, spent "a ton of dough" to adapt her house for Boyington's use. A den was built on and equipped with a large desk, where he answered the fifty or so letters he received every week from fans. In the basement, she installed special cabinets with wide drawers for storing prints.

In return, Boyington was generally the charmer she had been attracted to. He made time for golf, her passion, and on the eve of celebrity events would go out in the backyard and practice. Carl Christiansen said of Boyington's abilities: "He could do all those things, whether he was an artist or a painter; whatever he wanted to do."

She went on trips with him, or got friends to go when she

could not, unwilling to trust him by himself. Sometimes she went along but enlisted additional help, such as the time Hap Halloran joined them at Oshkosh in 1979. Boyington signed books and prints and talked with fans for ten straight days. It was exhausting, but he did it because he could never stop being Pappy. As the days wore on, and the air shows wore on, and the years wore on, the strain of maintaining the image became great. His moods became unpredictable.

Dean Keller was thirteen when he and some young friends spotted Boyington at Oshkosh in 1983. They first stopped to see George Gay, the sole survivor of a torpedo squadron in the Battle of Midway, who was autographing copies of his book in the booth next to Boyington's. "He seemed to be a very personable character," Keller recalled of Gay. "He willingly gave us autographs and talked with us like we all lived on the same block back home." Toting some model kits—a Corsair and a Zero marketed for the television series—Keller stopped at Boyington's table and asked him to autograph the boxes. The response scorched him: "If you want an autograph you can buy my book, otherwise forget it. And besides, anyone who believes that bullshit oughta be slapped."

Several years earlier, when Boyington was signing books in San Diego, twelve-year-old John Ford had endured a similar experience: "I stood in line with my father, and was getting excited. I came up to him and said, 'Mr. Boyington, would you please sign my book? And would you please write down your kills?' At which point he put the book down, and put the pen down, and looked up at me very indignantly. With lots of venom he said, 'It wasn't kills. We were not trying to kill the pilot; we were out to shoot airplanes down. They were victories. We always called them victories; we never called them kills.' He was very huffy about it, and I was shaking in my shoes by the time I left. It was an experience I'll never forget."

Even fellow fighter pilots sometimes got the treatment. James Hoisington, a dive bomber pilot prior to flying a Corsair over Omori and photographing Pappy Boyington

HERE! on the *benjo* roofs, saw the ace at an EAA fly-in. "I had read his book some time before and got one with his signature," he wrote. "I told him that I had been in on the first strike at Truk. He growled, 'Yah, you damn near killed me,' and took the next customer."

Others were privileged to meet a more congenial Boyington, the one blessed with an amazing memory for names. Irv Soble, copiloting a DC-10 in 1978, was informed that Boyington and his wife were passengers. He went back in the cabin and introduced himself, then mentioned that his fourteen-year-old son had just soloed a sailplane on his birthday, and would be thrilled to get an autograph. Apologetically, Boyington said he couldn't write because he had drops in his eyes, but he would send a note. Jo took down the name and address. On impulse, Soble gave the names of his other two children, who were living with their mother. "In truth," he said later, "I really didn't expect anything."

But a week later, his son Lee received a handwritten letter welcoming him to the pilot community, autographed by "Black Sheep One." The boy called his brother and sister, who had also gotten notes from Pappy. The kicker came a month later, when the Sobles went to Texas for the Confederate Air Force annual and stopped at Boyington's booth. Boyington not only greeted Irv, but without a prompt from anyone turned to his son, saying, "And you must be Lee."

Fans who sent letters were likewise amazed. Keith Osteen, sixteen when he first began corresponding with his hero in 1977, received a large stack of letters and pictures over the years. Calling it "treasured stuff," he later commented, "I was impressed that he would take the time to even acknowledge me, as I'm sure he was bombarded by letters at that time. My last contact with him was in late '86 or early '87 and he remembered who I was and even asked how my aircraft-mechanic training was coming."

Osteen's last contact coincided with the beginning of the end for Boyington. Two years earlier he had undergone prostate surgery, "old man's disease," he called it. By 1986 he was enduring chemotherapy, though he still went to air shows, hauling his books and folding tables around in a silver van. He still smoked constantly despite the fact that he couldn't even sit straight, not because his back was weak, but from hunching forward in an effort to draw more air into his diseased lungs. When he couldn't get enough oxygen, he brought out a portable bottle, but generally hid it from the public's sight.

He had grown even thinner by the middle of 1986, his diet no longer providing nourishment for him so much as feeding the cancer. The rest of him slowly wasted away. His clothing hung from his bony shoulders and arms, his sparse hair drooped, and he was constantly cold. Even in the desert heat that summer he wore a jacket—bright red, with the Marine Corps logo.

At the Yakima Air Fair in June, he gathered with a few of his relatives. Aside from Greg junior, there weren't many of his immediate family left. He had no relationship with Gloria, who had remained a Wickstrom until she married, and the Hallenbecks were gone. Grace had passed away at the age of ninety-three in a Eugene, Oregon, nursing home; Bill was just sixty-six when he died three years later in 1984. Quite a few years before that, Ellsworth had collapsed in his backyard, suffocated by emphysema. His granddaughters couldn't remember exactly when, and didn't care. His death had been "a happy day" for all of them.

Keith Boyington's family joined Pappy for a few days at Yakima, and Greg junior made the trip from California. He was divorced, and had retired from the military, but the similarities with his father ended there. He worked steadily for himself, renovating properties in Alameda to rent out, and had stayed away from the bottle. They talked, father and son, making their peace, if only on the surface.

Nineteen eighty-six was also a year of healing for some of the Black Sheep. After dozens of rejections, Frank Walton's manuscript for *Once They Were Eagles: The Men of the*

Black Sheep Squadron was published by the University Press of Kentucky. It had evolved into a then-and-now account of the original group, with fast-paced chapters about the squadron in combat and biographical sketches of each surviving member forty years later. Walton was justifiably proud of the achievement, which showed convincingly that the real Black Sheep were nothing like the misfits on television.

His coverage of Boyington was honest, even neutral, though he could have been vindictive, considering their final meeting in October 1980. During a gala event to commemorate a newly restored Corsair at the National Air and Space Museum, the two men met alone in a rest room. Walton extended his hand, so the story goes, hoping to begin a reconciliation. Boyington would have none of it. "Fuck you, Frank," he said, then turned his back and walked out. If Walton was tempted to vilify his former friend, his character was above that sort of smear. In private, however, he remained bitter about Boyington's behavior for the rest of his life.

The other Black Sheep had mellowed since that evening. Visiting regularly with several of them as he traveled around the country, Boyington would sit up late, drinking coffee while he told them about his life's battles. Almost to a man they came away with newfound respect, even compassion, for the demons he had endured.

After the prostate surgery he rarely undertook long trips, making the handful of air shows he attended in 1986 among his last. He no longer shook hands with fans, saving his strength for autographs. On one of his last journeys east, he returned to Pensacola for the seventy-fifth anniversary of naval aviation in May and, despite his weakness, powered his way through several hundred autographs while signing a commemorative print.

Hap Halloran, visiting Fresno a few times the following year, marveled at his ailing friend's spirit: "He was in pain and weak from the chemotherapy treatments. He never complained. Finally our golf games would consist of us riding a cart. I would play all the holes, he would play every fourth hole. He would never give up."

But there came a stage, after Boyington was in and out of the VA hospital several times, that nothing more could be done. As the cancer spread he continually weakened, until Jo was no longer able to cope, either mentally or physically. By the end of the year, a decision had been made—by whom is unclear—to move him to a hospice where he would receive full-time nursing care. They would keep him comfortable while he awaited the inevitable.

On the last day of 1987, a nonemergency ambulance transported him across town to a residential neighborhood on Fresno's northwest side. Along a quiet street in what used to be fig gardens, registered nurse Nancy Hines had modified a three-bedroom house for hospice use. One more remarkable irony was in store for Boyington. The hospice had only six beds, yet among the handful of patients was a Japanese man who had been interned in a U.S. camp while Boyington was a prisoner in Japan.

For the first part of his stay, Boyington did what he had done his whole life when facing adversity—he fought it. "I remember how difficult it was for him to admit to a terminal disease," Hines later wrote. "He had survived so many near-death experiences in his lifetime, surely he would survive cancer. It seemed like cancer was just another battle to be fought, not a war."

He stubbornly refused to quit smoking. The staff obligingly let him try, but he finally gave up when he could no longer inhale. He was still restless after dark, so Jeanne Brown and Jan Walters, the night nurses, took turns rubbing his back as he sat in a chair to watch television. "He was most courteous—'thank you,' 'please,' everything," said Brown. "If you're a cantankerous old thing during your life, you generally die that way, but he didn't. He was a nice fellow."

Boyington had come to the realization that the end was

rapidly approaching. Jo struggled to accept the accelerating decline in his condition, but he was at ease, surrounded by nurses and assistants who daily exhibited an extraordinary level of compassion. By the time Ned Corman and Fred Losch came to visit on the evening of Friday, January 8, he was able to say with complete sincerity: "Ah, here's a couple of my boys, coming to say good-bye."

His friends did not understand. The whole concept of hospices was still brand new in this country. "When I walked in and saw the living room, it looked just like a funeral parlor back East," recalled Losch. "There was a piano and three or four pews, like a church, which didn't lend itself to any confidence."

They were unprepared, too, for the shock of Boyington's appearance, but he showed a bit of his old stubbornness by struggling from the bed and sitting in an armchair when they arrived. It seemed to them that he was sedated. He kept nodding off, his chin falling to his chest. In reality, he was passing out as his oxygen-starved blood carried increasingly higher levels of carbon dioxide to his brain.

They soon bid him good-bye. Leaning over, Corman said, "You've just got to get your butt out of here," but from Boyington's expression he knew it would not happen. "I didn't break down while I was talking to him," he said later, "but when I walked out of that room the tears just streamed down my face."

Just two nights later, Boyington began "changing." His breathing became distressed, sometimes stopping for long periods, and his skin turned cold as circulation continued to drop. The body's last reflexive defense was to pool blood around the central organs—his last fight, though he was unaware of it. A little at a time, his body shut down until he drifted in and out of consciousness by the early hours of Monday, January 11.

Jeanne Brown and Jan Walters took turns sitting with him, holding his hand, talking softly to him in the darkness. No family members were present. Boyington was comfortable with the staff, who in the past ten days had shown as much unconditional love as he had known in seventy-five years. There were no profound last words. At about four o'clock that morning, Brown witnessed "a sense of his going away, without a great deal of anxiety."

She saw no fear.

Epilogue

Of all the cities that were important in Boyington's life, two stand out because of special flights. St. Maries was an uncomplicated little community, a magical backdrop for his first airplane ride in a barnstormer's biplane. Twenty-six years later, almost to the day, a four-engine transport flew him to Alameda, where he was lifted triumphantly onto the shoulders of his Black Sheep.

Now there was a last flight to accomplish. On this cold, gloomy Thursday morning, he was carried from the Fresno Airport terminal to a jet transport bearing the logo of the United States Marine Corps. Passing between two lines of marines, national guardsmen, and World War II veterans at attention, an honor guard shouldered his flag-draped casket across the concrete with slow, synchronized precision. His wife, son, and three of his grandchildren waited near the plane, as did his friend Hap Halloran, while his casket was placed aboard.

Overhead, three attack jets from the Black Sheep squadron streaked past in a ceremonial fly-by. Four had flown up from their desert base at Yuma, Arizona, the previous day, intending to perform the traditional Missing Man formation, but that morning one of the jets had suffered a mechanical problem. Boyington would have laughed; nothing with the Marine Corps ever seemed to go right for him.

454

After the jets passed overhead, Halloran and Boyington's family filed aboard the transport. The engines whined to a start, it pulled away from the terminal, then, as it taxied toward the departure end of the runway, onlookers were amazed to see a hole open in the overcast. Right on cue, sunlight burst through the clouds.

At eleven o'clock the next morning, another honor guard carried Boyington from the Fort Meyer chapel at Arlington National Cemetery to a waiting caisson. It was only fitting that a man who had earned a Medal of Honor, even if he stored it in his garage, should receive the full treatment of military honors, including the black caisson and its six-horse team for the last mile of his journey.

A few inches of snow blanketed the grounds, but the roads were clear and the winter air was warmed by a bright sun, so most everyone chose to walk with him. The commandant and the assistant commandant were there along with a ton of lesser brass, joined by seven Black Sheep, the family, well-wishers, and the press. Stirred by the cadence of Marine Corps drummers, the procession moved slowly through the wooded grounds to Section 7A, near the Tomb of the Unknowns.

The casket was placed at the gravesite, the chaplain read his service, then Hap Halloran presented a eulogy he had written during the flight from Fresno. He praised Boyington as an inspiration and a legend, "the original top gun." Folded national ensigns were presented to Jo and Greg junior, and the final honors were rendered: a twenty-one-gun salute, taps, a stirring flyover by four howling Phantom fighters from a marine detachment at Andrews Air Force Base. One pulled up and away—the Missing Man.

As the crowd began to disperse after the service, Fred Losch happened to glance at the inscription on the marble headstone he'd been standing beside. He almost laughed out loud. The name on the stone was Joseph Louis Barrow. It was Joe Louis, the great boxer.

Ol' Pappy wouldn't have to go far to find a good fight.

Appendix

The Roster of Boyington's Black Sheep

Countless individuals have claimed—some with clever layers of lies—to have belonged to the Black Sheep under Boyington's command. During his two combat tours with the Black Sheep, the following forty-nine pilots and two ground officers comprised the flight echelon of Marine Fighting Squadron 214.

Alexander, Robert A.	first tour	killed accidentally
Ashmun, George M.	both tours	missing in action
Avey, Fred V.	second tour	
Bailey, Stanley R.	first tour	
Bartl, Harry R.	second tour	missing in action
Begert, John F.	first tour	
Bolt, John F. Jr.	both tours	
Bourgeois, Henry M.	first tour	
Bowers, Glenn L.	second tour	
Boyington, Gregory	both tours	wounded in action, captured by the enemy
Bragdon, Robert M.	both tours	
Brown, John S.	second tour	
Brubaker, James E.	second tour	missing in action
Carnagey, Pierre	second tour	missing in action
Case, William N.	first tour	wounded in action
Chatham, Rufus M. Jr.	second tour	

Corman, J. Ned	second tour	
Crocker, William L.	second tour	
Doswell, Gelon H.	second tour	
Dustin, J. Cameron	second tour	missing in action
Emrich, Warren T.	both tours	
Ewing, Robert T.	first tour	missing in action
Ffoulkes, Bruce J.	second tour	missing in action
Fisher, Don H.	both tours	
Groover, Denmark Jr.	both tours	wounded in action
Harper, Edwin A.	both tours	wounded in action
Harris, Walter R.	first tour	missing in action
Heier, William D.	both tours	
Hill, James J.	both tours	
Hobbs, William A. Jr.	second tour	
Holden, Herbert Jr.	second tour	
Johnson, Alfred L.	second tour	
Johnson, Harry C.	second tour	
Lane, Perry T.	second tour	
Losch, Fred S.	second tour	
Magee, Christopher L.	both tours	
March, Marion J.	second tour	
Marker, Alan D.	second tour	injured in accident
Matheson, Bruce J.	both tours	wounded in action
McCartney, H. Allan	first tour	
McClurg, Robert W.	both tours	
Miller, Henry S.	second tour	
Moore, Donald J.	both tours	missing in action
Mullen, Paul A.	both tours	wounded in action
Olander, Edwin L.	both tours	
Ray, Virgil G.	first tour	missing in storm
Reames, James M.	both tours	
Rinabarger, Rolland N.	first tour	wounded in action
Sims, Sanders S.	both tours	
Tucker, Burney L.	both tours	
Walton, Frank E. Jr.	both tours	

Major Boyington*

The moon struck the runway
That rain-soaked dreary morn,
As the major gunned his engine
And flew into the dawn.

The bombers flew beneath them,
The Corsairs up on high,
The Hellcats in the middle
As the Warhawks scanned the sky.

Rabaul was for the army,
The runway for marines,
As onward flew the flying men;
A solid fighting team.

The sun blacked out, the Zeros dived;
The dogfights had begun.
The AA burst like city lights;
The bombers made their run.

Twenty-five had Boyington,
This man of fighting fame
Who flew into the Zeros,
And one came down in flames.

Rickenbacker's record,
And Foss's flying fame,
Had added Major Boyington
As homeward on they came.

The bombers' run had now been made;
They slowly banked and turned,
As Corsairs left the fleeing Japs,
The Zeros fell and burned.

* On January 3, 1944, the day Boyington failed to return to Vella Lavella,
a distraught marine wrote this ode to his hero.

The major's plane had not returned;
 His men cast worried eyes,
And listed was another man
 Who fought the Japs and died.

     James Cahill
     Corporal, USMC

Sources

The three largest collections of material on Gregory Boyington are located in government repositories, accounting for thousands of pages of correspondence, unit records, magazine articles, and news clippings. The box containing Boyington's medical and service records—which requires next-of-kin authorization for duplication—is stored at the National Personnel Records Center in St. Louis, Missouri. The Marine Corps Historical Center maintains several reference files at the Washington Navy Yard in Washington, D.C. Official records regarding Boyington's military units and POW experience are at the Modern Military Records, National Archives and Records Administration, in College Park, Maryland. The next largest source used for this book was Frank Walton's collection of war diaries, personal interviews, and scores of magazine and newspaper articles. The National Museum of Naval Aviation provided Boyington's flight training record, again after next-of-kin authorization was obtained. Two notable sources regarding Boyington's service in the AVG were Frank Olynyk, who copied flight records, action reports, and correspondence, and the Texas A & M University archives, which duplicated the AVG's Group War Diary (GWD) and personal diaries of George Burgard and Robert Keeton. Court records of marriages and divorces were obtained from Kootenai County, Idaho; King

County, Washington; and Los Angeles County and Fresno County, California.

The majority of Boyington's quotes were drawn from his 1958 memoir *Baa Baa Black Sheep* (BBBS) and his 1977 two-record audio recording (LP). Listed following are quotes from sources not cited in the text, or which were attributed to individuals who provided multiple sources. A complete bibliographic listing is provided separately.

Prologue
Ah, here's a couple of my boys . . . : quoted by Losch, interview, Jan. 23, 1999.

1: Rough and Tumble
All sorts of vile and vulgar names, and other quotes from Grace Boyington: court complaint, August 20, 1914; *Having intimate relations . . .* and quotes from Grace's letter to Hallenbeck: Charles Boyington, counter-complaint, August 14, 1920; *I was playing in my mother's bedroom . . .* : LP; *The window was open . . .* : Ibid.; *At any time during reasonable hours:* Judge R. N. Dunn, divorce decree, Mar. 4, 1915; *Were married at Spokane, Washington . . .* : Hallenbeck, court record filed Jul. 20, 1935; *The type that wasn't afraid to try anything:* Waterstrat interview; *For some reason . . .* etc.: LP; *They were familiar sights . . .* : Ibid.; *I seemed to have a penchant for climbing . . .* : Ibid.; *Was always a fighter,* etc.: quoted in *Ashland Independent,* Jan. 12, 1944; *Still a little kid . . . ,* etc.: LP.

2: A Trip Through the Air
hem-stitcher: LP; *at a kindergarten age,* etc.: *Ashland Independent; When I was six years old . . .* : BBBS, p. 308; *like the little boy . . .* : LP; *for a day of study,* etc: *St. Maries Gazette-Record,* Sept. 16, 1919; *Gregory, come back . . . ,* etc.: LP; *I tore off from the parked airplane,* etc.: Ibid.; *About dusk he came in . . .* : quoted in Johnstown *Democrat,* Jun. 14, 1945; *I was to pick these up one at a time . . .* : LP; *I couldn't see him . . .* : Johnstown *Democrat; He told me to be out . . .* : Johnstown *Democrat; Greg often said . . .* : Ibid.

3: Deeds

When I was in first or second grade, etc.: quoted by Schwalbe; *never missed school:* LP; *a band around his forehead . . .* : Ibid.; *I forget what I had done . . .* , etc.: Ibid.; *longest, steepest, most dangerous street . . .* : Mowreader, correspondence; *I recall going down this hill . . .* : LP; *There was a little breeze . . .* : Ibid.; *At our age . . .* etc: Ibid.; *I never flew so many different kinds of missions:* quoted in McGoldrick, p. 72; *They just seemed to go wild . . .* etc.: LP; *considered quite a plum:* Trummel interview; *sin spot of the Northwest,* etc.: *Look* magazine, Jun. 25, 1957; *What's life without spice . . .* : quoted in court record, August 20, 1914; *not a very nice man,* etc: Granath interview; *Christmas Day was repulsive to me . . .* : BBBS, p. 213–14; *Greg was so fascinated . . .* : quoted in *St. Maries Gazette-Record,* Oct. 14, 1976; *All the subjects I could take . . .* : LP; *composed of the most prominent boys . . .* : Doty interview; *Oh, Christ, I'm a mixture . . .* : quoted by Schwalbe; *I paid for these . . .* etc: LP; *Whenever Gregory made up his mind . . .* : quoted in *Tacoma News Tribune,* Apr. 13, 1978; *Greg wasn't a brilliant student . . .* : quoted in *Ashland Independent.*

4: Slipping the Surly Bonds

fairly uneventful and rather dull: LP; *I started out as a pledge . . .* : quoted by Lagana; *I soon discovered . . .* : LP; *a beautiful little biplane:* Ibid.; *It seemed to me like it was a chained animal . . .* : Ibid.; *an industrious worker . . .* : Kirsten, May 21, 1935 (NPRC); *an exceptional young man . . .* : Matthews, May 27, 1935 (NPRC); *the face of a Boticelli angel:* Quilter, interview; *struck by what a beautiful woman . . .* : Canavan, interview; *She was an orphan . . .* : Ibid.; *I should have considered myself very fortunate indeed:* LP; *the magnificent sum of $4.66 per week:* court affidavit, December 16, 1935; *I read in the paper . . .* : LP; *Why don't you go down to Pensacola . . .* , etc: Walton, *Pappy and His Black Sheep,* p. 16; *As fortunate . . .* : LP; *He was dumbfounded . . .* : quoted in *Chicago Daily News,* Jan. 7, 1944; *She started crying . . .* : quoted in *Tacoma News Tribune,* Apr. 3, 1978; *that he be found physically qualified . . .* : medical summary, May 16, 1935; *He never felt like doing anything . . .* : Walton, p. 15; *Let plane get away from him,* etc.: flight record, Jun. 18 and 25, 1935; *a good, average student:* Mangrum, July 3, 1935; *I was so happy . . .* : LP; *settled back into the dull routine . . .* : Walton, p. 17; *disregarded her marriage vows . . .* , etc.: complaint, Aug. 16, 1935; *The clatter of the stuff . . .* : quoted in *Boeing News,* Sept. 7, 1945.

5: Rats

with confidence: training record, Apr. 6, 1936; *dangerously skidded:* training record, Apr. 13, 1936; *some of the toughest check pilots . . .* : 1936 *Flight Jacket,* p. 54; *dreaded 25-hour check . . .* : Ibid.; *five foot minus:* 1930 *Lucky Bag,* p. 205; *very good feel:* training record, Jun. 4, 1936; *pleasant manner [and] willingness to help: Lucky Bag,* p. 205; *barely passing:* training record, July 27, 1936; *They sure as heck ruined Christmases . . .* : Boyington, public address, Oct. 25, 1958; *Studies came first . . .* : Nelson correspondence; *sober, honest . . .* : Stiley, May 22, 1935; *I figured I was at the opposite end . . .* : public address; *The fact that there's Irish and Indian . . .* , etc.: Ibid. *At this first cocktail party . . .* etc.: Ibid.; *blackouts are a very distinctive feature . . .* : Milam and Ketcham, p.108; *There were some people . . .* , etc.: public address; *Has a rather sullen appearance . . .* : fitness report, Apr. 9, 1937; *not sure of himself . . .* : flight record, Oct. 13, 1936; *fat son of a bitch:* BBBS, p. 206; *He had rattled me . . .* : Ibid., p. 144; *much improved after rest:* flight record, Jan. 12, 1937; *This regular commission . . .* : public address; *After two months at the beach . . .* : *Flight Jacket,* p. 64; *They made you feel . . .* : Reeder interview; *A little slow to learn . . .* : fitness report, Apr. 12, 1937; *Greg wasn't a brilliant student . . .* : quoted in *Ashland Independent.*

6: Adventures in Uniform

she did not keep clippings . . . : *St. Maries Gazette-Record,* Oct. 14, 1978; *A very bad reputation,* etc., and *a family filled with loners:* Granath interview; *a jolly fellow . . .* : Quilter interview; *Mac warned his men . . .* :

Barrow, p. 209; *Mac was very proud of all his boys* . . . : Ibid., p. 210; *I would like to toast* . . . : quoted in BBBS, p. 368; *beer barrel on roller skates:* Tillman, *Flight Journal; I always liked him* . . . etc.: Condon, correspondence to Warner Chapman, May 10, 1994.

7: Conduct Unbecoming

Each lady . . . : Quilter interview; *They were basically two naïve creatures* . . . : Ibid; *If you got over there* . . . : quoted by Galer; *a helluva long and expensive cab ride,* etc: Coon, *Air Classics; the people who wore those vulgar blue trousers* . . . : Quilter interview; *Helene was shaking* . . . : Quilter, correspondence; *I've never seen people drink like this* . . . : quoted in Quilter interview; *Hoffman's film* . . . : Quilter, C., *Fortitudine,* Winter 1977–78; *Not professionally qualified:* HMC correspondence to Boyington, Aug. 6, 1940; *The car he was driving* . . . : Quilter interview; *We figured* . . . : Boyington, public address; *This is just indebtedness* . . . : Boyington, correspondence to CMC, May 10, 1941; *If he were very sincere* . . . : A&P, correspondence to CMC, Jun. 27, 1941; *Your method of payment* . . . : CMC, correspondence to Boyington, Jun. 18, 1941; *I was instructed by the commandant* . . . : Boyington, public address.

8: Slow Boat to Burma

Flew another five hours today . . . : Weiland interview; *looking for an answer,* and details of hotel interview: Boyington, public address, Oct. 25, 1958. *I urge your attention* . . . : Aldworth correspondence to Chennault, Oct. 7, 1941; *I hereby tender* . . . : Boyington, correspondence to CMC, Aug. 8, 1941; *Acceptance of resignations* . . . : Mitchell, endorsement to CMC, Aug. 14, 1941; *never got the early scoop:* BBBS, p. 19; *plastered to the gills* . . . : Keeton diary; *like a busy elevator and getting stewed:* Burgard diary; *were pretty good eggs,* etc.: Burgard; *He seemed to direct* . . . : BBBS, p. 25; *much good wine:* Burgard; *gawking* . . . : Burgard; *pretty thin,* etc . . . : ibid.; *the lack of planes* . . . : quoted by Schwalbe; *a beautiful Balinese girl,* etc.: BBBS, p. 26-27; *a town the likes of which* . . . : Burgard; *the whiteness of the whites* . . . : BBBS,

p. 34; *did not conceal his contempt* . . . : Bond, p. 35; *I wandered about* . . . etc.: BBBS, p. 37; *although some were well stewed up:* Burgard; *we took the liberty* . . . : LP; *Outside of "Cokey" Hoffman* . . . : Rosbert, *Flying Aces,* Oct. 1944; *Little wonder* . . . : BBBS, p. 39; *Their work was serious* . . . : Ibid.

9: The Sharks of Toungoo

the size of a cantaloupe: BBBS, p. 39; *miles from nowhere* . . . : Greenlaw, *Lady and the Tigers,* p. 35; *After the first novelty* . . . : Ibid., p. 49; *to jazz up the planes:* Bond, p. 44; *I bounced to high heaven* . . . .: BBBS, p. 41-42; *With all the boys watching* . . . : Greenlaw, *Cosmopolitan; Even though Jim wasn't hurt* . . . : BBBS, p. 42; *I think the two most serious problems* . . . : Greenlaw, *Lady and the Tigers,* p. 56; *They were all grinning,* . . . : Ibid., p. 33; *Harvey is a man* . . . : Ibid., p. 14; *There used to be a running gag* . . . : Rossi interview; *one rainy afternoon,* etc.: Greenlaw, *Cosmopolitan; his eyes were large and dreamy,* and other descriptions: *Lady and the Tigers,* p. 33, 94, and 54 respectively; *I said, "Mr. Chennault* . . . ," etc.: LP; *Everyone got tighter than a tick:* Bond, p. 48; *to the great delight* . . . : Ibid., p. 49; *chasing natives* . . . : Keeton; *began to feel like a heel* . . . : quoted by Greenlaw, *Cosmopolitan; the British residents* . . . : Ibid.; *a grand windup* . . . : Bond, p. 50; *loafed the day away:* Burgard; *My plane is ready* . . . : Ibid.; *Many of us scan* . . . : Bond, p. 52; *in every emergency:* Greenlaw, p.75; *You can't imagine how dark it is* . . . : LP; *As we continued to fly northward* . . . : BBBS, p. 47

10: Fighting Tigers

I had to give Sandy all the credit . . . : BBBS, p. 47; *The name of our quarters* . . . : BBBS, p. 48; *As soon as I got our quarters* . . . : Greenlaw, p. 89; *I can't wait* . . . : quoted by Rosbert; *We asked him what should be done* . . . : Bond, p. 63; *it was no consolation* . . . : Burgard; *flew off the handle:* Bond, p. 63; *really attractive young belles:* Ibid., p. 65; *The self-made executive officer* . . . etc.: BBBS, p. 43; *like shooting ducks:* Olson, message to Kunming transcribed in Group War Diary (GWD); *Have few ships left* . . . : Olson to

Kunming, GWD; *How I envied . . .* : BBBS, p. 53; *our Adam & Evers . . .* : Ibid., p. 53; *Boyington, being a wrestle . . .* : Rosbert, interview; details of conversation with Olga: *Lady and the Tigers,* p. 108-09; *After drinking all the scotch I dared . . .* : BBBS, p. 56; *tiny islands . . .* : Ibid., p. 106; *I began to feel bitter . . .* : Bond, p. 78; *all in a dither:* Burgard; *On most of them . . .* : BBBS, p. 54; *In the lower latitudes. . . .* : Ibid. p. 54-55; *a bunch of buzzards . . .* : Neale; *one damn fool adventure . . .* : Ford, p. 203; *the guy who was leading . . .* and other quotes pertinent to the combat: BBBS, p. 58-60; *dream estates:* BBBS, p. 64; *carved Chinese chests . . .* : Rosbert, *Flying Aces,* Oct. 1944; *the delightful aroma . . .* : BBBS, p. 67; *clapping their hands in glee:* Bond, p. 84; *I became nervous . . .* etc.: BBBS, p. 60-61; *The largest part of the pilot . . .* : Ibid., p. 62; *two days after the first flubdub:* Ibid.; *This is for Cokey . . .* : Ibid. p. 63; *This Nip had committed hara-kiri . . .* : Ibid., p. 62; *the American drink:* Ibid., p. 65; *craving for excitement and women:* Ibid., p. 68; *His flight followed me . . .* : Bond, p. 94; *I caught a Jap flying along . . .* : quoted by Schwalbe; *The 1st Squadron unassisted . . .* : Sandell, message to Kunming, GWD; *He had been having some trouble . . .* etc.: Bond, p. 95; *Messages between Newkirk, Neale, and Kunming:* GWD; *No one will ever know . . .* : Neale diary; *I want to see what Bob Neale can do . . .* : quoted by Greenlaw, p. 139; *had a terrific load aboard:* BBBS, p. 68; *drink the RAF under the table,* etc.: Bond, p. 98; *Can't say that I blamed him . . .* : Burgard diary; *He does not seem to care . . .* : Bond, p. 100; *an incessant, frantic desire . . .* : Rosbert, *Flying Aces; The most pitiful sight I ever saw:* BBBS, p. 73; *[one] of the last alerts . . .* : Ibid., p. 74; *I was positive . . .* : BBBS, p. 105; *[We] decided to remain in the bar. . . .* : Ibid., p 104-05; *hoped that the missing boys . . .* : Greenlaw, p. 155; *I just simply did not know. . . . .* : BBBS, p. 82; *my apparent blunder:* Ibid., p. 86; *The colonel will die:* Burgard diary; *He's built like a bull:* Bond, p. 129; *stewed to the gills and details of tussle:* Ibid.

11: For the Good of the Service

It's all right to use that water . . . : BBBS, p. 98; *All right, you curly-headed fellows . . .* : Bond, p. 132; *What was passing by . . .* : BBBS, p. 98; *take shape in the semi-darkness:* Ibid., p. 99; *We intended to strafe . . .* : Geselbracht, combat report; *a line of planes . . .* and other details: from combat reports of Neale, Bartling, Boyington; *blurred forms jumping off wings . . .* : BBBS, p. 99; *one large fire . . .* : combat report; *uncomfortably close:* Bartling combat report; *After looking over combat reports . . .* : Neale diary; *Since each approved victory . . .* : Howard, p. 147; *Asiatic bums.* BBBS, p. 42; *written agreement back in Washington,* etc.: Ibid., p. 102; *I noticed it was not tracking . . .* : Schramm, p. 163-64; *Boyington cut slightly. . . .* : Olson, message to Kunming, GWD; *It just ran into a rice paddy . . .* : Schramm interview; *full of whiskey:* BBBS, p. 109; *Dear Mrs. G . . .* etc.: Greenlaw, p. 215; Details of Clare Booth Luce's visit and accusation: Ibid., p. 220-22; *Contemplating resignation. . . .* : Boyington, telegram to HMC, April 12; *There are a lot of things. . . .* etc. also, conversation with Neale: quoted by Greenlaw, p. 230-31; *At dinner I saw [Greg] . . .* : Bond p. 158; *Having terminated his contract . . .* : discharge letter, April 21, 1942; *After I got to hobbling around . . .* : Stolet, recollection in Schramm, p. I; *Dear Olga,* quoted by Greenlaw, p. 283.

12: About Face

Am unable to grant permission . . . : quoted in BBBS, p. 115; *closest I ever got . . .* : Ibid.; *shared the opinion . . .* : Greenlaw, *Cosmopolitan,* Apr. 1944; *full salary settlement . . .* : Wicks, deposition, May 12, 1942; *briefcase full of paper money:* BBBS, p. 112; *Laughing Boy:* Ibid., p. 115; *This tyrant . . .* : Ibid.; *in a couple of weeks . . .* etc: Ibid., p. 116; *In Karachi something happened . . .* : Greenlaw; *any number of export wives . . .* : BBBS, 116; *in front of two very attractive gams . . .* etc.: quoted by Callahan, Jan. 20, 1946; *Gosh, he was good to me:* Ibid.; *I was worried about my children . . .* : quoted by Callahan; *not be reappointed . . .* etc: Mitchell, correspondence to Holcomb, April 23, 1942;

but merely as a prelude . . . : BBBS p. 118; *the arrangements* . . . : Pawley, correspondence to Beatty, July 14, 1942; *as agreed to* . . . : Boyington, correspondence to CMC, July 17, 1942; *with the precedence* . . . : Mitchell, correspondence to Holcomb, July 21, 1942; *severely injured* . . . : quoted in Okanogan *Independent,* Aug. 7, 1942; *the excessive use of intoxicating liquors:* Boyington, affidavit, August 10, 1942; *Request information* . . . : Boyington, telegram to CMC, Sept. 1, 1942; *This pilot was a capable flyer* . . . : unidentified staff to Capt. Beatty, quoting Aug. 28 report from Mitchell to Holcomb, Oct. 13, 1942; *Reappointment to commissioned rank approved* . . . : CMC to Boyington, Sept. 3, 1942; *You don't mean it* . . . : quoted in BBBS p. 120; *Request details on lengthy delay* . . . : Boyington to CMC, Sept. 14; *It is extremely doubtful* . . . : staff to Beatty, Oct. 13, 1942; *a renowned son of a bitch* . . . : BBBS, p. 120; *Have been standing by.* . . . : Boyington to CMC, Nov. 8, 1942; *Owing to the length.* . . . : BBBS, p. 121; *They had to practice* . . . : Condon interview; *one of the great bases* . . . : Sherrod, p. 71; *the say of nothing,* etc.: BBBS, p. 126; *truly a gaunt specimen:* Ibid.; *months seemed to drag on:* Ibid.; *in the famous Hotel De Gink* . . . : BBBS, p. 127; *gave up the squadron:* Long interview; *back in harness* . . . etc.: *Chevron,* July 17, 1943; *I'm a psychopathic liar:* quoted in *Air Classics Quarterly Review,* Winter 1976; *never saw so much as a vapor trail:* BBBS, p. 127; *Greg had not changed.* . . . : Reinburg, p. 75-76; *There had been some doubt* . . . : BBBS, p. 129; *At the bottom* . . . : Reinburg, p. 76-77; *a sweet-flying baby* . . . : BBBS, p. 131; *by a superior officer* . . . : Boyington, forward in Porter, *Ace!; Who wants to wrestle, and I'm tired of this* . . . . : quoted by Long; *he be sent to a more temperate climate* . . . : medical history extract, Jun. 9, 1943.

13: Boyington's Bastards

a truly fine woman, etc.: BBBS, p. 137; *I could not beg or steal* . . . : Ibid., p. 139; *Choice scuttlebutt.* . . . : VMF-214 handwritten war diary; *There was a lot of heat* . . . and details of Black Sheep name: Case interview with Walton;

Half ass artist, etc.: Johnson, correspondence; *We're going to Cactus . . .* : Walton, *Once They Were Eagles,* p.19; *a complicated scene of destruction:* Ibid., p. 20; *If we attack . . .* : quoted by BBBS; *I was doing some tall hoping . . .* : BBBS, p. 146.

14: Touchstone of Victory

the monotony of flying herd . . . etc.: BBBS, p. 148-50; *showing the huge red roundel . . .* : VMF-214 war diary (WD), Sept. 16, 1943; *seemed like an eternity and . . . wet towel:* BBBS, p. 150; *It exploded so close . . .* : Ibid., p. 151; *a gentle turn to the left:* WD; *at extremely long range . . .* : Ibid.; *Not even the possibility . . . .* : BBBS, p. 154; *Charlie chose to be cagey:* Ibid., p. 174; *a good many thousand men . . .* : Walton, p. 36; *I don't feel comfortable . . .* etc.: quoted by Hill, interview; *They're firing at us . . .* etc.: quoted by Magee, interview; *a twin-tailed ship . . .* : WD, Sept. 27, 1943; *I pulled up . . .* : Case, interview; *cleared his guns,* etc.: WD; *an attitude . . .* : Hill; *chopped the Jap's tail to pieces:* WD, Oct. 4, 1943; *My outfit . . .* : quoted by Weller, *Chicago Daily News,* Oct. 18, 1943; *an ardent baseball fan . . .* : *Wenatchee Daily World,* Oct. 15, 1943; *Bailey ran the squadron . . .* : Begert, interview with Walton; *Boyington was a horror . . .* : Olander, interview; *lucky, wild-assed shot:* Case, interview; *in a heavy storm:* WD, Oct. 13, 1943; *It is recommended . . .* : WD, Oct. 15, 1943; *The weather was terrible,* also Boyington's radio transmissions: Bolt, interview; *It was a temptation . . .* : BBBS, p. 195; *He did a rather poor job . . .* and post-mission comments: Bolt; *When Jack Bolt finally returned . . .* : BBBS, p. 196; *It was my feeling . . .* : Moore, endorsement for award, Nov. 28, 1943; *We'll send a couple of your divisions . . .* etc.: quoted by Chapman, interview; *Major Boyington . . .* etc.: Walton, p. 55-56; *Off the end of the Kahili strip . . . ,* etc.: BBBS, p. 190-91; *We drowned out the lizards . . .* : Walton, p. 58; *They want planes . . .* : quoted by Begert, interview with Walton; *Never mind, Doc . . . ,* plus later exchange with Reames: quoted by Walton, *Pappy Boyington: Tragic Hero,* p. 15; *We needed an airplane . . . ,* and details of Boyington's visit: Chapman, interview; *a spark* . . . : De Chant, orig. manuscript, requested by *Collier's.*

15: Gramps

Black Sheep drinking song: Walton, p. 48; quotes and details of fight: Walton, *Tragic Hero,* p. 17-18; award recommendation: Hopper, correspondence to Twining, Oct. 25, 1943; *an idiot colonel,* etc.: Begert; *We figured on spending* . . . : Walton, *Once They Were Eagles,* p. 68; *Drink the beer, boys:* Olander, taping for documentary, Aug. 19, 1999; *Looks like he finally* . . . etc.: quoted by Walton, p. 75; *All officers of this group* . . . : quoted by Boyington, November 23, 1943; letter of commendation: Strother, D.C., Nov. 15, 1943; *He needed some booze:* Bowers; *You are hereby released* . . . : Smoak, correspondence to Boyington, Nov. 27, 1943; (footnote) *The flags were only pasted* . . . : Boyington, correspondence to Chance, Feb. 9, 1983; *The plane had cut a path* . . . : quoted in *Davenport Daily Times,* Dec. 24, 1943; *words would not come,* etc.: BBBS, p. 184; *a quagmire:* Olander, interview; *the most audacious* . . . : Moore, award endorsement; *Well Mom, you wrote* . . . : quoted in *The Washington Alumnus,* April, 1944; *All squadron commanders* . . . : Barakoma operations order, Dec. 15, 1943; *Seeing this, the major apologized* . . . : Bailey, Dan, press release, Jan. 11, 1944; *Come on down, sucker!:* quoted by Sakaida, p. 12; *They wouldn't come up* . . . : quoted in Walton, p. 87; *Far too many* . . . : WD, Dec. 17, 1943.

16: In a Rowboat at Rabaul

This is it, fellows: quoted in WD; Dec. 23, 1943; *Never before* . . . : BBBS, p. 214; *He was smart* . . . : Losch, interview, May 16, 1993; *I closed in on him* . . . : BBBS, p. 215; *and managed to get in* . . . : WD; *The minute his plane landed* . . . : Bailey, press release; *I caught this one on fire* . . . : transcript of interview with Hardin, Dec. 23, 1943; . . . *noisy, cheerful, and talkative* . . . : Bailey; *with a fine Irish brogue* . . . : Walton, p. 90; *I'll show you* . . . : quoted by Keller in *Foundation; Listen, Gramps* . . . : quoted by Walton, p. 90; *anything but happy:* Boyington, public address; *It's sure lonesome here* . . . : Walton, p. 91; *I asked him* . . . : Hampson, *Liberty; I was staggering* . . . : Boyington, public address; *a masterful tactical job:* WD, Dec. 27, 1943; *Thank you, Sgt. Hardin* . . . etc.: Walton, handwritten script; *The hunting was fine* . . . : quoted by Hampson; *It shouldn't have been anything* . . . : Bolt, interview with Walton, Dec. 11, 1981; *making such a wide sweep* . . . : WD, Dec. 28, 1943; *a terrific rate of climb:* Ibid.; *How about trading flights* . . . etc.: Carl, transcript of oral history, p. 125; *I was helpless,* etc.: BBBS, p. 223; *He went off by himself* . . . : Walton, p. 93; *Are you going to get another chance* . . . etc.: Ibid.; *Here's a ball* . . . : Reames, interview, May 12, 1993; *They certainly made* . . . : BBBS, p. 217; *a little tough luck* . . . : quoted by Walton, p. 95; *We had a little camp* . . . : Condon, interview; *He had only gone* . . . : WD supplement, Oct. 4, 1945; *the same as opening the door* . . . : BBBS, p. 231; *someone was heard* . . . : WD, Jan. 3, 1944; *I ended up in the water* . . . : Boyington, correspondence to Sakaida, Aug. 25, 1983; *pounding out some tune* . . . : BBBS, p. 234.

17: Mr. Prisoner

like the chill wind: Wenatchee Daily World, Jan. 7, 1944; *In the movies* . . . : Hampson, Liberty; *We knew he'd do it* . . . : quoted in *Daily World,* Jan. 6, 1944; *This Methuselah* . . . : Ibid.; *We are praying* . . . : quoted in *Daily World,* Jan. 7, 1944; *too young to understand* . . . : *Seattle Post-Intelligencer,* Jan. 7, 1944; *a shattered ankle,* etc.: BBBS, 243-44; *like tourniquets* and *snaky-eyed individual:* Ibid., p. 245; *physical description of Honda:* Arbuckle, deposition; *I came to like Suyako* . . . : BBBS, p. 245; (footnote) *I never did know the name* . . . : Boyington, correspondence to Col. Hersey, USA, Dec. 16, 1946; *a couple of gunnysacks:* BBBS, p. 249; *the usual slapping* . . . : Arbuckle, deposition; *I smiled to myself* . . . : BBBS, p. 256; *were herded* . . . and reference to Black Sheep: BBBS, p. 257-58; *a minimum of cotton clothing:* Arbuckle; *Well boys* . . . : quoted in BBBS, p. 272; *an honor and a pleasure* . . . : Halsey, award endorsement, December 25, 1943; *in case he should be available* . . . : Vandegrift, correspondence to

Hallenbeck, April 10, 1944; *Since Major Boyington . . .* : Smith, correspondence to Tinsley, April 14, 1944; *inspirational leadership . . .* : Manley, award recommendation, Jan. 20, 1944; *The purpose of this place . . .* : Boyington, public address; inventory of articles: McConnell, interview; *I know you are lying . . .* : quoted in BBBS, p. 308; *many a delightful conversation . . .* : Ibid., p. 307-08; *a man who just wanted . . .* : Ibid., p. 347; *I timed it . . .* : Condit, interview; *a cup of rice . . .* : Arbuckle, deposition; *You could stick your finger in your leg . . .* : Condit, interview; *They told us . . .* : Arbuckle; *I thought about going over the fence . . .* : McConnell, interview; *nicknames of guards*: postwar depositions, NARA; *He handed me . . .* : quoted in Washington, D.C. *News,* Oct. 3, 1945; *puffed out like a small barrel,* etc.: Boyington, *True,* circa 1946; *He was addicted to smoking . . .* and details of beating: Condit, deposition and interview; *because one of the prisoners . . .* : Cannon, deposition; *The captain was quite surprised . . .* : Boyington, deposition; *tasted like honey:* BBBS, p. 301; *little old civilian lady:* Ibid. p. 300; *cold, bitterly so:* Ibid., p. 302; *The cracks through the walls . . .* : Leibold, deposition; *technique for keeping warm:* McConnell, interview; account of drinking sake: Boyington, public address; *Deeds is alive . . .* : quoted by Hallenbeck, correspondence to Gen. Vandegrift, Jan. 5, 1945; *became even more brazen:* Boyington, public address; *I do not think . . .* : Leibold, correspondence; *I saw no beauty . . .* : BBBS, p. 322; *get out in the sunshine . . .* : Leibold, deposition; *The buildings were completely gone . . .* : BBBS, p. 325-26; *acts of kindness . . .* : Ibid., p. 332; *a sorrow . . .* : Ibid., p. 324; *just like muckers in a mine:* Ibid., p. 330; *I couldn't fathom . . .* : Ibid.

18: Chicken, Peas, and Bourbon

possible incursions and I won't do it . . . : Martindale, p. 231; *Roger and Harold . . .* : quoted by Stassen, correspondence to Johnson; *dropped a hundred feet . . .* : quoted in *Pittsburgh Press,* Aug. 30, 1945; *a lot of stories . . .* : BBBS, p. 348; *He is credited . . .* : *Congressional Record; a few minute particles* and *considering his time of confine-*

ment . . . : Cmdr. Hoot, (MC) USN, medical report; *I decided that I would smarten myself* . . . : BBBS, p. 348; *This is the most wonderful thing* . . . : quoted in *The New York Times,* Sept. 13, 1945; *It was truly fantastic* . . . : BBBS, p. 349; *My scalp was hanging* . . . : quoted in *San Francisco Chronicle,* Sept 12, 1945; *We just wanted to see Greg* . . . : quoted in *Seattle Post-Intelligencer,* Sept. 13, 1945; *It was not a boisterous party* . . . : *Life,* Oct. 1, 1945; *Greg, you're a worldwide hero* . . . : Walton, interview; *a veritable snowstorm: Post-Intelligencer,* Sept 18, 1945; *You've shown that you're glad* . . . : Ibid.; *You're looking pretty good . . . etc.*: quoted in *Seattle Times,* Sept. 21, 1945; *We believe the best way* . . . : quoted in *Okanogan Independent,* Sept. 27, 1945; *With days like years* . . . : Ibid.; *booby prize:* BBBS, p. 357; *Nothing is too good* . . . : Boyington, public address; verbal exchange during MOH ceremony: BBBS, p. 358; *Congratulations, Major:* quoted by Boyington, public address, Oct. 6, 1980; *Hey, Jim . . . etc.*: quoted by Condit, interview; *At each on of these places* . . . : Walton, interview; *took no pains* . . . : Callahan; *Dearest Lucy* . . . : quoted by Callahan; *She didn't want to drive it* . . . : Ibid.; *God Almighty . . . etc.*: Walton, interview.

19: The Low Road

I'll take you . . . etc.: Walton, interview; quotes from messages to Malcolmson: *Washington Post,* Jan. 9, 1946; *because it looked like a bargain:* quoted in *Washington News,* Jan. 10, 1946; *After two days of heated battle:* quoted in *Los Angeles Times,* Jan. 10, 1946; *the toughest air combat leader . . . etc.*: *Washington Times Herald,* Jan. 6, 1946; *Franny phoned* . . . : Walton, interview; *My client is on the verge* . . . : quoted in *Washington Post,* Jan. 9, 1946; answers to reporters: quoted in *Los Angeles Times,* Jan. 10, 1946; *composed of inexperienced pilots . . . etc.*: *Los Angeles Times,* Mar. 23, 1946; *My wife fixed us salads . . . etc.*: Walton, interview; medical extracts from Long Beach Naval Hospital and San Diego Naval Hospital: NPRC; *Honey, will you still love me . . . etc.*: quoted in *Time,* Sept. 2, 1946; medical and retirement board extracts: NPRC; *Shortly after the*

war . . . : BBBS, p. 372; *I set the business world* . . . :
Boyington, public address, Oct. 25, 1958; *Over the
years* . . . : Walton, interview; *I knew a big fat drunk* . . . :
Boyington, public address; *money-making hobby:* BBBS, p.
373; *milquetoast creatures:* Ibid., p. 376; *half blind from
vodka:* Ibid., p. 374; *They'd chase you* . . . : quoted in
Spokane Spokesman-Review, June 19, 1955; *a hotshot with
the Legion:* Foss, interview; *Three days after I started* . . .
etc.: Boyington, public address; *[He] became simply impossible* . . . : quoted in *Life,* Jan. 26, 1959; *[The doctor]
brought in* . . . etc.: Boyington, public address.

20: Tinseltown
craved sugar . . . , etc.: quoted in *Life; They used me* . . . ,
etc.: quoted in *Spokane Spokesman-Review,* Dec. 2, 1956;
short, very stocky . . . : Forbish, interview; *softpedaling the
rough parts* . . . : quoted in *Pomona Progress Bulletin,* Oct.
23, 1958; *Just name a hero* . . . : BBBS, p. 384; *Life* interviews: Jan. 26, 1959; *They only gave me* . . . : quoted in
Progress Bulletin; The hero . . . *aware of his own weakness* . . . : *Time,* Jun. 14, 1971; *peep show* . . . : review by
Bellman, Samuel, *Los Angeles Times,* Oct. 9, 1960; *strong
convictions* . . . : *Seattle Post-Intelligencer,* May 28, 1959;
the most photographed model . . . etc.: *Spokane Spokesman-
Review,* Oct. 18, 1962; *[Greg] used to drop in* . . . : Granath,
interview; *clawed, belted, and committed mayhem,* etc.:
Hollywood Citizen News, Mar. 31, 1964; *Do you know* . . . :
quoted in *San Diego Union,* Apr. 12, 1977; *I'm getting a divorce* . . . : quoted by Porter, interview; *The type of life I
lived* . . . : quoted in *Tacoma News-Tribune,* Mar. 13, 1972.

21: The Entertainer
pretty beat up: Price, interview; *Oh, that's great* . . . etc.:
quoted by Cannell, interview; *He was drinking wine* . . . :
quoted in *Tacoma News-Tribune,* Apr. 9, 1978; *When those
Corsairs taxied* . . . : quoted in *Air Classics Quarterly
Review,* Winter 1976; *correlate the script* . . . : *Fortitudine,*
Spring, 1977; *I was lied to* . . . : quoted in *National Enquirer,*
May 10, 1977; *That took care of that* . . . : quoted in *Los
Angeles Herald Examiner,* Jul. 22, 1976; *I had to pick out*

these guys . . . : quoted in *Air Classics Quarterly Review;*
loaded with humor . . . : Boyington correspondence to
Walton, March 9, 1976; *We asked . . .* : Walton, interview; *a*
big Polack . . . : Boyington, LP; *What are you looking so*
funny for . . . : Boyington, public address, Oct. 6, 1980; *Say*
you're at a convention. . . : quoted in *San Francisco*
Chronicle, Jul. 5, 1982; *like it was going out of style,* etc.:
Boyington, correspondence to Keith Boyington, Jun. 8,
1978; *were completely the same:* quoted in *Los Angeles*
Times, Feb. 23, 1977; *I said I would write . . .* : correspondence to Henry Sakaida, Jan. 12, 1977; verbal exchanges
with Kawato's girlfriend: quoted by Sakaida, correspondence to author, Jun. 11, 2000; *The tank on my right . . .* :
Kawato, p. 57; *ridiculous and disgusting:* statement issued
by ZFPA, Jun. 5, 1981; *It would seem . . .* : Boyington, correspondence to Losch, Dec. 11, 1984; I*t seems rather in-*
congruous . . . : quoted in *Air Classics Quarterly Review; a*
ton of dough: Porter, interview; *I was impressed . . .* :
Osteen, correspondence with author, May 19, 2000; *old*
man's disease: Boyington, correspondence to Strickland; *a*
happy day for all of them: Granath, interview; *Fuck you,*
Frank: quoted by Losch, interview, Nov. 23, 1999; *He was*
in pain . . . : Halloran, p. 147-48; *When I walked in . . .* :
Losch, interview, Jan. 23, 1999.

Epilogue:
the original top gun: Halloran, eulogy delivered Jan. 15,
1988.

Books
Barrow, Jess. *Marine Fighting Squadron Nine* (VF-9M).
 Blue Ridge Summit, PA: TAB, 1981.
Bond, Charles, and Terry Anderson. *A Flying Tiger's Diary.*
 College Station: Texas A & M University, 1984.
Boyington, Gregory. *Baa, Baa, Black Sheep.* New York:
 Putnam, 1958.
_____. *Tonya.* New York: Bobbs-Merrill, 1960.
Ford, Daniel. *Flying Tigers: Claire Chennault and the*

American Volunteer Group. Washington, D.C.: Smithsonian Institution, 1991.

Gamble, Bruce. *The Black Sheep: The Definitive Account of Marine Fighting Squadron 214 in World War II*. Novato, CA: Presidio, 1998.

Greenlaw, Olga. *The Lady and the Tigers*. New York: Dutton, 1943.

Howard, James. *Roar of the Tiger*. New York: Orion, 1991.

Kawato, Masajiro. *Bye Bye Black Sheep*. Phoenix: Printing Dynamics, 1978.

————. *Flight into Conquest*. Anaheim, CA: KNI, 1978.

Marshall, Chester, and Raymond Halloran. *Hap's War: The Incredible Survival Story of a WWII Prisoner of War Slated for Execution*. Collierville, TN: Global Press, 1998.

Martindale, Robert. *The 13th Mission: The Saga of a POW at Camp Omori, Tokyo*. Austin: Eakin Press, 1998.

McGoldrick, James. *One Man's Opinion of the Spokane Aviation Story*. Fairfield, WA: Ye Galleon, 1982.

Milam, James, and Katherine Ketcham. *Under the Influence: A Guide to the Myths and Realities of Alcoholism*. New York: Bantam, 1983.

O'Kane, Richard. *Clear the Bridge: The Patrols of the USS Tang*. New York: Rand McNally, 1977.

Olynyk, Frank. *USMC Credits for the Destruction of Enemy Aircraft in Air-to-Air Combat, World War 2*. Published by the author, 1982.

Orriss, Bruce. *When Hollywood Ruled the Skies: The Aviation Film Classics of World War II*. Hawthorne, CA: Aero, 1984.

Porter, Bruce, with Eric Hammel. *Ace! A Marine Night-Fighter Pilot in World War II*. Pacifica, CA: Pacifica, 1985.

Reinburg, Hunter. *Combat Aerial Escapades: A Pilot's Log Book*. Boynton Beach, FL: Star, 1966.

Rickenbacker, Edward. *Rickenbacker*. New York: Prentice-Hall, 1967.

Sakaida, Henry. *The Siege of Rabaul.* Saint Paul: Phalanx, 1996.

Schramm, Leo. *Leo the Tiger: True Stories about the Flying Tigers from WWII.* Camp Hill, PA: Green Shields, 1998.

Sherrod, Robert. *History of Marine Corps Aviation in WW II.* Rev. ed. Baltimore: Nautical & Aviation, 1980.

Tillman, Barrett. *The F4U in WW II and Korea.* Annapolis: Naval Institute, 1979.

———. *Wildcat: The F4F in WW II.* Annapolis: Naval Institute, 1990.

Walton, Frank. *Once They Were Eagles: The Men of the Black Sheep Squadron.* Lexington: University Press of Kentucky, 1986.

Weiland, Charles. *Above and Beyond.* Pacifica, CA: Pacifica, 1997.

Yoshimura, Akira. *Zero Fighter.* Westport, CT: Praeger, 1996.

Articles

Allen, Dub, and Frank Johnson. "Colonel Gregory 'Pappy' Boyington." *Air Classics Quarterly Review,* Winter 1976.

Boyington, Gregory. "I'll Buy the Drinks, Boys." *True* (no citation), circa 1946.

Bunzel, Peter. "Bright Days for a 'Bum.'" *Life,* January 26, 1959.

Callahan, Eileen. "Pappy Boyington in War and Peace." *Sunday World-Herald,* January 20, 1946.

Coon, Jerry. "The Fabulous Pappy Boyington." *Air Classics,* February 1979.

Greenlaw, Olga. "Pappy." *Cosmopolitan,* April 1944.

Hampson, Fred. "Boyington, Lost Ace." *Liberty*, July 1, 1944.

Keller, Robert. "Marion & Pappy: Remembering the Men behind the Legends." *Foundation,* Spring 2000.

Lagana, Gregory. "Gregory Boyington: Still a Legend, but Never a Hero." *Cross & Crescent,* March 1978.

Quilter, Charles, II. "'One-of-a-Kind' Marine Aviator 'Pappy' Boyington Dies." *Fortitudine,* Winter 1987–88.

Quilter, Elizabeth. "Those Vulgar Blue Trousers with the Red Stripes." *Fortitudine,* Fall 1988.

Rosbert, Joseph. "I Flew with Boyington." *Flying Aces,* October 1944.

Schwalbe, Timothy. "The Black Sheep's Pappy" (Pts. 1–3). *Military,* Sept.–Nov. 1985.

Tillman, Barrett. "Before There Were Cats." *Flight Journal,* June 1998.

_____ . "Five the Hard Way: Navy and Marine Corps Aces-in-a-Day; or, Numbers Do Count." *The Hook,* Fall 1993.

Walton, Frank. "Baa Baa Black Sheep Is Pulling the Wool over Our Eyes." *TV Guide,* April 23, 1977.

_____ . "Black Sheep . . . Run!" *Skyways,* July 1944.

Correspondence and Related Documents

Arbuckle, John. Deposition, conditions at Rabaul and Ofuna prison camps, September 26, 1946.

Bailey, Stanley. "Battling Black Sheep." Unpublished manuscript, circa 1945.

Boyington, Charles. Countercomplaint, August 20, 1914.

Boyington, Dolores. Correspondence to Keith Boyington and wife, January 26, February 14, April 12, and June 8, 1964.

Boyington, Grace. Complaint, August 20, 1914.

Boyington, Gregory. Affidavit, King County, WA, August 10, 1942.

_____ . Deposition, conditions at Ofuna and Omori prison camps, October 25 and November 26, 1945.

_____ . Correspondence to Frank Walton, March 9, 1976, and September 3, 1976; Hap Halloran, June 5, 1976, July 24, 1979, and December 3, 1981; Henry Sakaida, January 12, 1977, April 15, 1981, and August 25, 1983; Keith Boyington, June 8, 1978; Merritt Chance, February 9, 1983; Bob Strickland, April 3, 1984; Fred Losch, December 11, 1984.

Boyle, Donald. Deposition, conditions at Rabaul and Ofuna prison camps, September 23, 1946.

Burgard, George. Personal diary, September 24, 1941 to July 4, 1942.

Cannon, Carl. Deposition, conditions at Ofuna prison camp, May 16, 1947.

Carl, Marion. Oral history, History and Museums Division, USMC, 1978.

Eisele, Anthony. Correspondence to author, March 10, 1997.

Ford, Daniel. Correspondence to author, May 13, 1998.

Goad, Lloyd. Deposition, Omori prison conditions, September 20, 1946.

Greenlaw, Olga, et al. Group War Diary (AVG), December 8, 1941 to July 19, 1942.

Johnson, Pen. Correspondence to Frank Walton, May 26, 1986.

Halloran, Raymond. Eulogy for Gregory Boyington, January 15, 1988.

Hines, Nancy. Correspondence to author, April 26, 1999.

Hoisington, James. Correspondence to author, June 16, 1999.

Keeton, Robert. Personal diary, September 9, 1941 to August 23, 1942.

Keller, Dean. Correspondence to author, May 15, 1999.

Liebold, William. Deposition, conditions at Ofuna and Omori prison camps, October 26, 1945.

_____. Correspondence to author, February 21, 1999.

Malcolmson, Lucille. Correspondence to paymaster, USMC, January 22, 1944.

Mangrum, Richard. Flight training record entries, June 18 and 25, July 3, 1935.

Mowreader, Mikell. Correspondence to author, August 21, 1999.

Neale, Robert. Personal diary, January 1, 1942 to July 23, 1942. (Dan Ford collection.)

Olynyk, Frank. Correspondence to author, August 19, 1998.

Quilter, Elizabeth. Correspondence to author, February 9, 1999.

Sakaida, Henry. "Analysis of Pappy Boyington's Claims." Unpublished, 1995.

_____ . Correspondence to author, June 11 and July 10, 1999.

Sasaki, Kunichi. Testimony, war crimes trial, April 5, 1946.

Stassen, Harold. Correspondence to Alfred Johnson, March 7, 1989.

Walters, Jan. Correspondence to author, April 26, 1999.

Walton, Frank. VMF-214 War Diary entries, September 7, 1943 to January 8, 1944.

_____. "Boyington: Tragic Hero," unpublished manuscript, circa 1977.

_____. "Pappy and His Black Sheep," unpublished manuscript, circa 1945.

_____. "Let Them Sleep in Peace," unpublished manuscript, circa 1946.

Interviews and Audio Recordings

Anderson, Everett, December 9, 1998.

Anderson, Norman, March 17, 2000.

Begert, John (with Frank Walton), December 5, 1981.

Bickel, Carey, June 2, 2000.

Bolt, John, November 22, 1991.

Bourgeois, Henry, March 1, 1996, and March 19, 2000.

Bowers, Glenn, November 30, 1995.

Boyington, Gregory. *Pappy Boyington, World War II Ace: A Personal Reflection on His Life.* Mark 56 Records, 1977.

_____. Public address. San Francisco, CA, October 25, 1958.

_____. Public address. Washington, DC, October 6, 1980.

Boyington, Keith, May 23, 1998.

Britt, George, April 21, 1999.

Brown, Jeanne, April 5, 1999.

Canavan, Desmond, and Marie Canavan, February 24, 1999.

Cannell, Stephen, May 11, 1999.

Cartwright, Thomas, March 1, 1999.

Case, William, May 12, 1993.

_____(with Frank Walton), December 2, 1981.

Chapman, Warner, September 3, 1998.

Christiansen, Carl, July 21, 1999.

Condit, James, April 15, 1998.

Condon, John, July 3, 1996.

Conrad, Robert, April 24, 1999.

Cordell, Sandy, June 2, 2000.

Corman, Ned, May 13, 1993, and January 23, 1999.

Crowe, Betty (Smyth) February 2, 1999.

Dittman, Anne-Marie (Elwell), May 26, 1999.

Doty, Lamont, February 3, 1999.

Emrich, Warren, May 16, 1993.

Fisher, Don, May 15, 1993.

Forbish, Paula, March 19, 1999.

Foss, Joseph, December 22, 1998.

Galer, Robert, October 9, 1998.

Granath, Ramona, July 8, 1999.

Groover, Denmark, April 13, 1996.

Harper, Edwin, May 16, 1993.

Heier, William, May 16, 1993.

Hill, James, May 13, 1993.

Lane, Perry, May 13, 1993.

Layher, Robert, February 22, 2000.

Long, Herbert, March 20, 2000.

Losch Fred, May 16, 1993, January 23 and November 23, 1999.

Magee, Christopher, May 11, 1993.

Matheson, Bruce, May 15, 1993.

McCartney, Allan, March 15, 1996.

McClurg, Robert, May 11, 1993.

McConnell, Glenn, March 22, 1999.

McKellar, Everett, January 23, 1999.

Millington, William, January 24, 1999.

Nelson, Ronald, January 23, 1999.

Olander, Edwin, May 15, 1993.

Porter, Bruce, January 9, 1999.

Price, Frank, May 12, 1999.

Quilter, Elizabeth H., February 10, 1999.

Recder, Frederick December 4, 1990.

Rooke, John, May 19, 2000.

Rosbert, Joseph, May 2, 1998.
Rossi, Richard, October 22, 1998.
Schafhausen, John, June 16, 2000.
Soble, Irv, June 1, 2000.
Trummel, Julia (Theriault), May 17, 1999.
Walton, Frank, May 15, 1993.
Waterstrat, Paul, July 18, 1999.
Weiland, Charles, January 6, 1999.

Index

483

Don't miss this amazing account
of fury in the sky
by Peter Hunt

ANGLES OF ATTACK
An A-6 Intruder Pilot's War

*From the carrier launch in total darkness to the
gut-dropping rolls through enemy antiaircraft
fire, Peter Hunt puts you in the pilot's seat for
the flight of your life.*

Moments after Desert Storm began, bomber pilot
Pete Hunt was in the air over the Persian Gulf.
Tested to the max, flying all night, every night for
weeks on end, Hunt executed dozens of missions—
from carpet bombing to dropping deadly five-hun-
dred-pound cluster bombs with pinpoint precision to
supporting Marines on the ground. His A-6 jet was
a wide-open target for the antiaircraft fire streaking
up to destroy it. Escaping this threat made setting
the A-6 back down on a little deck in a big ocean
seem almost easy. But Hunt, like the rest of his
squadron, the VA-145 Swordsmen—honored as the
premier Attack Squadron in the United States Navy
for 1991—was just doing his job: keeping America
free.

Published by Ballantine Books.
Available wherever books are sold.

Don't miss the memoir of a man with just
as much "right stuff" as any astronaut—
Michael J. Novosel

DUSTOFF

The Memoir of an Army Aviator
With an introduction by W. E. B. Griffin

"A REMARKABLE READ . . . [Novosel's]
career is an inspiration to anyone who has ever
needed to overcome an obstacle or achieve a
desired goal. . . . A lively and universally
engrossing account."
—*Vietnam* magazine

After fast-talking his way into the aviation cadet
program (he was too short to pass the physical) and
earning his wings, Michael Novosel became a
heavy-bomber instructor for the Army Air Corps.
But it wasn't until Germany's defeat that the ace
pilot finally saw combat. He reached Tinian just
before the Enola Gay took off to end World War II
in the skies over Hiroshima. When the war in
Vietnam started, Novosel applied again for active
duty. The army decided that flying dustoffs (mede-
vac helicopters) in Vietnam was a perfect job for this
seasoned aviator. With two tours, 2,038 hours of
combat flight, 2,345 aerial missions that evacuated
5,589 wounded, and a Congressional Medal of
Honor, Mike Novosel is a genuine, 24-karat
American war hero.

Look for this page-turning, high-flying thriller by Joe Weber, *New York Times* bestselling author of *DEFCON One*

363

DANCING WITH THE DRAGON

From start to cliff-hanging finish, this is a gripping story that could have been torn from tomorrow's headlines.

"Heavy on high-tech thrills."
—*Publishers Weekly*

During routine night operations off Southern California, an F/A-18 from the USS *Abraham Lincoln* is inexplicably blown from the sky. The Pentagon wants to throw a blanket over the incident, but then another navy fighter jet is mysteriously destroyed in midair. The president orders an investigation to find out who is responsible for the attacks—and why. Tagged for the job: ex-CIA operatives and former military pilots Scott Dalton and Jackie Sullivan.

As Dalton and Sullivan proceed, they are surprised to learn that the loss of the navy jets is just the latest in a series of seemingly unrelated and previously unexplained losses of American combat aircraft. Yet their investigation soon uncovers a deadly conspiracy that seems to lead directly to the heart of Beijing.

Published by Presidio Press.
Available wherever books are sold.